DANTE
THE PHILOSOPHER

DANTE
THE PHILOSOPHER

By

ÉTIENNE GILSON

Translated by

DAVID MOORE

NEW YORK
SHEED & WARD
1949

.49-3435

"Ciò che è fuori della coscienza del poeta a noi non può importare."

MICHELE BARBI, *Studi Danteschi*, 1938, XVII, p. 48.

Preface

THE OBJECT of this work is to define Dante's attitude or, if need be, his successive attitudes towards philosophy. It is therefore a question of ascertaining the character, function and place which Dante assigned to this branch of learning among the activities of man. My purpose has not been to single out, classify and list Dante's numerous philosophical ideas, still less to look for their sources or to decide what doctrinal influences determined the evolution of his thought.[1] These are important problems; they have already been studied in part, and scarcely a year passes without our learning something fresh about them from scholars of the first rank. But our problem differs so widely from these that it inevitably requires a method specifically different from that to which they are subjected. Certainly, here

[1] It is arguable that the problem of the sources of Dante's work should be tackled anew in its entirety and discussed as a preliminary to any interpretation of his thought. A defence of this thesis will be found in BRUNO NARDI, *Sigieri di Brabante nella Divina Commedia e le fonti della filosofia di Dante*, published by the author, Spianate (Pescia), 1912 (from the *Rivista di filosofia neo-scòlastica*, April and October, 1911, February and April, 1912). In this article the author attacks the thesis upheld by Father Cornoldi, Father Mandonnet and a number of others, who practically identify Dante's thought with Thomism. His method is to single out the passages in the *Comedy* which attest the presence of non-Thomistic influences—for instance, Augustinism, Avicennism and even a few traces of Averroism. B. Nardi's interpretation of these passages has been discussed by G. BUSNELLI, S.J., *La cosmogonia dantesca e le sue fonti*, in *Scritti vari pubblicati in occasione del sesto centenario della morte di Dante Alighieri*, Vita e Pensiero, Milan, 1921 (pp. 42–84). Father Busnelli's conclusion is that Dante was a Thomist and that he has as much right to be so styled as any other member of the same school (pp. 83–84). Some reserves in respect of certain of the interpretations offered by Father Busnelli himself have since been made by P. MANDONNET in *Dante le Théologien. Introduction à l'intelligence de la vie, des oeuvres et de l'art de Dante Alighieri*, Desclée de Brouwer, Paris, 1935 (pp. 246–252). Add to these works that of E. KREBS, *Contributo della scolastica alla relazione di alcuni problemi danteschi* (in *Scritti vari . . .*, Milan, 1921, pp. 85–96), which stresses the Platonic influences, and also a number of essays collected in the important work, to which we shall have occasion to refer again, by BRUNO NARDI, *Saggi di filosofia dantesca*, Milan-Rome, Società anon. editr. Dante Alighieri, 1930–VIII. The last-named book is itself completed by BRUNO NARDI's *Note critiche di filosofia dantesca*, Florence, L. S. Olschki, 1938–XVI. All these works have performed a useful service and the ideas which they contain ought to be developed. It is still permissible, however, to bring up one other problem—that of Dante's attitude towards philosophy in general, and the place he assigns to it among the various activities of man, in particular politics and religion. I claim no precedence for this other problem; I merely say that it is another problem, and that it requires another method, more akin to doctrinal analysis than to the investigation of sources which the first problem demands.

vii

as elsewhere, analysis of our author's works should be our first consideration, but we shall bear in mind not so much their content, in other words the philosophy which they formulate,[1] as what they tell us of the way in which Dante conceived philosophy and of the use to which he put it. Here, moreover, unless I am mistaken, is the key to his true originality as a philosopher.

The circumstances in which I undertook these researches are merely of anecdotal interest and the reader would be none the better off for knowing them, but he is entitled to some explanation concerning the way in which the researches themselves have been conducted. To read Dante is a joy. To write about Dante is a pleasure, for it is impossible to write about him without reading him again more closely; but the effort needed to formulate one's conclusions on Dante is much greater, because one may legitimately hesitate between two methods, each of which has its advantages and its drawbacks. The first consists in stating simply one's conclusions on Dante, without troubling oneself about what others may have written with a similar purpose. The resulting books are short and unpretentious. To be sure, they are not necessarily devoid of a certain elegance and, whatever their value, it may fairly be hoped that the reader will not find them unduly tedious. Unfortunately this method is neither very honest in itself, nor very productive of lasting results. No one who discusses Dante can do so without remembering what distinguished expositors have said before him. Accordingly he has a debt to acknowledge, and how can he acknowledge it without enrolling himself modestly among their followers, in other words without admitting his familiarity with them instead of feigning an independence which in any case none can believe in? Moreover, unless he writes one of those books whose seeming originality cloaks an abundance of arbitrary notions, and which are addressed only to a defenceless public, how can he to-day adopt a positive attitude towards any problem relating to Dante in such a way that the informed reader does not recall other solutions, which seem to rule out in advance

---

[1] Some useful suggestions in connection with this problem will be found in M. BAUM-GARTNER's work, *Dantes Stellung zur Philosophie*, published in the *Dante-Abhandlungen*, Görres-Gesellschaft, Cologne, 1921 (pp. 48–71); and it is always interesting to re-read A. F. OZANAM, *Dante et la philosophie catholique au XIIIe siècle*, in Vol. VI of his *Oeuvres complètes*, Paris, 1872–1881.

the solution that is offered? If he ignores them, he is in effect
failing to establish his own thesis. To enumerate them and
discuss them one after the other is an endless, wearisome task,
the most obvious effect of which is to bury Dante beneath such
a mass of ideas which are foreign to his work that in the end
author and readers alike no longer know what or who is the
subject of discussion.

Inevitably, therefore, I have had to seek a middle course
between these two methods, in other words to select from the
debatable interpretations of Dante's thought those which, if
correct, would have implied directly that my own was radically
wrong. In the forefront was the fundamental thesis upheld
by Father Mandonnet in his *Dante le Théologien*. Accordingly
the reader will find it discussed with an insistence which, I fear,
will be to some unpleasing. And yet anyone who has read this
book knows very well that all the parts hang together and that
the closely-knit fabric of its reasoning must be unravelled stitch
by stitch if it is not desired that a portion which yields in one
direction should still be sustained by the countless threads that
link it to the remainder. May I at least be permitted to say
that where I seem perhaps to have indulged overmuch in controversy I have in fact done so only because of my belief that I
could not omit such passages without failing to justify the
interpretation of Dante's thought which this book offers. As
for the actual interpretation, it would be easy to imagine simpler
ones, but it would not, perhaps, be easy to find another of equal
simplicity which fits the same writings, taken in their obvious
sense and interpreted with the same directness. As we are here
concerned with Dante, I could not forget that the subject of this
study is one of the greatest names in literary history, but as it is
his ideas that are under discussion I have had to define them with
the sometimes meticulous exactitude which the analysis of ideas
demands. When a philosopher discusses literature he often
reveals a want of taste, but when a man of letters discusses ideas
he sometimes reveals a want of precision. By helping one
another we shall perhaps draw nearer to that state of grace in
which love increases as understanding becomes clearer, and
understanding is all the clearer as love is the more profound.
Great writers expect no less of us, for their ideas are bound up
with their art, and their very greatness consists in the fact that

after they have gone their thoughts remain inseparable from the manner in which they have expressed them.

It stands to reason, though perhaps the fact had better be stated, that this book is not presented as the work of a Dantologist. To love a foreign language, even as much as I love Italian, is unfortunately not the same as knowing it. Having worked merely with the knowledge of the Italian language that is indispensable to any self-respecting French historian, I must have made some mistakes; I offer my apologies, especially for the more unpleasing ones—those which I may have made while presuming to correct others better qualified than myself. As for the vast literature on Dante, I cannot think of it without experiencing a kind of dizziness. One cannot open an Italian review without saying to oneself: "Another book, another article that I ought to have read before expressing my opinion on this question!" It seems to me that I have covered vast tracts of this sea of commentaries, but I know that what I have gleaned from them is a mere drop in the ocean. That is all the more reason why I should at this point thank the Italian masters without whose aid I should have been unable to begin this work, let alone complete it. If I were not afraid that the responsibility for my shortcomings might be laid at their door I should like to record the full debt which my Dante studies owe to the learned scholars whose works have served to guide me: Signor Ferdinando Neri, whose *Letture dantesche* in days gone by revealed to me what it means to an Italian to understand Dante, and then Signori Luigi Pietrobono, Francesco Ercole and Bruno Nardi, whose books have never been long absent from my desk while I have been writing.

But I ought above all to refer to one master, who is a master even among masters. I mean Signor Michele Barbi, whose vast learning, shrewdness of mind and integrity of judgment have so often enlightened me where I was ignorant, put me on my guard against mistakes which I was on the point of making or corrected those which I had already made. His name will be found at the foot of some of the following pages, but far less often than it was entitled to appear, and I am anxious to say that, even where I part company with him, it is thanks to him that I have dared to do so. No circumstance that I know of or can fear could release me from this debt of gratitude or from the duty of making it public.

CONTENTS

I

Dante's Clerical Vocation and Metamorphoses of Beatrice

IT SHOULD be possible to write a book on Dante and philosophy without speaking of the *Vita Nuova*. At all events what may fittingly be said of it would amount to very little: a few words on two or three chapters of this work, in which Dante says he has consoled himself with philosophy for the loss of Beatrice. This facility is, however, denied us, since on the threshold of Dante's work a new *fera* mounts guard. I mean *Dante the Theologian*.[1] If Father Mandonnet is right, no one hitherto has ever understood the character of Beatrice, or, in consequence, the *Vita Nuova*, which this exquisite figure lights up throughout with its radiance. This would be grave enough, but not the gravest thing, for it is impossible to subscribe to Father Mandonnet's conclusions without at the same time admitting that the *Vita Nuova* is from beginning to end the book of a theologian. If that were true, all that one may have to say besides on Dante's philosophy would necessarily be affected; and not only on his philosophy, but on his personal history, on his life, on himself. In short, one can no longer go into the poet's work without first demanding an explanation from the theologian who claims the

[1] Father Mandonnet early interested himself in Dante's work, not only through personal taste, but also because the study of the *Divine Comedy* forced itself on him for his researches on Siger of Brabant. Besides what he says of it in the memorable book which he has dedicated to this philosopher—a book to which we shall often have to return—Father Mandonnet has published the following works on Dante himself: *Dante théologien* in *Revue des Jeunes*, May 25, 1921 (11th year, No. 10), pp. 369–95; *Theologus Dantes*, in the *Bulletin du Comité Catholique français pour la Célébration du VIe centenaire de la mort de Dante Alighieri* (1321–1921), No. 5, January, 1922, pp. 395–527. This last work forms the body of the volume later published under the title of *Dante le Théologien. Introduction à l'intelligence de la vie, des oeuvres et de l'art de Dante Alighieri*, Paris, Desclée de Brouwer, 1935.

Throughout each of these works Father Mandonnet's position is established as constant. Save in cases where it may be of interest to verify that Father Mandonnet has constantly maintained a certain point of view, we shall simply refer the reader to the volume which finally reproduces his thought: *Dante le Théologien*. For his work on Siger of Brabant, see below, Chap. IV.

I

privilege of introducing us to it. One may accept or reject this entirely new Beatrice: one cannot disregard her.

I. Beatrice Metamorphosed into Theology

There are, says Father Mandonnet, three Ladies in the work of Dante. All three are introduced in the *Vita Nuova*: Beatrice, Poetry and Philosophy. Two are introduced in the *Banquet*: Beatrice and Philosophy. One only remains in the *Divine Comedy*, which she illuminates throughout with her smile: Beatrice. Now none of them represents a real personage, but all are mere symbols, as Father Mandonnet proceeds to demonstrate.[1] The first proof is that of these three Ladies two are anonymous and must be so by the very reason of the name borne by the third— a revealing name, furthermore, and one that suffices to show what she is: "Beatrice, beatitude, no other name must appear beside that one."[2]

This argument introduces us straight away to Father Mandonnet's method. A Thomistic theologian, he argues frankly as a Thomist, as if it were understood in advance that Dante himself could not have reasoned otherwise. Now it is quite true that for St. Thomas Aquinas there is only one beatitude, but it unfortunately happens that for Dante there were two. Dante has said so in Latin, in the Monarchy: Man's aim is twofold, *hominis duplex finis existit*, because he has two *beatitudines*, to the first of which we attain through philosophy, while the Christian revelation leads us to the second;[3] he had already said so in Italian, in the *Banquet*: *Onde, con ciò sia cosa che quella che è qui l'umana*

[1] We shall not discuss in this work the problem of the reality of Beatrice, except in terms of the new arguments advanced against it by Father Mandonnet. For a comprehensive study of the principal interpretations of Beatrice, see EDW. MOORE's excellent work, *Studies in Dante*, Second Series, Oxford, Clarendon Press, 1899: II, *Beatrice*, pp. 79–151. The interpretations will there be found classified under three principal heads: symbolist theories, idealist theories, realist theory. The author is in favour of the last, which he defends, with all the necessary nuances and limitations, by means of excellent arguments, pp. 129–149. Let us note, as a matter of curiosity, that Beatrice has represented, successively or at once: Wisdom (Biscioni); the Emperor (G. Rossetti); the ideal Church (Gietmann); Dante's Thought-word, his sectarian faith, his soul and spirit personified (Aroux); the active intellect (Perez); the ideal woman (Bartoli; Renier), etc., etc. Father Mandonnet has therefore done nothing, as will be seen shortly, but enrich this already rich collection by one item, itself polyvalent and the origin of several others.

[2] P. MANDONNET, *Dante le Théologien*, p. 37.

[3] *De Monarchia*, III, 16. We shall cite this work according to R. ALLULI's edition, *Dante Alighieri, De Monarchia*, C. Signorelli, Milan, 1926.

natura non pur una beatitudine abbia, ma due.[1] Whatever one may pretend to explain in the name of the principle that there is only a single beatitude, it is not an explanation that can claim the authority of Dante.

Even supposing Dante had admitted that there is only one beatitude, it is not very clear what that would prove so far as regards Beatrice. The fact that this name signifies "beatitude" does not permit us to conclude that a woman bearing this name and loved by Dante did not exist. One may love a woman named Beatrice; one may even love her, among other reasons, because her name is Beatrice; finally, one may love a woman, and name her Beatrice because one finds one's happiness in loving her and because this name means "she who gives happiness", but nothing of all this can have the effect of eliminating her. The echoes that a woman's name awakes are not extraneous to the love that she inspires. It is conceivable that a woman called Beatrice should be not only the well beloved, but the well named, for a soul thirsting for happiness as was Dante's; it is likewise conceivable that Petrarch, passionately ambitious for the poetic laurel, was in love with a woman called Laura, but if one concludes from her name that Beatrice was only beatitude, it will likewise be necessary to conclude that the Laura of Petrarch was only a laurel.

And even if, finally, all that has just been denied were conceded, what would be the result? If there is only one beatitude and if it is desired to symbolize this beatitude by a fictitious personage, it is conceivable that this symbol should be named Beatrice, and that no other personage figuring in the same work should also bear this name, but it is not clear why the other personages that appear in the same work should not themselves be entitled to bear other names. Yet this is what we are asked to admit in the name of logic: Beatrice means beatitude; now there is only one beatitude; therefore no one else is entitled to bear a name. This curious paralogism would be inexplicable if it were not an entirely spontaneous defensive reaction against the secret protestations of a good sense which refuses to let itself be stifled. Here is a book in which appear three Ladies, one bearing a name, the other two bearing none; if a supposition of any kind is made

---

[1] *Convivio*, II, 4. We shall cite this work according to P. PAPA's edition, *Dante Alighieri, Il Convivio*, C. Signorelli, Milan, 1926.

on this subject, it will undoubtedly be thought that the one who bears a name is a real woman, whereas the other two are mere symbols. As soon as one thinks about it, good sense is immediately reinforced by a positive argument of great weight: if Beatrice were but a mere symbol, she would be a unique case in Dante's work, for there is no other certain example in it of a mere symbol designated by a proper name. This fact assuredly does not prove that Beatrice really existed, but it suggests it; in any case, it cannot be asserted that it suggests the contrary thesis, the very one that it is desired to make it prove.

What is concealed behind Father Mandonnet's argument is his fixed, unshakable conviction that Beatrice is a mere symbol of that which confers on man beatitude, namely the "Christian Revelation or, more exactly, the supernatural Christian order in all its concrete reality: historical facts, cultural doctrines and practices".[1] A sufficiently broad symbolism, as is clear, and one that will permit us later to identify Beatrice with the most varied things; but also—and it is this that concerns us at present —a symbolism that suggests an explanation of the strange reasoning that we have seen. If Beatrice is the Christian life in

---

[1] P. MANDONNET, *Dante le Théologien*, p. 37. See another exaltation of Beatrice, but without elimination, in L. PIETROBONO, *Il poema sacro. Saggio d'una interpretazione generale della Divina Commedia*, 2 vols., Bologna, N. Zanichelli, 1915. Basing himself on the symbolism of *Vita Nuova*, XXX, to which we shall return, L. Pietrobono judges that "Dante would consider Beatrice *as another God incarnate*" (p. 79; underlined in the text). Cf. below: "il poeta . . . ha premesso che Beatrice è un altro Dio incarnato" (p. 81). All this because Dante has said of Beatrice that she is a miracle whose root is the admirable Trinity. If it causes astonishment, that is undoubtedly because the theology of grace has been forgotten. Grace has the effect of making man "deiform", that is of "assimilating" him to God. St. Bonaventure counts twelve "novenaries" in the soul subject to the hierarchy of grace (*In Hexaemeron*, Visio IV, collatio IV, n. II, ed. F. Delorme, Quaracchi, 1934, pp. 264–265), which then becomes "the abode where God dwells, the daughter of God, His bride and His friend, a member of the head of Christ, His sister and co-heiress" (*Itinerarium mentis in Deum*, cap. V, 8, in *Tria opuscula*, Quaracchi, 1911, p. 330). As to L. Pietrobono's question: "Do you picture a God Who marvels at a human soul and feels desire for it?" (*op. cit.*, p. 81), the answer must be given to him that in admiring and loving a soul in a state of grace, God admires and loves always Himself alone. Yes, God desires us, and it was, indeed, He Who loved us first, as St. John (1 *John*, IV, 19) and St. Bernard (*De dil. Deo*. VII, 22) say. "Tu te ipsum amas in nobis", says Guillaume de Saint-Thierry to God (*De contemplando Deo*, VII, 15; Pat. Lat., vol. 184, col. 375B). In short, grace has as its ultimate effect the "deification" of man through God (cf. E. GILSON, *La théologie mystique de saint Bernard*, Paris, J. Vrin, 1934, pp. 114–146, 155, 229, 232, 237), and this is not without cause, for it is for this end that God has created him. And not only created, but re-created to make of him a heaven in which He may live: "pugnavit ut acquireret, occubuit ut redimeret . . . Et beata cui dicitur: *Veni electa mea, et ponam in te thronum meum* (Ps. 131)" (ST. BERNARD, *In Cant. Cant.*, XXVII, 9). The soul of the just man would not be the *sponsa Dei* if God did not covet it.

its beatific function, and if the two other Ladies, Poetry and Philosophy, are claimants to the exercise of this same function, they are not entitled to bear its name, since they are not entitled to exercise it; and since they figure in the *Vita Nuova* and the *Banquet* only as usurpers of the function designated by this name, not only are they not entitled to bear the name of her who exercises it, but they are not entitled to bear any name. Thus understood, the argument would assuredly cease to be a paralogism, but only because it presupposes the very thesis which it is trying to prove.

As soon as he enters upon such a road, and whatever, moreover, the thesis which he maintains, a historian runs great risks. Unless a happy intuition has led him directly to the truth, and unless all the facts and passages then come of themselves to his thesis like doves to the dovecote, his initial error is going to bring him into fatal conflict with a capital fact or a capital passage from which he will disengage himself only at the cost of a second hypothesis, no less vain than the first, and once this second hypothesis is in conflict with other facts or other passages, it will be necessary to invent a third, and so on indefinitely. The truth is that historical reality has a fibrous structure: it may only be followed along the thread; whoever takes it slantwise is bound to tear it.

Himself convinced of the clearness of his thesis, Father Mandonnet naturally judged that "Dante, in short, has not made research very difficult for us",[1] and that with a little attention any reader of average perspicacity will quickly understand this fact, which the poet is working to make himself understand: Beatrice never existed. Thus, in the *Banquet*, Dante shows himself "very explicit in this respect", since he says he has written this work in order to purge himself of the "infamy" inflicted on him by those who took him for a mere singer of the human passions.[2] Certainly, but, in the first place, the passage in the *Banquet* in which Dante makes this remark does not refer to Beatrice; it expressly refers to quite a different personage, with whom we shall have to make closer acquaintance, and bearing the name of the *Donna gentile*. Now this *Donna gentile* is really but a mere symbol, and we may this time be certain of it because it is Dante himself who tells us so. The *Donna gentile* is neither more nor

---

[1] P. MANDONNET, *op cit.*, p. 37.   [2] P. MANDONNET, *op. cit.*, pp. 37–38.

less than Philosophy.[1] What, then is the "infamy" of which Dante wishes to purge himself? That which would justly attach to his name if it could be believed that this "second love" were a carnal passion. Because he is a poet, Dante likes to imagine Philosophy in the guise of a Lady full of charm and beauty, but he is not at all willing to let us believe that what he loves after Beatrice is a woman.[2] Here again, what is the simplest hypothesis? Undoubtedly it is that Dante has meant to tell us: I am not betraying the dead Beatrice in loving the *Donna gentile*, for the latter is not a woman. Philosophy is not the sort of successor a woman fears. What made this very natural inference unacceptable to Father Mandonnet was that it implies the real existence of that Beatrice of whom it is desired to make a mere symbol. Here indeed is the passage that cannot be reconciled with the thesis, and only a new hypothesis will enable us to surmount it.

It will be supposed, then, that Dante has meant to tell us: Having loved Beatrice, that is to say the Christian life in its supernatural and beatific reality, I should bring disgrace on myself if I let it be believed that I am betraying it for a carnal passion. Now the argument here propounded to us is as unnatural as the first was natural. To love another woman after loving Beatrice as the Dante of the *Vita Nuova* says he loved her would have been, especially for a chivalrous poet, to bring disgrace on oneself, but it was not a betrayal to seek in philosophy the means to allay an undying grief. If, on the contrary, it is supposed that the ardent love of the poet of the *Vita Nuova* was addressed to the supernatural beauty of grace, it is very clear that, when he specifies that he is not betraying it for a woman, he mitigates his disgrace, but it is not clear that he purges himself of it. To forsake the Christian life of grace for philosophy is still to betray it. To console oneself with philosophy for having deserted the Christian life is to betray it just the same. If, then, it is admitted that Beatrice was a real woman, Dante truly excuses himself by his precise statement that his "second love" is only addressed to philosophy; if, on the contrary, it is admitted that Beatrice symbolized the Christian life, Dante does not justify himself

---

[1] DANTE, *Convivio*, II, 12. On the symbolism of the *Donna Gentile*, see below, Chap. II, pp. 137–156.
[2] DANTE, *Convivio*, I, 2. The expression "second love" occurs, *op. cit.*, III, 1.

when he says that he consoles himself for her loss with philosophy. Very far from excusing himself in gratuitously giving us this information, he accuses himself. One does not purge oneself of an infamy by publicly accusing oneself of it.

The thing is so clear that good sense has had to seek again to make itself understood, but, again, we shall only discern its protestation through the arguments which stifle it. Since it is clear that, if Dante's first love had not been a real woman, he would not justify himself at all by saying that his "second love" was not one, it must be proved at all costs that the fact that Dante's "second love" is not a woman implies that the first was not one either. "If, in accordance with Dante's affirmation, the truth contained under the symbol of his second love, or of his second lady, is Philosophy, his first love, or his first lady, can only be a reality of the same order; but a reality superior to Philosophy: Theology."[1] *Non sequitur.* From the fact that the second lady introduced by Dante is a fiction that he himself proclaims as such, it in no way follows that his first lady, whom he names Beatrice and of whom he has never said that . he was a fiction, was one for all that. And that too is so clear that Father Mandonnet could not fail to notice it; whence he has been led to invent an additional pseudo-fact to give substance to his argumentation: Beatrice cannot have been a woman because "if love of Philosophy killed the love in Dante's soul for Beatrice, she cannot be a young Florentine girl or indeed another woman, but another science placed higher than Philosophy; otherwise we move into the realm of absurdity".[2]

I do not know if it is absurd to think that love of philosophy may have killed the love in a man's heart for a woman: it would be necessary to consult the wives of philosophers on that point. But we may spare ourselves this inquiry, for Dante has never said, either in the *Vita Nuova* or elsewhere, that his love of Philosophy has "killed" the love in his heart for Beatrice. Quite the reverse, it was because he still loved Beatrice passionately even after her death that he turned first towards philosophy in order to console himself. Philosophy was very far from having killed in him a love of which the mere thought still carried him off into an ecstasy;[3] so much so that Dante addressed himself

[1] P. MANDONNET, *op. cit.*, p. 39.   [2] P. MANDONNET, *ibid.*
[3] DANTE, *Convivio*, II, 7.

to the philosophers, and in particular to the authors of philosophic Consolations, as the custodians of the only effective remedy for such afflictions. That is what the poet himself says: I sought to console myself, *cercava di consolarme*; I desired a remedy for my tears, *a le mie lagrime un remedio*.[1] Beyond doubt, and precisely because it was well chosen, the remedy was effective in the end; philosophy, or, as he defines it himself, amorous association with wisdom, in the end suppressed their cause. Let us add finally that even if it were true—and it is false: *Purg.*, XXX, 48—that Dante ever ceased to love Beatrice, it would not be true that Dante put forward his love of philosophy as having caused the death of his love for Beatrice. What he says, on the contrary, is that the persistence of his love for Beatrice has led him to the readings and studies from which his love for philosophy sprang. Thus are created the pseudo-facts charged with masking the joints which false hypotheses make necessary. We have, alas, not yet seen the last.

These deductions, which proceed implacably straight ahead, creating at every step the reality they pretend to discover, would in the end compel recognition merely by virtue of their internal coherence if, from time to time, they did not run into obstacles of such a sort that any unprejudiced mind must perceive them. Such is the case here. What the arguments of Father Mandonnet set out to prove is a very simple conclusion touching the hidden meaning of the *Vita Nuova*. He alleges that, under a veil of transparent symbols and poetic fictions which could only be taken literally by a somewhat obtuse mind, Dante's first book does not tell us the story of his love for a young Florentine girl, but of his desertion of theology, which was his first love, for human wisdom: "Dante is, then, a deserter from Theology who has gone over to Philosophy? Yes, and that is the *smarrimento*, as Dante says, addressing his soul, *nel quale se' caduta vilmente per questa donna che è apparita*" (*Conv.*, II, 10).[2]

Father Mandonnet's thesis not only has the instinct of self-preservation; it has all its creative fecundity. Here the expedient consists in not translating the word *smarrimento*, as if this unmysterious term were heavy with implications, then in commenting upon it with a passage in which the adverb *vilmente* is encountered. The impression is thereby created that this

<hr />

[1] DANTE, *Convivio*, II, 12.   [2] P. MANDONNET, *op. cit.*, p. 49.

smarrimento into which the coming of Dame Philosophy has igno-
miniously plunged Dante is something like a love that is disgraceful
and shameful in itself. Now in his commentary Dante himself
has translated this word for us; the agitation or confusion that he
designates is really fear: *la temenza*. And what fear? That
experienced by his first love when it saw itself all at once threatened by the birth of the second. The *Canzone* upon which the
Second Treatise of the *Banquet* comments described in this
passage the dialogue of a divided soul torn by two passions. A
"spirit of love", that is, according to Dante himself, the interior
voice of his nascent love for philosophy, harangues his soul in
these terms: "This fair lady, to whom thou hearkenest, has
transformed thy life to such a degree that thou art affrighted and
dost become fearful . . . But if thou deceivest not thyself, thou
shalt see her adorned with so many marvels, that thou wilt say:
Love, true lord, behold thy handmaid; do what pleaseth thee."
Thus, far from reproaching himself for his "second love" as if
it were a base thing, Dante has reproached himself for his first
hesitation in welcoming it as for an act of cowardice. Less
brave than Mary, Dante's soul could not say to the herald of
this new birth: "Behold the handmaid of the Lord; be it unto
me according to thy word."

Not only is it a complete perversion of this passage thus to
make Dante's second love bear the shame that he feels at having
welcomed it so timidly, but it is a formal contradiction of the
poet's testimony, and that in this same *Banquet*. Dante, we are
told, is a deserter from theology who has gone over to philosophy;
that is the whole story which the *Vita Nuova* and the *Banquet*
tell us. It is impossible to misrepresent the poet's words more
brazenly: "And as it happens often enough that a man sets out
in quest of silver and, not having thought thereon, finds gold
that is offered him by some hidden cause, and not perhaps
without divine ordinance, likewise also I who sought to console
myself found not only a remedy for my tears but words of
authors, sciences and books: whereon reflecting, I verily judged
that philosophy, which was the lady of these authors, sciences
and books, was a supreme thing. And I imagined it made like
a noble Lady . . . And because I imagined it thus (*da questo
imaginare*), I began to go where it was demonstrated truly,
namely in the schools of the friars and in the disputations of those

who practise philosophy; in such wise that after a short time, about thirty months, I began to feel so much of its sweetness, that its love drove away and destroyed every other thought. That is why, feeling myself carried away from the thought of the first love by the virtue of this one, it was with wonder that I opened my mouth to utter the words of the *canzone* in question . . ."[1]

This is the only passage in Dante which authorizes us to speak of the history of his studies otherwise than by inventing it ourselves. By a happy chance, this passage is perfectly clear. Dante has just said that he has lost Beatrice and that, in order to console himself, he has addressed himself to the philosophers. At this period he could not yet enter into the meaning of these authors except in so far as his understanding and his knowledge of the art of grammar allowed him: *quanto l'arte di grammatica ch'io avea e un poco di mio ingegno potea fare.*[2] Thus, like all his contemporaries, Dante did not go to philosophy from theology, but rather from grammar. Furthermore, this crystal-clear passage assures us, what one would moreover have surmised, that Dante did not study theology before philosophy any more than he studied it before grammar. In fact, if one looks closely at the passage, Dante does not even say that he studied theology at all at that time, but only that he went to the monastic schools to study philosophy. The sole issue here is therefore courses of philosophy organized in monastic *studia*. Of course, no one wishes to contest that Dante was from childhood instructed in his religion, or that as early as that period he assimilated some theology, whether through having learnt it by himself, or through having mixed with the theologians. To hear a sermon is to learn theology. It is evidently not of this that the writer intends to speak when he describes Dante as a deserter from theology who has gone over to philosophy; now, according to this unique passage which has just been quoted, Dante began to frequent monastic schools only at the very time when he began to study philosophy and in order to find philosophy there. How, then, could he have betrayed for philosophy a theology which he had never studied? More, since Dante only entered the schools of the theologians to seek philosophy, it was his love for Dame Philosophy that led him in their direction; he cannot therefore be made to say that he betrayed them for her.

[1] DANTE, *Convivio*, II, 12.   [2] DANTE, *ibid.*

It may be because he refuses to say so in this way that the writer attempts to make him say so differently. It is imagined, then, that at the beginning of the *Banquet* Dante has excused himself for having deserted that of the theologians and offering his readers only a philosophers' repast: "Besides, as early as the first page of the *Convivio* . . . Dante compares two feasts, another and his own . . . What he is about to serve up is his philosophic *Banquet*. The other, it is hardly necessary to say, is that of Theology."[1] Poor Dante! What has he not been made to say ? Because he speaks here of a table at which " the bread of the angels" is served, certain people conclude that it can only be that of the theologians, while others say that since it is evidently a question of philosophy throughout this passage Dante here raises the science of the philosophers to the rank of an ultimate beatific science and treacherously substitutes it for theology. In fact, I believe that it is really a question here of philosophy, a science that is indeed beatific in Dante's eyes—as will be seen later on—but not at the expense of theology. It matters little, moreover, for the question we have to settle is not that. We are told that Dante here opposes two banquets, his own and another, but whence comes the idea that there are two?

In Chapter I of the *Convivio* Dante first recalls that, as Aristotle says, all men naturally desire knowledge, "because learning is the ultimate perfection of our soul, in which our ultimate felicity resides". Then he adds that, although all desire it, many are cut off from this perfection, whether through evil disposition of the soul, or because their affairs or their absence from any school prevent them from working. Also "very few remain those who can succeed in possessing that which all desire, and almost countless are those who, thus prevented, live in a perpetual hunger for this food". Such is the contrast rendered by the image that immediately follows: "How happy they are, the small number who sit at this table where the bread of the angels is eaten! And how unhappy those who only share the food of the herd!" Now, concludes Dante, "I who do not sit at the blessed table, but, having escaped from the pastures of the vulgar, gather up, at the feet of those who sit there, part of that which they let fall"—I wish to remember my former companions in misery and to set before them that which I have put aside for them. As

---

[1] P. MANDONNET, *op. cit.*, p. 40.

may be seen, Dante is speaking here neither of Theology nor of Philosophy, whether to unite them or to contrast them. He in no way suggests that what he is about to serve up is of a different kind from this bread of the angels on which scholars feed; on the contrary, he says explicitly that his own banquet will consist of the remains from this same table at which the bread of the angels is eaten. In a less generous and less pure form it is therefore *the same food* that he is about to serve up to the disinherited of knowledge. If, therefore, taking one's stand on *Par*. II, 11, one were to claim that even in the *Convivio* the "bread of the angels" designates Theology, it would be necessary to conclude that, since the remains of this bread of the angels are served up there, the feast served up by Dante is also a theological feast. From this would follow two equally unacceptable consequences: one, that the *Convivio* was a work of theology, whereas Dante there constantly invokes Dame Philosophy and celebrates her cult; the other, that Dante had betrayed Theology in writing a book to initiate in that science those who have not had the time or the means to study it.

Thus, like a knight in the service of the Beatrice whom he has created, and with whom he is literally in love, Father Mandonnet for her sake challenges passage after passage to single combat. Always defeated, but never discouraged, when a passage bends beneath him be bestrides another, and so on indefinitely. After all, he is himself well aware what enormous objections await his exegesis. If one maintains, as he does, that " Beatrice is indeed, in her immediate signification, Theology" and that "this first lady has been succeeded by a second, philosophy", it is necessary by that very fact to maintain "that Alighieri had dedicated himself to Theology before Philosophy and that he forsook one for the other." Whereupon the objection comes forward of itself: Why does Dante nowhere say in the *Banquet* that his first lady was Theology, when he says "explicitly and many and many a time that his second lady . . . is Philosophy"?[1] It is a very amusing question. If we did not protest, we should end by wondering, with Father Mandonnet, why, since an anonymous lady whom we know to be a mere symbol of philosophy is presented to us as philosophy, another lady, who bears a proper name and is nowhere reduced to the state

[1] P. MANDONNET, *op. cit.*, p. 42.

of a symbol, is not presented to us as being theology. Perhaps it is simply that she is not theology, but Beatrice.

Not a bit of it, nevertheless objects Father Mandonnet; Beatrice is really only theology, but Dante does not want to say so, because he is none too proud of what he is relating: "Dante is not anxious to cry from the house-tops that he has been a cleric and that he has abandoned the pursuit of his vocation."[1] Why did he not keep silent if he did not wish it to be known? But what, then, had he after all to be so ashamed of? We are in the Middle Ages, that is to say at a time when the study of philosophy was essentially the work of a cleric. St. Albert the Great and St. Thomas Aquinas, illustrious theologians, did not hesitate to interrupt their theological work to write long commentaries on the philosophical works of Aristotle. These men never thought that they had betrayed their clerical vocation in so doing. Dante had not so much theology to lose; but above all, let us remember that it was through love of philosophy that he penetrated for the first time into the monastic schools. To imagine that he judged as dishonourable a step that was natural in itself and in such conformity with the customs of the time is to write his history topsy-turvy, in a topsy-turvy mediaeval world in which it seems to be supposed that Dante lived.

When it is so sure of itself, an exegesis is never without resources. Father Mandonnet's ingenuity is apparent not only in the ease with which he finds solutions to the problems he creates, but also in the art with which he arranges his arguments and graduates his effects. After passing through a series of probabilities, each of which leaves room for doubt, one is brought abruptly face to face with the massive, tangible, irrefutable proof which cannot fail to compel assent. Remembering, then, the doubts which had assailed him, the ingenuous reader reproaches himself for them as though they were unjustified prejudices; all probabilities become for him demonstrations. This indeed is the blow that Father Mandonnet was keeping in reserve. You are unwilling to believe the foregoing demonstrations? Very well, but then how do you explain that Dante himself has said, of the Ladies who people his work: "These are not women"? And, indeed, that definitely settles the question, provided he has said it.

[1] P. MANDONNET, op. cit., p. 42.

According to Father Mandonnet, not only has Dante said that his ladies are not women, but he has said so twice. What first strikes our historian is "the systematic omission of the name of *woman* which could have been attributed to the Dantesque ladies" and which even should have been attributed to them if they had been either "veritable women" or even "real women used after the event as symbols". They are therefore "exclusively mere symbols, created out of nothing for their allegorical office".[1] That, he adds, is "a material and explicit proof of this fact". Yet, in order to remove all hesitation, Dante has uttered this name of *femmina* but twice only and, in both cases, "it was just to affirm that these ladies are not women. Speaking of Beatrice, the protagonist of the *Vita Nuova*, Dante has written explicitly: 'That is not a woman'—*quella non è femmina* (Chap. XXVI). And the others? The others also are not women: *non sono pure femmine* (Chap. XIX). Thus women are mentioned in the *Vita Nuova* only twice, and then in order to say that the ladies . . . are not women, as much as to say that they are but mere symbols".

Let us refer to these two passages and, since Father Mandonnet says that he uses the text and translation of H. Cochin, let us consult them in this edition. So far as regards Beatrice, we there read, Chap. XXVI, p. 119: "Many used to say, after she had passed: This is not a woman, but she is one of the most fair angels of heaven." Of the women who hear themselves called " angels", very few expect to be treated as "symbols". But let us pass on. And the others, as Father Mandonnet says? This is what the poet tells us of the others, in Chap. XIX of the *Vita Nuova*, in a passage where he is simply concerned to say why the *canzone* upon which he is commenting begins with the word *Donne*. His reply is that, to speak of such a noble subject as Beatrice, he must address his *canzone* "not to all ladies, but solely to those who are noble, and are not merely women".[2] Thus Father Mandonnet begins by not even following the text or the translation which he cites; furthermore, he extends to all the other ladies in the *Vita Nuova* what Dante says only of the ladies to whom he addresses this *canzone*; finally, having to translate *a coloro che sono gentili e che non sono pur femmine*, instead

---

[1] P. MANDONNET, *op. cit.*, pp. 54–55.

[2] DANTE ALIGHIERI, *Vita Nuova*, following the critical text prepared for the *Società Dantesca Italiana* by Michele Barbi, translated with an Introduction and notes by Henry Cochin, Paris, Champion, 2nd edit., 1914, p. 69.

of translating: "to those who are noble [in the sense of "Noble lady", as in "Nobleman"] and who are not merely women", he extracts from these words, by an incomprehensible feat of conjuring: "these are not women". A lady does not cease to exist because she is separated from common women any more than a real woman dissolves into a symbol by the fact that she is called an angel. Moreover, Father Mandonnet must have been indeed infatuated with his hypothesis not to have seen in this same sentence an answer to the question he was propounding. Why does Dante never use *femmina*, but *donna*, when he speaks of these ladies? Because they are not simply women, but ladies; their very rank forces him to use this word.

After that, what are we to say of the confirmations with which Father Mandonnet seeks afterwards to reinforce his thesis? He asserts that, having twice denied that his ladies are real women, the poet has intentionally declared twice that the Virgin Mary herself was in reality a woman, by which Dante means (he alleges) to say to his reader: "Do not imagine that if I have not said of my ladies in the *Vita Nuova* that they are women it is due to forgetfulness or chance. The proof of the contrary is that in speaking of the mother of Christ I affirm, apparently without reason, that she was in reality a woman; and I say it twice, for symmetry, because in the *Vita Nuova* I have also said twice that my ladies are not women. Will you finally understand the difference that exists between my ladies and real women?"[1]

Ah, no! I still do not understand it. First, what symmetry can there be between two facts which exist and two facts which have been seen not to exist? Moreover, where are these two facts which exist? In an early passage in the *Banquet*, IV, 5, in which he is speaking of the time of the Incarnation, Dante says simply that God had foreseen the birth of a woman superior to all others: *una femmina ottima di tutte l'altre*. He therefore does not say that Mary was "really a woman", as this so-called symmetry would have it, but he simply comments upon the word of St. Paul, *Galat.*, IV, 4: *At ubi venit plenitudo temporis, misit Deus filium suum, factum ex muliere* ("But when the fulness of time was come, God sent forth His Son, made of a woman"). Since St. Paul has said it, why should Dante not say it? There remains the other passage, that in *Convivio*, II, 5, in which it is

[1] P. MANDONNET, *op. cit.*, p. 57.

said that the Emperor of the universe is Christ: " son of the
sovereign God, and son of the Virgin Mary (in reality a woman
and daughter of Joachim and Adam), a real man, who is dead . . ."
Whereupon Father Mandonnet asks us: "Why emphasize, twice,
that the Virgin Mary is in reality a woman? In the history of
the Church and of theology no one has ever doubted it, and
Dante's insistence appears at first sight devoid of reason."[1]
Perhaps, but there is no need to explain either why Dante has
said it twice, since he has said it only once, or why he insists
on it, since in fact he does not insist. Most certainly, he has
indeed said once that the Virgin Mary was really a woman, but
the very structure of his sentence explains why. In adding to:
*figliuolo di Maria Vergine, femmina veramente e figlia di Ioacchina e
d'Adam,* the two words: *uomo vero,* Dante gives us to understand
that if Christ was a real man, it was because His mother was
really a woman. As St. Cyril had said, and as St. Thomas repeats
after him: "The Word of God is born of the substance of God
the Father; but since He has put on the flesh, it must necessarily
be recognized that, according to the flesh, He is born of a
woman."[2] I do not see that Dante himself meant to say anything
else. Moreover, whatever may have been his intention, this
passage alone leaves us very far from the four passages of Father
Mandonnet and their symmetry. It is difficult to imagine in
what way the statement that the Virgin Mary was a real woman
can signify that Beatrice was not one.

II. BEATRICE METAMORPHOSED INTO A NUMBER

Beatrice, then, for Father Mandonnet, is the symbol of theology,
but, since she represents the Christian life in its entirety, this
cannot prevent her from symbolizing something else besides.
Now it happens that Dante himself attached a definite symbolism
to the character of Beatrice and that he has explained it to us.
This time, then, we are on sure ground. In the first place, it is
certain that the *Vita Nuova* conceals an allegorical meaning under
the cloak of the literal meaning; the fact would be easily perceived, even if Dante had not said as much. It is likewise certain,

---

[1] P. MANDONNET, *op. cit.,* p. 56.
[2] ST. THOMAS AQUINAS, *Summa theologica,* Pars III, qu. 35, art. 4, ad. 2m.

since Dante himself has taken care to notify us of it, that as early as the *Vita Nuova* Beatrice takes on a religious symbolism, that of the number nine, of which the root is three, that is to say, "the admirable Trinity".[1] What Dante does not say—though Father Mandonnet wishes at all costs to make him say it—is that Beatrice is nothing more than her name symbolizes. One can make him say it simply by stressing one half of a sentence of his in order to obliterate the other half from the reader's mind "Thinking thereon more discerningly, and *in accordance with the infallible truth, this number was her very self;* I speak figuratively, and my meaning is this . . ." etc.[2] But the stress might be altered: "Thinking thereon more discerningly, and in accordance with the infallible truth, this number was her very self; *I speak figuratively*, and my meaning is this . . ." etc. We may even do as Dante did, stressing nothing at all and read his sentence as he wrote it. In that case its sense is as follows: The number three was not only the lucky number of Beatrice: it was Beatrice herself—by analogy, I mean, etc. Whence it follows naturally that Beatrice was not a number in reality, but that she was one symbolically, which is rather different.

In another passage in the *Vita Nuova*, Dante says that he had written a letter in the form of a *serventese*, quoting in it the names of the sixty most beautiful ladies in the town in which Beatrice lived, and that the name of Beatrice refused to occupy any place in this list but the ninth.[3] It seems to me beyond dispute that Dante is here invoking the sacred symbolism of Beatrice. We must say so, then, and undoubtedly it is wise to leave it at that. This is not what Father Mandonnet does; he scents mysteries of quite a different order underneath. "A downcast spirit," he observes, "would find that sixty beautiful ladies constitute an exaggerated figure, even for a town like Florence, in which everything—people and things—is famous for its beauty, but which was not very large at the time of Dante." In reality, he adds, this number sixty happens to be the symbol of the natural and scientific order, as may be inferred from St. Thomas, *Quodlib.*, VIII, 1. On the other hand, in the *Banquet*, II, 14, Dante likens the sciences to the sixty queens mentioned by King Solomon, above whom Theology sits enthroned. Consequently it is

---

[1] *Vita Nuova*, XXIX.   [2] P. MANDONNET, *Dante le Théologien*, p. 46.
[3] *Vita Nuova*, VI.

impossible to doubt that the sixty ladies are the sixty parts of philosophy and that Beatrice, who sits enthroned above them, is Theology.[1] Numerical symbolism and theological symbolism here conspire to assure us of it.

How are we to unravel the skein of this symbolist arithmetic? We think we are´pulling out a thread, and that thread is in itself a skein. To understand the reasoning that precedes, we must not only admit that numbers may have a symbolic value, which no one disputes, but also (1) that the multiples of a number havè the same symbolism as that number; (2) that 1 symbolizes indifferently God or the natural order,[2] which fact vastly extends its field of application; (3) that, since philosophy belongs to the natural order, any number which symbolizes that order also symbolizes philosophy. Starting from this point, it is easy to find any number and to make it signify what one wishes. Here, the number we have to find is 60; let us say, then, that 1 (God) x 10 = divine perfection, and since St. Thomas teaches that 6 symbolizes the completion of the Creation, we may reckon thus: 10 (divine perfection) x 6 (Creation) = 60. But sixty what? Father Mandonnet knows: by multiplying the perfection of God by the number of days occupied by the Creation, one obtains indifferently the number of the prettiest women in Florence at the time of Dante, the number of King Solomon's Queens and the number of the parts of philosophy. And I am quite willing to admit that all this only makes one, but these arguments strongly resemble the famous problem: Given the tonnage of a boat and the number of knots it makes, find the age of its captain. Let us again read Father Mandonnet: "The number sixty is composed of ten, the perfection of unity and the symbol of the unity of God, together with the figure six, the symbol of the Creation as being completed in six days. *That is why* there are sixty ladies, *that is to say* sixty subdivisions of the scientific order."[3] Now, not only is all this gratuitously laid to Dante's account, but, even if we were to concede the premises, the desired conclusion

---

[1] P. MANDONNET, *Dante le Théologien*, pp. 49–50. Father Mandonnet's statistics seem to me here a little arbitrary, for he does not quote any figure. According to Villani, Florence was in 1339 a town of 90,000 inhabitants (see G. SALVEMINI, *Florence in the Time of Dante*, in *Speculum*, July, 1936, Vol. XI, No. 3, p. 318); but how can one know the number of inhabitants Florence must have in order to contain sixty pretty women?

[2] P. MANDONNET, *Dante le Théologien*, p. 188, note 1.

[3] P. MANDONNET, *op. cit.*, p. 48, note 1. On this passage from the *Banquet*, see below, Chap. II, p. 116.

would not always emerge from them. For it is a question not only of obtaining sixty, but of proving that, if the sixty queens are sixty sciences, and if the queens are ladies, the sixty ladies are sixty sciences. This cannot be demonstrated, for two reasons. The first is that, Beatrice being reckoned among the sixty most beautiful women in her town, they are in fact only sixty in number, whereas, since King Solomon's "dove" hovers above the sixty queens, their total amounts to sixty-one. They cannot therefore be compared. The second reason is that, if we were to be entitled to compare the two passages, the Beatrice of the *Vita Nuova* would have to be to the sixty ladies as the Theology of the *Banquet* is to the sixty queens, standing for the sciences. Now, in the *Vita Nuova* Beatrice refuses to occupy any rank among the ladies but the ninth: she is, therefore, certainly one of them; in the *Banquet*, on the contrary, Theology hovers like a pure dove above the sixty queens, standing for the sciences: it is therefore not one of them. Since the ratio " Beatrice: sixty ladies : : Theology: sixty sciences" does not hold good, it is impossible to deduce from it either that the sixty ladies are the sixty sciences, or that Beatrice is Theology.

Once he has succumbed to the bemusing influence of numbers, our historian will never be able to stop. Indeed, Father Mandonnet very appropriately remembers that in a sonnet to his friend Guido Cavalcanti Dante identified another lady by a number. Nay more, he "called his Lady 'No. 30' ".[1] Perhaps the reader hastens to conclude: "I know this Lady! The number 10 is Creation in its perfection; the number three is the Trinity; 10 x 3 = the miracle of Creation—Beatrice." But how stupid

---

[1] The allusion is to the sonnet to Guido Cavalcanti: *Guido i' vorrei . . .* It will be found in any edition of Dante's *Canzoniere*. In the one that I have before me—*Tutte le opere di Dante Alighieri*, Florence, G. Barbèra, 1919—it is classified among the *Rime Amorose*, XV, p. 153. I permit myself the observation that the present note is the thirty-first in this chapter; 31 = 3 (divine Trinity) + 1 (divine unity); that the sonnet to Guido is the fifteenth in this edition: 15 = 1 + 5 = 6, number of the creation, because it is a creation of Dante's; 15 is half 30, which is the number of the science of ethics. Finally— and this fact seems to me of considerable significance—the edition I am citing is dated 1919, a number itself formed of two others: 1 twice repeated and 9 twice repeated, to indicate, by a duplicated symbol, the unity of Dante's work and its wholly sacred character. On the other hand, if we take separately each of these two groups of numbers, that is to say 19, we obtain twice 1 + 9 = 10, that is to say the duplicated affirmation of the creature symbolized by the number one, but taken in its perfection, which is 10, because, being a likeness created by God the Creator, Dante's art is, in the order of artistic creation, a perfect counterpart of the divine art. I prefer to forestall my critics, since every objection that tends to cast doubts upon these obvious facts will find me unshakable.

we are! Mrs. No. 30 cannot be Beatrice, since Beatrice is already
Mrs. No. 9! We know, moreover, that there are sixty ladies,
so the newcomer must be the thirtieth of the sciences. Which
one? As Dante has never given the names of the sixty queens,
the sixty sciences or the sixty ladies, the problem is difficult to
solve. It is so, at all events, for us, but not for Father Mandonnet.
Thirty, he says, is half sixty, therefore science No. 30 is the middle
science, that is to say Ethics.[1] To which it will first be objected
that, in the hierarchical classification of the sciences which Dante
himself has left to us, and to which we shall return at our leisure,[2]
he did not assign to Ethics the number 30, but the number 1.
Moreover, it is not even true that in the sonnet in question Dante
"called his Lady 'No. 30' ". He says simply that she is "quella
ch'è *sul numero* del trenta", or even, as the edition of G. Barbèra
has it, "con quella ch'è in sul numer delle trenta".[3] Who was
this lady? Guido Cavalcanti knew, without a doubt. But, to anyone who has read Cavalcanti, what a pleasure it must be to
imagine him reading for the first time this Dantesque sonnet as
revised by Father Mandonnet! Dante there hopes for a pleasant
meeting, at which the friends will speak endlessly of love with
Monna Vanna, Monna Lagia and—Ethics. Let us conclude
with Dante: "And each one of them would be content, as I verily
believe that we also would be." Indeed, with two Florentine
women and Ethics, Dante and Guido could not fail to amuse
themselves! Cavalcanti at least, as he is portrayed to us, would
willingly have dispensed with Ethics.

There is no conceivable reason why these numerical exegeses
should ever come to a stop. Their possibilities are like those
of number itself—unlimited. If it is pointed out to Father
Mandonnet by way of objection that Dante never enumerated
the sixty famous subdivisions of philosophy, our historian replies:
That is true, but he named a score of them in the four books of
the *Banquet* that he wrote; now this work was to number fourteen
books; Dante would certainly have found means to name the
other forty sciences in the ten books which he did not write.[4]
How can we deny it? Still, Dante did not need fourteen books
to name these sixty sciences; sixty words were enough for him,

---

[1] P. MANDONNET, *Dante le Théologien*, pp. 52-53.
[2] See below, Chap. II, p. 99.
[3] *Tutte le opere* . . ., p. 153.
[4] P. MANDONNET, *Dante le Théologien*, p. 50.

and the moment at which it is maintained that he counted sixty of them was really the moment when he should have named them. These ten books that Dante did not write comfortably accommodate the suppositions of his interpreters. Everything in them is symbolic, *even the fact that they do not exist*. Do not think that I am making this up—it is Father Mandonnet who says it: "It does not appear certain, moreover, that Dante had the intention of finishing the *Convivio*. I believe that he treated a part of it in order to signify symbolically that philosophy is an imperfect thing, never complete."[1] If there is a symbolism even of nothingness, it is really not clear why Beatrice should not be reduced to the symbolism of a number. Is theology itself, then, a perfect thing, always complete? If it is not so either, why did Dante finish the *Divine Comedy*? But let us pass on. We shall be left with the certainty of this—that, if he had wished, Dante could have named the forty sciences that are missing, in ten books which he perhaps never intended to write. And, indeed, the ratio $40 : 0^{10}$ may symbolize anything.

III. BEATRICE METAMORPHOSED INTO BAPTISM

When, eventually, he makes his own approach to the account which Dante gives of his life in the *Vita Nuova*, Father Mandonnet begins by settling several points which seem to me beyond dispute and which, I feel, few of his interpreters would dream of contesting. The first relates to the difference in kind between the division of the ages of life in the *Banquet* and in the *Vita Nuova*. In the *Banquet* Dante follows, or adapts to his own ends, a recognized classification of the ages of man; in the *Vita Nuova* all the events occur and all the stages of life are marked off in periods of nine years. If we remember that nine is the "lucky number" of Beatrice, and that the root of that number is the Trinity, we cannot doubt for an instant that the computation of the *Vita Nuova* is symbolical and that it should in consequence be treated as such. As Father Mandonnet very well says: "The chronology of either work refers to a wholly different order of things";[2] and since the times in the *Vita Nuova* are divided throughout into periods of nine years—9–18 and 18–27—

[1] P. MANDONNET, *Dante le Théologien*, p. 50, note 2.   [2] *Op. cit.*, p. 69.

we must conclude with Henry Cochin that Dante intended "to express the ages of his life in terms of the number nine, which is the perfect number and the basis of his whole narrative and of his whole argument on the subject of Beatrice".[1] All this is excellent.

This, of course, is still not enough for Father Mandonnet, who adds forthwith that "it is certain that here again *Vita Nuova* means *ninth life*—life beginning at nine, of which nine is the symbol, the light, the key".[2] How *nova* can mean "ninth" in Italian is a riddle to which the creative power of Father Mandonnet holds the clue. Everyone knows that "ninth life" could be rendered in Italian only by "vita nona", *nona* being as distinct from *nova* in Italian as the word *neuvième* is from the word *nouvelle* in French.[3] What is more curious is that the desire to link these two words is probably the only reason for which Father Mandonnet has been led to prefer the form *nova* to *nuova*. It is true that Henry Cochin had adopted it before him, but he did so simply "for the convenience of the French reader".[4] In any case this detail is of little importance. Even the exact meaning of the title—*Youth, New Life*—is of little importance; Dantologists do not agree on this subject, and we are not qualified to decide between them. The only point that interests us is what Father Mandonnet will deduce from the premises that we have seen him put forward.

First of all—and we might have expected it—the sense of this title holds no ambiguity for him. *Vita Nuova* means first and foremost "new life", and "what constitutes the novelty in Dante's life is that at the age of nine he saw and loved Beatrice for the first time".[5] "The realists take the statement at its face

---

[1] H. COCHIN, *Vita Nova*, p. 182. Nevertheless there is, as it seems to me, an exception to this rule, and it occurs in the *Vita Nuova*. It is the date assigned by Dante to the death of Beatrice—June 8th, 1290. As a matter of fact, this date lends itself so reluctantly to the symbolism of the number nine that, to find such a symbolism in it, Dante has been obliged to have recourse to three different calendars: the Arabic calendar for the day, the Syrian calendar for the month, the Italian calendar for the year. It is hard to believe that, if a real date were not involved, Dante would not have been capable of inventing one more favourable to his symbolism. As has been pointed out, that fact is a very strong argument in favour of the genuineness of this date and of the reality of Beatrice. See on these various points EDW. MOORE, *Studies in Dante.* Second Series, Oxford, Clarendon Press, 1899: II, *Beatrice*, p. 114 and pp. 123–124.

[2] P. MANDONNET, *Dante le Théologien*, p. 67, note 1.

[3] Nova, nouvelle = new; nona, neuvième = ninth (*Translator's note*).

[4] H. COCHIN, *Vita Nova*, p. 183.

[5] P. MANDONNET, *Dante le Théologien*, p. 71. Let us recall, as a reminder, that *vita nuova* certainly signifies "youth" in *Purg.*, XXX, 115.

value. The child Dante was beguiled by the beauty and the per-
fections of a young Florentine woman of his own age." To
avoid such foolishness let us search the supernatural and Christian
order for "the symbolism of Beatrice at the age of nine".[1]

Following in this the opinion of some Dantologists, Father
Mandonnet chooses first to apply to Beatrice the words of Dante
in a *canzone* which, however, he did not include in the *Vita Nuova*:
"On the day when she came into the world, according to what
is contained in the book of the mind, which is prone to error,
my small person suffered a new passion."[2] Since Dante was
only six months older than Beatrice, it would be absurd to
suppose "that he, a child of some six months, fainted because a
little Florentine girl, if Florentine she was, came into the world".[3]
The only plausible explanation of these lines is that "the day
on which the Lady came into this world was none other than
the day on which Dante received baptism, or the sanctifying
grace, which made him a Christian . . . Consequently, nothing
could be clearer than the sequence of the words and ideas in
the *canzone*".[4]

This rejoicing is premature, for, after all, if the *Vita Nuova* is
such a rigidly composed work as we are told, Dante must have
had his reasons for not including this *canzone* in it. By what
right do we ordain that the Lady in question should be Beatrice?
Many Dantologists uphold this theory, some dispute it, but none
knows for certain. Dante does not tell us the Lady's name, so
we do not know who she was. If she is someone other than
Beatrice, there is no longer any reason to suppose that Dante
was six months old on the day she was born. If she is indeed
Beatrice, the possibility arises that her birth coincided with
Dante's baptism, that Dante, then, was not baptized until he
was five or six months old and even, as we are told, that the
date of the baptism was postponed because baptism was effected
by immersion. This is, indeed, possible, but since the date of
Dante's baptism is not known, we cannot tell if that is what
happened.

This, moreover, is not the real question. Why seek theological
explanations so far afield? One is amazed to think that Dante
may have fallen in a faint on the day a little girl was born,

---

[1] P. MANDONNET, *op. cit.*, p. 74.
[2] P. MANDONNET, *op. cit.*, p. 76.
[3] P. MANDONNET, *op. cit.*, p. 77.
[4] P. MANDONNET, *op. cit.*, p. 78.

because it is improbable that *a child five or six months old* would
faint for such a cause. This is, indeed, improbable; but at what
age would it first become probable? That a chivalrous poet like
the author of the *Vita Nuova* should indulge in these poetic
fictions is not surprising, but one can suggest no other explanation
without entering the realm of improbability and, of all the
surprising explanations, the one which makes the birth of Beatrice
coincide with the baptism of Dante is not the least difficult to
accept. The first thing that the poet tells us of the emotion
which he felt then is that it filled him with fear: *Una passion
nuova, Tal ch'io rimasi di paura pieno.* So the little Alighieri,
when five or six months old, was filled with fear by the liberating
grace of baptism, and with such fear that he was still to remember
it when grown up? Nay more: this new passion paralysed
Dante's faculties with such suddenness that he fell to the ground:
Sì ch'io caddi in terra.[1] Must we believe that the child was
dropped by his nurse? But it was he, not his nurse, who was
being baptized. Or else are we to suppose that Dante walked
by himself at the age of five or six months? That would be an
interesting biographical discovery. Or, finally, are we to say
that the small person of whom Dante is speaking in this *canzone*
was not the body but the "soul" of this child?[2] Although the
theology of this seems to me doubtful—for it is not souls that
are baptized, but men—I am quite willing to feign agreement.
Shall we have to admit, then, that Dante's soul fell to the ground?
In whatever way this exegesis is defended, I confess that I do not
understand.

Let us, however, rest assured that Father Mandonnet has not
understood either. Having cut short the text of the *canzone* at
the convenient place, he considers himself rid of the difficulties
raised by the rest. Any text suits him up to the point where it
ceases to accord with his thesis. Thus early it is clear that the
Lady of the *canzone* must be Beatrice, and this Lady must also
be the grace of baptism, because, if that is regarded as proved, it
will have been proved at the same time that "Dante's Lady is
merely a fiction";[3] now "Dante's Lady" is a fiction, therefore
all this is proved. Father Mandonnet is so sure of it that he even

[1] DANTE, *Tutte le opere . . .* ; *Rime Amorose, Canz.,* XXIII; p. 155, l. 57 *et seq.*
[2] P. MANDONNET, *Dante le Théologien,* p. 80.
[3] P. MANDONNET, *op. cit.,* p. 83.

knows why, although the "baptismal *canzone*" (*sic*) refers to
Beatrice, Dante did not include it in the *Vita Nuova*.[1] The reason,
he says, is that "Beatrice, the personification of the grace received
at baptism, belongs to all Christians alike and on that account
cannot signify a modality peculiar to the life of Dante". That
is why, leaving this *canzone* aside, the poet will only begin the
story of his life in the *Vita Nuova* at about the age of nine. But
since we do not know if this *canzone* applies to Beatrice, and it
is not clear how the effects of the passion that it mentions could
have been those of baptism, the fact that is to be explained seems
to be a product of the very mind that explains it. However,
let us continue on our way. All this will perhaps become clear
when we are acquainted with "the modality peculiar to the life
of Dante" with which the poet chose to begin his narrative.

IV. BEATRICE METAMORPHOSED INTO THE TONSURE

With the first encounter of Dante and Beatrice we in fact
enter into the actual narrative of the *Vita Nuova*. After making
good-natured fun of the "realists" who do not find love so
improbable in a child of nine, "especially if he is precocious",[2]
Father Mandonnet offers his own explanation of this famous
passage (*Vita Nuova*, II): The encounter with Beatrice marks
the moment when "Dante turns his gaze towards the ecclesiastical
life and begins to prepare for it by the study of grammar, probably followed by a grounding in theology".[3]

I am quite ready to acknowledge that the age of nine can
hardly be accepted as authentic, for the simple reason that it
clearly forms part of a symbolical computation, of which Dante
himself has handed us the key. I modestly confess that I am
credulous enough not to deem *impossible* the birth of a violent
passionate feeling in a child of nine, especially if his name is
Dante. But the question is here of no interest. Once it is admitted that the computation of the *Vita Nuova* is symbolical in
its very essence, all the chronological details of that work must
be regarded, if not as historically false, at all events as historically
suspect. Yet the question whether the facts themselves are

---

[1] P. MANDONNET, *op. cit.*, pp. 83–84.   [2] P. MANDONNET, *op. cit.*, p. 72.
[3] P. MANDONNET, *op. cit.*, p. 84.

pure symbols because they are allotted symbolical dates stands where it was. Father Mandonnet's observations on this point remain somewhat obscure. After all, it *is* the text of the *Vita Nuova*, Chapter II, that is the subject of this discussion. Dante there says that he met her whom he will call Beatrice at a time when she was almost at the beginning of her ninth year, and he almost at the end of his. This encounter lasted only as long as an encounter does last, and it was *in quel punto,* at that point, that a terrible thrill passed through his veins and affected his vital spirits. When someone says that this date marks the moment, or the approximate moment, at which Dante turned his gaze towards the ecclesiastical life and applied himself to the study of grammar, and that he began ere long to study theology, undoubtedly he does not think that he did all this at the moment of an encounter. But, in that case, what does he think? Since he tells us nothing else, we are driven to conclude that that is what he does think; or rather, since that would be absurd, that he does not even ask himself what he would have to think in order to be able to say what he does say.

What justifies such a fear is that from this point onwards Father Mandonnet's interpretation becomes so arbitrary that one can hardly discuss it politely. Passing at once to the second encounter with Beatrice, our interpreter notes that this Lady appeared to Dante nine years later "between two noble ladies who were of more advanced age", that is to say, manifestly, "Poetry and Philosophy, which are older than the Christian Revelation". And upon my word, that is quite possible. It is next recalled that this admirable Lady greeted him. Her greeting, we are assured, is "Dante's admission into the clerical profession".[1] Once again, it might be so! After receiving this greeting, Dante withdrew from the world and shut himself in his room in order to think of this Lady. In fact, it is explained, he obeyed the word of the Gospel: *Non estis de mundo* ("Be not of the world"). Nothing in all this is impossible; since the hypothesis does not contradict the text, it is gratuitous, but not impossible. Accordingly, we find Dante in his room. There he has a vision which Father Mandonnet interprets as "the epitome of the vicissitudes of his clerical career, which will be abandoned".[2] It is here that things go wrong, and we shall be wise to interrogate the poet

---

[1] P. MANDONNET, *op. cit.,* p. 84.   [2] P. MANDONNET, *op. cit.,* p. 85.

himself about this vision, of which Father Mandonnet relates only so much as he pleases.

Dante first of all sees a cloud the colour of fire; from within this cloud, a Lord, who is terrible to behold but is himself full of joy, utters some obscure words of which Dante understands only a few, notably these: *Ego dominus tuus*—"I am thy master". In the arms of this Lord sleeps Beatrice; she is naked, and wrapped only in a pale red cloth. In one hand she holds a flaming heart. Next, this Lord wakens Beatrice and wishes to make her eat the burning heart. She only does so after some hesitation. Soon afterwards, the joy of this Lord turns to tears, and, gathering up the Lady in his arms, he seems to depart heavenwards with her. Thereupon Dante wakes up and writes a sonnet—for he is already a writer—to the "famous *trouvères*" of the time. The sonnet interprets his dream thus: This Lord is Love, who holds Dante's heart in his hand, makes the terrified Beatrice devour it and finally departs in tears. This sonnet, concludes Dante, evoked many different answers, among which he mentions in particular the *Vedesti al mio parere onne valore* of Guido Cavalcanti. This marked the beginning of the friendship between the two poets.[1]

If it was obscure at the time, the meaning of this sonnet was to become clear to the simplest when Dante's love for Beatrice became known. To us, at all events, it is so, since Dante himself has taken the trouble to interpret it to us. To this interpretation Father Mandonnet pays no heed. What interests him is his own, which is as follows: Through the medium of the terrible Lord with his obscure words, "Dante indicates that he did not entirely realize the significance of the obligations that the clerical vocation entails".[2] Yet he understands *Ego dominus tuus*, and, in fact, "it is the idea expressed, and almost the formula uttered, by the cleric when he receives the tonsure: *Dominus pars hereditatis meae . . .*" ("The Lord is part of mine inheritance"). After which, says Father Mandonnet, the rest of the vision is easy to understand. After some time (a year or more) "the Lord, who carries the sleeping Beatrice in his arms, makes her eat Dante's heart. She eats it at first hesitatingly (*dubitosamente*); this is Dante's uncertain frame of mind at the time when he took Minor

---

[1] *Vita Nova*, III; ed. H. Cochin, pp. 9–15.
[2] P. MANDONNET, *Dante le Théologien*, p. 85.

Orders. A short time afterwards her joy turns to tears of great bitterness. She nestles in the Lord's arms, and both seem to depart heavenwards". The worst has happened. Beatrice, that is to say Dante's clerical vocation, is dead; Dante will not go beyond Minor Orders, he will never assume the subdiaconate.[1]

This ingenious commentary has only one fault: it does not explain the text. Who is this Lord whose words Dante does not wholly understand? He is, I imagine, God. And who is this woman who sleeps in his arms? We are told that she is Dante's clerical vocation. Very well. Why is she naked? And why wrapped in a pale red cloth? We are not told. This Lord holds in his hand Dante's burning heart. For what purpose does this heart burn? If it is for the Lord, or for his vocation, one ceases to understand how his vocation is uncertain. True, it is Beatrice herself who seems to hesitate, but since the heart which is offered to her is aflame with love, why does this vocation hesitate? There is nothing in Father Mandonnet's very un-Freudian *Traumdeutung* to explain this strange phenomenon of a vocation which is offered a burning heart, accepts it and then becomes discouraged. It really looks here as if Dante's vocation is a person lacking any connection with him, having feelings that take no account of his. Father Mandonnet assures us, moreover, that, as soon as she has devoured Dante's heart, this lady's joy "turns to tears of great bitterness. She nestles in the Lord's arms, and both seem to depart heavenwards".[2] It is unnecessary to discuss this interpretation, because here Father Mandonnet gets visibly muddled in his story. It is the Lord, not Beatrice, who sees his joy turned to tears; it is the Lord who gathers up Beatrice in his arms to take her away, and not Beatrice who nestles against him in order that he may take her away. And I am well aware that Father Mandonnet would explain this version as easily as the other, but his explanations resemble the text of Dante as much as *Ecce Dominus tuus* ("Behold thy Lord") resembles *Dominus pars hereditatis meae* ("The Lord is part of mine inheritance"). To be satisfied by such concordances one must be truly easy to please. For their part, the requirements of these preconceived theses are, on the contrary, insatiable. Nothing would be gained by admitting Father Mandonnet's theory that in meeting Beatrice Dante really met the tonsure of the clericate. The symbolist

[1] P. MANDONNET, *op. cit.*, p. 86.   [2] P. MANDONNET, *op. cit.*, p. 86.

exegesis demands much more of us, as we shall be able to establish in a moment.

V. Beatrice Metamorphosed into Minor Orders

The reader has doubtless noted the bold affirmation that Dante not only assumed the tonsure but took Minor Orders, and stopped only on the threshold of the subdiaconate. What convinced Father Mandonnet of this was a sentence in the *Vita Nuova*, XIV: "I have set my feet at that point of life beyond which none may advance with the will to return." Indeed, he observes, the obligation of the subdiaconate is irrevocable and, besides, in the ordination of the subdeacon, the ordinand expresses his decision by taking a step.[1]

To a mind already persuaded that the meaning of the *Vita Nuova* is entirely theological, Dante's words are certainly an irresistible temptation, but to anyone who merely wonders what they mean their sense appears different. It is true that the aspirant to the subdiaconate takes a step forward to signify his decision and that the last step thus taken is irrevocable; but Dante mentions nothing of the sort. Since he tells us that he "set his feet" at a point beyond which another step would have been irrevocable, it follows that the step he took was still revocable, in direct contrast to the one that the subdeacon has to take. What emerges, then, is simply this, that Dante tells us, not indeed that he took a step, but that he "restrained his feet" (*io tenni i piedi*), that is to say that he found himself at the extreme limit of that point in life whence return is possible, and that, when being ordained a subdeacon, the ordinand takes a step forward to set his feet at that point whence there is no return. These two facts are unrelated. Yet, Father Mandonnet would say, since Dante speaks of a point beyond which another step would be irrevocable, he is thinking of the minor cleric in face of the subdiaconate. The objection would hold good if this were the only point in life beyond which none may pass with any hope of returning; but there is at least one other, and we shall see that this is the one of which Dante is speaking. Moreover, Father Mandonnet's

---

[1] P. Mandonnet, *op. cit.*, pp. 86–87.

interpretation is incomprehensible, and its very origin is inexplicable, unless ascribed to a curious error. His mind full of his hypothesis, he thinks only of the subdeacon's step; thus, he tells himself, since Dante did not take this step, it follows that he had already taken another one, after which he could have taken this one; he had therefore taken Minor Orders. Unfortunately, he who takes Minor Orders takes no step. To argue as Father Mandonnet does, therefore, one must interpret Dante's *tenni i piedi* as signifying minor ordination, in which no step has to be taken, because, in major ordination, which Dante did not undergo, a step has to be taken which Dante did not take.

In any case, why should we let ourselves be trapped in this labyrinth? We need only return to Chapter XIV of the *Vita Nuova* to see that some other question is involved and that Father Mandonnet's interpretation does not hold good. Dante there represents himself as being "thunderstruck" at the sight of Beatrice, whence he experiences a violent crisis in which he thinks that he is dying and from which he emerges "transfigured". This, Father Mandonnet assures us, is "the taking of Minor Orders, which Dante calls his *new transfiguration*".[1] Thus, on the one hand, we are told of "Dante's uncertain frame of mind at the time when he took Minor Orders",[2] and, on the other hand, we are told that this taking of Minor Orders was for him a "new transfiguration". In the first case his vocation is lacking in urgency because Beatrice, who symbolizes it, hesitates to devour his burning heart; in the second case the mere sight of Beatrice, that is to say of his vocation, plunges him into an emotional crisis so violent that it is almost fatal and transfigures him—as though Dante's text says at every juncture what the commentator wishes to make it say in order to justify the hypothesis that he wishes to establish.

What Dante actually does say remains, however, clear enough. The poet recovers his senses after the terrible emotion caused by the sight of Beatrice: " Then, somewhat calmed, my dead spirits being revived and those which were driven out of their domain having returned, I spake unto that friend of mine these words: I have set my feet at that point of life beyond which none may go with the intention of returning." Whereupon Father

---

[1] P. MANDONNET, *op. cit.*, p. 87.　　　[2] P. MANDONNET, *op. cit.*, pp. 85–86.

Mandonnet concludes: "I do not know what explanation Danto-logists provide of the words quoted above, but I find it hard to believe that any acceptable one may be offered except from within the set of ideas which we have in mind."[1] I am not a Dantologist, but I shall venture to take up the challenge. The " words of Dante quoted above" do not mean: "I took the step which has not to be taken in order to assume Minor Orders"; they signify precisely this: "A little further, and I should have died."

VI. BEATRICE METAMORPHOSED INTO A CORD

After exploiting the contiguous fields of the *Vita Nuova* and the *Convivio*, Father Mandonnet was bound to carry his hypo-thesis into the domain of the *Divine Comedy*. I shall leave aside the general discussions that we find in his arguments, confining myself to the positive proofs which he himself declares to be alone capable of settling the question: "Has Dante provided us with any positive indication in the pages of the *Comedy* as to the reality of his clerical vocation?" Such is the issue from now on. Father Mandonnet will, moreover, limit himself to two points, the most decisive of all and consequently the ones that we must examine with him.

Here is the first. In the *Divine Comedy*, St. Lucy, "the symbol of Providence", speaking to Beatrice about Dante, refers to him in the following terms: "He who loved thee so much, that for thy sake he left the vulgar throng" (*Inf.*, II, 105). Whereupon Father Mandonnet begins by asserting that *schiera* means "militia"; then that *militia* is used of laymen and clerics; finally that this line means: "He who for thy sake left the lay militia." Whence it follows quite naturally that, leaving the lay militia, Dante entered the clerical militia.[2]

The first Italian dictionary consulted has given me as the meaning of *schiera*: line, group, band, row. There is no mention of "militia". Furthermore, Dante himself has made use of this word elsewhere, notably in *Inf.*, IV, 101, in a passage in which it assumes a capital importance for our problem. Virgil is con-ducting Dante through Limbo; four great shades come towards

[1] P. MANDONNET, *op. cit.*, p. 87.   [2] P. MANDONNET, *op. cit.*, p. 94.

them: Homer, Horace, Ovid and Lucan; these shades render homage to Virgil as the *altissimo poeta* and form the group of "lords of that sublime flight of song which soars above all others like the eagle"; after conversing together for a little while these four poets turn to Dante, proffer him a friendly greeting at which even Virgil rejoices and, finally, do Dante the honour of admitting him to their group, with the result that he finds himself the sixth member of this immense Wisdom:

> Che sì mi fecer della loro schiera,
> sì ch'io fui sesto fra cotanto senno.
> (*Inf.*, IV, 101–102.)

Here, then, is a *schiera* of which, to our certain knowledge, Dante regarded himself as a member. Virgil, Homer, Horace, Ovid, Lucan, Dante himself. Is this a "militia"? It is not clear in what sense such a group would be one. Is it a "vulgar throng"? At all events Dante did not think of it as such. This *schiera* is "the throng of masters of that sublime flight of song which soars above all others like the eagle"; in short, it is that of the great poets. And for whom, through whom, has Dante become one of them? For and through Beatrice. We have noted that, according to the *Vita Nuova*, III, Dante entered the world of the famous *trouvères* of his time and formed a friendship with Guido Cavalcanti when he published the sonnet, *A ciascun' alma presa*, on the dream which he had after his second encounter with Beatrice. It was therefore certainly *for* and *through* Beatrice that Dante left *la volgare schiera*, that is to say the common throng, to enter that of the poets. This interpretation is so natural that Father Mandonnet has felt the need to eliminate it. Here, then, is his objection: "Was it because Dante became a poet? But Dante loved Beatrice at the age of nine and did not write verses until the age of eighteen. And so?"[1] And so, supposing that the chronology of the *Vita Nuova* has any historical value whatever, Dante left the vulgar throng when, through and for Beatrice, he took his place among the most famous *trouvères* of his time. He was then not nine, but eighteen.

The second indication of Dante's clerical vocation furnished by the *Divine Comedy* is given, according to Father Mandonnet,

[1] P. MANDONNET, *op. cit.*, p. 96.

in this passage from *Inf.*, XVI, 106–111: "I had a cord girt about [my body], and with it I thought, once, to catch the panther with the spotted coat. After I had removed it from me, as my guide had bidden me, I handed it to him gathered into a ball." What is the symbolism of the panther? Sensual pleasure. With what can sensual pleasure be captured? With chastity. The cord of which Dante speaks is therefore chastity. More precisely, it is and can be only "the symbol of ecclesiastical celibacy, to which he had pledged himself provisionally by his adoption of the clerical profession".[1] Since Beatrice is Dante's clerical vocation, this is she, metamorphosed into a cord.

Not, however, into *any* cord, for Father Mandonnet has his own idea on that point, and he who shows himself so easy to satisfy when it is a question of proving his theses becomes, on the contrary, extremely exacting in face of any fact which might embarrass him. Among the candidatures for the title of the Dantesque cord, Father Mandonnet first of all objects to that of the Penitent Friars, for the reason that they wore not a *cord* but a *strap*. He objects likewise—and how spiritedly!—to the Franciscan cord. In fact, the Franciscan cord symbolizes poverty; now what we need is a symbol of chastity; this, then, is not the right cord. *If it could be thought* that Dante was attached to any religious order, *his cord would tend rather to identify him with the Dominicans,* among whom the custom of wearing the *lumbare* had been introduced. In short, if this were a monastic cord, it would without a shadow of doubt be a Dominican one, but there is no reason to assert that Dante was bound to a monastic order. How, then, can we evade the difficulty? Very simply: "On the other hand, *Dante was a cleric,* and the cord—the symbol of continence—is pre-eminently the sign of ecclesiastical celibacy." This is proved by the fact that the priest, after putting on the alb to celebrate mass, puts a girdle about his loins.[2]

Let us greet sympathetically the appearance on the stage of this new character, the girdle, which Father Mandonnet has just adroitly substituted for the cord, the only thing that Dante has mentioned. *Corda* no more means *cordiglio* in Italian than *corde* means *cordon*[3] in French. If our exegete does not hesitate to transform a cord into an ecclesiastical girdle, the reason is that,

---

[1] P. MANDONNET, *op. cit.*, p. 102.   [2] P. MANDONNET, *op. cit.*, p. 102.
[3] *Corde* = cord, *cordon* = girdle. (*Translator's note.*)

wholly under the spell of his favourite thesis, his delight in the contemplation of it far exceeds his zeal for the task of proving it. What he was concerned with establishing was that the cord under discussion in *Inf.*, XVI, 106 proves that Dante was a cleric. And that is what Father Mandonnet would in fact have established, if he had first proved that this cord was in reality a girdle, the symbol of continence, instead of proving, as he has just done, that this cord is a girdle, the symbol of continence, because Dante was a cleric. Add to this, moreover, that, even if its form were adjusted, the argument would still prove nothing. It is not desired that the cord should be that of a Penitent Friar, or of a Franciscan, or of a Dominican, because Dante was not a monk. Why, then, should the girdle be that of a priest, seeing that he was not one? This argument is·excellent as a proof that Dante was a priest, which is universally denied, but it is valueless as a proof that he was a cleric. The symbol of clerical continence is neither a girdle nor a cord, but the tonsure.[1] Certainly, it is not easy to trap a panther with a tonsure; yet that is the only symbol of continence which Dante, as a cleric, would have had at his disposal for the purpose of attempting such an exploit.

Once assured that Dante was not a mere layman, Father Mandonnet no longer fears any difficulty in the interpretation of Dante's symbolism, for this symbolism "could not be more coherent and more simple, once it is unlocked with the key of the clericature".[2] The difficulties which some might still find in his explanations are due solely to their own obstinacy in not admitting that Dante was a shaveling and even a Minorite. Admit it, on the contrary, and everything is explained with the utmost ease. Yes, everything—even, if there is still any doubt, the famous girdle. For after all—Dante himself affirms it— Beatrice rescued him from the common militia. Since she rescued him from it, it is true that he was in it. But how can one tell a militiaman? By his belt: "The special emblem of the militia is the *cingulum militiae*, the military belt." The passage in which Dante says that Beatrice extricated him from the common

---

[1] "Tonsurae autem ecclesiasticae usus a Nazareis exortus videtur, qui, prius crine servato, denique ob vitae continentiam caput radebant . . ." PETER LOMBARD, *Sent.*, lib. IV, dist. 24, cap. 4; ed. Quaracchi, Vol. II, p. 893. This quotation signifies that, whatever commentary on P. Lombard's *Maxims* is consulted, a repetition will there be found of the statement that the tonsure is the symbol of clerical continence.

[2] P. MANDONNET, *Dante le Théologien*, p. 103.

militia therefore finds its complete explanation in this other passage in which we see him undo the cord with which he is girt. Indeed, to leave the lay militia, Dante had to gird on another belt: "The one that he donned on leaving the *militia saecularis* (lay militia) was the *cingulum continentiae et castitatis*" (the belt of continence and chastity). In saying that he parted with the cord with which his loins were girt, Dante simply means that he laid aside "the cord of the clerical profession"—in short, that having lost his vocation, he "re-entered the *schiera volgare* from which Beatrice had extricated him in the first place".[1]

To tell the truth, all this seems to me the most extraordinary story of belts that has ever been told. Just as certain warriors spontaneously divide men into two classes, civilians and soldiers, Father Mandonnet divides them naturally into two other classes, laymen and clerics. On the other hand, all, whether clerics or laymen, are in his eyes soldiers, serving in two distinct militias and recognizable by the belt that they wear. Thus, whether layman or cleric, Dante must wear a belt. Whereupon the reader will ask simply this: When, in *Inf.*, XVI, 106, Dante takes off his belt, how may one be sure that the belt in question is really a clerical belt, and not one of those ordinary military belts which have never passed for symbols of continence? True, Father Mandonnet assures us that by this time Dante has changed his belt. He says so, but what does he know about it? That is just the point in question. Now Dante himself suggests nothing of the kind. The only thing that we learn from him is that his body was girt with a cord, with which he had once tried to catch the panther, and that, at Virgil's bidding, he parted with this cord and offered it to him rolled into a ball. That is all. Dante does not say that the cord is a girdle, that the girdle is a belt, that the belt is the emblem of a militia, that the militia is the clerical militia. On the contrary, he says: It was at my guide's injunction that I handed him this cord: *Sì come il duca m'avea comandato*. Now Virgil is here only Dante's guide on the road to paradise: is it in order to lead him more surely to heaven that he makes him abjure his clerical vocation? Moreover, Virgil is here only Beatrice's ambassador to Dante. If, therefore, we were to pursue Father Mandonnet's exegesis, we should arrive at

[1] P. MANDONNET, *op. cit.*, p. 104.

this surprising conclusion, that after Beatrice had caused Dante to leave the vulgar throng, she herself caused him to re-enter it.

VII. Beatrice Metamorphosed into a Bishop —Death of Beatrice

In the eyes of a historian who does not discern the presence of these obstacles, the thesis that Dante was a cleric may be regarded as being so firmly established that one is entitled to wonder when and how he carried on his studies. Father Mandonnet begins, then, by submitting as a certainty that Dante entered the clerical profession at the age of eighteen, that is to say in 1283. On the other hand, the date of Beatrice's death, "that is to say his renunciation of the clerical profession", is 1290. Whence it follows that Dante was a cleric for about seven years. The problem therefore finally amounts to this: "What form did his studies take between the ages of eighteen and twenty-five?"

We may feel astonished to encounter such a deduction in a book which assumes that the whole of Dante's work is purely symbolical; for, as a matter of fact, it happens that, in this precise respect, it is. If we admit, as we should, that all the arithmetic of the *Vita Nuova* is based on the symbolism of the number three, we forfeit the right to treat its chronology as a series of dates with any historical value. After transforming into a mere symbol a character whom Dante represented as real, it would be somewhat paradoxical to regard a series of numbers, with a symbolism that has been explained to us by Dante himself, as signifying actual dates. Let us say, then, that we do not know at what age Dante entered the clerical profession, assuming, incidentally, that he ever did enter it.[1] We are therefore likewise ignorant as to how long his studies lasted, and it is rather futile to try to find out what he may have learned between the ages of eighteen and twenty-five. At all events it is futile to try to

---

[1] The hypothesis is formally contradicted by the evidence of Giovanni Villani, *Cronica*, lib. IX, 136: "Questo fue grance letterato quasi in ogni scienzia, tutto fosse laico." This passage will be found in G. L. Passerini's compilation, *Le vite di Dante*, Florence, G. C. Sansoni, 1917 (p. 3). Father Mandonnet eliminates this obstacle, *op. cit.*, p. 106.

find it out by this method or for these reasons, and it was, more-over, purely for reasons of his own that Father Mandonnet adopted this method.

We shall, in fact, discover here, with no possibility of mistake, one of the secret laws by which the Dantesque exegesis of Father Mandonnet, O.P., is most strictly governed: *Of two historically equivalent hypotheses on the subject of Dante, the one that tends rather to identify him with the Dominicans should be taken as correct.* The confirmations of this law are in actual fact innumerable. Un-doubtedly Father Mandonnet does not claim that Dante was attached to the Dominican Order. *He does not even wish to insinuate it,* since, to be entitled to do so, he would need a positive documentation which, *at present,* does not exist.[1] And what need have we of documentation on this point, since "Dante, by virtue of his entire intellectual evolution and his philosophical and theological convictions, is a Thomist, that is to say a Domini-can". Thus, every Thomist is a Dominican by right. Convinced that Dante was both, Father Mandonnet sees proof of it every-where. First, that daughter of the poet whom her father had named Beatrice dons the religious habit at the Dominican convent of Ravenna. Why? Because her father "had un-doubtedly directed her on to this road, in order to give to the Church, in the person of one of his children, that which he had himself taken away by his clerical defection".[2] In fact, Dante was not a monk, but, *if he had been,* he would have been a Dominican. That is why, *if the cord of* Inf., *XVI, 106 were a monastic girdle,* it would not be a Franciscan girdle, but a Domini-can *lumbare.*[3] It is the same here: to make up for the defection of a father who not only should have remained a cleric but should have become a Dominican, a Dominican nun was needed. That, finally, is why, in the analysis that he gives us for the famous dream described by Dante (*Vita Nuova,* XII), when he arrives at the passage where a young man appears, clad in "pure white garments", Father Mandonnet does not hesitate: first, this young man is a monk, then he is a Preaching Friar, finally

---

[1] P. MANDONNET, *op. cit.,* p. 101.

[2] P. MANDONNET, *op. cit.,* p. 101.

[3] Of course, it may with equal ease be proved that the reference is to the Franciscan girdle. It is in connection with this cord that Francesco da Buti has written: "Fu frate minore, ma non vi fece professione, nel tempo della fanciullezza"; *Commento,* Vol. I, p. 438, Pisa, Nistri, 1858; and Vol. II, p. 735; quoted by L. PIETROBONO, *Il poema sacro,* Vol. I, p. 13, note. Cf. PIERRE-GAUTHIEZ, *Dante,* Paris, H. Laurens, 1908 (pp. 69–70).

this Preaching Friar who comes and sits with such familiarity beside Dante "can only be his spiritual father".[1] Needless to add, Dante himself does not say a word of all this. We do not learn from him if this young man is a monk, or if his white garments are those of a Dominican or a Cistercian, still less if this Dominican is a visiting director. The whole of this interpretation is merely a reverie about a dream, and we are still far from having pursued it to the end.

In order to elucidate Dante's dream, Father Mandonnet begins at the famous episode in the *Vita Nuova*, X, where Beatrice refuses her greeting to Dante. This starting-point is well chosen, since Dante's emotion after Beatrice had refused to greet him was in fact the occasion of the dream whose interpretation is in question. Let us carefully note that Dante himself has been at pains to tell us, in Chapter XI, that Beatrice's greeting was for him an "intolerable bliss" whose nature and effects he describes in detail. Disregarding this authentic explanation, Father Mandonnet interprets Beatrice's "greeting" as being "the seven orders, of which the last is the priesthood". Thus, in refusing to greet Dante, Beatrice was unreservedly refusing him the seven orders, both minor and major, from that of gate-keeper to the priesthood. This Beatrice is truly the most capricious of religious vocations, for if it is understandable that a man should have a vocation, and that he should refuse to adopt it, it is less easy to understand what sort of a vocation it can be that persistently refuses to be adopted. The only way out of the difficulty is to effect a new dispensation of the symbolism of Beatrice by choosing, within the "Christian life", which she represents, the person who has the authority to refuse ordination. This is clearly the Bishop of the locality. So here we have Beatrice transformed into the Bishop of Florence. Since to refuse to greet Dante is tantamount to refusing him ordination, and since only the Bishop of Florence could refuse him this, he is necessarily Beatrice. Dante's religious vocation is therefore not only a historical fact

---

[1] P. ·MANDONNET, *Dante le Théologien*, p. 118. In the opinion of L. PIETROBONO (*Il poema sacro*, Vol. I, p. 55) this personage is identical with Love, which is possible, although Dante does not say so. Moreover, it is (he avers) a hallucination, and even an "autoscopy", a splitting or a "quasi-projection of oneself", like that attributed to Guy de Maupassant (*op. cit.*, pp. 52–53). And that too is quite possible. What is not? Between Dante and Guy de Maupassant there is, however, this difference, that of the two only the second died insane. When there is a question of crediting someone with autoscopic hallucinations, the point is not without interest.

of whose existence, broadly speaking, we are aware, but we also know this precise detail about it—that there was a time when his Bishop refused him the Minor Orders for which he was a candidate.[1]

Furthermore, we may ascertain the exact cause of this refusal simply by translating into plain language the dialogue between Dante and his "spiritual father", a symbolical conversation to which Dante's clerical vocation gives us the key. After contemplating Dante for some time, the young man with the white garments seems to say to him: "My son, it is time to renounce our images." He says "my son", so Dante really is his "spiritual son. As to the *images* which it is time to put aside, they represent the studies that are not of first importance for his vocation. Philosophy is a mere image in comparison with theology".[2] The reason for this visit is then understandable. At heart, this "spiritual father" is very annoyed. Dante's negligence puts him in a false position, between a candidate for Orders who neglects his theology and a Bishop of Florence who complains of the fact. This, moreover, is what he explains to Dante when he says to him: " I am situated at an equal distance between you and the ecclesiastical authority, in whose eyes I am responsible for you. You cannot judge your case from the same point of view as I." This, at all events, is how Father Mandonnet understands it, happier in this respect than Dante who, for his part, confesses simply that he does not understand at all and asks the young man the reason for this obscurity. "Ask no more about it than is to your advantage," the vision answers him. Without losing heart, Dante asks his spiritual father "why Beatrice has refused him her greeting, that is to say why he has not been admitted to ordination. That, comes the answer, would have been a source of vexation."[3] A slightly surprising answer and one which the "spiritual father" might easily have made clearer by saying: It is your Bishop who refuses, because you neglect theology. However, everything is about to come right, for we very soon learn some new historical details about this stormy experience of clerical life: "The intervention of Dante's director seems to have reassured the ecclesiastical authority, and the young man

[1] P. MANDONNET, *Dante le Théologien*, pp. 117–118.
[2] P. MANDONNET, *op. cit.*, pp. 118–119.
[3] P. MANDONNET, *op. cit.*, p. 119.

was admitted to Minor Orders."[1] We even know that, having refused to take the subdeacon's step, Dante never went any further. We knew it, but we have just learned the cause. Dante tells us, indeed, that his spiritual father is dead,[2] which fact Father Mandonnet, who doubtless finds him a little young to die, regards as signifying "perhaps only his absence from Florence". At all events, "this departure, whatever the circumstances, was to exert a notable influence on Alighieri's vocation. It is, indeed, in the following chapter that Dante relates simultaneously his moral death and that of Beatrice, which are, as it were, merely one and the same event".[3]

The calm assurance of Father Mandonnet as he writes these words is literally hallucinative. Such certainty is all the more contagious as, after being subjected to his influence for more than a hundred pages, the reader has completely lost sight of Dante's *Vita Nuova* and is now thinking only of Father Mandonnet's. Add to this that the very magnitude of the fallacies on which this interpretation is based makes it in practice impossible to suspect their existence. They are there none the less and it is they that save us from the spell of a conviction that is supremely skilful in the art of persuasion. Here, for example, we might concede all that we are told about this young man with the white garments: that he was Dante's spiritual father, a Dominican, an intermediary between Dante and his Bishop, a sponsor of his clerical vocation and the cause of his Minor Ordination. There is nothing in all this that offers enough historical substance to provide grounds even for a denial. On the other hand, it may be affirmed with absolute certainty that if the young man in Chapter XII of the *Vita Nuova* is really all this, it is not he who dies in Chapter XXII of the same work. It is enough, moreover, to refer to the text to be convinced of it: "After a few days had elapsed, as it pleased the glorious Lord Who did not refuse to die Himself, he who had been the father of the mighty marvel that this most noble Beatrice was seen to be, departed this life, and passed in very truth to eternal glory."[4] Dante then describes the great grief of Beatrice, the excellent daughter of this good

---

[1] P. MANDONNET, *op. cit.*, p. 120.
[2] Father Mandonnet, in a note (p. 121, 1), refers the reader to *Vita Nova*, cap. XXII, ed. H. Cochin, p. 85.
[3] P. MANDONNET, *op. cit.*, p. 121.
[4] DANTE, *Vita Nova*, ed. H. Cochin, p. 85.

man. There is clearly no connection between these two "fathers". Moreover, if Dante had claimed that they were one and the same, we should ask ourselves in amazement how, in the course of the seven years which, according to Father Mandonnet, separate Dante's clericature from the final loss of his vocation, the young man in Chapter XII could have become the father of a young girl of more than twenty. It is useless to try to find out, since there is nothing of all this in the text of Dante; but it is worth while trying to find out how it all became fixed in the mind of Father Mandonnet.

We may at all events make a guess, provided only that we participate in the game by which his imagination is captured. According to the rules of this game, what is Beatrice? In this passage she is Dante's clerical vocation. And what is Beatrice's father? He is the father of Dante's clerical vocation. But what, finally, is the young man with the white garments? He is Dante's spiritual father, that is to say the father of his clerical vocation. It only remains to formulate the equations. If Beatrice is Dante's clerical vocation, the father of Dante's clerical vocation is also the father of Beatrice; now the young man in Chapter XII is the father of Dante's clerical vocation, therefore he is the father of Beatrice, and since, finally, the father of Beatrice dies in Chapter XXII, it is of necessity the young man with the white garments who dies in this chapter. All this is so obvious in Father Mandonnet's eyes that he does not make the slightest effort to explain it to us. In fact, he does not even dream of doing so, but those who are not, like him, obsessed by his system, and consequently find themselves abruptly confronted with the many-headed monsters begotten of his exegesis, may perhaps be excused a feeling of astonishment.

Let us hasten to the end of this lugubrious story. The "young man-father of Beatrice" being dead, for "Beatrice-vocation" herself it only remains to die. This she does not fail to do in Chapter XXVIII, which begins with these words: *Quomodo sedet sola civitas plena populo! Facta est quasi vidua domina gentium* ("How desolate is the city that was full of people! The mistress of the nations is well-nigh deserted"). Dante has finally lost his clerical vocation; he will never be a subdeacon: there is nothing astonishing in the fact that the whole town is in mourning! Surprising as it is, this thesis is none the less one of those to which

Father Mandonnet clings most tenaciously, for the simple reason that it alone enables one to imagine why Dante might thus have concealed his personal history under the veil of allegory. After all, to what would the obscure narrative of the *Vita Nuova* then amount? This personal history of Dante would be the history of a fall from grace, since it would recount the loss of his vocation. That, we are told, is why the *Vita Nuova* does not say that Beatrice is merely a symbol of theology: "Dante is not anxious to proclaim from the house-tops that he has been a cleric and that he has abandoned the pursuit of his vocation." Such would be, once more, the real meaning of this work and its symbolism: Alighieri has forsaken Theology for Philosophy, or, if one prefers it, "love of Philosophy has put an end to love of Beatrice".[1]

I wish I knew a polite way of saying of a textual interpretation that it flatly contradicts almost every page of the text on which it comments. If such a way exists, I make my excuses for not having found it, but this is indeed a just estimate of Father Mandonnet's exegesis. If its conclusions were justified, it would in the first place be incomprehensible that Dante should have written the *Vita Nuova*. A fallen cleric, and one who feels so little pride at his fall, has no reason to recount it. It is pointed out to us that he does not, as a matter of fact, recount it, "but he wishes us to infer it". If he is ashamed of it, why should he desire this? Since Dante knows that "the attentive and alert reader will certainly find the clue to the riddle in the end",[2] the way in which he sets about recounting this ecclesiastical tittle-tattle makes no difference to the question. Add to this, moreover, that even if we were to concede this point, two far more re-doubtable obstacles would still stand in the way of Father Mandonnet's thesis.

Here is the first. It is insisted that the death of Beatrice was merely the death of Dante's clerical vocation, an event which he did not care to make public. Now in Chapter XXVIII of the *Vita Nuova*, the very one in which he relates the death of Beatrice, Dante says that he will not treat of her death, for three reasons. The first is that, if reference is made to the preamble of the *Vita Nuova*, it will be seen that this event does not form part of the subject of his book. The second is that, even if it did

---

[1] P. MANDONNET, *Dante le Théologien*, pp. 42–43.
[2] P. MANDONNET, *op. cit.*, p. 42.

form part of his subject, Dante would not be capable of treating of it in the requisite way. "The third is that, even if both of these conditions were fulfilled, it is not seemly for me to treat of it, for this reason, that, in treating of it, I should have to give praise to myself, which thing is above all else blameworthy in him who does it."[1] Commentators have made many a conjecture as to the reason which Dante might have had for praising himself in this connection. I hold no opinion on the subject. Yet I say that, whatever the reason may have been, and even if we admit that Dante is here merely using a literary artifice, it is difficult to maintain simultaneously that by the death of Beatrice Dante was symbolizing his fall from the estate of a cleric, and that he refused to comment on the death of Beatrice because he could not have done so without praising himself. This is all the harder to maintain as there is presented to us a Dante whose pride in having abjured his clerical vocation was so small that he did not speak of it save in veiled terms.

This first obstacle to Father Mandonnet's thesis is a small thing compared with the second. It is impossible that Dante symbolized the loss of his clerical vocation by the image of a woman whom, from the day on which he saw her first until the day of her death, and even beyond death, he never ceased to love. If Beatrice is Dante's clerical vocation, Dante passionately cherished that vocation. If Beatrice is the symbol of the "seven orders of which the last is the priesthood", never was the priesthood more tenderly loved. Short of refraining completely from discussion of these things—and that would perhaps be the wisest course—we should at all events have to agree as to the minimum probability required of a textual interpretation for it to be tenable. Here, for example, it seems reasonable to think that, if Beatrice represented Dante's clerical vocation, and if the *Vita Nuova* related how, after many hesitations, he finally came to abjure it, some trace of his hesitations and of his abjuration should be apparent in his feelings for Beatrice when alive. It is enough, however, to re-read any part of the *Vita Nuova* to establish that nothing of the sort is to be found there. Certainly, Beatrice dies in the end, but in no passage does Dante consider himself responsible for her death. He does not leave her: she departs. Beatrice died the object of Dante's adoration. At the moment

[1] DANTE, *Vita Nova*, ed. H. Cochin, p. 127.

when this terrible news reached him he had just written two of his most beautiful sonnets[1] for her and, reproaching himself for having there depicted the object of his love without describing its effects, he had just begun the *canzone* of Chapter XXVII:

> So long have I been held in thrall by Love
> And inured to his sovereignty,
> That, as formerly he wielded his power over me,
> So now I feel his gentle presence still in my heart.
> Therefore, when he robs me of my courage,
> So that my spirits seem to fly from me,
> Then is my frail soul pervaded by a feeling
> So tender that my face turns pale . . .

If it was to his clerical vocation, disguised under the name of Beatrice, that Dante addressed these words, it is hard to understand how she died as a result of seeing that she was forsaken. Yet this was the exact moment at which she died, as Dante himself tells us: "I was still planning this *canzone*, and had completed the stanza written above, when the Lord of Justice summoned this most noble Lady to dwell in glory (*a gloriare*) beneath the standard of that holy queen, the Virgin Mary, whose name was deeply revered in the mouth of this blessed Beatrice."[2] Thus, if Father Mandonnet is to be believed, that which, by an inexplicable theological cataclysm, suddenly expires before our eyes, is not only the most devotedly pursued of vocations: it is a vocation entrusted to the Blessed Virgin Mary.

That, however, is not the last surprise that this incomprehensible tale has in store for us, for a vocation which died when most fervently cherished, but which (according to the story) Dante is supposed to have abjured, has his love no less in death than it did in life. What cries of love does he not send after it even into the world beyond!

> Poscia piangendo, sol nel mio lamento
> chiamo Beatrice, e dico: "Or se' tu morta?"
> e mentre ch'io la chiamo, me conforta.
> (*Vita Nuova*, XXXI.)

A year later, on the anniversary of the death of Beatrice, Dante writes a poem for her in which his love declares itself to

---

[1] DANTE, *Vita Nuova*, XXVI. They are the sonnets *Tanto gentile e tanto onesta pare*, and *Vede perfettamente onne salute*.

[2] DANTE, *Vita Nova*, tr. H. Cochin, p. 125 (slightly modified in this last passage).

be as intense as ever.[1] It is only later that he is tempted in his heart to betray Beatrice for philosophy and another betrayal is perpetrated. Neither the *Vita Nuova* nor the *Banquet* is very explicit about it, but light will be shed upon it by other passages to which we shall have occasion later to refer. Whatever the facts, since it occurred after the death of Beatrice this betrayal can in no sense be identified with it nor can it have been the cause of it. After a period of indiscretions, whose gravity will later become apparent, Dante nevertheless regains possession of himself in the end, his *tribulazione* is allayed[2] and the *Vita Nuova* ends with an oath of fidelity. To identify Beatrice with Dante's clerical vocation, one would have to admit that a vocation can die without having been betrayed and that it can be betrayed even after its death.

VIII. Beatrice Metamorphosed into the Light of Glory

Having ceased to exist as a vocation, this Protean Beatrice returns to life immediately in a new form which, happily for us, will be the last of her metamorphoses. On her return to heaven, she there becomes, it appears, the *Lumen gloriae* (light of glory) of the beatific vision, which is conceived exactly as it had been by St. Thomas. Let us accept the thesis provisionally, and see how the writer claims to prove it.

I think I have said elsewhere that the gravest danger awaiting the historian of ideas—and there is not one of us who has not succumbed to it—is the commentary on the misinterpretation. Here it is different. One would say rather that the misinterpretations sprout from the commentary as from their common stock. Father Mandonnet cites as a strictly theological definition of the "light of glory" the line from *Purg.*, VI, 45: *Che lume fia tra 'l vero e lo 'ntelletto*. Even if the light of glory ought to be thus defined, there is nothing in the text of Dante which says that that is what he intends to define. The subject is indeed Beatrice, but here she need only symbolize faith for Dante to describe her as a light between the truth and the intellect. Further-

---

[1] Dante, *op. cit.*, XXXIV.   [2] Dante, *op. cit.*, XXXIX and XL.

more, if Beatrice is thus designated *qua* the light of glory, why does this designation occur immediately after, following her return to contemplation, she has caused her place at Dante's side to be taken by another guide, St. Bernard of Clairvaux? Finally, the writer assures us unreservedly that this verse defines, in a strictly theological way, the light of glory. Not being myself a theologian, I can only acquiesce, not, however, without asking the experts for some explanations. How can we identify a light that is interposed (*fra*) between the truth and the intellect with the light of glory, seeing that St. Thomas defines the *lumen gloriae* (light of glory) as being not *between* the Truth and the intellect, but *in* the intellect? For that, indeed, is how I have understood him: to see God in *essence* means that no light is interposed between God and the intellect, even for the purpose of revealing Him, in this vision in which *ipsa essentia Dei fit forma intelligibilis intellectus* [1] ("God's very essence becomes the intelligible form of the intellect"). "The eyes of Beatrice," we are told, "shed the vision of the Divinity into the eyes of Dante."[2] This is quite possible, but it proves conclusively that Beatrice is not the light of glory. Since it must be said of this light *quod non est medium in quo videatur*,[3] it is no Beatrice who sheds it, but God Himself. If Beatrice symbolizes a light of glory between God and the intellect, it seems to me that she symbolizes something which does not exist.

The only justification that Father Mandonnet offers of his truly singular doctrine deserves particularly to hold our attention. The truth is, he says, that "Dante, shrewd man that he is, makes his symbolism conform to the Thomistic doctrine which locates the formal, or specific, element of beatitude in the vision of the intelligence and not in the act of love which follows it, as the Augustinian school demanded".[4] That is true, but it is only half the truth, and it is only too clear what hides the other half from the eyes of Father Mandonnet. In this crucial point of his thesis, he himself, in his own person, confirms in the sight of all the cause of his mistake, for it is equally true to say that we only love what we know and only know what we love. The only weakness to which, here and elsewhere, that great historian,

---

[1] St. Thomas Aquinas, *Sum. theol.*, Pars. I, qu. 12, art. 5, Resp.
[2] P. Mandonnet, *Dante le Théologien*, p. 217.
[3] St. Thomas Aquinas, *Sum. theol.*, Pars. I, qu. 12, art. 5, ad. 2m.
[4] P. Mandonnet, *Dante le Théologien*, p. 218.

Father Mandonnet, was a prey, was that he always loved St. Thomas at once for himself and in despite of someone else. If he had loved him only for himself he would have loved him better; he would also have understood him better and the fatal error that we here see him commit would not have been made. This error is as follows: The better to make Beatrice dissolve into the light of glory he has had to interpret the whole of the end of the *Divine Comedy*, from the departure of Beatrice onwards, as a description of the fruition of love resulting from the sight of God; whereas in reality it describes the asceticism of love required for this vision. The whole secret of his negative attitude towards St. Bernard lies in this. To anyone who here identifies Beatrice with the light of glory, her departure cannot signify that something else is beginning but that this moment marks the term of Dante's celestial pilgrimage. What follows is that which Beatrice-light of glory causes another who comes *after her* to do: to love the God Whom she makes known and Who is loved only because she reveals Him. In short, St. Bernard is here only an executor of the works of Beatrice: the love which follows the vision.

This, however, is not the way in which matters present themselves, either in the *Divine Comedy* or in the *Summa theologica*. It is a good thing to be a Thomist because one is a Dominican, but it is better to be a Dominican because one is a Thomist. A Dominican of this type soon perceives that, like St. Thomas himself, he is at the same time a Cistercian. It is, indeed, an authentically Thomistic doctrine that, precisely because the light of glory is not interposed between God and the intellect, but is the light of the divine essence itself, the differences in degree of perfection that may exist between beatific visions cannot proceed from the light of glory taken by itself. They therefore proceed from the fact that the intellects of the blessed have a greater or lesser share in this light, those who have a larger share in it seeing God more perfectly. And who, then, has a larger share in it? *"Plus autem participabit de lumine gloriae, qui plus habet de caritate, quia ubi est major caritas, ibi est majus desiderium, et desiderium quodammodo facit desiderantem aptum et paratum ad susceptionem desiderati. Unde qui plus habebit de caritate, perfectius Deum videbit, et beatior erit"*[1] (" Moreover, *the greater*

---

[1] ST. THOMAS AQUINAS, *Sum. theol.*, I, 12, 6, Resp.

a man's charity, the greater will be his share in the light of glory,
because where there is greater charity, there too is greater desire;
and desire in some way makes him who desires fit and prepared
to receive that which he desires. Hence, the greater a man's
charity, the more perfectly will he see God, and the more blessed
will he be"). A St. Bernard of Clairvaux can easily be fitted
into this formula, which fact proves once more that one never
loses another saint through loving St. Thomas—not that his
saintliness comprises all their saintly qualities taken together,
which would be an absurd thing to say, but because the office
and the special form of his saintliness consist in making us understand every other form of saintliness in its essence and in the
special function that devolves upon it.

In the mind of anyone who understands this, the rôle of St.
Bernard in the *Divine Comedy* assumes an intelligible aspect and
at the same time that of Beatrice appears in its true light. The
outcome of the sacred poem is nothing else than the union of
the soul with God, the image of the beatific vision. If Beatrice
were the light of glory, the *Divine Comedy* would conclude with
a look from her eyes and a smile from her lips. But Beatrice
retires and appoints in her place this man whom love has transfigured into the image of Christ, Bernard of Clairvaux. From
this moment onwards there is no lack of indications on the part
of the poet to the reader. There is *la vivace carità* of him who,
in this world, through contemplation, enjoyed the peace of the
world beyond (*Par.,* XIII, 110–111); there are the names of the
three who sit on the summit of the Empyrean, just below the
forerunner, St. John the Baptist: Francis, Benedict and Augustine
(*Par.,* XXXII, 35); there is Bernard's prayer to the Virgin,
which inflames Dante's soul with *l'ardor del desiderio* (*Par.,*
XXXIII, 48), because, as St. Thomas was telling us just now,
ubi est major caritas, ibi est majus desiderium ("where there is greater
charity, there too is greater desire"). Then, but only then, there
appears in the sacred poem something that resembles the light of
glory; but it is not the light which proceeds from the eyes of
Beatrice: it is the direct, immediate ray of the divine light itself:
lo raggio dell'alba luce che da se è vera (*Par.,* XXXIII, 53–54).
Thus, born of Cistercian charity, the supreme, brief vision is
prolonged in this same charity, absorbed in "the love that moves
the sun and the other stars". Nothing could be more Cistercian

—nor, for that matter, could anything be more Thomistic: *Qui plus habet de caritate, perfectius Deum videbit et beatior erit* ("The greater a man's charity, the more perfectly will he see God, and the more blessed will he be").

It is evident here in what way the fetish of system, if applied to a point affecting the balance of the whole of the *Divine Comedy*, may destroy the meaning of the poem. It is very true that, regarding essential points, Dante has referred to St. Thomas as to the surest doctrinal rule. This is, indeed, especially true where the nature of beatitude is involved. Father Mandonnet has seen and demonstrated in an irrefutable manner[1] that, following St. Thomas, Dante formally locates beatitude "in the act of the understanding, which apprehends God, and not in the act of the will, which only follows the understanding". As regards this precise point Dante has taken the part of the Thomistic doctrine against the others, but neither he nor St. Thomas has ever said that beatitude would be possible without the charity which prepares the way for it, and accompanies and follows it. If we add to this that the concluding part of the *Divine Comedy* does not describe the beatific vision of one of the elect, but the unitive ecstasy of the Christian mystic, we shall have no difficulty in understanding that Dante has contrived to make notions of Cistercian, Victorine or Franciscan origin hold good in a Thomistic setting. St. Thomas's genius, comprehensive as it was, had already accepted them, since, inflexible on the subject of the cognitive *nature* of mystical rapture or ecstasy, he had expressly taught that its *cause* at all events may be affective, and that it had been so in the case of St. Paul: *Unde et Apostolus dixit se raptum non ad tertium coelum, quod pertinet ad contemplationem intellectus, sed etiam in paradisum, quod pertinet ad affectum*[2] ("Hence the Apostle likewise said that he had been transported not to the third heaven, which pertains to intellectual contemplation, but to paradise itself, which pertains to the will"). That, indeed, is why the rapture of St. Paul took place in a momentary light of glory: the light of paradise itself. The more one desires to make Dante simply a Thomist, the more necessary it is to think of Thomism in its widest sense. Beatrice at all events did not misunderstand it. When the hour of the *dénouement* approaches, far from taking

---

[1] P. MANDONNET, *Dante le Théologien*, pp. 273-274.
[2] ST. THOMAS AQUINAS, *Sum. theol.*, Pars. III, qu. 175, art. 2, Resp.

herself for the beatific vision of another, she turns back for good
and all to the eternal source of her own:

> Poi si tornò all'eterna fontana.
> (*Par.*, XXXI, 93.)

Yet Beatrice does not leave Dante bereft. She it is who sends
to him this Bernard, fired with divine love, and he, Bernard,
well knows the name of her by whose holy love he is sent:
A che priego ed amor santo mandommi (*Par.*, XXXI, 96). In
face of the living unity of mystical knowledge and love, it is
possible, without forgetting or rejecting salutary niceties, to
welcome this charity and this light, each with the other, each
within the other. It is possible, and beyond a doubt it is even
necessary, if only to understand Dante. For after all, we can
never repeat too often, with Signor Michele Barbi: "The
supremely important thing is to understand the poetry of Dante."[1]
That is indeed the question! "That, then," concludes Father
Mandonnet calmly, "is why the understanding is named thirty
times in the *Comedy* and the will only ten times, as we have seen
above."[2] Even if this were true it would undoubtedly not signify
very much, but, as we shall see later, it is not even true.

IX. BEATRICE'S MISSION

In aspiring to outline the characteristics of a Beatrice more
closely resembling the real one we should be guilty of presumption if we did not at the outset specify what must be
understood by the real Beatrice. It seems to me that she is the
Beatrice whom for centuries countless readers of Dante have
immediately recognized and comprehended, because they were
the very public for whom Dante had written. The real Beatrice
is the Beatrice of the *Vita Nuova*, the *Banquet* and the *Divine
Comedy*. She is the creation of an artist. We know nothing
and can know nothing of her apart from what we derive from

---

[1] M. BARBI, *Nuovi problemi della critica dantesca*, in *Studi Danteschi*, Vol. XXIII, 1938,
XVII, p. 5. Pp. 5–7 will repay study; the sage opinions which they contain should
always be borne in mind, especially by the historian of ideas who is concerned with
those of Dante.

[2] P. MANDONNET, *Dante le Théologien*, p. 275.

that artist, and it is impossible to perceive her real nature unless we perceive her real nature as a work of art. The cultured reader who, having sufficiently elevated literary tastes, but no special erudition and no particular historical proficiency, surrenders himself to the genius of the poet and accepts Beatrice as Dante reveals her to him, is in little danger of being deceived as to the meaning of this radiant figure. We cannot fail to be deceived, on the contrary, once we seek the explanation of the work of art elsewhere than in itself and try to elucidate it by the light of a system which is not its own. The sciences that are handmaids of the history of letters and of the arts become detrimental rather than useful once they abandon their proper rôle, which is to be the handmaids of delectation. To paint Beatrice from nature is therefore to paint her as Dante wishes her to appear to us, for she has no other nature than that. This is what we would attempt to do, remembering that, since she is the creation of a poet, the key to the understanding of Beatrice can only be found in the poetic signification which is her *raison d'être*.

It is therefore advisable first of all to eliminate carefully what might be termed the infra-Beatrices. They abound in the works of scholars, but they are also encountered in the commentaries of artists, some of whom pride themselves on their utter contempt for these scholars even though, like everyone else, they do not refrain from making use of them. So, for example, it is with Giovanni Papini, who, in a book which is otherwise full of the most just intuitions, takes credit to himself for questioning Beatrice about her feelings towards Dante and for obtaining answers from her. Did she pity Dante? Did she understand him? "I am referring," says Papini, "to the living, real Beatrice, to the Beatrice of flesh and blood, clothed in white or red, lawful daughter of Folco Portinari and Cilia Caponsacchi, to the second wife of Simone dei Bardi." In short, we are concerned here not with Beatrice transfigured into a symbol, but with the Florentine Beatrice, "daughter and wife, who was born in 1266 and died in 1290 in the month of June", with a "physical, earthly and visible" Beatrice "who would have existed even if Dante had not loved her, even if Dante had not sung of her", even if he had not made her play the part of a sort of vicar of the Virgin Mary.[1]

[1] G. PAPINI, *Dante vivo*, tr. J. Bertrand, Paris, Grasset, 1934; Chap. IX, pp. 51-52.

That there existed a woman loved by Dante under the name of Beatrice and that this woman was Bice Portinari is, with all due deference to the adherents of Father Mandonnet, possible and even probable.

Unless he has laid down in advance, for abstract reasons and in pursuance of a fixed exegetic system, that Beatrice can have been merely a symbol, no historian will reject as totally devoid of value the testimony of Boccaccio in his *Vita di Dante*. It is only the belated testimony of a man too young to have known Dante, and of an artist whose narrative has the same charm and the same documentary value as an allegory of Botticelli; yet the names, dates, and places mentioned by Boccaccio tally with the text of Dante and, if we object to this witness as being too far removed from the facts to which he refers—and he was a Florentine of the fourteenth century—what, then, shall we say of ourselves? Let us rest assured that if Boccaccio had denied the existence and the reality of Beatrice, the defenders of this thesis would crush us beneath the weight of his testimony. Whatever may be said on this subject, the text of Boccaccio constitutes favourable presumptive evidence of a very serious kind, not in favour of the details of an anecdote which was undoubtedly reconstructed by his imagination, but in favour of the identification of Beatrice with Bice Portinari.[1]

It is not here that the difficulty lies. Rather, the problem is whether, even to an interpreter of Dante who regards this identification as beyond question, Bice Portinari is the true Beatrice. I think the answer must be "No" and that this "No" should be maintained with the utmost energy against all opponents, past, present or future. What is involved is the very aim of literary studies which, as in every domain of the history of the arts, is and should remain identical with the aim envisaged by the public to which the artist addresses his work. Now of all the known ways of replacing it with another, the most dangerous consists in causing the artist's characters to be doubled by real persons, as if the world of art were not governed by laws of its own, so essentially different from those of nature that the two sets of laws cannot be considered as applying to a single set

---

[1] The text of Boccaccio is translated in PIERRE-GAUTHIEZ, *Dante, essai sur sa vie d'après l'oeuvre et les documents*, Paris, H. Laurens, 1908, pp. 23-25. For the original text see BOCCACCIO, *Della origine, vita, costumi e studii di Dante Alighieri di Firenze e delle opere composite da lui*, cap. 5 (in G. L. PASSERINI's compilation, *Le vite di Dante*, pp. 18-20).

of facts. Bice Portinari, or any other real woman whom one may like to substitute for her, may well have been the woman loved by Dante; it remains none the less true that Beatrice was born of the genius of Dante, not of the marriage of Folco Portinari and Cilia Caponsacchi. The assertion of the right to argue from one to the other as if it were a question of one and the same person results from a confusion that is fatal to our studies. Bice Portinari is a historical personage whose shadow discreetly accompanies the eternally living Beatrice whom Dante alone has created. Of this shadow history knows practically nothing, and it speaks of it only because Dante has enriched the nature of that eminent reality which is Beatrice, the work of art created by him; but even if history were capable of telling us everything about Bice Portinari, the birth of Beatrice would be in no way explained thereby. Now the historians are here disarmed. There is no tomb to be violated, there are no drawers to be forced that the dead may be robbed of their secrets, no intimate joys or woes to be prostituted to the public for money. Bice Portinari has, thank God, no history, but if she had one it would only be the history of the young Florentine girl who was encountered by Dante, became the second wife of Simone dei Bardi, and died in the month of June, 1290. If Bice Portinari had left us any letters, memoirs or some intimate diary, we could write her history. If Dante had written a *Secretum*, as Petrarch was to do, we could divine, beneath the surface of the *Vita Nuova*, something of the reality which it treats poetically. In fact, we have nothing of all this. We do not even know if Dante had a *Secretum* to write, and there is nothing that authorizes us to suppose that his relations with Beatrice were more involved than he says. It is true that someone or other called Bice Portinari would have existed even if Dante had not sung of her, but that is precisely the reason why, even if we had the material with which to write it, her history would not be that of Beatrice. The interpreter of Dante need not therefore concern himself with it.

In contrast to the infra-Beatrices, the ultra-Beatrices obstinately solicit our attention. Instead of reducing an artistic creation to the dimensions of a historical personage, these latter transfigure it into mere symbols, as if the artistic value of Beatrice did not essentially imply that she is presented as a reality. All that we know of this story we derive from Dante, and the story he tells us is a love-story. One apologizes for harking back to such baldly obvious facts, but it is really necessary, since so many people forget them. If the *x* specified as Beatrice is a clerical vocation, an active intellect, an emperor or Joachimite spiritualism, it is hard to understand how an artist can have found the accents of Dante to sing of the passion with which such objects could inspire him. Whatever may be the truth on this point, the fact remains that Dante tells us that he loved a woman and found in his love for that woman the source of his song. The fact that what the poet says is in harmony with the most elementary good sense is not an adequate reason for rejecting it. The only Beatrice known to the interpreter of Dante is the one that he can find in Dante's works, and it is there that we must look for her.

To know Beatrice as she is we must therefore believe of her what Dante has intended to make us believe of her and think of her as he has intended to make us think of her. Now he has certainly intended that we should think of her as a real person, a woman whom he has met, whom he has loved, whom he has lost in the flesh and found again in spirit. When Dante intends to speak of grace, he writes *grazia*; to signify faith, he says *fede*, and if by chance he intends to treat some abstraction poetically, as he has done in the case of the *Donna Gentile*, Dante warns us that what is there involved is an imaginary character: he describes it, but he does not name it. On the contrary, Dante names all the others, and not only the three ladies to whom some have chosen to reduce the feminine company of the sacred drama, but many others who appear in it, although they do not mention them to us: Mary, Anne, Lucy, Francesca da Rimini, all the women of history and legend who people Dante's work have retained their names in it. The only two exceptions to this rule would be the Matelda of the Earthly Paradise, if it were proved that there was no real person corresponding to this character, and Beatrice, if it were proved that she was only a symbol. In naming her alone between two other unnamed ladies, one of whom at least he describes as a mere symbol, Dante has treated Beatrice exactly like all the feminine characters in his work whose historical reality is beyond doubt. To regard Beatrice as a real woman is certainly to understand her as Dante has intended that she should be understood and to defer to his intention.

There are other indications besides. Many symbolical meanings can be made to serve a single image, but not all can. It is rather a simple artifice thus to set Beatrice between two anonymous ladies in order to dissolve her in their unreality. Beatrice has never paraded between these symbols: they only appear after her death. When she advances towards Dante with Monna Vanna, it is Guido Cavalcanti's Giovanna with whom she comes forward:

> Io vidi monna Vanna e monna Bice
> venire inver lo loco là ov'io era,
> l'una appresso de l'altra maraviglia.
> (*Vita Nuova*, XXIV.)

This Giovanna, surnamed Primavera—was she too, then, a symbol? She seems, however, to be the very one who reappears in the Sonnet to Guido, this time in the company of their friend Lapo, Monna Lagia—this same Florentine versifier's lady—and the famous "Lady No. 30" whom commentators are unwilling at any price to accept as Beatrice.[1] The real ladies do not begin with the *Divine Comedy;* as early as the *Vita Nuova* Beatrice is in their midst and appears as one of them. But above all, even after the *Vita Nuova*, the transfigured Beatrice will always remember that she was a woman. The blessed soul of the *Paradiso* has not forgotten its body, and this is excellent theology; she even remembers that she was beautiful, which is excellent psychology; and she says so quite simply, because it is true, as Dante says quite simply that he is in his place beside Homer, because it is true: "Never did nature or art offer you pleasure so great as did the fair limbs in which I was encased and which are at present scattered about the earth" (*Purg.*, XXXI, 49-51). It is rather strange that after seeking hidden meanings in the smallest words of Dante's text commentators should purely and simply eliminate such declarations. If Beatrice is only a symbol, she is a symbol whose body, after its death, was brought to earth, where it resides, at the time when Dante is writing these lines, in expectancy of its future glorification. We are assuredly yielding to the most urgent suggestions of Dante himself if we see in Beatrice a human being, composed like us of a soul and a body, her soul being in heaven and her body on earth; a being who, since she is actually dead, has actually lived.

[1] Sonnet: *Guido, i' vorrei che tu e Lapo ed io . . .*; ed. cit., *Rime amorose*, XV, p. 153.

It does not, however, follow from this that, being an actual woman, Beatrice represents nothing and symbolizes nothing besides herself in the work of Dante. Here again, we have no other means of avoiding error except to follow the indications of the poet. If we resign ourselves to it, one fact seems to dominate the whole of this inquiry; it is that *among the works of Dante, taken in the completed form in which the poet has bequeathed them to us, there is not a single one in which Beatrice is not charged with a religious symbolism.* The remark is of importance only as regards the *Vita Nuova*, but as regards this work its importance is capital. The problem of this work's composition belongs essentially to literary history. It has been the subject of much discussion and I am not qualified to intervene in these arguments. The one fact that we must remember is, however, incontestable, since it emerges clearly from a bare inspection of the text: The sequence of prose pieces and poems of which the *Vita Nuova* consists is made up of two series of passages which do not date from the same period. As H. Cochin has very well said, Dante "only composed the narrative in prose in order subsequently to set within it some poems which already existed".[1] To carry out this plan, Dante had to choose from his *Canzoniere* those of his poems which he had written for Beatrice or saw how to relate to her or to reconcile with her history. It is not even impossible that he may have written some of the poems at the time, even though he represents them in his commentary as dating from a former period. The most beautiful of all, *Donne ch'avete intelletto d'amore*,[2] which Dante relates to the time preceding the death of Beatrice, so clearly anticipates her death, the transfiguration which followed it and the beloved woman's mission of redemption, that one cannot help wondering if, like the commentary that accompanies it, this poem was not composed after the event. Unhappily, we do not know, and the most learned literary dissertations on this point will never be anything but learned reflections on our uncertainty. In the *Vita Nuova* as we know it, all other reflections being, after all, purely hypothetical, Beatrice is already dead and Dante already speaks of a *mirabile visione* which induces him to celebrate her in a manner worthy of her, as if he had even then conceived some

---

[1] H. Cochin, *Dante Alighieri, Vita Nova*, Introduction, p. vi.
[2] *Vita Nova*, XIX, ed. H. Cochin, pp. 68–73.

vast project. In short, as soon as we are introduced to her, Beatrice appears to us as a miracle of nature and grace, she who is loved by the number nine and whose life seems to bend like herself to the law of that sacred symbol. Already beatified in the *Vita Nuova*, Beatrice remains so in the *Banquet* and it is in the *Divine Comedy* that her glory will reach its height. If we except the pieces in the *Canzoniere* not utilized by Dante but capable of referring to Beatrice, or the poems in the *Vita Nuova* which were certainly written before the commentary—and our conjectures on these points seldom border on certainty—we have absolutely no grounds for speaking of any other Beatrice than this one.

None at all, save only this, that, according to Dante himself, Beatrice really existed. It is a small thing, but this single fact justifies conclusions of extreme importance, and first of all this one, that before she was to Dante one of the blessed in heaven, Beatrice was to him a woman on earth. If he loved this earthly Beatrice, he loved her as a woman. More exactly, Dante loved Beatrice primarily as a chivalrous poet of his time loved a Lady of his time. Some interpreters of Dante have difficulty in admitting the fact. They cannot conceive that a man in his right mind can have spoken of a human being as Dante has spoken of Beatrice. The truth undoubtedly is that they have difficulty in conceiving what chivalrous love was and what part was played in the Middle Ages by this sentimental emotion, so different from those that we experience. It existed none the less. We know that its creators and interpreters were the Provençal troubadours, soon followed by the *trouvères* from the North, and everyone knows that even Dante, who makes the troubadour Arnaut Daniel speak in Provençal in *Purg.*, XXVI, 140–147, at first ranged himself, in the *Vita Nuova*, III, among the *trovatori* of his time. Much has been written on chivalrous love, and those who speak of it know hardly anything about the subject. Some, moreover, do not even understand what others say of it, perhaps because the very thing of which they speak is too fluid to admit of definition, but perhaps also because they do not always speak of the same thing.

Happily for us, the responsibility of interpreting chivalrous love as a whole does not devolve upon us. We are interested only in the form that it has assumed in Dante, and we have to attempt here the analysis of this form alone, without aspiring in addition to distinguish those of its essential characteristics which might be peculiar to it from those which it possesses in common with the other forms of this sentiment. The few comparisons that we may make in the course of analysis will therefore aim at nothing but the elucidation of some characteristic of chivalrous love as it is presented in Dante, and not at all at the definition, even by way of comparison, of any form but this one.

The most general and, I think, most striking of these characteristics is what might be called the autonomy of this sentiment in Dante's life. In a certain sense the poet's whole work was affected by it. There his love for Beatrice has more or less coloured all his other sentiments, save, perhaps, one—the only other one that may be compared with it for depth, intensity and duration: his political passion. It is therefore not a case of saying that Dante's life remained isolated from his love for Beatrice, which would be palpably absurd, but rather that his love for Beatrice forms in Dante's life a sort of emotional order complete in itself, self-sufficient and containing within it all the elements required not only for its existence, but for its justification.

People have often remarked, sometimes for the humour of it, how little the material history of this love amounts to. In order to kindle this devouring fire in Dante's heart Beatrice did nothing more than cross his path when he was nine years old. The only things we know about the sequel of this encounter are that from that moment onwards Dante sought many a time to see her again; that he met her nine years later, flanked by two other ladies, and that, turning her eyes towards where he was standing *molto pauroso*, she greeted him courteously; that Beatrice, who seems to have continued to greet him, one day refused him her greeting, "for fear of being a cause of annoyance": *temendo ne fosse noiosa*; that Dante saw her one day at a gathering at which many other ladies were present, which was enough to cause his "new transfiguration"; finally, that after losing her father, Beatrice herself died.[1] That is what the part she played in Dante's life in the course of her earthly existence amounts to so far as we are concerned, and can it be said that she really played even this part? Never did she speak to him, and the only sentence she is reported to have uttered on the subject of Dante is the

[1] DANTE, *op. cit.*, II, III, X, XII, XIV, XXVIII.

classic reply of the woman whose patience is exhausted by the
petrified suitor whom she meets at every street-corner: she
wants to remain courteous, but courtesy ceases at the point at
which, being mistaken for something else, it is in danger of
causing complications. In speaking of the loves of Dante and
Beatrice people seem to forget that in this story Dante acted the
cavalier seul.

Perhaps, moreover, it ought to be said that he did not even
act the *cavalier* at all. Not only did Dante obtain nothing from
Beatrice, save the casual greetings which she proffered him, but
he did not ask anything from her, he does not even seem to have
desired or hoped for anything else. One wonders, moreover,
how he would have endured more—he who one day fainted
merely at her presence. But Dante himself has intended that
we should not be able to make any mistake about it and, in order
to define in a rigorous way the exact nature of this sentiment,
he has made a woman friend of Beatrice ask him what was the
meaning of his attitude. "With what object dost thou love this
lady of thine, since thou canst not bear her presence? Tell us,
for certainly the object of such a love must be very unusual."
Whereupon, the ladies—who had, incidentally, been making
fun of Dante—having all fixed their eyes on him in expectation
of his reply, he told them simply that the object of his love
had hitherto been the greeting of Beatrice, but that, since that
greeting had been refused him, there remained to him another
object, the former one being ruled out: praise of Beatrice.[1]
So that was the single and "quite unusual" object which Dante's
love had before it, even during the lifetime of Beatrice. I admit
that this seems strange. Nevertheless, as soon as they heard his
reply, Dante's women friends stopped laughing, and we shall
see later that they did right.

From now on our attention is arrested by a fact which enables
us to understand the autonomy of this love in Dante's life. It
is assuredly the love of a man for a woman: neither Dante nor
Beatrice is a disembodied soul; it is even a profoundly carnal
love, since it is accompanied by physical emotions of extreme
violence, but it is a carnal love of which the object is not itself
carnal and which is directed far less towards the beloved woman
than towards the work which she inspires; in short, it is the

[1] DANTE, *op. cit.*, XVIII, tr. H. Cochin, pp. 64–67.

poet's love for the woman whose presence liberates his genius
and makes his song burst forth. We will not enter here into the
labyrinths of the psychology of genius: those without genius
have nothing to say of it and those who have it generally have
other things to do than to speak of it.[1] Yet we are not rising
above the level of the most elementary observation in saying
that there are artists whose inspiration requires incentives of this
kind and that lyrical poets are generally among them. Of these
poets, some do not hesitate, if they can, to sacrifice the higher
interests of the artist in them to the pleasures of the man: by
following a carnal emotion where its natural bent leads them,
they deprive it soon enough of all virtue as an incentive. Others,
who are often among the greatest, exist only for their work.
They sacrifice everything to it, even the pleasures of the man,
of which they have better use to make than to dissipate their
virtue by succumbing to them. We see them, then, studiously
capitalizing their most intense emotions, stemming them in
order to increase simultaneously their power and their depth,
using admirable skill to prolong their duration with a view to
increasing their efficacy. Who shall ever say to what point the
creative instinct to which some artists are literally a prey can
push its demands? That, if Richard Wagner and Mathilde
Wesendonk had sated their passion, we should only have one
more item in the life of Wagner, and no *Tristan* in his work, is
scarcely a hypothesis. What is a hypothesis, but by no means an
impossible one, is that in the case of Richard Wagner the artist
raised between the man and his desire the obstacle that was
necessary for the birth of *Tristan*. That Beatrice, a real woman,
was to the poet that was Dante this inexhaustible source of profound and stimulating emotion; that she enjoyed this singular
privilege—which often astonishes the very women who possess
it and sometimes embarrasses them—of liberating in him the
flood of lyrical inspiration, is what Dante himself says in every
chapter and almost on every page of the *Vita Nuova*. That the
object of his love for Beatrice was to sing of her is what he has
said at least once, but this once is enough. "Where, then, is thy
beatitude?" the women friends of Beatrice ask him. And Dante
gives them this reply: *In quelle parole che lodano la donna mia.*

---

[1] Some great artists have nevertheless done so, especially in modern times. For some
details on this point see Éclaircissement I, *Of Poets and Their Muses*, pp. 282–288.

This is the object of his love, *che non mi pote venir meno*. The thing which cannot fail him is the actual poetic enthusiasm with which the mere sight of Beatrice fills him. To give to Dante what he expected from her Beatrice had only to exist.

It is easy to understand from this how two lives so distinct from each other were nevertheless so intimately united. They were so at any rate in the person of Dante the artist, that is to say in that creative life whose duration does not coincide with that of the man either in meaning or in rhythm. This is why Dante's family life unfolded in accordance with a plan completely separate from that of his artistic life. Of the two women who appear in his life, Dante owes to one the inspiration from which his finest works sprang: this is Beatrice, through and for whom Dante became a poet; he owes to the other the fact that he knew for a time the life of the domestic hearth in the love of man for woman and of a father for his children. These two plans never converge; the image of Beatrice is as completely absent from Dante's hearth as is that of Dante's wife from the *Divine Comedy*. Gemma Donati, whom Dante probably married in 1295, five years after the death of Beatrice, had spent a long time waiting for him, if, at least, it is true that Dante and Gemma were betrothed by their families as early as the year 1276. But we shall shortly see that Dante then had other urgent reasons for marrying.

The chivalrous love of Dante for Beatrice is not only that of the poet for the fount of his inspiration, but also the love of the man for a woman whose nobility of soul he exalts to such heights that he who loves her cannot abase himself without betraying her and rendering himself unworthy to love her. The theme, classic in chivalrous literature, of the Lady who is the source of "valore" and of virtue, is here introduced into the analysis of Dante's feelings—not at all like the announcement of an oft-repeated literary theme that is taken up once more to be embroidered again in words, but as the expression of a living reality in the heart of Dante himself. Dante's most original contribution to the history of chivalrous love is perhaps the fact that he lived it so intensely.

There are, indeed, a number of signs which tempt us to think that the death of Beatrice in 1290 was the cause of a grave moral crisis in Dante's life from which he recovered only with great difficulty. Of this crisis the *Vita Nuova* itself retains barely a trace; and if we had only this document to go by, there would be nothing to lead us to suspect the gravity of the crisis.[1] Dante, indeed, there says simply that a little more than a year after the death of Beatrice he began to be attracted by another lady and soon came to delight in seeing her. However, after courageously joining battle with this temptation, it appears that Dante was aided by a triumphant return of the memory of Beatrice and reverted, full of remorse and shame, to the cult of his love.[2] It was, we gather, some time afterwards that the *mirabile visione* which seems to be the germ of the *Divine Comedy* finally appeared, and that is the stopping-point of this story, in which one cannot help feeling that Dante reproaches himself very harshly for having thought for some while of replacing Beatrice by another Lady of his thoughts.

When we turn to his other works, there are many things which, on the contrary, lead us to think that the *Vita Nuova* did not mention everything. No doubt the time had not come for Dante to confess his sins, but when we read the series of six sonnets exchanged between Dante and Forese Donati, any confession becomes superfluous. The accusations levelled by Forese against Dante are of little importance: they are insults which must be taken as such, especially as they are offered in a country where the insult itself is an art the rules of which prescribe a sort of lavish magnificence. What is far more disconcerting to

---

[1] I do not even see anything in the *Vita Nuova* which could, with any degree of certainty, be interpreted as an allusion to moral disorders resulting from the death of Beatrice. The episode of the *donna gentile* was to be explicitly related by Dante himself, in the *Banquet*, to philosophy (see below, Chap. II, p. 141). I know that high authorities dispute this point; at all events we cannot regard the contrary as certain. Nor do I consider myself bound to interpret Guido Cavalcanti's famous sonnet to his friend—*I' vegno il giorno a te 'nfinite volte* (DANTE, *Il Canzoniere*, in *Tutte le opere, ed. cit.*, p. 175)—as being directed against any moral degradation. Not only do I not think, with G. APPEL, *Das Sonett Guido Cavalcantis . . .* (in *Mélanges Wahlund*, Mâcon, Protat Frères, 1896), that in this sonnet Guido is speaking throughout in the name of Beatrice, but I do not see that Guido is there censuring any moral disorders in his friend. The whole of this sonnet suggests rather that Guido is reproaching Dante for neglecting his talent, letting his genius sleep and consorting with undesirable people, for whom he would formerly have had only contempt. Taking one hypothesis with another, I could quite readily picture Cavalcanti expressing disgust with a Dante who, instead of continuing to write, consorts with those untouchables, the clerics and the philosophers—a disgust something like that of the lettered nobleman for pedants. However that may be, the expression *anima invilita* does not here necessarily designate moral degradation any more than it ordinarily designates it in the writings of Dante himself; cf. for example, *Vita Nuova*, XXXV, and F. TORRACA, *La "vile vita" di Dante*, in *Nuovi studi danteschi nel VI centenario della morte di Dante*, Naples, P. Federico e G. Ardia, 1921, pp. 40–48.

[2] *Vita Nuova*, XXXIX.

us in this exchange of sonnets is the part played by Dante himself
—not what is said to him, nor even what he says, but the fact
that it is he who says it. It is idle to point out that Dante was a
man like any other and a Florentine with as sharp a tongue as
any other Florentine—the fact remains that the public insults
offered by Dante to Forese's mother[1] go a very long way beyond
the limit of what is justified in the name of rhetorical satire and
Florentine vivacity. The sonnets of Dante and Forese Donati
are an exchange of filthy abuse for which Dante, who began it, is
primarily responsible, and the tone of which is very precisely
that used by two tavern brawlers. How can we doubt, after
this, that it is here a question of one of those verbal affrays that
are only too frequent between companions in debauchery?
That the men were such the *Divine Comedy* itself attests. In the
passage in *Purg., XXIII*, 115–117 in which Dante replies to Forese,
who died before him and whom he is prudent enough to put
only in Purgatory, he begins with these words: "If thou recallest
to thy mind what thou wast to me and what I was to thee, the
recollection will even now be painful to thee." What, then,
had they been to each other? The Franciscan Serravalle explains
to us in Latin which it is better not to translate: *Nam ipsi
fuerunt socii in rebus aliquibus lascivis, quas fecerunt invicem
et insimul.*[2] How can we tell if the good Minor Friar is guilty
of betrayal or calumny? The passage in the *Divine Comedy* is
complete in itself; even if we do not interpret it in the extreme
sense—which we cannot deny, moreover, that it suggests—Dante's
sentence cannot mean that the relations between the two friends
were honourable. Certain of his historians refuse to believe it,
others, virile commentators and full-blooded he-men, dub the
former simpletons and are delighted at it for the sake of Dante,
his work and ourselves. All betray Dante. For it is true that the

---

[1] DANTE, *Il Canzoniere*, in *Corrispondenze in versi*, ed. cit., pp. 173–174. The explanation of these passages bristles with difficulties, even for specialists; cf. F. TORRACA, *La
tenzone di Dante con Forese*, in *Nuovi studi danteschi nel VI centenario della morte di Dante*,
Naples, P. Federico e G. Ardia, 1921, pp. 1–40. It is not necessary, however, to understand them in detail in order to perceive their tone; Dante's third sonnet to Forese
especially is only too clear in this respect.

[2] For a moderate interpretation, cf. DANTE, *La Divina Commedia*, Scartazzini's edition,
revised by Vandelli, U. Hoepli, 1920, *ad. loc.* (*Purg., XXIII*, 116): "*Qual fosti meco*
etc.: the life thou ledst with me, and I with thee. That the allusion does not turn so much
on the relations between Dante and Forese and their objectionable attitude towards
each other as on a life of sin led by both in common is proved by line 118: *Di quella vita*,
etc. And the tension between Dante and Forese is actually proof of vicious living."

poet acted thus, but no less true that he is ashamed of it: let us believe, then, that he so acted, and suffer with him.

The remainder of this passage is, moreover, of capital importance for the interpretation of Dante. We must therefore read it without adding anything to it or taking anything from it: "This was the life from which I was diverted by this man who is walking before me, the other day, when the sister of him yonder (and he pointed to the sun) appeared round. This man has led me through the deep night of those verily dead, with the very body, which accompanies him. From thence I have been extricated through his aid, climbing and ever and anon circling the mountain which sets you up again—you whom the world has distorted. He has told me that he will bear me company until I reach the place where Beatrice is: at that place it is fitting that I remain without him. Virgil is he who spake to me thus" (*Purg.*, XXIII, 118-130). So this life of debauchery with Forese (*di quella vita*) is nothing more nor less than the starting-point of the *Divine Comedy*. Read again the first three lines of the sacred poem: "In the mid-way of our life, I found myself in a dark forest, for the right way was lost." Many things have been sought in the symbol of this forest: ignorance, philosophy, the political anarchy of Florence, Dante's exile, and heaven knows what else.[1] Why should we not listen to Dante himself, seeing that he has told us what it was? Dante, full of sleep as he was at the time, no longer remembers how he entered this forest, scene of the destruction that wasteth at noonday. "Lord," says another great poet, "save us from the first sin that we commit when we are taken by surprise." The fact remains that Dante is horrified by the recollection of this place, which is so bitter that death is hardly more so. It is there, after a night of anguish, and when the sun is already lighting the slopes of a high hill, that Dante, who is making his way towards it in order to scale it, sees rising before him the three beasts: the panther (or lynx, *lonza*), the lion and the she-wolf. In this crisis Virgil appears, sent specially to Dante's aid by Beatrice, who wishes to save her friend. *L'amico mio*, she says; and she is explicit: It is I, Beatrice,

---

[1] That the *Selva oscura* represents not the corruption of original sin, as some inter-preters will have it (L. Pietrobono, L. Valli), but that of sin actually committed, seems to me quite certain in the light of this passage. Other arguments, tending in the same direction, are propounded by M. BARBI, *Nuovi problemi della critica dantesca*, in *Studi Denteschi*, Vol. XXIII, 1938–XVII, pp. 26–28.

who send thee to him: *Io son Beatrice che ti faccio andare* (*Inf.*, II, 70).

To understand what has happened it only remains to combine these two passages as Dante himself bids us do. Since the dark forest of vice is nothing more nor less than his life of debauchery with Forese, we know, because we have it from Dante's lips, that Beatrice has extricated him from it, and that she has extricated him from it through Virgil. In saying this we are adding not a single idea to those which the passages in actual fact contain. On the other hand, if we wonder besides how Beatrice has saved Dante through Virgil, it is impossible to answer without adding to the passages something which they do not expressly say. In such a case we not only ought to represent as a conjecture what is nothing more—we ought in addition to seek the simplest conceivable interpretation and, in short, reduce the conjectural element to the bare minimum.

To satisfy this requirement the hypothesis to be chosen should be the simplest that takes account of all the following facts: Beatrice has freed Dante from a dissolute life; in order to free him from it she has had recourse to the *parola ornata* of Virgil (*Inf.*, II, 67); Dante is not surprised; Virgil is his master, the poet *par excellence* (*Inf.*, I, 85), whose work he has long studied and loved; this is therefore the moment for him to be recompensed (*Inf.*, I, 83: *vagliami* . . .); Virgil fulfils his mission in undertaking again, for Dante's sake, the "descent into Hell" which he has already made in the past for the sake of Aeneas. These, it seems, are the essential data of the problem. Now we know, on the other hand, since Dante has said it himself in the *Vita Nuova*, that he has had a wonderful vision, which induced him to speak no more of Beatrice before he was in a position to speak of her worthily, "to say of her what was never said of any woman". It has been said that these words from the last chapter of the *Vita Nuova* are a subsequent addition by Dante to his work. That may be, but it in no way alters the fact that Dante wrote them. Furthermore, we know from the *Banquet*, II, 7, something of the tenor of this vision and of the effects which it had on him: "That is to say that I contemplated in thought the kingdom of the blessed. And I state at once the last reason for which I climbed aloft in thought, when I say: *Ove una donna gloriar vedia*; in order to let it be understood that it was because

I was certain, and am certain, through her gracious revelation, that she was in heaven. Hence it is that thinking thereon oft-times, as I was able, I used to go as it were into an ecstasy: *me n'andava quasi rapito*." Here, then, is a Christian poet, beset by a moral crisis, whom the image of Beatrice, though obliterated from his mind by all his transgressions, impels none the less to think of heaven and to contemplate her blessedness. What Christian can think of heaven, if his state is Dante's, without thinking also of its tragic alternative? And what is, in actual fact, the sole concrete image of Hell that arises in the mind of a man of the Middle Ages, and an avowed disciple of Virgil,[1] if not Book VI of the Aeneid? Virgil Dante's guide through Hell, Beatrice Dante's guide through Paradise—that is very nearly the *Divine Comedy* itself. Without pretending to reconstitute the psychological genesis of the work, we may say that its author himself invites us to seek its origin in this direction.

It has been said—and how rightly!—that remorse is one of the most certain sources of the sacred poem's inspiration. Perhaps we must go further and say that, as a work and as an act, the *Divine Comedy* is a work of penitence—the incomparable *amende honorable* of a poet of genius to his Muse whom he has betrayed, and to the God Whom he has wounded in betraying her. Like every true act of penitence, Dante's was also the remedy which saved him; not only his expiation, but his redemption. To make expiation, he had to awaken in the fallen man the poet whom his friend Cavalcanti strove to recall to life, but in vain, for only Beatrice could do so. To make himself worthy to grapple with such a task, he decided to keep silent as long as the necessary preparation lasted—throughout the years of initiation into philosophy and theology mentioned in the *Banquet*. Finally, to write such a work, which smashes its way through the low ceiling of courtly poetry like an arrow shot at the sky, Dante had to re-adjust his moral life by marrying the patient Gemma Donati: then, in spite of the thousand and one set-backs caused by civil war, domestic separations and exile, he had to grow to

---

[1] There has been a suggestion of Moslem sources with regard to this point (Señor Asin Palacios). It goes without saying that I do not intend here to express any opinion on a thesis which this is not the place to examine. I endeavour to confine myself to what is certain. Now it is certain that Dante was long familiar with Virgil, and, whatever we may think of the thesis of Señor Asin Palacios, we cannot ascribe to it a comparable degree of certainty.

the stature of this marvellous work, into which he poured his loves and hates, his feelings of tenderness and of wrath, his remorse and his highest Christian hopes, and in which his voice rang out in tones the world had never heard before.

In so far as it is an act and a work in Dante's life, the *Divine Comedy* is certainly bound up with the history of his own religious life. It figures in it in the rôle of an event. It is the tragedy lived by a Christian between damnation and salvation, the tragically outstretched arm of the drowning man, the hand that feverishly clutches the hand of salvation. This hand Beatrice alone could proffer. She did so, but we need only recall her first meeting with Dante in Purgatory to realize that she will not save him without an effort on his part. She does not welcome him with words of love; she casts in his face the recollection of his unworthiness: "Regard me well, 'tis indeed I, 'tis indeed I, Beatrice. How wast thou able to approach the mountain? Knowest thou not that here is man blessed?" (*Purg.*, XXX, 73–75). Dante does not miss the point; he bows his head and, seeing his reflection in a limpid pool, averts his eyes and looks at the grass that he may no longer see himself, so great is the shame that oppresses his brow: *tanta vergogna mi gravò la fronte!* What, then, is this Psalm XXXI, the *In te Domine speravi*, which the angels intone immediately after the last words of Beatrice, if not one of the Psalms of Penitence? And the issue involved here is not the notion of penitence as required of Christians in general, but the actual penitence due from Dante for the personal sin of Dante with which Beatrice charges him personally. The brand with which she marks him has nothing in common with those homilies on sin in general to which we listen without worrying because we apply them to the sins of others. Dante knows perfectly well that the moment has come to explain his conduct, that he can no longer avoid doing so, and he knows what errors he is required to explain. As soon as the angels have finished their chant, through the efficacy of the psalm tears of repentance well from his eyes, but the pitiless Beatrice denounces the offender in front of the angels: "For some while I sustained him with the sight of my face: by letting him see my youthful eyes, I led him with me on the right road. As soon as I was on the threshold of my second age and passed to the other life, this man took himself from me and set his heart elsewhere. When I ascended from

flesh to spirit, and grew in beauty and in virtue, I was less dear
to him and less welcome; and he turned his steps towards a road
that is not the true one, following false images of good which
never wholly fulfil their promise. I gained nought by praying
for divine intercession, through which, in dreams and in other
ways, I called him back; so little did he reck of it! He fell so
low that all remedies aimed at his salvation were ineffectual, save
to let him see the folk that are lost" (*Purg.*, XXX, 121–138).
That is why, concludes Beatrice, I visited the realm of the dead
and sent Virgil to him with my prayers; but the divine law would
be violated if, before crossing the purifying waters of the river
Lethe, he did not first shed the tears of repentance.

It is rather curious that the classic commentaries on the *Divine
Comedy*, Scartazzini's for example, even in Vandelli's amended
version, calmly say by way of a note to line 127: He turned
altrui, towards another lady, the *donna gentile* of the *Vita
Nuova*, 36–39. Let us say, if we like, that he turned towards the
less worthy things that such an image can symbolize. And as
for the notion that this storm of abuse from Beatrice, this dreadful
shame felt by Dante, can refer to nothing but philosophical
excesses committed by a cleric, that is really hardly possible.
The words that he uses when addressing Forese forbid us to accept
it. It is true that, farther on, Beatrice reproaches Dante for other
errors, and that the words she uses irresistibly suggest the idea
that it is there a question of doctrinal errors, but Dante may have
committed both misdemeanours,[1] and for the moment we are
concerned with the one of which he actually accuses himself.
In fact, Dante has just told us more here than he has yet said
about the story of his misdemeanours: he has been not only a
sinner, but a hardened sinner. It is not a vision, or a dream, or
divine intercession that has rescued him from the path of evil:
Beatrice has had to insist in order to make herself understood
and, what is more, the only decisive argument capable of breaking
down his resistance has been furnished not by the heaven of
Beatrice but by the hell of Virgil. That is what this passage says,

[1] There is, indeed, reason to believe that he did commit both. As we shall see, the
Convivio strongly suggests that after the death of Beatrice Dante passed through an
intellectual crisis. The only way in which we may conceive this crisis, having regard to
the relevant passages, is to picture it as a period of profound forgetfulness of religious
truth and aims. In short, Dante was supposedly affected for a time by a more or less
acute spell of "philosophism", the nature of which we shall, moreover, have ample
cause to reconsider.

and if we do not believe what Dante himself there relates of his
own history, even though it accords with all that we know of
it from other sources and the very structure of the *Divine Comedy*
confirms it, it is quite vain for us to imagine another truth more
agreeable than that revealed by him. After all, what advantage
could it be to him to invent such a story? There was nothing in
it to boast about.

What has just happened here before our eyes is nothing less
than the transfiguration by Dante's genius of the chivalrous theme
of the lady who is the inspiration of "valore". Because he never
lives among abstractions, but among things and people, Dante has
never thought either that he could save his genius without saving
himself, or that the source of his personal salvation could be
different from the source of his genius. Had he been swallowed
up for ever in the mire of vice, Dante would not have drowned
himself alone in it: he would have drowned this *Divine Comedy*
which he had to create in order to escape from it. The choice
between Forese Donati and Beatrice had to be made. Dante
chose Beatrice. Thus, *just as she was invested with a religious symbolism as early as the* Vita Nuova, *Beatrice is still, in the* Divine
Comedy, *the woman whom he has loved and the inspiration of his
song*. The whole of Dante's work suggests that Beatrice remained
the liberating force of his lyrical powers, because she had formerly
presented to his gaze that excruciating beauty possessed by some
bodies which promise more than a body can hold and something
other than a body can give. When such emotions degenerate
into desire it is an admission that their object is not worth while,
for they themselves are not desire-emotions, but contemplation-
emotions.

> Laying his respect on her beauty like a veil,
> He loved her without desire.

That which the beloved woman thus presented to Dante's
gaze in the light of her face, the smile in her eyes and the charm
of her greeting, was—attuned to his sensibility through a myster-
ious affinity—the beauty of the flesh as signifying beauties of a
more exalted kind. I believe that in the whole of Dante's work
not a single case could be found in which the salutary intercession
of Beatrice does not owe something of its efficacy to the sight
or the memory of her bodily beauty. She herself has just reminded

him of it in the passage from the *Divine Comedy* which we have
quoted: As long as I was visible to thee, I kept thee on the right
road; no sooner didst thou lose sight of me than thou didst begin
to stray. It is Dante himself who addresses to his genius this
exhortation on the part of Beatrice to ascend like her from
flesh to spirit, and the *Divine Comedy* stands as its answer to the
appeal.

Moreover, the sacred poem has many features which tempt
one to think that the blest woman who saves the poet is still the
woman whom he formerly loved. In the passage in *Purg.*,
XXXI in which Beatrice publicly confesses a penitent Dante,
what she reproaches him for is his failure to understand, after the
death of the woman he loved, the vanity of earthly things, and
the fact that, instead of following her in her transfiguration, he
exposed to further blows an already wounded spirit; but it is
precisely there that she recalls to him the dazzling beauty of the
body that the poet formerly loved, those "fair limbs" the sight
of which, in his eyes, nothing in nature or in art could replace.
Is it not, moreover, this same unbearable emotion that causes
the poet's frame to tremble—for it is certainly a man, not a soul,
that goes on this journey beyond the grave—when there appears
to him for the first time, in Canto XXX of the *Purgatorio*, this
triumphant Beatrice whom he has never yet seen? To him she
is always the same—the woman without whom his genius is
powerless, but whose presence he cannot endure. Exactly as in
the *Vita Nuova*, his body trembles, consciousness deserts him, his
eyes grow dim: there can be no mistake about it—this is not
merely a symptom of love, it is love itself: *D'antico amor sentì la
gran potenza;* and when Dante turns to his guide in order to tell
him that he recognizes the signs of the old-time flame that still
burns in his veins, it is a line of Virgil that he chooses to quote
to Virgil: *Adgnosco veteris vestigia flammae*[1]   ("I recognize the

[1] VIRGIL, *Aeneid*, IV, 23. Cf. *Purg.*, XXX, 48: "Conosco i segni dell'antica fiamma".
The objection that Dante's imagination enabled him to make even a mere symbol live
seems to me here beside the point. I do not know if Dante *could have* given life to a
mere symbol: I do not wish, therefore, to deny it. On the other hand, I state as a fact
that, leaving aside the case of Beatrice, none of the characters in the *Divine Comedy* is a
mere symbol, that the coefficient of reality which accompanies their names does much
to make them live for us and that in effect they speak, move, feel and act in Dante's
work like living people. To add that if, to Dante, Beatrice does not correspond to any
real being, she is an exception in the *Divine Comedy*, is simply to state a fact. To say,
with Father Mandonnet, that Dante made Mahomet and Virgil live, although he had
never seen them (*Dante le Théologien*, p. 62), is not even to touch on the question. The

signs of the ancient flame"). Dante probably knows of what love he is thinking when he makes it speak the language of Dido.

The problem of whether such emotions are pure is one that does not fall within the province of history, but philosophy solved it long ago. Yes, they are pure, *provided that they do not betray their essence* and in the precise degree in which they are faithful to it. It is their misfortune that, since they are human emotions, this degree very seldom remains constant. For the common run of men, prudence consists in helping them to subside; for the philosopher, Plato in his *Banquet* has made some rather strong remarks as to the means of bringing them to their state of purity and maintaining them in it; but there are two classes of men whose redemption is effected as if of its own accord: the saint, who perceives all beauty as a reflex of divine beauty, and the artist, who, incarnating these emotions in his works, creates for them a body made to measure in order that they may express themselves in it and survive it.

Dante was not a saint, but he was a Christian artist of pro-digious power. It was as a Christian and as an artist, together and undividedly, in a unique act of creation and salvation, that, having seen every human substitute for Beatrice leading him to debauchery, Dante saved his work and his soul at one stroke. For him there never was, there never would be, another Beatrice; since she was dead, he must, after singing of her as she once was, praise her in the glory that was now hers. To Dante, was not to praise her or to love her the same thing? But one cannot love and praise a woman who is among the blessed without at the same time loving and praising the source of her beatitude. And how can one love it without wishing to share in it oneself? To tear himself away from the kind of places where the sonnets to Forese Donati would be written, Dante had no course open to him but to return to Beatrice. His Muse was one of the blessed, and so he had to sing of one of the blessed; the woman

---

problem is not whether Dante saw them, but whether, to him and to his readers, their names answered the question *quis* or the question *quid*. Mahomet exists, Heresy does not exist; Virgil exists, Poetry does not exist. Mahomet and Virgil are concrete beings, objects of love or hate; *everything passes off as if* Beatrice were one as well. That is all we can say, and I do not see that literary analysis can lead us any further; but we have already taken a big step, and we must not, in spite of it, argue as if such analysis invited us to infer the contrary. An imaginary Beatrice is less probable in a world of real beings than she would be, for example, in a *Roman de la Rose*—a work crammed with avowed allegories.

beloved of the poet was one of the blessed, and he had to love her henceforth as one of the blessed. This is very precisely what Dante did, and the very existence of the *Divine Comedy* is proof of it. What prevents so many interpreters from acknowledging this obvious fact is their inability to conceive such a transfiguration of a real being as possible even in the imagination of a poet. Since they refuse to take even Dante's word for it, there is little hope of making them understand it, but we may none the less try.

X. Transfiguration of Beatrice

The first point that we must remember, as we approach the problem, is that with Dante imagination had no part to play in the matter. As a Christian, he believed that the soul of Beatrice, like that of each and every human being, was an immortal substance whose final abode after the death of the body could only be heaven or hell. As a man, he knew from personal and unquestionable revelation that Beatrice was in heaven. These are the fundamentals of his problem as Dante himself conceived them; to understand how he solved it in this way we must attribute to them the same reality as he himself attributed to them. Some of his interpreters willingly accept the blest woman, but they refuse to remember that, to make a blest woman, the first essential is a woman; others do indeed believe in the real existence of this woman, but, less Christian than Dante, cannot take seriously the love of a poet for a blest woman. To these doubts no answer can be given, except that they render the *Divine Comedy* incomprehensible and dry up the source of the very beauty which makes us read it. If the sacred poem still lives, it is because its creator has peopled it only with living beings. Himself in the first place, by a unique decision which no poet had ever dared to take or has ever taken since. Then all the others, for not only have all the characters that move in it lived in history or legend, but they live in the poem more intensely than ever, in their individual essence as finally manifested by the inflexible law of divine justice. There is not a single dead man in the whole of the *Divine Comedy*. That is why the text of Dante has nothing in common with any *Pèlerinage de Vie Humaine*, *Roman de la Rose*, or other allegorical rubbish with its poverty of human stuff. When people tell us that "the *Roman de la Rose* ought to be studied here as Dante Alighieri is studied in the institutes of Rome and Tuscany", they are simply and solely confusing art with philology. When Jean de Meun chances to tell us of Charlemagne, Abelard and Heloise, we fall greedily upon these drops of water in his desert of allegories, but Slander, Giving-Too-Much and Mad Bounty soon reassert their rights, and Jean's few profoundly human lines on Guillaume de Loris and on himself are quickly buried beneath the chatter of Fear, Shame, Danger and Hypocrisy. The adventures of these proper names leave us cold and we no longer read what they say because it is completely and utterly insipid, but we shall always read Dante because the *Divine Comedy* is the story of a living being in the midst of other living beings and, among these living beings, there is none more real than Beatrice.

Let us note carefully that she is incomparably more so in the *Divine Comedy* than in the *Vita Nuova*. All social conventions being done away with, every equivocality of the flesh being removed, Dante and Beatrice no longer have to avoid each other in a square in Florence or content themselves with greetings exchanged from opposite sides of the street. As soon as they meet in Purgatory, they at last speak for the first time, and they do so in order to confess to each other all that has been weighing on their hearts for so long. Beatrice knows that Dante has loved her for her womanly beauty: she tells him so at last. What reason could there now be for not speaking of these things? Dante had debased himself because of losing her, whereas the loss should have ennobled him: she tells him so, and he listens with downcast eyes, for his blush of shame is truly due to his being in this state *in her presence*. If it were only a question of personal remorse, Dante could have recourse to the art, so prevalent among men, of self-purification through forgetfulness, but so long as Beatrice knows and Dante knows that she knows, nothing can prevent his shame from persisting—nothing short of a request for pardon and the obtaining of it. That is why, in this "other life", which is still in a true sense "life", with no severance, no break, but, on the contrary, with a perfect continuity of essence under diversified conditions, the Beatrice whom Dante meets in Purgatory is not a duplicate of Beatrice any more than he himself is a duplicate of Dante; it is truly they themselves who meet again there and it is truly their own story that is continued. A number of Dante's interpreters are astonished or even shocked that he could say what he did say of Beatrice the blessed if it is true that to him she was first a woman. Assuredly Dante exalted his Muse to the pinnacle of human grandeur, but did he go too far?

In order to approach the discussion of this problem through its most superficial aspect, we may fittingly note first that of all styles of language none was more familiar to Dante than that of the Scriptures. To him, as, for that matter, to his contemporaries, the Bible was not a book reserved exclusively for the use of priests when they conduct services in their churches. If the Biblical formulas have for him a special meaning, they owe it to the sacred origin of the book in which they are found; but every truly great event in human life, be it happy or tragic, has a sacred meaning of its own; to mark its true greatness we may therefore express it in a sacred style of language. This is what Dante often did and, with the lack of false modesty for which he is well known, he applied the process to himself first.

If, we are told, Beatrice was really only a woman, Dante could not, "without blasphemy", have written of her as he did. To which the answer should be that we must resign ourselves to the facts: if they are such, Dante was a blasphemer. For it can hardly be doubted that he at all events was a real man; now it was he himself, and he himself as a pilgrim from the earthly city, *not* the blessed being that he might one day become, whom Dante fearlessly caused Virgil to greet in these terms: "Proud soul, blessed is she who conceived thee!" (*Inf.*, VIII, 44–45). In this *Beata colei che in te s'incinse!* who could fail to recognize the passage from the Gospel: *Beatus venter qui te portavit* ("Blessed is the womb that bare thee") (St. Luke, XI, 27)? Here, then, is Dante's mother, whom he hardly knew and never mentioned, likened to the Virgin Mary, and Dante himself doing as much honour to his mother as if he had been Jesus Christ! Undoubtedly it will be conceded that the poet never had this truly blasphemous intention. At the distance at which we are in time from his work, we cannot form an exact opinion of the impression produced on a contemporary of Dante by formulas of this kind. Were they in general use and did people speak the language of the Bible as those who are brought up on the sacred

text are fond of doing? Was the expression a little too strong
for the fastidious? Or was it frankly an error of taste? It is hard
to tell. But these words have never been cast in Dante's teeth
as a blasphemy. However high an opinion he may have had of
himself, he never took himself for God.

The words that he uses in connection with Beatrice, or even
in connection with other characters of less importance, should
not be otherwise interpreted. Moreover, Dante did on one
occasion reveal his secret to us. In order to stimulate the belief
that he felt great sorrow at the departure of a lady whom he
pretended to love, Dante had decided to speak of her *alquanto
dolorosamente*; otherwise, he said, no one would believe in his
sham. What better way to succeed than to write a *lamentanza*, in
other words a lamentation? So we see him in the process of composing a lamentation of Jeremiah; and what words has he not
chosen! The most sacred, because they directly apply to the
passion of Christ:

> O ye that pass along the road of love,
> Pause and see
> If there be any grief as heavy as mine. . . .
> (*Vita Nuova*, VII.)

This "road of love" introduced into the text of Lamentations,
I, 12, solely in order to deceive the reader, suggests that Dante
was not precisely scrupulous in these matters. We shall not be
surprised, after this, that the poet has again assumed the voice
of Lamentations (I, 1) to announce the death of Beatrice,[1] but
we shall be still less surprised that he has spoken to us of Beatrice
the blessed as in fact he has done.

The surest way to settle this problem would perhaps be to
begin by agreeing as to what may and what may not be said
of a soul that is blessed. To this question I offer the following
answer: We may praise it in terms as lofty as we please, provided only that we do not identify it with God. I was almost
about to add "and even . . . !"—for one could easily quote
passages which, if such an idea was not in their authors' minds,
seem nevertheless to express it. But we need not go so far in
order to understand Dante's words concerning Beatrice; they
can usually be explained simply by reference to the power

[1] DANTE, *Vita Nuova*, XXVIII.

of grace, whose nature and effects no Christian can fail to know.

Yet, to give ourselves the right to adopt this principle of explanation, we must not begin by laying down *a priori* what Dante must have thought of Beatrice. If we were to decide, for example, that Beatrice was Revelation, there would be some reason for saying that "in Dante's mind it would be a profanation to make a real woman the symbol of Christian Revelation";[1] but there would only be reason for saying so if to Dante Beatrice really had been the symbol of Revelation. The fact that she could not be a woman if she symbolized that which perhaps she does not symbolize does not imply that she is not a woman. This is not all. To draw a conclusion of any kind from what are called "all the concrete notions which form the outline of Beatrice *qua* woman", we must begin by enumerating them *all*.[2] That is not what is done, and it is a pity. If one has failed to do it, one can reach no conclusion from arguments like the following, which has a hollow sound in spite of its massive appearance: "The qualifying terms bestowed by Dante on Beatrice are neither equivalent nor interchangeable. What Dante says, or appears to say, of Beatrice *qua* lady may always be applied to Beatrice *qua* doctrine, but not *vice versa*."[3] In fact, this assertion is false, and, if we confine ourselves to the first part of it, it is even palpably so. If what Dante says of Beatrice *qua* woman always applies to theology, it must be said that theology was born in Dante's lifetime, that it had well-shaped limbs, that the father of theology is dead, that theology itself followed this excellent father to the grave, that its death was bewailed by the whole town, that its body has been interred, but that its soul is in the heaven of the blessed. The truth is that, to resort to the familiar language of the author of this thesis, Beatrice *qua* woman must indeed have an "outline", because she exists, whereas Beatrice *qua* Revelation has none, because she does not exist. If Revelation had one in the *Divine Comedy*, it would only be that of Beatrice *qua* woman, whose body, grace and smile Revelation borrows; whence we arrive, moreover, at the real problem: Is it true that, *vice versa*, what Dante says of Beatrice *qua* doctrine may not always apply to Beatrice *qua* woman?

[1] P. MANDONNET, *Dante le Théologien*, p. 60.   [2] P. MANDONNET, *op. cit.*, p. 63.
[3] P. MANDONNET, *op. cit.*, pp. 63–64.

If this is true, it rests with those who maintain it to prove it. I would gladly help them to do so, but I do not remember a single passage in Dante concerning Beatrice which has seemed to me to raise such a theological problem. That is probably because I am simple enough to believe that a woman who enjoys the sight of God face to face is decidedly an excellent person. Not only that, but I believe also that a young Florentine girl who has received the grace of baptism is already, even before she has reached a state of beatitude, a being of supernatural dignity whose spiritual beauty passes imagination. The fact that I believe this is important only to myself; but Dante also believed it, and that is extremely important to the interpreter of his work. That is why I cannot admit that one "plumbs the depths of absurdity" if one thinks that Dante wrote of a Christian woman that she was "a miracle of the Trinity, surpassing all that nature and art can produce". This thesis is altogether strange, especially coming from a theologian, and a theologian in whose mind Dante's thought and that of St. Thomas are confused. It is true that Dante is afterwards made to say: "So that between the first day and the last night of the world, God made nothing like her," a thing which, indeed, "cannot be said of any woman, since it implies superiority even to the angels."[1] But here our theologian's conclusion is a little too hasty, for there is at least one woman whom God created superior to the angels: the Virgin Mary.[2] And of Beatrice Dante never wrote this. In fact, he first of all said, in the *Vita Nuova*, XXIX, that this Lady Beatrice was, *per similitudine*, a number 9, that is to say a miracle, whose root, that is to say the root of the miracle (*cioè del miracolo*), exists only in the Holy Trinity. Now St. Thomas teaches, like every theologian, that man is an image of God. He does not even make any difficulty about admitting that in certain respects "the image of God exists more in man than in the angels".[3] If, as St. Thomas afterwards proves, that is true of every man, but especially of him who is *imago per conformitatem gratiae*,[4] and if this image of God exists in man "not only with respect to the divine nature, but also with respect to the Trinity of the Persons",[5]

[1] P. MANDONNET, *op. cit.*, p. 64.
[2] ST. THOMAS AQUINAS, *Sum. Theol.*, Pars. III, qu. 27, art. 5, Resp.
[3] ST. THOMAS AQUINAS, *op. cit.*, I, 99, 3, Resp.
[4] ST. THOMAS AQUINAS, *op. cit.*, I, 99, 4, Resp.
[5] ST. THOMAS AQUINAS, *op. cit.*, I, 99, 5, Resp.

it is not only Beatrice, but each one of us who, compared with the forces of nature and of art, *excedit omnem aliam naturam*.[1] So what, finally, is the root of all these marvels which transcend nature, if it is not the Trinity that creates and deifies?

Dante was therefore entirely right to glorify Beatrice—and, moreover, in another passage—by praising her as one of the marvels of the Creator: *Questa è una maraviglia; che benedetto sia lo Segnore, che si mirabilmente sae adoperare!* (*Vita Nuova*, XXVI). It is not of this passage, however, that Father Mandonnet is here thinking, but rather of the one which he elsewhere applies to Beatrice: "Between the last night and the first day (of the world) no work so great and so magnificent ever . . . existed or will exist."[2] A decisive passage indeed, if it did apply to Beatrice; unfortunately, these words are uttered by Beatrice herself, and she is speaking of the mystery of the Incarnation and the Redemption. Thus, through allowing himself to be dominated by the fetish of system, Father Mandonnet has gone so far as to invent false passages and even of ceasing to understand the obvious meaning of the true ones. He has lost in the process not only his Italian, but also his theology.

Above all, he has lost, what those who enter upon similar paths will lose with him, the deepest joy—one that is truly beatific of its kind—that communion with a genius through the medium of his work offers to the simplest reader. If one were deluding oneself in persisting in the assertion that a woman who is blessed is still a woman, and that she may remain so for the man who loves her, one would be guilty of a misinterpretation of Dante's work more inspired than that work itself. Such a thing has been known; but one cannot take the credit for adding to Dante what he himself never ceases to suggest. One is astonished to see a real woman undergo such a transfiguration; but unless she were real, how could Beatrice be transfigured? One is astonished again that a woman transfigured by glory should think, speak and love as a woman and that it should be as a woman that she is still loved; but if she were no longer a woman,

---

[1] St. Thomas Aquinas, *op. cit.*, Ia IIae, 112, I, Resp.

[2] *Par.*, VII, 112–114; quoted by P. Mandonnet, *Dante le Théologien*, p. 213. On the same page, Father Mandonnet describes as inapplicable to a blest woman the following remark: "God alone can appreciate her thoroughly because He alone has a thorough knowledge of her." What else, then, could Dante have said, short of asserting that any creature may know another creature as thoroughly as its Creator knows it?

how could she be a transfigured woman? What Dante here asks us to understand and to admit is precisely that, on the strength of the love that he bore her, Beatrice is exclusively marked out to be his intercessor with God. If God can win him back, it will be through her, and it is surely because Dante loves her still that God sends her to him. This man Dante will undoubtedly follow her, though he would follow no one else! And, in fact, he does follow her, in the character that she has now assumed— that of the mediator between his soul and God.

Such, indeed, combined with her glorification in heaven, is the transfiguration that Beatrice has undergone in the poet's soul. He himself says so time and time again, and it is because they have not taken him at his word that people have finally lost the meaning of his work. What kind of a person, then (they ask), is this Beatrice who, after coldly abandoning the young Alighieri to wed Simone dei Bardi, makes herself ridiculous by addressing "scathing reproaches to Dante, who is lawfully married and the respectable father of a family"! And the most unconscionable thing is that after obtaining from Beatrice, from start to finish, two greetings in nine years, Dante "should still be infatuated with Beatrice, and more so than ever. What psychology"![1] Alas! Yes, what psychology! But whose? And what kind of psychology can it be which does not appreciate that Beatrice the blessed is still a living woman—*quella viva Beatrice beata*[2]—but one transfigured into glory, and, when she meets Dante in purgatory, busied in her mind with something else besides involving him in a domestic scene at the cost of good sense and morality? She reproaches him with something quite different; through a failure to appreciate the fact, a misunderstanding has been inevitable as to the meaning of the entire work.

In order to understand Dante's attitude towards Beatrice, as, for that matter, that of Beatrice towards Dante, one need only remember that not all the saints are in the calendar. Like so many other Christians, Dante thinks that, if he has a personal chance of salvation, it consists not in the intercession of the

---

[1] P. MANDONNET, *Dante le Théologien*, pp. 92–93. The argument had already been employed by E. V. ZAPPIA, *Studi sulla "Vita Nuova" di Dante*, Rome, E. Loescher, 1904, p. 344. Zappia's book is discussed by M. BARBI, *La questione di Beatrice*, in *Problemi di critica dantesca*, Prima serie (1893–1918), Florence, Sansoni, 1934–XII, pp. 113–139.

[2] DANTE, *Convivio*, II, 8.

great saints, men and women, of the whole Church, but in that
of his own saint. Now let us not forget that Dante *knows* that
Beatrice will live henceforth as a saint among the saints. Why,
then, should she not be to him what to so many Christians
those beloved beings are, to whom they *know* that they can
pray, and to whom they do pray? As a means to the discovery
of Love, how should they not first think of those whom they
love still, and by whom they are loved? In this man's past, the
mother whom he lost when so young—at about the age of six—
is too indistinct a figure for him to think of turning to her. For
him there is really no woman elect of God to whose personal
intercession his love entitles him but this *Beatrice beata* whom,
with that instinct which makes so many Christians pray to their
mothers, Dante has made his mediator. If he undertakes a
journey to the lands beyond the grave, what blessed soul does
Dante hope to meet first to receive him on the threshold of heaven
and lead him in? None but Beatrice. And she is, in fact, there.
But Dante is not unaware of what he would first have to confess
and expiate at this meeting. To find out, he had only to ask
himself how, each time he felt that he was beneath her gaze, the
associate of Forese Donati faced the soul of Beatrice:

> As those little ones, who, filled with shame and speechless,
>   remain with their eyes fixed on the ground, listening,
>   conscious of their guilt and contrite,
>
> so was I; and she said: "Since
>   it is painful to thee to hear me, raise thy eyes:
>   thy distress will only be the greater as thou beholdest me."
>   (*Purg.*, XXXI, 64–69.)

But Dante well knows in whom he trusts, for when in the
eighth heaven the sudden clamour of the triumphant spirits
makes him sick with terror, like a frightened child that in-
stinctively runs straight to her on whom it relies more than on
anything in the world, Dante turns at once to Beatrice. But here
nothing can take the place of his text:

> Oppresso di stupore, alla mia guida
>   mi volsi, come parvol che ricorre
>   sempre colà dove più si confida;

e quella, come madre che soccorre
subito al figlio palido e anelo
con la sua voce che il suol ben disporre

mi disse: "Non sai tu che tu se' in cielo?"
(*Par.*, XXII, 1–7.)

And what does she say to the pale, breathless little one—this succouring mother "whose voice is ever a solace to him"? Simply these divinely maternal words: "Thou knowest not, then, that thou art in heaven?" We are, I fear, rather far from the learned deductions from which it transpires that Beatrice never existed, save as a symbol of baptism, the clerical vocation, Minor Orders, continence or the light of glory. But we are very close to Dante.

If Beatrice was not a real woman, loved by the poet as long as she dwelt on earth, still living in his heart after she had quitted this world, lost for a time during which his moral outlook was in the grip of a crisis which even threatened his genius, then rediscovered as a heavenly protectress whose intercession saved at once the man and the work bequeathed to us by the poet —if, I say, Beatrice was not this to Dante, it may be said that the *Divine Comedy* has systematically deceived us, and that it has unworthily deceived us by using the magic of the most splendid genius in order to make us believe in imaginary confessions, in which false loves converse with feigned remorse and pretended griefs with a hope that has no object. Once again, this is not impossible, but to be credible it would have to be proved. The fact that every attempt to prove it leads to flagrant contradictions of the works as they stand, then to distortion of the passages to which it is desired to give the form that they ought to have, finally to innumerable misinterpretations and justificatory sophisms, which abound as if of their own accord as soon as one enters upon this road, is perhaps enough to turn us from it.

There are two works in which Dante has not made a public confession: the *Vita Nuova* and the *Banquet*. If we only had these, we should have to take him for a chivalrous poet whom grief at the loss of his lady has led to philosophy. But we have others: the pieces of evidence constituted by the sonnets to Forese, and the public accusation of Dante by Beatrice in the *Divine Comedy*. All these works were certainly written by the same man, but not at the same period of his life. Whatever estimate one forms of the sonnets, they fit in more easily with the fault of which the author of the *Divine Comedy* accuses himself than with the feeling that leads him to accuse himself of it. Such a personal work, in which the author is the chief actor, and in which we find him in the midst of a reality that may be verified in all its aspects, surrounded by friends and enemies whom he names and whom, moreover, we know, full of political passions and desires for vengeance, but also of forgiveness, remorse and hopes the objects of which we may identify—if that is not the whole truth regarding Dante (he himself did not know the whole of it and no man ever tells all that he knows of the truth about himself), it is at least, in the primary intention of its author, something of the truth about things which he himself regards as realities. If such is the case, the *Vita Nuova* certainly does not tell us of the downfall of a cleric or a theologian, but of the life of a young poet and his love for his Muse, whom he celebrates, loses and finds again transfigured. So there is here no question of theology. Even if, as I think—though it is debatable—the *Donna gentile* already symbolizes philosophy in this work, the matter in no way enlightens us as to the function which Dante attributes to it, apart from that of consoling him. To find out what Dante really thought of the philosophers and their wisdom, we must address ourselves to the work in which he himself says explicitly what he thinks of them—the *Banquet*.

II

Philosophy in the *Banquet*

THE PRESENT controversy about the meaning of the *Convivio* is perhaps destined never to end, first of all because scholars only rarely interpret this work for its own sake. They have their general idea about Dante's thought; they know who Beatrice is and what she is not; they have made up their minds about the *Donna gentile* who appears in this work, and about her relations with all the other equally *gentile* ladies who may figure elsewhere; they are certain that Dante has lied and that, to cover his lie, he has refashioned other works, the original text of which has thus disappeared; but they know what this original text contained, with the result that they interpret the text that we have in the light of one that we lack. This little game serves in a high degree to provide material for teaching from university chairs, but it has no reason to end, for it is only too true that the works of Dante are not always easily reconciled in our minds. Indeed, we shall be able one day to reach agreement as to the probable way in which they were reconciled in his only on the express condition that we do not alter these works in order to reconcile them the more easily in our own. Yet this is what is done. Whence it follows that the discussions of the Dantologists no longer turn on one single *Banquet*, that of Dante, but on multifarious hypothetical *Banquets*, everyone defending his own against others, with which he cannot even compare it.

There is a second cause of difficulty which is peculiar to the authentic work itself. The *Banquet* of Dante is incomplete. As Dante had conceived it, the work was to comprise a general introductory treatise, followed by fourteen treatises, every one of which would have been composed of a poem with a copious commentary in prose. Dante only wrote the Introduction, the first three poems with their commentaries and several poems intended to furnish the material of the other treatises which he did not write. Scholars do not always agree in their choice of poems from Dante's *Canzoniere* which should be considered as intended for the *Banquet* as it would have been when once completed.[1] We possess, all told, only four out of the total of fifteen treatises contemplated by Dante. Now if we had only the second of the treatises written, without the fourth, we could demonstrate the truth of interpretations which, in the light of the fourth, are manifestly complete misconstructions of the poet's thought. What would the position be if Dante had written the following eleven? For this reason alone, it will always be difficult to reach any absolutely rigid conclusions as to the ultimate meaning of the theses contained in the *Banquet*.

There is a third source of difficulty which results from the very character of this composition. It is a work full of philosophical and even theological ideas, and it is written by an author who is, technically speaking, neither a philosopher nor a theologian. When he writes this work, his erudition in these matters is of somewhat recent date.[2] That is perceptible from the way in which he inserts, just as they stand, chunks of doctrine of varying origin, without always smoothing or adapting them as he ought. For that matter, Dante had nothing more to do, given the actual character of this composition. He conceived it as a work of learning for the masses. The *Banquet* has as its aim the initiation in philosophy of those worthy folk who are

---

[1] With regard to the *canzoni* which Dante wrote for the *Convivio*, giving only the text, without the commentaries, see N. ZINGARELLI, *La vita, i tempi e le opere di Dante*, F. Vallardi, Milan, 1931, Chap. XV, Vol. I, pp. 337–368. For a general introduction to the *Convivio* and to the problems bound up with it, see *op. cit.*, Chap. XXI, Vol. I, pp. 527–564. The date of the work's composition is located between March, 1300 and May, 1308, but it varies greatly with different authors. With regard to the text of the treatise, see EDW. MOORE, *Studies in Dante*, Fourth Series, Oxford, 1917: *Textual Criticism of the Convivio*, pp. 1–133 and pp. 288–295. For a critical edition of the text see *Dante, Il Convivio . . .*, comm. da G. Busnelli e G. Vandelli, con Introduzione di M. Barbi, F. le Monnier, Florence, two Vols., 1934 and 1937. For reasons of practical arrangement I have made use of the following edition: DANTE ALIGHIERI, *Il Convivio*, con Prefazione di Pasquale Papa, C. Signorelli, Milan, 1926. This is the standard edition of the text: I made use of it to begin with for a large number of years, and I have finally remained faithful to it, because its faults, if it contains any, at least have the merit of being the result of accidents which may counterbalance one another, instead of all tending in the same direction, as do those of certain editions in which the criticism is sometimes inspired by previous interpretations.

[2] It is, moreover, necessary to remember that, according to Boccaccio's remark, Dante never enjoyed the leisure of a speculator. In addition to his "fierissima et importabile passione d'amore" for Beatrice, he had a wife and family, played a political rôle and, above all, lived for a long time a life of exile and poverty. These elementary facts are too often neglected. Cf. BOCCACCIO, *Della origine . . .*, IV; in G. L. PASSERINI, *Le Vite di Dante*, Florence, Sansoni, 1917, pp. 17–18.

usually prevented by their public duties, their family responsi-
bilities or simply material circumstances from instructing themselves in these matters and extracting from them the benefits
to which they are entitled. If what we shall say below of philosophy as conceived by Dante seems true, it will be understood
how the actual idea of such a treatise is organically bound up
with his idea of philosophy.

This science is in his eyes a laymen's science, without which
they cannot attain the temporal aims which are their prerogative.
It is indispensable to them in order that they may live happily
after their way; it is therefore necessary that some at least among
them should be acquainted with it, and since these laymen
cannot conveniently go and learn it from the clerics who teach
it, it is necessary that one of them should write for the others
this "philosophic initiation" for worldly folk which is precisely
what the *Banquet* is. Undoubtedly Dante has availed himself of
the opportunity to express personal ideas, principally the one
which I have just mentioned and which is by a very long way
the most important; but for that very reason we must be careful
always to interpret the chunks of doctrine which Dante utilizes,
not according to what they contain or what they imply in the
philosophies from which he borrows them, but according to the
justification which they provide for the personal thesis which
Dante wishes to uphold. In other words, if we wish to understand Dante in the *Convivio*, we must not install ourselves successively in each of the positions through which he passes, nor
probe each of them to its depths or diverge from each of them
in all the directions which, taken by itself, it suggests; we must
pass through them in his company, with the same motion as
that with which he passes through them, as if they were halting-
places at which we may linger a moment to enjoy the scenery,
none of them, however, being the goal.[1]

To avoid these various dangers, the wisest course will be to

---

[1] With regard to Dante's general attitude in the *Banquet*, there is everything to be
gained from reading the three wise remarks made by M. Barbi in his *Introduction* to the
critical edition of G. Busnelli and G. Vandelli. It will also be profitable to consult the
numerous philosophical and theological works cited in notes by these two editors; but
such works may be utilized without danger only on condition that one discerns clearly,
beneath their analogies or their verbal coincidences with the text of Dante, the profound
differences of thought due to the clearly defined use which Dante makes of them. Dante
did not envisage, or we are not sure that he envisaged, anything save what he says in
his text, certainly not anything of what the other authors cited by way of comment say.
This has sometimes been forgotten.

proceed unceasingly by way of analysis, at the very least as regards those thought-developments in the *Convivio* which manifestly form a group. To detach a sentence from them in order to justify a comprehensive interpretation of the work, or even of the thought-development to which it belongs, would always be a risky procedure. Now in that part of his work which Dante has bequeathed to us we find, essentially, a justification of the symbol by which he represents philosophy, a study of the aim and of the chief parts of philosophy, a description of the effects of wisdom on the philosopher's soul, a definition of the relationship between philosophy and one of the other two authorities that govern human life : the Empire. These questions here intermingle, as they intermingle in reality; a score of times they seem to be submerged in some digression, but they remain the constant guiding rules which regulate the progression of the work. Therefore, given the clearly defined object of our own inquiry, they should also regulate our study of this treatise.

I. THE *DONNA GENTILE*

Philosophy is represented in the *Banquet* by the symbol of the *donna gentile*. How did this lady find her way into Dante's life? The beginning of this story, as he relates it in the *Banquet*, dates from the death of Beatrice and is linked with his conviction of her heavenly beatification. This is the starting-point to which he always comes back: *Appresso lo trapassamento di quella Beatrice beata* (II, 2)—after the passing of that blest Beatrice. In order, therefore, to link up the *Banquet* with the *Vita Nuova*, it is natural to admit that at the moment when this new fragment of his story begins Dante has already had the vision with which, in the forty-second chapter, the *Vita Nuova* ends. True, some posit as an obvious fact that the last part of this work, from Chapter XXIX to the end, inclusive, forms a distinct entity which the author has added to the rest. " Everyone can see it," we are assured, "everyone knows it, everyone agrees about it."[1] As I do not see it, or know it, or agree about it, I find myself greatly embarrassed. Being unable either to bow to a fact the obviousness of which escapes me, or to contest what is a fact by general

---

[1] L. PIETROBONO, *Il Poema sacro*, Vol. I, pp. 101–102.

consent, I will simply say that, whether or not it has been added to the original text, the end of the *Vita Nuova* remains what it is and says what it says. Addition does not signify fabrication, still less falsehood, trickery or falsification. Dante has, then, assured us in the *Vita Nuova*, whatever the period of his life at which he may have said it, that he had a vision relating to the dead Beatrice, that this vision inspired him with the desire to celebrate her in a unique way, but that he would need a few years to realize this project. On the other hand, Dante asserts in the *Banquet* (II, 7) that he knew, through a gracious act of revelation on the part of Beatrice herself, that she was in heaven; that while thinking of heaven as he was able he used to go as it were into a rapture; that this thought, by its sweetness, inspired him with the desire to die so that he might go and join her there, but that another thought, opposed to the first, suggested to him that he should love another lady, and promised him her notice and her greeting. This lady Dante names a little further on: she is the wisdom of the philosophers. Being a chivalrous poet, Dante personifies her in the image of a Lady, the *donna gentile*, but this time it is no longer a question of anything but a poetic fiction, as he himself explicitly states when he intentionally repeats that she was born of his imagination: *E imaginava lei fatta come una donna gentile, e non la poteva imaginare in atto alcuno, se non misericordioso* (II, 12). Finally, Dante declares that we have already met this imaginary *donna gentile* in the *Vita Nuova*, where she had appeared to him with the same aspect and the same character: she is that merciful lady who, a little more than a year after the death of Beatrice, offered to console him. To assure ourselves that the *gentile donna*, who looks at him so piteously— *sì pietosamente*—in *Vita Nuova*, XXXV, is indeed already philosophy, we need only refer to the *Banquet*, II, 2: "I say, then, to begin with, that the star of Venus had completed two revolutions in that circle which would make it appear in the morning and in the evening, according to the different seasons, after the passing of that blest Beatrice who lives in heaven with the angels and on earth with my soul, when that gentle lady, of whom I made mention at the end of the *Vita Nuova*, appeared for the first time before my eyes, accompanied by love, and took a certain place (*prese luogo alcuno*) in my mind." What fascinated him about her, then, was the consolation which she offered to

his widowerhood. This new love, adds Dante, had some difficulty
in taking root within me, because "the love of this glorious
Beatrice still held the citadel of my mind". Yet it finally prevailed,
at least for a time, until the vision narrated in *Vita Nuova*, XXXIX,
had freed Dante from it by restoring him to Beatrice.

    Such are the facts. When he himself refers us from the *Banquet*
to the *Vita Nuova*, Dante does not merely authorize us to base
our conclusions on both works, he compels us to do so. The
donna gentile of the *Banquet* is only a symbol; now the *donna
gentile* of the *Vita Nuova* is the same woman; therefore she also
is only a symbol. Yet, like everything that Dante himself may
have said about his work, this capital point is debated. It is even
discussed by him who, by unanimous consent, knows as none
other does the work of Dante, not having set aside a line of it
without examining it from every angle, speaking about it with
almost miraculous good sense and discussing it with an urbanity
that no attack can ruffle. I mean, of course, Signor Michele
Barbi. According to this master in Dantesque criticism, it cannot
be true that the *donna gentile* of the *Banquet* is the same as the one
of the *Vita Nuova*, because, in the *Banquet*, Dante loads her with
praises, whereas in the *Vita Nuova* he loads her with his scorn. It
is therefore not possible that Dante was referring to the same
thing in the two works: "Can we really believe that this love
for the *donna gentile* which, in the *Vita Nuova*, is styled *the
adversary of reason* and *most base* is that same love for Philosophy
which is declared to be so noble in the *Banquet? . . .*" The contradiction between the two works lies not so much in the
appraisal of the two ladies as in the love that the poet feels for
them: in the *Vita Nuova* too the lady is *gentile*, but the thought
that causes the heart to give her its assent is very base (*Vita
Nuova*, XXXVIII), whereas she is noble in the *Banquet*. No one
has said of the *donna gentile* of the *Vita Nuova* that she is represented as the adversary of reason. What is " the adversary of
reason" in that early work is the love for this merciful lady; and
it is so termed not because the desire would be—speaking in a
general and an abstract sense—the adversary of reason, but
because such a love is opposed to the " constancy" which here
reason itself should exhibit (*op. cit.,* XXXIX). The contradiction
between the *Vita Nuova* and the *Banquet* consists in the fact that
in the former it does not appear reasonable to abandon Beatrice

for the *donna gentile*, but such an idea is represented as evil desire and vain temptation (XXXIX), whereas in the *Banquet* the new lady is said to be of such great virtue that "all firmness of spirit may be considered fickle in comparison with it" (III, 1). Since the opposition is there established between the lady who is Beatrice and another lady, merciful and gentle, but not superior to her, it is the poet's duty to remain constant in his first love; here, on the contrary, it is a question of turning to wisdom, and it would scarcely be a sign of nobility to persist in the love of the senses, however virtuous it may be: where the love for philosophy shines forth (it is fitting to repeat here the exact words of Dante), "all other loves are obscured and extinguished, because its eternal aim puts to flight and transcends other aims out of all proportion" (*Conv.*, III, 14).[1]

It may, in truth, well be said that Dante has no luck. If he asserts that Beatrice is a woman, Father Mandonnet and E. Aroux say that she is only a symbol;[2] if he asserts that the *donna gentile* is only a symbol, Signor M. Barbi maintains that she is a reality. In short, only Dante himself never knows to what he is referring. Happily for him, and above all for us, to contest a conclusion reached by Signor M. Barbi is in no way comparable to refuting those of Father Mandonnet. Here the analysis is at once so precise and so finely shaded that, if error there be, the very premises of Signor M. Barbi's argument should suffice to show where it lies. Indeed, as this excellent historian has seen, it is not at all a question of what the *donna gentile* symbolizes, but of the feelings which Dante himself says he experienced towards her. This is precisely the reason why the fact that these feelings are not the same in the two works in no way implies that the *donna gentile* is not the same in each of them. We must here remind this master of a fundamental principle which he has himself instilled into us: Although the works of Dante are related like the daughters of a common father, each of them exists

---

[1] M. BARBI, *La questione di Beatrice*, in *Problemi di critica dantesca*. Prima serie (1893–1918), Florence, G. C. Sansoni, 1934–XII, pp. 118–119. Cf. the same author's *Razionalismo e misticismo in Dante*, in *Studi danteschi*, Vol. XVII, p. 14 and pp. 17–18.

[2] The symbolism of Beatrice is, moreover, entirely contradictory in the two cases. We have seen that to Father Mandonnet she symbolizes "the Christian life"; according to E. Aroux, whose work was dedicated to Pope Pius IX in 1853, Beatrice symbolizes "the hypostatized heretical thought" of Dante, or again "heresy incarnate" and, to be quite exact, the heresy of the Albigenses. See the very recent reprint of this book: E. AROUX, *Dante hérétique, révolutionnaire et socialiste. Révélations d'un catholique sur le moyen âge*, Paris, éditions Niclaus, 1939.

independently and demands to be treated as a separate individual. One need only conform to this wise precept to see that the alleged contradiction may not, after all, exist.

Let us first place the facts before our eyes. In the *Vita Nuova*, Dante has just lost Beatrice; without waiting for a vision to assure him of the fact, he already knows that she is in heaven among the elect. Beginning, then, from this moment, to love Beatrice is to love her in heaven and as she is in heaven. At all events that is what it means to love her *as he ought*. Meanwhile another love is offered to him—that of a noble and merciful lady who promises to console him. Dante is sorely tempted to give way. In fact, if it is wrong to do so, he consents to the wrong: his eyes begin "to delight overmuch in seeing her" (*Vita Nuova*, XXXVII). He actually reproaches himself for this weakness: he regards himself as despicable—*assai vile*—and the word *vile* certainly has here its full moral sense; Dante battles against this feeling, which is so strong that his condition seems to him horrible: *questa orribile condizione*. Thus the poet is on the point of forgetting Beatrice, the lady whom death alone should make him forget, and it is at the moment when this "adversary of reason" is perhaps on the point of triumphing for ever that the first appearance of Beatrice drives away in time this evil desire: *cotale malvagio desiderio* (*op. cit.*, XXXIX). All Dante's thoughts then return to Beatrice, his tears well up anew, he is saved.

Such are the facts. Let us suppose that this *donna gentile* is, as Dante affirms, only the symbol of philosophy; how does this affect our problem? Simply in this way, that after loving the earthly Beatrice, then remaining faithful for more than a year to the heavenly Beatrice, Dante consented for some time to console himself with philosophy and to seek in this new love forgetfulness of the first. But the first has returned, it has found its original strength and henceforth nothing can endanger it. What, then, is this evil desire, contrary to reason, of which Dante accuses himself? It is the desire to *substitute* the love of an earthly thing, even though it were as beautiful, as noble, as beatific as philosophic wisdom, for the love of a heavenly thing like Beatrice and her beatitude. For that is certainly the question here—whether or not Dante is going to pursue the supreme beatitude where the heavenly Beatrice invites him to seek it, or forget it and seek only earthly beatitude in the footsteps of Aristotle.

Dimenticare does not merely signify in Italian that passive thing which we term forgetfulness: it connotes, at least in its root, the act of dismissing a certain memory from one's thoughts. What philosophy sets out to do in the *Vita Nuova* is to lead Dante to forget that he is bereft of Beatrice: *Ed ora pare che vogliate dimenticarlo per questa donna* (*Vita Nuova, XXXVII*). Nothing could be clearer in this connection than the sonnet in Chapter XXXVIII: " The soul says to the heart: 'Who is this who cometh to console our thoughts, and is his power so mighty that he letteth no other thought remain with us?' " The dilemma that the whole context creates is here clearly defined: Either philosophy, or Beatrice. At the end of this crisis we know that the *donna gentile* has not displaced Beatrice. What has been cast out is rather, indeed, the evil desire—opposed to the constancy of reason—to displace Beatrice. Dante will never forget this from now on.[1]

The *Vita Nuova* does not say and does not ask that we should admit anything more. Under what conditions would other works by Dante contradict its testimony? It is not enough that when they are compared difficulties of chronology arise. As a poetic autobiography, the *Vita Nuova* may permit itself foreshortenings or extensions of perspective according to the poet's taste. We have no need to feel disturbed because what is there termed "a few days" may elsewhere be termed thirty months or more. The indications of duration in a work wherein the reckoning is manifestly symbolic cannot enter into the same system of calculation as the seemingly historical indications of duration in the *Banquet*. What matters here is the *nature* of the facts and their *sequence*. If another work by Dante is to contradict the *Vita Nuova* on this point it must either deny the reality of the so called philosophical crisis, or deny the ultimate triumph of Beatrice, or, finally, deny the sequence of these events as it *emerges* from the *Vita Nuova*: death of Beatrice, love of the heavenly Beatrice, temptation to substitute for her the love of philosophy, final return of Beatrice. The eulogies of philosophy which may be found elsewhere, exaggerated as they are, do not create any difficulty. As Signor M. Barbi very justly says, the question is not one of *philosophy*. Like the one in the *Banquet*,

---

[1] This point has been excellently expounded by F. ERCOLE, *Il pensiero politico di Dante*, Alpes, Milan, 1928; Vol. II, pp. 301-302.

the lady in the *Vita Nuova* is *gentile*, she is *bella molto*, she is *pietosa*, her love is *nobilissimo*, and not only does Dante wonder whether this comforter is not sent to him by Beatrice herself, but she resembles her as one form of beatitude resembles another: *Onde molte fiate mi ricordava de la mia nobilissima donna (Vita Nuova,* XXXVI). The question is one of Dante's feelings towards her; now philosophy has presented itself as a substitute for Beatrice —here is an evil desire and one contrary to reason if ever there was one—but Beatrice has never presented herself as a substitute for philosophy in Dante's soul; there is therefore no contradiction between Dante's condemnation of his idle desire to renounce Beatrice in favour of philosophy and his subsequent exaltation of a philosophy that is mindful of the rights of Beatrice. To be able to love both simultaneously, Dante only needed to find a place for each of them and to keep them there. Is that what he did?

Let us first recall that at the time when Dante was writing the end of the *Vita Nuova*, as at the time when he was writing the *Banquet*, the whole of this story was complete. In other words, in these works as we know them Dante has already described the circle Beatrice-philosophy-Beatrice. In the second place, if, as we think, there was in Dante's life a period of moral transgression, neither the *Vita Nuova* nor the *Banquet* makes any allusion to it: the only crisis of which the poet there seems to speak is the one which led him from the love of Beatrice to that of philosophy. Thirdly, Dante's position in the *Banquet* is that of a man who, knowing already *through a gracious act of revelation on the part of Beatrice* that she is in heaven, is nevertheless going to confine himself in this work to the field of philosophy, not, to be sure, exclusively, but principally. If we are to observe all these basic ideas simultaneously, what must we do? We must admit that they are all correct, if that may be done without creating an impossible situation. Now it may be done. It may be that after the death of Beatrice, apart from less wholesome distractions to which he does not here intend to confess, Dante sought oblivion in a new passion for philosophy and that, for a time, he found it; in consequence of which, at the instance of that Beatrice "who dwells ever with his heart", the memory of the beloved woman, now transfigured by beatitude, raised him from the love of philosophic truth to that of religious truth, from which she is henceforth inseparable. Now to rise from philosophy to religion does not necessarily mean that one repudiates philosophy, but only that one transcends it. If, therefore, we were to try to define Dante's possible position in the *Banquet*, so far as these basic ideas enable us to gauge it, we should arrive at the following conclusions: So far as may be judged from the only parts of the work that he wrote, Dante speaks there as a man who has already been won back by the heavenly Beatrice, a man who therefore cannot doubt the preeminence of religion over philosophy, but who, convinced that philosophy remains none the less legitimate in its own sphere and for its special purpose, undertakes to become its interpreter. In other words, we should be dealing with a Dante who has already emerged from a crisis of pure philosophism—which, moreover, he unequivocally admits that he experienced—but who is convinced that a legitimate place remains for philosophy, and is bent on defining it.

It seems that this is indeed the attitude which Dante has adopted in the *Banquet*. After the death of Beatrice he had the idea of turning to the specialists in consolation in order to seek a remedy for his ailment. "I began," he says, "to read that book, not known to many, by Boethius, in which, while a captive and in disgrace, he had found consolation. And learning, moreover, that Cicero had written another book, in which, treating of friendship, he had said something of the consolation of Laelius, a man of the highest merit, upon the death of his friend Scipio, I read it."[1] Such, then, was the starting-point of Dante's interest in philosophy. He already had many philosophic ideas before studying these works, but they were ideas that he had found in his own mind, without study, and which he "saw, so to speak, only as in a dream, as may be seen in the *Vita Nuova*". This lack of technical knowledge made it difficult for Dante at the start to enter into the thought of Boethius and Cicero. He therefore understood only that part of it which he could understand with the implements at his disposal: the grammatical and

---

[1] Dante therefore read BOETHIUS, *De consolatione philosophiae*, and CICERO, *Laelius sive de Amicitia*. On the history and influence of these works see H. R. PATCH, *The Tradition of Boethius. A Study of His Importance in Medieval Culture*, New York, Oxford University Press, 1935, pp. 91–92; CH. FAVEZ, *La Consolation latine chrétienne*, Paris, J. Vrin, 1937; and P. COURCELLE, *Etude critique sur les commentaires de la Consolation de Boèce (IXe–XVe siècles)*, in *Arch. d'hist. doctrinale et littéraire du moyen âge*, 14e année (1939), pp. 5–139.

literary make-up of the grammarian and the natural resources of his mind.[1] What happened, however, was this, that, seeking consolation for his grief, Dante found something quite different. The study of these works revealed to him the existence of a language that was new to him—the language of these authors, of these sciences and of these books. The Wisdom promised by the philosophers at once fascinated him and it was this that he imagined in the semblance of a *donna gentile*, of whom it is merely the poetic symbol (II, 12).

Hence the special function and the specific nature of philosophy in the *Banquet*. It is essentially a giver of human happiness and, as such, it tends there to be centred upon ethics. Everything conspires, moreover, to orientate the work in this direction—the public to whom it is addressed, since it is a question of inculcating a love of philosophy into a public of noblemen, politicians and men of action whose lives it is to guide; the primary aim pursued by Dante himself, since he asks it above all to console him and to save him. At the precise moment at which it enters his life Dante is beginning to love it for the promises of consolation which he reads in its face: *Lo mio secondo amore prese cominciamento de la misericordiosa sembianza d'una donna* (III, 1). In short, what this lady represents above all in his mind is philosophy in its function as a comforter.

Nothing could fulfil this function better than philosophy. One love drives out the other, and it happens, in fact, that the very definition of philosophy requires that this science should be a love: the love of wisdom.[2] In writing the *Banquet* Dante insists with satisfaction on the purity of such a love, and let

---

[1] See, on this point, M. BAUMGARTNER, *Dantes Stellung zur Philosophie*, pp. 49–51, and ROCCO MURARI, *Dante e Boezio. Contributo allo studio delle fonti dantesche*, Bologna, Zanichelli, 1905 (especially Chaps. IV and IX).

The expression "l'arte di grammatica" should be understood here in the sense attributed to it in the Middle Ages, following QUINTILIAN, *Oratoriae Institutionis*, lib. I, cap. 4: "Haec igitur professio, quùm brevissime in duas partes dividatur, recte loquendi scientiam plus habet in recessu quam fronte promittit." In fact, it was Dante's literary taste that was first won over to philosophy, understood in the humanistic sense, by the music of Cicero. Moreover, Dante began the Canzone in *Convivio* II, with the well-known line: *Voi che 'ntendendo il terzo ciel movete*, in which, as we shall see, the third heaven symbolizes Rhetoric, and the word *voi* designates the movers of that heaven, especially Boethius and Cicero: "Boezio e Tullio, li quali con la dolcezza di loro sermone inviarono me, come detto è sopra, ne lo amore, cioè ne lo studio, di questa donna gentilissima, Filosofia" (*Convivio*, II, 15).

[2] DANTE, *Convivio*, II, 15. Cf. III, 11, and especially III, 14: "Filosofia per subietto materiale qui ha la sapienza, e per forma ha amore, e per composto de l'uno e de l'altro, l'uto di speculazione."

us note carefully that, although he does not say everything, he is not lying in what he does say. If, as we have reason to fear, something else has happened, it is not to that that he is referring in this passage. Dante is therefore justified in saying that his life in spiritual union with this gentle lady—*l'unimento de la mia anima con questa gentil donna*—that is to say the love of philosophy, which had just cured him and consoled him, contained nothing that was not noble (III, 1 and 2). Now it was this new love, as we have seen, that led Dante to attend the schools of the theologians and the discussions of the philosophers. Where did Dante carry on his studies? We do not know. Those who positively insist that he betook himself to Paris have every opportunity of seeking here for confirmation of their thesis.[1] But for us this is not the important point: much rather is it the permeation of Dante's spirit by philosophy in consequence of those studies on which it is fitting for us to reflect.

Dante, indeed, expresses himself in a truly remarkable way when he describes the impression produced on him by this belated initiation in philosophy. At the end of about two and a half years of study this new love drove every other thought from his heart and by its power expelled the memory of his former love. It was then that he wrote the famous *canzone, Voi che 'ntendendo il terzo ciel movete*, his hymn to Philosophy. In this poetic eulogy what titles does Dante bestow on it? He calls it the daughter of God (*figlia di Dio*) and the queen of the universe (*regina di tutto*) (II, 12). These are rather strong expressions. Add to this that what the new love expels from Dante's thoughts is not only the memory of Beatrice the woman, the poet's human Muse, but actually that of Beatrice the blessed. Let us re-read the second

---

[1] See, on this point, PIO RAJNA, *Per l'andata di Dante a Parigi*, in *Studi Danteschi*, Vol. II (1920), pp. 75–87. That Dante stayed in Paris is, let us remember, asserted by G. VILLANI, *Cronica*, lib. IX, 136: "Et andossene allo Studio di Bologna, e poi a Parigi, et in più parti del mondo", in G. L. PASSERINI, *Le Vite di Dante*, Florence, Sansoni, p. 3; next by BOCCACCIO, *Della origine* . . . , IX, ed. cit., p. 28, and the very precise text of the *Trattatello*, II, ed. cit., p. 85; then by FIL. VILLANI, *De vita et moribus Dantis poetae comici insignis*, V, ed. cit., p. 185. The tradition is therefore ancient, but we do not know if these authors do more than gloss the text of the *Banquet*. For the arguments tending in the opposite direction see H. HAUVETTE, *Etudes sur la Divine Comédie*, Paris, H. Champion, 1922, pp. 206–214. Of these arguments none seems to me decisive. To say that Dante may have collected in Italy all the information about France that his work contains is tantamount to saying that the content of his work does not enable it to be proved that he went to France, not that he did not go there. Ultimately, therefore, the problem is whether or not we place reliance on the testimony of G. Villani; it is a matter of free choice; the problem therefore remains open by the very nature of the basic ideas that define it.

stanza of the poem, and we shall see that it cannot be interpreted
otherwise.

So there was indeed in Dante's life—and the *Banquet* too bears
witness to it—a period of enthusiasm and passionate desire for
questa donna gentilissima Filosofia. Enthusiasm for the pure intellectual beauty of a science which, by the love that it inspires,
frees the soul from grief; desire for a beatific form of learning
which literally snatches man from the cares of material life
and confers on him at one and the same time light and peace.
Let us note the fact carefully—Dante does not here speak of
philosophy as if it were capable of assuring the eternal salvation
of man, nor even as if it conferred on man a temporal beatitude
which would relieve him from the need for the other kind. What
has taken place in his mind, therefore, is something quite different:
in the discovery of philosophy, and in the enthusiasm with which
that discovery filled him, *Dante forgot all else.* That, moreover,
is why this new love could console him for everything, even
for the loss of the object of his former love. Dante does not
mean anything else in the passage which I am about to quote
in full. It is a little long, but I remember once hearing it said by
an Italian *cantatrice* that when an Italian carter sings he never
breaks off his phrase in the middle: he sings it right to the end.
How can we deal any less respectfully with the thread of the
following glittering period? "And where the *Canzone* says:
Let him who wishes to see salvation fix his eyes on the eyes of this lady,
the eyes of this lady are her proofs, which, being fixed on the
eyes of the understanding, capture the heart, which is freed
from its conflicts. O most sweet and ineffable images, sudden
ravishers of the human mind that appear in the teachings of the
eyes of philosophy when she reasons with her lovers! Verily
in you lies that salvation through which he who beholds you
finds bliss and is saved from the death of ignorance and corruption.
Where I say: *But he doth not fear the anguish of sighing,* the meaning
is: If he fear not the toil of study and the conflict of doubts which
arise in plenty as soon as this lady fixes her gaze, but afterwards,
as her radiance persists, vanish like the light mists of the morning
before the sun, and the familiar understanding is left free and
full of conviction like the air when it is purified and illuminated
by the rays of noon-tide" (II, 15). We feel behind this enthusiasm the presence of a very recent personal experience which,

perhaps, endures even yet: Dante glorifies philosophy as a source of bliss because he has just discovered the joy of understanding rational truth and the happiness of having it at his command.[1]

The fact that, in the joy of this discovery, Dante for a time forgot all else, is not very extraordinary in itself. We know what forms the ardour of the neophyte may take. On a far humbler, but not dissimilar plane, who among us does not know what it is to discover a writer, to become enthusiastic about him, to read none other but him for a time exactly as if there no longer existed any other, until, saturation-point once reached, we put him respectfully in a corner of our library in the limbo where those we have loved slumber? As M. Barrès used to say: Another squeezed lemon! Intellectual crises are more profound than crises of literary taste; they also last longer; but they are not essentially different. Beatrice has formally accused her penitent one of having in the past followed a false doctrine. When Dante asks her why her words go so far beyond the range of his understanding, Beatrice replies: "So that thou mayest know that school which thou hast followed [*conoschi . . . quella scuola c'hai seguitata,*] and see how its doctrine may follow my word, and see that your way is as remote from the divine way as is that heaven which hastens on its course in the highest from the earth" (*Purg.,* XXXIII, 85–90). Since it is here a question of a *school* and a *doctrine*, Beatrice cannot have been speaking of moral transgressions in this passage. Furthermore, in order to explain why Dante's reason cannot comprehend her words, Beatrice replies that he should know, because he has followed a school whose way—*vostra via*—is as inferior to that of the divine word as is the earth to heaven; unless it has the object of re-minding him that he has in the past counted too much on the

---

[1] It is precisely to this period of philosophic ecstasy, which coincided with his discovery of human wisdom, that reference is made in the passage in the *Convivio*, II, 15, where Dante says "che non dee l'uomo, per maggiore amico, dimenticare li servigi ricevuti dal minore". There was, then, a time when Beatrice was to Dante a "lesser friend" and philosophy a "greater friend". I am unable to share the astonishment to which this passage gives rise in the mind of L. PIETROBONO (*Il poema sacro*, Vol. I, p. 96). The illustrious Dantologist seems to assume as an obvious fact that "Dante's return to Beatrice", if it had taken place, would necessarily have excluded from the poet's heart the love of philosophy. Never will Dante assume that one love must exclude the other —not even in the *Divine Comedy*, where we know the place he allots to Siger of Brabant. There was, at a certain stage, a reversal of the hierarchy of these two loves in Dante's heart, and even a temporary oblivion of Beatrice, but the return of Beatrice never entailed his exclusion of the *donna gentile*, which—as, moreover, we shall see later (Chap. III) —would have entailed the exclusion of the Dantesque ideal of the Empire.

power of reason, it really is not clear what this could actually signify.[1] According to his threefold testimony, therefore, Dante really experienced this crisis. It remains to be seen whether, in the *Banquet*, Beatrice has really triumphed. There are conceivably three different solutions to this problem: Dante is still in the throes of the crisis when he writes this work; Dante has already emerged from the crisis, which has ended without leaving any trace; Dante has already emerged from the crisis, but his thought bears the mark of it. Between these three hypotheses we are not entitled to make an *a priori* choice, but we may consult the actual text of the *Banquet* and expect it to decide for us.

---

[1] For a long time now Signor Michele Barbi has maintained that the transgressions of which Beatrice accuses Dante in *Purg.*, XXX, 124-145, are essentially the same as those of which she accuses him in *Purg.*, XXXIII, 85-90. In his eyes Dante has simply declared himself to be guilty of seeking worldly goods and their vanity. His favourite argument is that "if the *straniarsi* of Dante (*Purg.*, XXXIII, 92) is that which he has already lost from memory in Lethe, how can it be different from that with which he is reproached in Canto XXX and which he has so bitterly lamented? Why should Beatrice have waited until now to reproach him with a second transgression? And how could Dante have drunk the waters of oblivion without first paying the scot of repentance? "(M. BARBI, *Problemi di critica dantesca*, Prima serie, pp. 134-139). The matter is open to argument. First of all, the fact that Beatrice refers to these transgressions separately is more easily explained if they are not the same than if they are; and as to the forgiving of a transgression of which there has been no repentance, I believe it is really going too far to read the passage in *Purg.*, XXX, as if it were actually a question of a general confession. Dante does not there confess his sins: Beatrice accuses him, and she afterwards purges him in Lethe of the transgressions which he has committed, not merely of those of which she has accused him. Furthermore, Signor M. Barbi's interpretation is at variance with the actual text, and it is the text which must finally decide. In *Purg.*, XXX, Beatrice reproaches Dante with having fallen to that estate in which we find him, together with the three beasts, at the beginning of the *Divine Comedy*—an estate so low that only the fear of hell could now reform him. In *Purg.*, XXXIII, she reproaches him with adherence to a "school" whose "doctrine", as Dante now sees clearly, cannot follow her "word", and whose way (*vostra via*) is as remote from that of God as is the earth from heaven. Whereupon Signor M. Barbi raises the objection that Dante cannot have been accusing himself of an unduly exclusive love for philosophy, that is to say "of an intellectual aberration which is never apparent in his works" (*Razionalismo e misticismo in Dante*, in *Studi Danteschi*, Vol. XXI (1937), p. 42). That is not the point, for, if Dante were accusing himself of it, we should be relieved from the necessity of trying to find out how he could have been guilty of it; but, most important, signs of this intellectual aberration are often apparent in Dante's works, even where he himself has not recognized them as such. A thinker who, up to the end of his life, has regarded moral philosophy and politics as autonomous and separate orders to the point of exempting them from the jurisdiction of theology and the Church may perfectly well have passed through a crisis of pure philosophism of which this remnant of separatism is the sign. There is a small part of Dante which has never really been immersed in the waters of Lethe. Beatrice did not notice it, because Dante himself never noticed it. He believed that he was rising above his philosophism by re-establishing Revelation and the Christian life above his ethics and his philosophy, but he never consented actually to subordinate one of the two orders to the other, although he was prepared to fit them into a hierarchy (see below, pp. 129 seq.). With regard to the various solutions to this problem which have been offered, consult EDW. MOORE, *Studies in Dante*, Third Series, Oxford, 1903: *The Reproaches of Beatrice*, pp. 221-252.

II. The Primacy of Ethics

The place occupied by Beatrice in the *Banquet* is most curious and one is not surprised that it has been the subject of commentaries of the most varied kinds. Here, however, the commentators find themselves on some of the surest ground that is to be met with in this work of Dante. Everywhere else we may wonder: Yes, that is what he says, but what would he have added in the treatises which were not written? Here, on the contrary, we have all that Dante would have said about Beatrice even if the eleven missing treatises had been written. Beatrice disappears from the work in the First Treatise, and, in Dante's intention, she was never to appear in it again: "But since we are speaking here of the immortality of the soul, I will make a digression in order to discuss it; because, in discussing it, it will be an excellent thing to finish speaking of that living and blest Beatrice of whom it is my firm resolve to speak no more in this book" (II, 8). Whereupon some interpreters unhesitatingly conclude that Beatrice has lost the struggle, since Dante seizes the first opportunity he finds to get rid of her.

This is a very hasty way of settling the problem. In declaring that he will never speak of her again *per proponimento*, Dante suggests that he is eliminating from his work one whom he cannot eliminate from his thoughts. That is what the French call "to refrain from speaking of something", and we only refrain from speaking of that of which we are thinking and of which we should even like to speak. Furthermore, Beatrice is here explicitly termed *viva*, and this living woman is at once in heaven and in Dante's heart, as he himself has told us. If he who speaks of the quasi-ecstasies into which he went through contemplation of the heavenly abode of Beatrice decides to keep silent about her, assuredly it is not because he has nothing further to say of her, but because he has definite reasons for not speaking of her any more.

So true is this that the real problem is not why Beatrice quits the *Banquet*, but why she came to it. If Dante invited her, were it only to make a fleeting appearance, he probably did so with a definite intention.[1] One cannot imagine the *Vita Nuova* or the

---

[1] For the same line of thought see F. Ercole, *Il pensiero politico di Dante*, Alpes, Milan, 1928; Vol. II, pp. 301–302.

Divine Comedy without Beatrice: she is the soul of those two works; but a *Banquet* without Beatrice was no more inconceivable than is the *Monarchy* without her. Dante is going to speak of the *donna gentile*, that is to say Philosophy; philosophy has not a great deal to say about the next world, and since Beatrice is dead, philosophy will have done for her almost all that it could do in proving that she is still alive in a world beyond about which, *qua* philosophy, it lacks precise information. The supreme homage paid by the *donna gentile* to Beatrice consisted in proving that she was immortal. She rendered it to her, after which she ceased to speak of her. But she only rendered it to her because Dante was expressly bent on rendering it to her. The whole narrative of the Second Treatise which we have analysed has the immediate object of placing the entire work under the patronage of Beatrice and, as it were, invoking her protection for it. Perhaps the truth is that in effect, in a treatise on philosophy as Dante understands it, the place due to theology lies above that science, entirely above it even, but just as clearly outside it. Let us see, then, if this is not also the reason why Beatrice, having received from the *donna gentile* the preliminary homage to which she is entitled, defers to the counsels to which her eminent dignity gives her access and, leaving Philosophy mistress in its own house, goes her way.

The *donna gentile* is not long, moreover, in taking cognizance of her departure. Proceeding like the philosopher she is, she first busies herself with putting her house in order, assigning to each of the sciences the definite place that is its due. An excellent opportunity to specify that which is due also to theology, and we shall shortly see that Dante very well knew in what way he intended to obtain from it the privileges but for which philosophy could not have rendered him the definite services that he expected of it.

Dante has, *ex professo*, treated the problem of the classification of the sciences by way of commentary on the line in the poem on which is constructed the whole of the Second Treatise of the *Banquet: Voi che 'ntendendo il terzo ciel movete.* In order to explain what the third heaven is, we must first explain the meaning of the word "heaven" in the poem in which Dante has just employed it. *Heaven* there signifies *science*; the various heavens, then, are the various sciences. Just as, in fact, each heaven revolves around its centre, each science revolves around its subject, as around a motionless centre. Furthermore, just as each heaven illuminates visible things, each science illuminates intelligible things. Finally, just as, in the opinion of all the philosophers, the stars influence material things when the latter are suitably disposed, conferring upon them the degrees of perfection which they are capable of receiving, so also the sciences confer upon us the various degrees of perfection which enable us to contemplate truth, that is to say our ultimate perfection, as Aristotle says in the passage in the *Ethics*, VI, where he says that truth is the good of the intellect.[1]

No problem is raised by this general comparison, but two arise as soon as we try to identify each particular science with a particular heaven. By adding together the sciences of the trivium and those of the quadrivium, we obtain seven sciences; by adding to these physics and metaphysics, ethics and theology, we arrive at a total of eleven. On the other hand, by adding together the heavens of the seven planets, the two moving heavens that surround them and the motionless heaven that envelops the whole, we obtain the number ten. There is therefore one science too many, and we shall of necessity have to assign two distinct sciences to a single heaven. Furthermore, the problem arises as to what is the ascending order in which the sciences will be classified. Since the highest heavens are those whose influence is most universal, they are at the same time the noblest; to classify the sciences by relating them to the various heavens is therefore tantamount to grading them according to a hierarchy. Not only has Dante not avoided these difficulties, but he has provoked them—a sure sign that he had something

---

[1] DANTE, *Convivio*, II, 13. I have not found this passage in ARISTOTLE, *Ethic. Nic.*, VI. On the other hand, St. Thomas Aquinas, in his *In X libros Ethicorum Aristotelis ad Nicomachum expositio* (ed. A. M. Pirotta, Turin, Marietti, 1934), says: "Et hujus rationem assignat [Aristoteles], quia omnia consonant vero. Et hujus ratio est, quia, ut dicetur in sexto hujus, verum est bonum intellectus" (*ed. cit.*, lib. I, lect. 12, No. 139). In fact, we read in lib. VI, lect. 3–4, No. 1143: "Quamvis enim per ista duo quandoque verum dicatur tamen contingit quod eis quandoque dicitur falsum, quod est malum intellectus, sicut verum est bonum intellectus." As this formula, which occurs twice in St. Thomas's commentary, is not in the text of Aristotle, it seems that Dante is here quoting Aristotle according to that commentary. It may even be conjectured that his reference is borrowed from the former of the two passages from the commentary that we have just reproduced: *in sexto hujus*. Dante has understood *hujus libri*; hence the formula that he uses: "la veritade . . . che è l'ultima perfezione nostra, sì come dice lo Filosofo nel sesto de l'*Etica*, quando dice che 'l vero è lo bene de lo intelletto" (*loc. cit.*). Dante thought St. Thomas said that Aristotle had said it; he therefore confidently asserted that Aristotle had said it.

definite to say and that he was seeking an opportunity to explain his views on this subject.

The correspondence between the first seven sciences and the seven planets is established in the easiest possible way, provided at least that we accept without question some rather unexpected alliances, whose acceptance, however, the universally recognized order of the seven liberal arts compelled. We obtain in that case the following hierarchy:

$$
\text{Trivium} \begin{cases} \text{Grammar} & = \text{Moon} \\ \text{Dialectics} & = \text{Mercury} \\ \text{Rhetoric} & = \text{Venus} \end{cases}
$$

$$
\text{Quadrivium} \begin{cases} \text{Arithmetic} & = \text{Sun} \\ \text{Music} & = \text{Mars} \\ \text{Geometry} & = \text{Jupiter} \\ \text{Astronomy} & = \text{Saturn} \end{cases}
$$

There is no need for us to analyse the reasons that justify, if one may use the term, these alliances. As we know beyond any possible doubt that it was the list that dictated the reasons and not *vice versa*, we may, without wronging Dante, regard them as arbitrary. It is not the same with the last four sciences and the last three heavens. The problem then arises of distributing four sciences (physics, ethics, metaphysics and theology) amongst three heavens (the Firmament, the Crystalline and the Empyrean). How are we to effect this distribution?

For the moment at least we may eliminate the Empyrean because it does not normally fall within the natural classification of the heavens.[1] The Empyrean is a heaven unknown to philosophers and scholars; it is the theologians who affirm its existence, and that for purely theological reasons. In fact, the natural universe, beyond which the supernatural world begins, stops short at the Crystalline. That is what Dante clearly suggests when, after enumerating the heavens of the seven planets, the Firmament and the Crystalline, he adds: "Outside all these, *the Catholics* situate the Empyrean heaven" (II, 3). Quite obviously, this heaven does not exist so far as scholars, *qua* scholars, are

---

[1] Regarding the Empyrean, consult BRUNO NARDI, *La dottrina dell'Empireo nella sua genesi storica e nel pensiero dantesco*, in *Saggi di filosofia dantesca*, Milan, Perrella, 1930–VIII, pp. 187–238.

concerned. For the same reason we may for the time being eliminate theology, for it equally is not the kind of science of which knowledge is secured by natural means. Let us, then, place this science and this heaven in a temporary position where we may anticipate that they will not fail to meet, and turn to the two heavens and the three sciences that remain: how are we to divide physics, ethics and metaphysics between the Firmament and the Crystalline?

I sincerely believe that I am not twisting the relevant passages to suit any thesis when I say that, if the question is put to any philosopher who is familiar with scholasticism, his answer will be as follows: Since metaphysics is the loftiest of the sciences, it must be matched with the highest heaven, in other words the Crystalline, which would lead one to assign physics, as also ethics, to the Firmament. In fact, Dante's procedure is quite different. The Firmament, he says, offers to our eyes two main spectacles: first a great number of stars, then the Milky Way, that white circle which the people call St. James's Road. Furthermore, it displays to us one of the poles, whereas it keeps the other one hidden. Finally, it carries out one movement from east to west, then another, from west to east, which it is hardly possible for us to discern.

Let us first consider the multitude of stars which appears in the Firmament. Egyptian scholars say that there are 22,000. This number is composed of three others: two, twenty and a thousand. *Two* means local movement, which necessarily supposes a point of departure and a point of arrival. *Twenty* signifies movement of alteration, that is to say change; in effect, the number ten can change by augmentation only through the addition of the other nine, or of itself, and the most beautiful of these changes is that which it undergoes when it is added to itself; *twenty*, which represents the perfect change of ten, therefore admirably symbolizes physics, which is concerned with change. Thus, just as *two* symbolized local movement, *twenty* symbolizes movement of "alteration"; now *a thousand* happens to symbolize a third kind of movement, that of "augmentation", because a thousand marks a limit beyond which we cannot go save by multiplying it. The number 22,000 is therefore made up of three numbers which, combined, symbolize the three kinds of movement which form the subject of Physics, as Aristotle teaches in Chapter V of Book I of the treatise that bears that title.[1] On the other hand, in so far as it displays the Milky Way to the eyes of man, the Firmament closely resembles metaphysics. Indeed, after recording several different explanations of this fact, Dante adheres to one of those which the ancient translation of Aristotle attributes to that philosopher: the Milky Way is merely a conglomeration of fixed stars, so small that we cannot distinguish them, but productive of that glimmer which we call the Milky Way: "That is why, as the Milky Way is an effect of those stars which we cannot see and which we know only by their effects, and since metaphysics treats of the primary substances, which likewise we can comprehend only by their effects, it is manifest that the Firmament bears a close resemblance to metaphysics."

After this excellent proof, it is a simple matter for Dante to show that the visible pole of the Firmament signifies visible things, to which physics alludes, whereas the invisible pole signifies invisible substances, which are the subject of metaphysics; finally, that the diurnal revolution of the heavens, which begins and is completed in a day, signifies the natural and corruptible things with which physics deal, and that the almost imperceptible movement of a degree in a hundred years which the heavens make from west to east signifies the incorruptible things which were created by God in the beginning and which will have no end: those things to which metaphysics alludes (II, 14).

Dante dwells at leisure on the symbolical justification of his thesis. Consequently, there can be no question here of a mistake, and it is with full knowledge of the case that after according second place *ex aequo* to physics and metaphysics he raises ethics to the first rank. It is the last named, indeed, that corresponds to the Crystalline heaven. The analogy between them is obvious, for the Crystalline is what is also called the *Primum Mobile*. Now this heaven has a very evident connection with moral philosophy,

---

[1] DANTE, *Convivio*, II, 14. I can find nothing on this subject in ARISTOTLE, *Phys.*, I, 5; but Dante himself, or a copyist, must simply have transposed the two numbers, for a passage which corresponds perfectly to the ideas here expressed by Dante occurs in *Phys.*, V, 1, 225 b 5–9. The passage in the *Convivio*, II, 14, which we have just quoted should therefore read: "E questi tre movimenti soli mostra la Fisica, sì come nel primo del quinto suo libro è provato." It is rather curious that, in their commentary on this passage, G. Busnelli and G. Vandelli (*ed. cit.*, Vol. I, p. 216, note 8), undoubtedly because they found nothing in *Phys.*, I, 5, have concluded that, by *Fisica*, physics in general must here be understood. But, in physics in general, there is no "quinto del primo", in other words no Chap. V of Book I.

for the latter, as St. Thomas says in his commentary on the
Second Book of the *Ethics*, moves and guides us towards the
other sciences.[1] Nay more, Aristotle himself says, in Book V
of the *Ethics*, that "legal justice ordains the study of the sciences,
and that, lest the latter be abandoned, it commands that they
be learned and taught".[2] Similarly, the Crystalline heaven, or
Primum Mobile, ordains by its motion the daily revolution of all
the other heavens, a revolution that enables them to receive and
transmit to the earth each day the efficacy of all their parts.
If the revolution of the *Primum Mobile* ceased to make the other
heavens go round, we should see but a faint part of them on
earth and we should feel their influence but slightly. There
would no longer be in the world any reproduction of living
animals and plants, or any distinction of day or night; there
would be no weeks, or months, or years, but the whole universe
would be in disorder and the motion of the other heavens would
be in vain: "And likewise, if moral philosophy ceased to be, the
other sciences would for a while be eclipsed, there would be no
survival of felicity, nor would life hold any happiness, and these
sciences would have been formulated and discovered of old in
vain. Whence it is very clear that this heaven is connected
with moral philosophy" (II, 14).

The thesis which Dante here maintains is quite extraordinary
for the Middle Ages. Taken literally, it amounts to the maintenance of the primacy of ethics over metaphysics, a doctrine
which at any rate could not claim the authority of Aristotle and
perhaps still less that of St. Thomas Aquinas. It is impossible to

---

[1] ST. THOMAS AQUINAS, *In II^m lib. Ethic.*, lect. I, ed. Pirotta, No. 245: "Et ratio ordinis
est, quia virtutes morales sunt magis notae, et per eas disponimur ad intellectuales." I
confess that I do not see the necessity here for the hypothesis propounded with reference
to this passage by A. GILBERT, *Dante's Conception of Justice*, Durham, North Carolina,
1925, p. 183, and adopted again by G. BUSNELLI and G. VANDELLI, *ed. cit.*, p. 223, note 5.

[2] I have been unable to find this passage in *Ethic.*, V. But we find the same idea sum-
marily indicated in *Ethic.*, I, 1, 1093 a 27–1093 b 2, and commented upon by St. Thomas
with a distinction to safeguard the primacy of the speculative sciences, in *In X libros
Ethic.*, lib. I, lect. 2, ed. Pirotta, Nos. 26–28. This passage is reproduced in full by
G. BUSNELLI and G. VANDELLI, *ed. cit.*, p. 224, note 1. Dante's formula may also be
compared to the following passage in Averroes: "Videtur autem esse potissima artium,
et maxime principantis: et hujusmodi quidem est ars gubernandi civitates. Etenim haec
ars principatur omnibus artibus, cum determinet quas artes et scientias oportet esse in
civitatibus, in quas artes et scientias oportet exercere quosdam hominum, et usque ad
quem finem oportet discipulos pervenire in discendo artes. Cum igitur haec ars taliter
se habeat ad reliquas artium, est principalior earum" (AVERROES, *In Moral. Nicom.*,
lib. I, cap. 2, in *Aristotelis Stagiritae libri moralem totam philosophiam complectentes*, Venetiis,
apud Juntas, 1550; vol. III, fol. 1, v. 2).

doubt that to these two philosophers the supreme, chief and architectonic science is metaphysics, a theoretical, purely speculative science, which knows only the ultimate cause of everything, that is to say what is best in the whole of nature, the cause of causes: God.[1] St. Thomas is as steadfast on this point as is Dante in the inverse sense: "All the sciences and all the arts aim at one thing alone, the perfection of man, which is his beatitude. It is therefore necessary that one of them should govern all the others—that one which with good reason arrogates to itself the name of wisdom", for, since it deals with the most universal principles, it is also the most intellectual of all and, as a final consequence, it is their governor: *est aliarum regulatrix*.[2]

It is difficult to believe that Dante can have been unaware, if not of these passages, at any rate of the absolutely fundamental thesis to which they point. It may even be because he knew them in an admirable degree that he found in them the means to adapt them to the personal aims which he was pursuing. Such, indeed, is the exaltation of metaphysics in Aristotle that one ultimately finds it a little disturbing. Properly speaking, metaphysical wisdom is a contemplation of the pure intelligibles, positing a life entirely free from the needs of the body and the constraints of social life. It is not the life of a man, but rather that of a god. Aristotle concludes that man has no right to be master of such a science and, without agreeing with the poet Simonides that God alone seems worthy of such an honour, he at all events thinks that it is the noblest of all the sciences, because, being the most divine, it is also the one that deserves most respect. More divine than any of the others, metaphysics is so for two reasons: it is the science of which God is master, and it deals with divine things. It is therefore the goddess of the sciences—*dea scientiarum* —which is tantamount to saying *quod non sit humana* (that it is not human), because knowledge of it is not, strictly speaking, *humana possessio* (within the competence of man).[3]

In Dante's view, that is certainly the root of the question. In order to understand his attitude on this point we must remember

---

[1] St. Thomas Aquinas, *In Metaphysicam Aristotelis Commentaria*, ed. M.-R. Cathala, Turin, P. Marietti, 1915; lib. I, lect. 2, Nos. 50–51.

[2] *Op. cit.*, Prooemium.

[3] Aristotle, *Metaph.*, I, 2, 982–983. St. Thomas Aquinas, *op. cit.*, lib. I, lect. 2, Nos. 60 and 64. That the supreme science must be speculative, not active, is demonstrated in No. 53.

the starting-point of his treatise. The *Banquet* is, in fact, based entirely on the principle, or, if one prefers, on the hope, that man is able, thanks to philosophy, to find consolation for his miseries in the beatitude of the sage. The question whether, *in itself*, metaphysics is or is not a superior science to theology seems from this point of view almost purely academic. What does the perfection of this science matter to us? If it is the science of God, one imagines that it may constitute His beatitude, but, for that very reason, it cannot constitute ours on earth. Why, then, instead of classifying the sciences according to the order of their absolute perfection, should we not classify them according to their increasing capacity for beatifying us? To do so means committing ourselves to place at the summit of the hierarchy not the most divine of all sciences, but the most human of all sciences: not metaphysics, but ethics.

There are numerous indications—and they are extremely precise—which urge us to think that Dante has followed this line of reasoning. The *Banquet* derives the materials of which it is composed from manifold and even somewhat heterogeneous origins, but if there is one source from which it has drawn more than from any other, and whose influence, by its continuity and abundance, has imposed upon it a real unity, it is assuredly Aristotle's *Ethica ad Nicomachum*. It is true that Dante read this work, not only in the Latin text which was then in use, but in conjunction with the commentary furnished by St. Thomas Aquinas. The fact is not unimportant, for St. Thomas's commentary, objective as it is in general, is not innocent of modifying the compass, balance and relative values of the text that it explains, with the object of facilitating the insertion of Aristotelianism in the doctrinal synthesis which its author endeavours to elaborate. In the case under review, Aristotle can place above ethics and physics only a rude natural theology, reduced exclusively to its own resources and cruelly inadequate to its purpose. The Greek metaphysician of the Aristotelian brand has lost his Platonic illusions: he knows that all his knowledge is of sensible origin and that, even if there were a world of Ideas, access to it would be denied him; but he has not yet conceived the Christian hope; no divine Revelation is present, either to bolster up his tottering metaphysic, or to supplement it with a faith which, without merging with it, infinitely increases its compass. That is why,

in a hierarchy of the sciences like that of St. Thomas, in which
natural theology is subordinated to a theology of Revelation, but
profits by this very subordination, the speculative value and the
practical efficacy of metaphysics as a science that beatifies man in
this life are far superior to those of Aristotle's metaphysic. This
truth, which St. Thomas says is the good of the intellect, is still
of the same kind as Aristotle's, but it is rife in Thomism, in which
it multiplies itself in the doctrine of the divine ideas, divine
providence, the divine will, divine love, the justice of God and
the power of God, the equivalent of which would be looked for
in vain in the metaphysic of Aristotle. In spite of its inherent
deficiency in the science of intelligible things, the Thomistic
metaphysic is quite different in scope from the Aristotelian metaphysic; it is therefore much more fitted to beatify the metaphysician in this life.

Let us, on the contrary, take a man who has been restored by
a preponderance of reading and contemplation of the *Ethica ad
Nicomachum* to Aristotle's point of view. What attitude will be
forced upon him by the influence of this work? Like Aristotle
himself, he will inflexibly maintain the absolute superiority of
the *goddess of the sciences,* which is also the science appertaining to
God, but, being unable to depend for his beatification in this
life on a science which in this life is not his to comprehend, he
will transfer his reliance from what he lacks to what he has,
from what he cannot properly do to what he can do well. In
short, he will seek beatitude in this life in the order of activities
which best suits man as he is in this life; no longer, therefore,
in metaphysics—the diffused glimmer of that Milky Way whose
stars no man can see, the invisible pole of a world of which
physics is the visible pole, the sidereal revolution that is almost
imperceptible in comparison with the diurnal revolution which
can be seen by all—but rather in ethics, and even, since man is a
social animal, in a political philosophy moulded by ethics.

The reasons for thus descending once more from the Thomistic
plane to the Aristotelian plane are as numerous in Dante's thought
as they are strong. He is a man who suffers and seeks in philosophy the means to console himself; he is an author who addresses
himself to men of action in order to teach them to mould through
philosophy lives that are essentially practical and hardly in any
way speculative; he is a citizen of Florence, in one of the most

disturbed periods in the history of a town that has known so
much disturbance in the past, and no one will make Dante believe
that man can be happy contemplating intelligible things at a
time when the plunder of his possessions is impending, when
his life in society is being moulded by hatred and violence, and
when he has awaiting him the exile that will drive him from his
native land, far from the domestic hearth, beside which his wife
and children will live without him in misery. To such a man,
what an inspiration it must have been to discover those *Ethica
ad Nicomachum* whose author had known so well the miseries
of civil discord that he had died in exile at Chalcis, whither he
had fled from Athens so as not to let the Athenians "sin twice
against philosophy"! Every book and almost every chapter of
the *Ethics* is a eulogy of "political" virtue, an appeal to the civic
virtue *par excellence*—that creator of order and human happiness
which is Justice. For justice is not simply an individual virtue
among the rest; properly speaking, it is virtue in its entirety.
If he had not read Aristotle, Dante's political passions would
have been neither less compelling nor less violent, but they
would have lacked what they needed in order to found themselves
in reason, to define themselves in doctrine and above all to
discover the remedy for the evils which had been their cause.
Dante knew this, and that is why the *Banquet* places at the summit
of the heaven of the sciences that appertain to man *qua* man the
saving science of men as they are in this life, that science which,
like the Crystalline, is the *Primum Mobile* whose supreme influence
moulds, orders and renders fruitful the workings of all the other
sciences: Ethics. The author of the *Divine Comedy* was not the
man to neglect his chance of finding God, and we shall see that
even the author of the *Banquet* avowedly cherished it, but, in the
meantime, Dante talks like a man who is conversing about
human life with men: here on earth, it is better to be a perfect
man than an inadequate god.

As soon as he opened the *Ethica ad Nicomachum*, suggestions
with this bias came crowding into Dante's mind in profusion. In
his book, as its very subject requires, Aristotle reasons always
from the point of view of the conditions of the moral life. When
he defines the ultimate purpose of man, what he means is the
purpose of moral activities, and when he grades the sciences
according to a hierarchy, it is from this point of view that he

classifies them. Now from this clearly defined point of view the supreme and architectonic science is that which he calls πολιτική, and which the Latin translation and the commentary of St. Thomas call *scientia politica* or *scientia civilis*. Not only does it govern human life, but it even governs the use of the sciences, since it prescribes what sciences must be learned, in what towns they must be taught, who should learn them and up to what point everyone should pursue the study of them.[1] Now the purpose after which this virtue strives in thus ordering all the sciences and all the arts—military, economic, rhetorical and others—is the purpose which contains the individual purposes of all those arts and all those sciences: the good of man, τὸ ἀνθρώπινον ἀγαθόν, the *humanum bonum* of the Latin translation, upon which St. Thomas comments with great precision when he says that "the purpose of politics is human good, that is to say the best purpose *in human affairs*".[2] In short, the particular subject of the *Ethica ad Nicomachum* is, to be precise, the nature of that supreme virtue which is called πολιτική.[3]

Such, too, is the particular subject of the *Banquet*, in so far, at least, as this work speaks of the virtues and classifies them. Unless he specifically indicates the contrary, Dante's attitude here is that of the philosopher speaking of human good and of the human virtues as such. Now these human virtues are essentially the moral virtues, because the latter call for the simultaneous exercise of the two parts of the human synthesis, the soul and the body. The metaphysic of a philosopher is the better in proportion to the degree in which he transcends his body, and is

---

[1] ARISTOTLE, *Ethic. Nic.*, I, 1, 1094 a 27–1094 b 2.

[2] ARISTOTLE, *Ethic. Nic.*, I, 1, 1094 b 7. Cf. ST. THOMAS AQUINAS, *In X lib. Ethic.*, lib. I, lect. 2; ed. Pirotta, No. 28. I would not wish to appear to twist the relevant passages to suit my interpretation, for I am truly anxious not to do so. I shall not be doing so, however, if I make this statement: By way of commentary upon the three lines in which Aristotle asserts that, in the moral order of human good, the supreme and architectonic science is ethics, St. Thomas has written two paragraphs with the object of specifying clearly, first that ethics is only entitled to govern the use of the sciences, not their substance (*ed. cit.*, No. 27), then that Aristotle calls "politics the supreme science, not absolutely, but in the *genre* of active sciences, which deal with human affairs, of which politics conceives the ultimate purpose. For if it is a question of the ultimate purpose of the whole universe, it is the divine science that conceives it, the science that is supreme in comparison with all the others. If Aristotle says that it is the concern of politics to conceive the ultimate purpose of human life as he defines it in this book, that is because the doctrine of the book contains the primary elements of political science" (*ed. cit.*, No. 31). The commentator's insistence on specifying a distinction which nothing in the text suggests is quite easily explained: Aristotle was not versed in theology and had no beatific vision to safeguard.

[3] ARISTOTLE, *Ethic. Nic.*, I, 3, 1094 b 11.

thereby more of a god and less of a man; but the ethics and the politics of a moralist are the better in proportion as they are more in harmony with the special nature of the human being as such. Dante is so profoundly convinced of this that he has not scrupled to put Aristotle into verse in order to make him say it:

> I say that every virtue, taken at its source,
> comes from a single root:
> that virtue, I mean, which makes man happy
> in his activity.
> And it is, as the *Ethics* has it,
> a disposition firm in election,
> which keeps solely to the golden mean,
> and those are its words. [1]

Now, commenting on the passage, in the dual capacity of Aristotle and Thomas Aquinas, Dante defines its meaning thus: This passage signifies two things, first that every virtue proceeds from a single source, then that by *every virtue* must be understood the moral virtues that are here in question, as is indicated, moreover, by the reference to the *Ethics*: "In which connection it should be known that the fruits which are eminently ours are the moral virtues, because in all respects they are in our power." This formula—*però che da ogni canto sono in nostra potestade*—should be to us a ray of light which illuminates the fundamental nature of Dante's thought as distinguished from the thought of Aristotle and that of St. Thomas Aquinas. [2] For his personal attitude is that of neither; it is that of a man situated between the two, inclined by virtue of his political preoccupations to treat the good of the city as an ultimate purpose, just as Aristotle would desire, but inclined by virtue of his Christianity to safeguard what pertains to a transcendent and truly supreme purpose, just as St. Thomas Aquinas desires. To satisfy these two allpowerful inclinations, Dante has sought his middle way in a distinction between the two orders that is much more emphatic than it could be in Aristotle, in whom the religious plane is rather faintly marked, or than it was in St. Thomas, in whom distinction between these orders implies the subordination of one to the other and bases the jurisdiction of the superior

---

[1] DANTE, *Convivio*, IV, *Canzone*. Cf. ARISTOTLE, *Ethic. Nic.*, II, 6, 1106 a 15–29.
[2] DANTE, *Convivio*, IV, 17.

on the inferior. Dante, on the contrary, has tried to distinguish the two orders in such a way that their mutual independence should be as complete as possible. That is why we find him here describing as eminently human the virtues which, *precisely because they are only human,* are in no sense outside the range of man's nature, govern the special function of man *qua* man, and assure him of the human happiness that is *humanum bonum* in the proper sense through the exercise of the human function *par excellence*: the correct voluntary choice of an intelligent being. Such is the meaning of this extraordinary classification of the sciences and of the primacy which it reserves for ethics. Undoubtedly—and Dante is well aware of it—there are nobler sciences than ethics, but these nobler sciences are also less our preserve than that science which is concerned with what man can do, by purely human means, for the happiness of man. In a human classification of the sciences, the most perfect of human intellectual attainments should occupy first place. And theology? it will be asked. To this question the answer is simple: The science that appertains to God certainly comes first in a divine classification of the sciences, but, as we shall now see, it cannot count in the general rating of our human sciences because, being supernatural in its origin, it hovers above them but does not mingle with them.

III. TRANSCENDENCY OF THEOLOGY

There remain to us now only one heaven and one science: the Empyrean and theology; we cannot, then, do other than pair them off. It may be said, moreover, that their very nature predestined them to be associated in Dante's thought. In using the word "heaven", we may intend to signify two things that are essentially distinct: either a heaven understood according to the concept of the astronomers and philosophers, or else a heaven understood according to the concept of the theologians.

The astronomers recognize nine heavens: the seven heavens corresponding to each of the seven planets that we can see, the Firmament or heaven of the fixed stars that we can also see, and finally the Crystalline, which we cannot see, but which we postulate as the only conceivable cause of visible effects. The theologians recognize another, which is, in point of fact, the Empyrean. Not only do the astronomers not recognize it, but it cannot even be said that all theologians recognize it, since, according to St. Thomas, only Basil, Strabo and Bede have affirmed its existence.[1] As for St. Thomas himself, he does not think the reasons adduced to prove that this heaven exists are very convincing, but he proposes to take its existence for granted, if only on grounds of theological expediency. The Empyrean would then be conceived as something created in the very beginning in a state of glory, first-fruit of the future glorification of the body, just as, since the commencement of the world, the Angels have been in a state of glory, first-fruits of the future glorification of the soul. The name of this heaven is borrowed from that of fire, not that it has its heat, but because it has its light. Thus conceived, this heaven lacks any close connection with the others. As Basil says, it is *extra mundum* ("outside the world"); it is essentially a place of peace and repose: *quietis domicilium*. It is therefore understandable that some theologians, speaking of the Empyrean as the destination of those bodies which are in a state of glory, have maintained that it exerts no influence on the inferior bodies, which belong to another order, that of the natural course of things. However, St. Thomas himself is of a different opinion. It appears to him more likely that, although without motion, the Empyrean exerts an influence on those bodies which move. It must be added that this cannot be a positive action, whether exerted by direct motion, or resulting indirectly from some movement. As we have said, if this heaven exists it is without motion. But we might attribute to it a fixed, stable action, for instance a containing or causal property, or something of the same kind with an implication of dignity.[2]

Such was the constant attitude of St. Thomas on the question. Dante appears to have been a little more knowledgeable than he in this connection. Above the Crystalline heaven, he asserts, Catholics postulate the existence of the Empyrean heaven, that is, a heaven of fire, or else of light, and they postulate it as without motion, because it possesses in each of its parts what its substance

[1] Cf. BRUNO NARDI, *La dottrina dell'Empireo* . . . , in *Saggi di filosofia dantesca*, pp. 204–227.
[2] ST. THOMAS AQUINAS, *Sum. theol.*, Pars I, qu. 66, art. 3, Resp. and ad 2m. Cf. ST. BONAVENTURE, *In II Sent.*, 14, 2, 1, 3, Concl., ed. Quaracchi, Vol. II, p. 356.

requires. This heaven, Dante assures us, is the cause of the very rapid movement executed by the *Primum Mobile* (or Crystalline): indeed, each part of the Crystalline, the heaven immediately below the Empyrean, has such an extreme, burning desire to be united to each of the parts of this most divine heaven of repose that, under the stress of this desire, it moves with a speed that almost passes understanding: "This place of calm and peace is that of the supreme Deity Which alone has a complete vision of Itself. It is the place of the blessed spirits, as the Holy Church has it, which cannot lie; and Aristotle seems to think the same, to whoso understands him clearly, in Book I of the *De caelo et mundo*. This heaven is the summit of the edifice of the world; within it the whole world is contained, and outside it there is nothing; and it has, itself, no location, but was formed solely in the first Thought, which the Greeks call Protonoè. This is the splendour to which the Psalmist refers when he says to God: Thy splendour is exalted above the heavens."[1]

We need not ask how Dante was able to find in the *De caelo et mundo* the creation of the Empyrean, the heaven of God.[2] The essential thing is that he did find it there and that, because of the peace and calm that reign in it, this divine heaven is related in his mind to theology.[3] For theology too is a place of calm and quietude: "The Empyrean heaven, in its peace, resembles the divine science, which is full of all peace and suffers no conflict of opinions or of sophistical arguments, because of the most excellent sureness of its motif, which is God. And speaking of it He says to His disciples: *Peace I leave with you, my peace I give unto you* (St. John, XIV, 27), when He gives and leaves to them His doctrine, which is that science of which I speak. Solomon has said of it: 'There are threescore queens, and fourscore concubines, and virgins without number. My dove, my undefiled, is but one' (*Song of Songs,* VI, 8-9)."[4] A passage rich in pointers and one whose full sense we shall have difficulty in extracting,

---

[1] DANTE, *Convivio,* II, 3. Cf. the extended treatment accorded to the Empyrean in the *Letter to Can Grande,* in *Tutte le opere . . . , ed. cit.,* Epist., XVII, 24-27, pp. 440-441. On *Protonoè,* see G. BUSNELLI and G. VANDELLI, *ed. cit.,* p. 116, note 5.

[2] On the passage in ST. THOMAS AQUINAS, *In de Caelo et Mundo,* lib. I, lect. 21, which seems to have suggested to Dante the idea that Aristotle, too, assumed the existence of an abode of the blessed, see *ed. cit.,* p. 116, note 1. The whole of this syncretistic cosmography is that of a poet rather than a philosopher.

[3] ". . . e al cielo quieto risponde la scienza divina, che è Teologia appellata" (*Convivio,* II, 13).

[4] DANTE, *Convivio,* II, 14; *ed. cit.,* p. 60.

for it abounds in implications of the most subtle kind and we should neither allow them to be lost nor force their meaning.

Let us note first—for we shall see its importance later on—the identification of theology with the teaching of Christ: *dando e lasciando a loro la sua dottrina, che è questa scienza di cu' io parlo.* Without wishing to credit Dante with ideas which perhaps he did not have, we may say almost with certainty that he intends here to recall that, in its origin, and consequently in its essence, theology is simply the word of God which has been handed down to us through the Holy Scriptures. In insisting on the peace that is brought to him by his unshakable certainty of Revelation, Dante recalls besides that it ought not to suffer from the conflicts of opinions which disturb the other sciences. Unless we suppose him to have been totally ignorant of the theological teaching of his time, when what he calls *lite d'oppinioni o di sofistici argomenti* most certainly was not lacking, we cannot believe that he intended these words as a definition of the state of theology as it was. What Dante defines in these terms is its state as it should be. It is therefore permissible to think that the theology whose peace he likens to that of the Empyrean is an ideal theology, strictly based on Christian faith in the doctrine of Christ.

This is not all. To the quotation which he borrows from the Gospel of St. John Dante immediately adds a quotation from the *Song of Songs*, applying its meaning to theology. The majority of the commentaries on the *Banquet* see no difficulty in this; some even admire the perfect compatibility between this passage and the doctrine of St. Thomas Aquinas. We need, however, only compare these two conceptions of theology to conceive doubts as to their compatibility.

In the article in the *Summa theologica* in which he explains his views on this point, St. Thomas too adduces, as the basis of his own thesis, a passage from the Scriptures, but it is not the same one: *Misit ancillas suas vocare ad arcem* ("She hath sent her maids to invite to the tower") (*Prov.*, IX, 3). Beyond any doubt, however, St. Thomas knew the passage from Solomon, but he does not quote it. Conversely, Dante probably knew this doctrine of St. Thomas and the passage from *Proverbs*, but he prefers to quote another: *Sexaginta sunt reginae, et octoginta concubinae, et adulescentularum non est numerus: una est columba mea, perfecta mea* ("There are threescore queens, and fourscore concubines, and virgins without number. My dove, my undefiled, is but one" (*Song of Songs*, VI, 8–9). Since he is made out to be so faithful and well informed a Thomist —and he was at any rate well informed—Dante undoubtedly did not prefer one Solomon to another without reason. The fact of the matter is that the symbolism of the passage chosen by St. Thomas makes the other sciences out to be so many hand-maids of whom theology is queen, whereas the passage chosen by Dante makes theology out to be a pure dove, but not a queen, and the other sciences queens, and not handmaids. This passage from the *Song of Songs* therefore illustrates admirably Dante's idea on the point.

This idea is not, as some would like to make us believe, that "the sacred science, Theology, is above all the other sciences, which are its attendants and handmaids".[1] If Dante had wished to maintain, as St. Thomas does, that the other sciences are the handmaids of theology—*quod aliae scientiae dicuntur ancillae hujus* —he would not have failed to quote the same passage as St. Thomas had utilized. The one that he quotes says, in actual fact, something else, to wit, that theology is a dove, because it enables us to see perfectly the truth in which our souls find their rest. As for the other sciences, they are all queens, favourites and handmaids: *tutte scienze chiama regine e drude e ancille, e questa chiama colomba . . . e perfetta* (II, 14). If we reckon theology —*questa*—among the other sciences, we shall have to say that it is one of the queens, and the purest at that, but not their queen. If we reckon it separately from the other sciences, the "divine science" will be distinguished from them as a dove is distinguished from queens. In whatever way we interpret this passage, not only shall we not find there the Thomistic doctrine of the sub-ordination of the sciences to theology, but we shall find rather the intention of avoiding it. Whether we say, according to our preferred interpretation of the passage, that there are sixty queens, of which one is theology, or that there are sixty queens

---

[1] The passage in which St. Thomas quotes the text of *Prov.*, IX, 3, occurs in *Sum. theol.*, Pars I, qu. 1, art. 5, *Sed contra.* On the alleged accord between Dante and St. Thomas on this matter see P. MANDONNET, *Dante le Théologien*, p. 50. G. BUSNELLI and G. VANDELLI, *ed. cit.*, Vol. I, p. 30, note 8, apropos of the word *ancille*, refer the reader to St. THOMAS AQUINAS, *loc. cit.*, without any comment, as if Dante were here only reproducing the doctrine of St. Thomas.

in addition to a dove which is theology, in either case we deny the theological monarchy of the teaching of St. Thomas Aquinas. Between St. Thomas's phrase—*aliae scientiae dicuntur ancillae hujus* —and Dante's—*tutte scienze chiama regine, drude e ancille*—it seems that a choice is imperative. If there is only one queen, there are not sixty; to maintain that Dante is here in accord with St. Thomas Aquinas, we must be satisfied with an accord based on a contradiction.

Yet this is still only a first indication, certainly valuable as a means of putting us on the right road in the interpretation of Dante's thought, but insufficient to enable us to define it. Happily, and although he does not neglect to be prudent in the expression of his personal thought, Dante seldom forgoes the pleasure of expressing it in full. When he is speaking of questions that are near his heart, he even gives proof of a remarkable continuity of purpose. Now the decision which we have seen him take placed him in a difficult position, from which he had to escape at all costs. On the one hand, Dante evidently desired a theology which, like the peace of Christ, should not be of this world: that is why he is so very anxious that it should not mingle with the sciences, even for the purpose of ruling them. On the other hand, he was not ignorant of the doctrine of St. Thomas, which makes the sciences the *ancillae* (handmaids) of theology. That Dante profoundly admired and loved St. Thomas cannot be doubted, not only on account of the glorious part that he is to make him play in the *Divine Comedy*, but because, even in the *Banquet*, where he will have for him one of those terms of familiarity and affection which have the ring of sincerity,[1] Dante's work is based as much on the commentary of St. Thomas as on this passage from Aristotle. How, then, are we to fit in the desire not to make the sciences, in other words philosophy, handmaids of theology, without denying that philosophy can render theology the services which the latter expects of it? Dante set himself this thorny problem, and the most remarkable thing is that he found what he needed to settle it in the very root from which, so far as he was concerned, the question sprang.

With a riposte no less brilliant than his scriptural parry to the passage from Solomon, Dante simply replied that, to aid

[1] See below, p. 158.

theology, philosophy has nothing else to do but exist. Thus, the less it forgoes the complete exercise of its rights, the truer will it be to itself, the more too, incidentally, will theology be the gainer. Dante meant this not merely in the sense that philosophy must first exist as philosophy to be able subsequently to serve theology, which would be the genuine Thomistic solution to the problem, but in the more radical sense that its existence as philosophy is essential if that science is to give theology adequate help in the work of human salvation.[1]

What, indeed, is the basis of theology, if not faith in the Revelation of Jesus Christ? And what is it that proves that we should have faith in this Revelation? The miracles accomplished by Christ. But again, what is it that proves that we ought to believe Christ wrought miracles? For, after all, many people have the greatest aversion to believing what they do not see, and they did not see these miracles. Let such, then, turn their eyes towards philosophy! This *donna gentile* arrives at this point in

---

[1] "E però ultimamente dico che *da eterno*, cioe etternamente, *fu ordinata* (*sc*. questa donna gentile) ne la mente di Dio in testimonio de la fede a coloro che in questo tempo vivono" (*Convivio*, III, 7). Dante is here alluding to *Prov*., VIII, 23: "Ab æterno ordinata sum et ex antiquis antequam terra fieret"; but in thus applying to philosophic wisdom that which all the theologians of his time applied to the eternal Wisdom, which is the Word, Dante was certainly adopting an entirely personal attitude to the question. In this connection G. Busnelli and G. Vandelli quote in their commentary (*op. cit.*, p. 343, note 6) a long passage from ST. THOMAS AQUINAS, *Cont. Gent.*, III, 98, in order to establish that even miracles are subject to God's providence. Undoubtedly: and no one was unaware of it; but what it would have been interesting to find would have been a passage in St. Thomas saying (1) that philosophy is something miraculous; (2) that it is that wisdom of which it is said in *Proverbs*, VIII, 23: *Ab aeterno ordinata sum*; (3) that it was thus predestined by God to render the miracles of the Gospel more credible to sceptics. Of course, nothing of the kind occurs in his works. By accumulating passages from St. Thomas at the foot of pages which contain nothing Thomistic, one presents Dante's thought in a false setting, at the risk of leading the reader into error as to the authentic meaning of the doctrine thus annotated. I wish to make it clear that this remark does not apply to the passages in the *Convivio* where Dante does draw his inspiration from St. Thomas, and where, in consequence, the commentary of G. Busnelli and G. Vandelli is often very useful. It becomes dangerous where it leads the indulgent reader to "agree" what Dante says with what St. Thomas says. Thus, in dealing with *Conv.*, III, 8, where Dante says that the revival of nature through the beauty of philosophy is *miracolosa cosa*, these commentators explain that such a revival is one of those things which St. Thomas calls *praeter naturam*, like those that are brought about through miracles, not *quantum ad substantiam*, or *ad subjectum*, but *quantum ad modum* (*op. cit.*, Vol. I, p. 363, note 7). Now the passage from St. Thomas quoted in support of this distinction (*Sum. theol.*, Pars I, qu. 105, art. 8, Resp.) gives, as an example of the lowest form of miracles which are only miraculous *quantum ad modum*, the sudden cure of a fever by God, a sudden fall of rain that can be attributed to no natural cause, and *hujusmodi*. The moral correction of a man by philosophy is a wonderful, but natural, effect produced by a natural cause; for St. Thomas at all events it is not a *hujusmodi*. Hence, to suggest to the reader that an accord exists where one knows very well that it does not exist is to set him on a false trail.

time to aid faith, in other words to give the support of her
testimony to that science which is above all others conducive
to the salvation of the human race—theology, which saves man
from eternal death and endows him with eternal life. And how
can she here aid Revelation? By the fact that, because she is
herself "something visibly miraculous, of which men's eyes
may daily have experience, and because she makes other miracles
credible to us, it is manifest that this lady aids our faith by her
wonderful aspect" (III, 7). Indeed, philosophy was eternally
destined, in the mind of God, to testify in favour of faith before
the men of to-day. And philosophy thus bears witness to faith
not only through the light with which it illuminates the intellect,
but also through the moral beauty with which it ennobles the
soul. By this means God gives us to understand that the splendour
of wisdom "has the power to revive the nature of those who
contemplate it, which is a miraculous thing. And this confirms
what was said above in the previous chapter, in the passage where
I say that it is an aid to our faith" (III, 8).

There is not the barest allusion in all this to any sort of collaboration on the part of philosophy in the evolution of a
theological science as St. Thomas Aquinas understood it. Nor
do we find there a single word about the subordination of
philosophy to theology of which the basis, in the *Summa
theologica,* was furnished by the text of *Prov.,* IX, 3: *Misit
ancillas suas vocare ad arcem* ("She hath sent her maids to
invite to the tower"). Philosophy appears in Dante as a
collaborator far prouder and far more independent. It is through
its splendour and magnificence, as a daughter of God, *by virtue
of the miracle of its own existence and of the effects which it produces
on man through its special quality,* that philosophy, a miracle to
be seen every day, helps us to deem possible the miracles of
Christ which we did not see. No one will deny that this aid can
indeed benefit Christian faith with its efficacy, but it will undoubtedly be recognized that it does not conform to the canon
of Thomistic apologetics. To suggest that the miracles of Christ
in the Gospel become *possibili* when one sees how divinely
miraculous are the splendour of philosophical knowledge and the
efficacy of the philosophical ethic, is to make the credibility of
the miracle dependent on the beauty of the natural order, itself
conceived as a miracle. Whatever the doctrine from which

Dante may here be drawing his inspiration, it is certainly not that of St. Thomas Aquinas.[1]

In fact, and if we try to define Dante's position with regard to the nature and function of theology, we find ourselves faced with the following facts: It is a supernatural science situated above, but outside, the order of the natural sciences, as the Empyrean is a supernatural heaven, situated above, but outside, the order of the natural heavens; just as the Empyrean does not exert on the world of nature any positive action, but moves the *Primum Mobile* through the love with which it inspires it, we may think that, although he does not say it,[2] Dante admits that theology, without exerting any direct action - on philosophy, may be a sort of call summoning it to the heights; finally, Dante has nowhere said or suggested that the philosophical sciences are in any way subordinate to this supposed queen, theology, but he has said, on the contrary, that there are at least sixty queenly sciences, not counting favourites and handmaids. Everything, then, tempts one to think that Dante regards theology as being exalted beyond the limits of the world by virtue of its very perfection and separated from nature through its supernatural dignity.

[1] In their commentary on these passages G. Busnelli and G. Vandelli have naturally had no difficulty in finding passages in St. Thomas calculated to confirm that miracles —supernatural acts—are the principal grounds of our belief in a Revelation that is itself supernatural (*op. cit.*, Vol. I, p. 342, note 7), that God has chosen to create our reason inferior to His power (*loc. cit.*, note 9), and that the saints perform their miracles in the name of Christ (*loc. cit.*, note 10); but, according to their note on the words *e questa donna sia una cosa visibilmente miraculosa* (*op. cit.*, p. 343, note 3), they have failed, and with good reason, to find any passage to quote in which St. Thomas has said that philosophy is something "miraculous" to the extent that it *faccia a noi possibili li altri*. The passages in St. Thomas which the two commentators quote to elucidate this passage say first that the purpose of visible miracles is to confirm our faith, then that it is of the essence of the miracle that it should excite our wonder, because it seems to us, when a miracle occurs, that what happens is the contrary of what ought to happen. Now St. Thomas greatly admired philosophy, but he certainly did not regard the intellectual and moral effects of this natural knowledge as contrary to the habitual order of nature. When it produces such effects on man, what happens is exactly what naturally should happen.

[2] I permit myself to ask the reader to be good enough to check this point by referring to *Conv.*, II, 14: "Ancora lo Cielo empireo . . ." I think, however, that Dante would not deny that theology has a practical influence on philosophy, with the proviso that it is not a positive influence, but one like that which he attributes to the Empyrean: causing motion by the mere fact of being loved. The identification of theology with this heaven as it is described by Dante at any rate tempts one to imagine so.

IV. Limits of Metaphysics

As it emerges from the preceding analyses, the head of the table of the sciences according to the Dantesque classification assumes the following aspect:

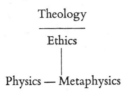

Theology here seems to hover in a sort of splendid isolation, to which we shall find, however, that there are limits; with ethics, which corresponds to the *Primum Mobile*, begins, on the contrary, the order of motive influences and direct positive actions which pervade the entire order of natural sciences, down to the modest but indispensable science of grammar. All taken together form Wisdom, and because ethics summons and prescribes them, and directs them towards their goal, it is ethics that endows them with harmony and beauty: *La moralitade è bellezza de la sapienza* (III, 15).

If we reflect on this doctrine, we see clearly enough *why* Dante came to prefer it, but we do not see *how* he was able to make up his mind to uphold it. All external influences conspired to deter him: Aristotle on the one hand, who never hesitated to keep metaphysics at the summit of the hierarchy of the sciences; St. Thomas on the other, who insisted on this even more strongly than Aristotle had done, because he had to vindicate the claims of another and even higher speculative theology, that of Revelation. We cannot, then, imagine how Dante was able thus to relegate metaphysics from the first place, which belonged to it traditionally, to the second place, which he assigns to it, without modifying the conception of it in order to make it conform to the new part which it is desired to make it play. Not only did Dante do this, but in the process he expended a wealth of ingenuity, and an ingenuity of the highest quality, because it is in the service of an idea that is very precise but hard to express.

At the risk of slightly stretching Dante's thought, but with the object of bringing out what seems to me the idea which a great number of passages suggest, I am going to say, in definitely stating that the formula is not his, that metaphysics as conceived by Dante remains *in itself* the loftiest and most perfect of the sciences, but that it is not so *as far as we are concerned*. Hence the two groups of passages, all authentic, which confront each other and join battle in book after book and in commentary after commentary, each one of those which take up their position being perfectly sure of the justice of its cause, and with reason, but forgetful that its adversaries are likewise so, and with no less reason. There was nothing contradictory in maintaining that, by its very superiority, metaphysics passes our understanding, so that though it is in itself the noblest of the sciences naturally accessible to man our mastery of it is too incomplete for it to be the noblest of *our sciences*, that is to say of those whose subjects we dominate instead of feeling dominated by them. The noblest of our sciences is that of man's happiness *qua* man: ethics; as for metaphysics, we should certainly place it first if our mastery of it were equal to our mastery of ethics. Its only fault is that it is a little too much for us.

This conviction appears to me to make itself felt in the majority of the passages in which Dante compares the respective teachings of philosophy and theology on a single problem. The result of these comparisons is that in the long run the conclusions of metaphysics always agree with those of theology, but that, concerning each of the points treated by human wisdom, divine wisdom knows much more and knows it much better. Dante's exaltation of theology therefore seems to have had the primary effect of giving him a keener sense of the inherent shortcomings of our metaphysic, as if the latter could only strive more or less successfully towards what is, in fact, the special goal of theology and, straining towards a goal that lies beyond its reach, were often condemned to remain a sort of inadequate theology.[1]

---

[1] Dante's attitude to these questions sometimes resembles that which has lately been ascribed to Siger of Brabant by F. VAN STEENBERGHEN, in *Les oeuvres et la doctrine de Siger de Brabant*, Brussels, Palais des Académies, 1938. See especially the excellent pages 174–175. Formulas like Siger's—"Non tamen videtur quod possit ad plenum satisfieri intellectui humano" and "Homo de separatis errat faciliter et ideo decipitur" (*op. cit.*, p. 175)—have an entirely Dantesque ring. On the other hand I do not know a single equivalent in Dante of the numerous passages in which Siger propounds a certain thesis as philosophically irrefutable, although the contrary is true in the light of faith:

In certain cases however, even when thrown back upon its own resources, metaphysics emerges with great credit. That is what happens in connection with the immortality of the soul, a problem which was forced on Dante's thought by the ever living memory of Beatrice. It is true that philosophy is here satisfied at small cost: "Of all follies (*bestialitadi*) the most stupid, the basest and the most pernicious is the belief that there is no other life after death; in point of fact, if we refer to all books, those of the philosophers as well as those of the other sages who have written on the subject, all agree on this point, that there is some part of us which is immortal." In support of which assertion Dante cites Aristotle, *De anima*; all the Stoics; Cicero, *De Senectute*; all the pagan poets; all the religious laws, those of the Jews, the Saracens, the Tartars and that which is common to all men in whatever part of the world they live. If all had deluded themselves the result would be an impossible situation of which the mere mention provokes a shudder. This impossible situation would consist in the fact that, although man is the most perfect of beings here below, he would die like all the other animals, in spite of the hope of another life with which he is buoyed up; now if he were deluded in this natural hope, man, that is to say the most perfect of creatures, would be at the same time the most imperfect, which is the more impossible as in that case it would be reason, the highest perfection of man, that was the cause of his imperfection (II, 8).[1]

For these reasons, and for others too, Dante is therefore quite certain of the immortality of the soul. None the less he adds this one: "Moreover, the infallible doctrine of Christ assures us of it, that doctrine which is the way, the truth and the light

---

"Et istae rationes sunt Commentatoris, quasi indissolubiles; tamen oppositum verum est per fidem" (*op. cit.*, p. 174). To Dante, reason may often be out of its depth in philosophy, but its necessary conclusions are never the opposite of the teaching of faith. Even on a point such as the inability of the most virtuous heathen to be saved without faith, Dante does not say that it is unjust from the viewpoint of reason, but just from that of faith, that a man who has never heard of Christ should be reproved for not having believed in Him, but that, aided by faith, reason may see that that is just: "Quaedam enim judicia Dei sunt, ad quae etsi humana ratio ex propriis pertingere nequit, elevatur tamen ad illa cum adjutorio fidei eorum quae in Sacris Litteris nobis dicta sunt, sicut ad hoc, quod nemo, quantumcumque moralibus et intellectualibus virtutibus et secundum habitum et secundum operationem perfectus, absque fide salvari potest, dato quod numquam aliquid de Christo audiverit. Nam hoc ratio humana per se justum intueri non potest, fide tamen adjuta potest" (*De Monarchia*, II, 7).

[1] Regarding these arguments, consult BRUNO NARDI, *Note critiche di filosofia dantescha*, Florence, L. S. Olschki, 1938–XVI, pp. 28–42.

[St. John, XVI, 6]: the way, because by it we pass without let to the happiness of this immortality; the truth, because it is not liable to err; the light, because it illumines us in the darkness of the ignorance of this world. This doctrine, I say, makes us certain of it more than all other reasons, because He Who gave it to us is He Who sees our immortality and sets its bounds. We cannot, indeed, see it perfectly so long as the immortal in us is mingled with the mortal. But we see it perfectly through faith, and, through reason, we see it in a shadow of darkness due to the mingling of the mortal and the immortal. And this should be a most potent proof that both are in us; and I, for my part, thus believe, thus affirm, and am thus certain of passing after this life to another and better one, to the abode of that glorious lady [*sc.* Beatrice] of whom my soul was enamoured . . ." (II, 8).

This passage contains a small difficulty of construction. After writing, with reference to immortality, that "we cannot see it [*feminine*] perfectly so long as the immortal in us is mingled with the mortal", Dante continues: "But we see it [*masculine*] perfectly through faith . . .", etc. If we follow the thread of the sense our interpretation will be: "But we see through faith that man is immortal." If we follow the grammar, we shall have to relate the *lo* of *vedemolo* to *the immortal*, and our interpretation will be: "But we see it [*sc.* the immortal in us] perfectly through faith." In both cases the sense remains the same, for the question propounded by Dante is in fact whether, in this life, we see perfectly through reason *la nostra immortalitade.*[1]

<hr/>

[1] In their commentary on this passage G. Busnelli and G. Vandelli make *vedemolo* refer to *il nostro immortale* (*op. cit.*, Vol. I, p. 164, note 4), which is correct. But, carried away by the desire to refute a remark of Bruno Nardi (in *Giornale storico della letteratura italiana*, XCV, 83), according to whom Dante considers that "the arguments advanced by Thomas in favour of the immortality of the soul would not suffice to make us absolutely certain of it", the two commentators want this sentence to signify besides: "We do not see perfectly through reason the essence of what in us is immortal." As it is the soul that is immortal, and as St. Thomas denies that we have in fact any knowledge of our souls *per essentiam*, Dante finds himself thus brought back within the barriers of Thomistic orthodoxy, outside which he is forbidden to go. This interpretation is doubly unwarranted. It is so in the first place in view of the letter of the text; for Dante wrote: "La quale [immortalitadè] noi non potemo perfettamente vedere mentre che 'l nostro immortale col mortale è mischiato; ma vedemolo per fede perfettamente . . ."; even if we translate: "But we see it [*sc.* the immortal in us] through faith, perfectly . . .", it is clear that the assertion is an answer to what precedes: "But we cannot perfectly see our immortality . . ." It is therefore not a question here of the possibility of seeing the essence of our immortal souls, but of the possibility of seeing perfectly the immortal in ourselves as such. This interpretation is, furthermore, impossible in the light of the very thesis which it upholds. For it is true that St. Thomas denies that we have a direct·

His answer to this question is embodied in the following points: (1) The immortality of the soul is a rational certainty universally accepted; (2) we cannot deny it, moreover, without acknowledging a monstrous inconsistency in nature in general and in the nature of man in particular; (3) yet we do not see our immortality perfectly through reason alone; (4) we do, however, see it perfectly through faith. There is no trace, however slight, of incoherence in this series of propositions. A universal feeling of certainty is a powerful indication of truth, yet it is not conclusive, for men feel their immortality, but they do not *see* it. Similarly, the argument based on the natural desire for immortality may well make the contrary thesis incredible to us, but such a demonstration is not based on the actual nature of the soul, and so it does not enable us to *see* its immortality. As St. Thomas says, it is a *sign* that we are immortal,[1] not a proof. Thus, Dante formally teaches that we have no perfect rational knowledge of the immortality of the soul, but that faith makes us perfectly sure of it.

How are we to classify this doctrine? To be sure, St. Thomas laid it down as a rule that, if we judge certainties from the point of view of their causes, certainty based on faith is the supreme certainty. Indeed, the cause of certainty based on wisdom, science and even intellection is of a human order, whereas the cause of certainty based on faith is the authority of God. He added, however, that if we classify certainties according to what the informed individual can understand of them, those based on faith are less absolute than those based on the intellect,

---

knowledge of the essence of the soul, but he adds that it may be proved that it is an immaterial substance and that, when this has been proved, its immortality becomes obvious merely by virtue of the principle of contradiction: "Impossibile est autem quod forma separetur a seipsa, unde impossibile est, quod forma subsistens desinat esse" (*Sum. theol.*, Pars I, qu. 75, art. 6, Resp.). In short, the philosopher, in St. Thomas's view, sees the immortality of the soul as one of those *communes animi conceptiones* the contrary of which is philosophically unthinkable: ". . . communis animi conceptio dicitur illa cujus oppositum contradictionem includit, sicut: Omne totum est majus sua parte, quia non esse majus sua parte est contra rationem totius. Sic autem animam rationalem non esse, non est communis animi conceptio, ut ex dictis patet; sed naturam animae rationalis non esse corruptibilem, haec est communis animi conceptio" (*De Potentia*, quaest. disput. V, art. 4, ad 7ᵐ). Thus, to St. Thomas the immortality of the soul is a rationally obvious fact; when, therefore, Dante says that it is only imperfectly seen in this life through reason, he shows either that he is ignorant of St. Thomas's thesis, or that he knows it, but rejects it. In either case Signor Bruno Nardi is fundamentally right: Dante here is not in agreement with St. Thomas.

[1] ST. THOMAS AQUINAS, *Sum. theol.*, Pars. I, qu. 75, art. 6, Resp.: "Potest etiam hujus rei accipi signum ex hoc . . ."

precisely because they are outside the range of the intellect, but that this does not prevent knowledge founded on faith from remaining, strictly speaking, the surest knowledge.[1] Dante undoubtedly admitted all this, but he adds here something else, for he maintains not only that faith makes us more certain of the immortality of the soul than reason does, but that it enables us to see it perfectly, whereas reason only enables us to see it somewhat dimly. Now to St. Thomas the immortality of the soul is not essentially a truth revealed by faith; it is essentially a philosophic truth, and it is even an obvious philosophic fact inseparable from the definition of the soul as a spiritual substance. How can we ascribe to St. Thomas the thesis that faith enables us to see obvious philosophic facts more perfectly than they are revealed to us by natural reason? In authentic Thomism such a proposition is meaningless. "The Soul of man," says St. Thomas, "is naturally incorruptible."[2] We therefore need only define the nature of the soul correctly in order to see, with perfect rational certainty, its immortality.

Is this Averroism? There is the objection that Averroes does not admit the immortality of human souls endowed with a personal intellect, whereas Dante admits at one and the same time the existence of such personal intellects and their immortality. It is therefore not the Averroism of Averroes himself. Nor is it the Averroism of the Latin Averroists, who consider that philosophy naturally decides *against* personal immortality, and accept this thesis only as an article of faith. Dante, on the contrary, admits that there are very strong philosophic reasons *in favour of* the personal immortality of the soul; on this point, therefore, he is not reduced to the light of faith alone.[3]

---

[1] St. Thomas Aquinas, *Sum. theol.*, Pars. IIa IIae, qu. 4, art. 8, Resp.

[2] St. Thomas Aquinas, *Sum. theol.*, Pars I, qu. 98, art. 1, Resp.

[3] Compare the following three passages: (1) St. Thomas Aquinas, *Sum. theol.*, Pars. I, qu. 98, art. 1, Resp.: "Est ergo considerandum, quod homo secundum suam naturam est constitutus quasi medium quoddam inter creaturas corruptibiles et incorruptibiles: nam anima ejus est naturaliter incorruptibilis, corpus vero naturaliter corruptibile"; (2) Dante, *De Monarchia*, III, 16: "Sciendum quod homo solus in entibus tenet medium corruptibilium et incorruptibilium . . . Nam homo, si consideretur secundum utramque partem essentialem, scilicet animam et corpus: corruptibilis est, si consideretur tantum secundum unam, scilicet corpus; si vero secundum alteram, scilicet animam, incorruptibilis est"; (3) the attitude of Latin Averroism, which is the attitude of Siger of Brabant: "Sed nunquam invenitur Philosophus determinare de his quae sunt animae separatae et statu ejus. Quare non videtur eam opinari sic esse separabilem totaliter a corpore" (*Quaest. de anima intellectiva*, qu. VI; in P. Mandonnet, *Siger de Brabant et l'averroïsme latin au XIIIe siècle*. 2nd ed., Louvain, Institut supérieur de philosophie de l'Université,

His attitude has been compared, with a greater semblance of truth, to those of Duns Scotus and Ockham, who consider the immortality of the soul more probable on rational grounds than the contrary thesis, but fully certain only on grounds of faith. Yet here again it is advisable to use discretion, for Dante's attitude in no way implies his adherence to what is implied by the corresponding attitudes of Duns Scotus or Ockham in the doctrines, otherwise so different, of those two thinkers. Even if he says something similar, his words have not the significance of the same formula in Duns Scotus any more than that formula signifies in Duns Scotus what it does in Ockham. It is more vital to understand Dante than to classify him. Now what he says here is simple enough, if, at least, we confine ourselves to what we are certain he did say: the universal reason of men, including the philosophers, is unshakably convinced of the immortality of the soul, but it does not see it with perfect clearness, whereas we see it perfectly through faith.

This, moreover, is not the only case of the kind that is to be met with in the *Banquet*. It is not very unusual for Dante to stress the inadequacy of the resources at the disposal of metaphysics for the attainment of its loftiest objectives. Why should he have refrained from doing so? Does not Aristotle himself say that our intellect can know nothing beyond what we can perceive through the senses and picture by means of the imagination? Now, as a matter of fact it happens that none of the supreme objectives of metaphysics—the pure Intelligences, the pure Intelligibles, and God—can be either perceived through our senses or conceived by our imagination. Whereupon it will undoubtedly be asked why God wills that these objectives should escape the grasp of our intellect and why He is pleased to impose such a rigorous limitation on our knowledge. If we knew, the question would no longer have any *raison d'être*, for such a limitation would itself not exist. It is therefore this limitation that gives rise to the question and prohibits us from seeking the answer to it: "I say that owing to the inadequacy of the faculty from which it derives its images—an organic faculty,

---

Part II, p. 164). Dante, on the contrary, is convinced that Aristotle preached the immortality of the soul: "E questa massimamente par volere Aristotile in quello [*sc.* libro] de l'Anima . . ." (*Convivio*, I, 8). To him, then, what is involved is a thesis that is philosophically certain (in this he differs from the Averroists), but not perfectly intelligible (in this he differs from St. Thomas Aquinas).

namely the imagination—there are some things to which our intellect cannot rise (because the imagination cannot aid it, not having the means to do so), such as substances that are independent of matter; for although we may have some knowledge of them, we cannot understand or comprehend them perfectly. And for that man is not to be blamed, for this reason, I say: that *he* is not the cause of the defect; the responsibility for that lies with the universal nature, in other words God, Who has chosen to deprive us of that light in this life. As to the question why God has done this, it would be presumptuous to discuss it" (III, 4). A very interesting passage, and one that sheds light on the preceding problem.

What, in fact, did Dante say of the darkness that clouds our vision of the immortality of the soul? That its cause lies in the union, and, as it were, the mingling, of our soul and body in this life. Now this is precisely the reason which he has just assigned here to our inability to understand perfectly the nature of independent substances. But to conceive of the soul as immortal is exactly the same as to conceive of it as an independent substance; and so there is nothing surprising in the fact that we are incapable of it. Dante's attitude seems in consequence to amount to this: Knowing, on the authority of Aristotle himself, that metaphysics has too limited a range to apprehend fully its loftiest objectives, he establishes in addition that on these same objectives theology sheds a light complementary to that shed by metaphysics. He therefore finds himself almost in the position of an Aristotle who, acquainted with the Christian Revelation, establishes the extent to which he has been justified in noting the inherent limitation imposed on our metaphysics by the sensible origin of our knowledge.

Hence the extreme reserve of which Dante gives proof each time he finds himself faced with one of these objectives whose nature so radically transcends our own: independent substances, primary matter, God.[1] It is these very things that constitute "the bread of the angels", for "angel" here means nothing else than "independent Intelligence", and the intellect of the metaphysician is that of a man compounded of body and soul who

[1] "Ondè e da sapere che di tutte quelle cose che lo 'ntelletto nostro vincono, sì che non può vedere quello che sono, convenevolissimo trattare è per li loro effetti: onde di Dio, e delle sustanze separate, e de la prima materia, così trattando, potemo avere alcuna conoscenza" (*Convivio*, III, 8).

claims to understand the nature of independent intelligible objectives, created for independent intelligences. In fact, when we try to attain such objectives, our aim is too high for our shafts. The philosophers seek, for example, to discover the cause of the Firmament's revolution from east to west. They wonder whether this movement should be attributed to a motive Intelligence or to the love felt by this sphere for the Prime Mover. An excellent question, to be sure, but only God knows the answer to it: *Dio lo sa, che a me pare presuntuoso a giudicare* (II, 5). This conviction, deeply rooted in Dante's heart, that our philosophic wisdom has great shortcomings when it is pitted against pure intelligibles, explains how he was able to justify in his own eyes the destitution which his hierarchy of the sciences brought upon metaphysics and the primacy which it attributed to ethics. We shall, however, shortly see how dangerous it is to presume to systematize Dante's position merely on the basis of one of his principles, and how much more flexible, and also more complex, is the doctrinal equilibrium which he himself sought than those which are commonly ascribed to him by his historians.

V. PRIMACY OF CONTEMPLATION

When, after placing ethics above metaphysics in the hierarchy of the sciences, a thinker tackles the problem of the relation of action to contemplation, we naturally expect him to affirm the primacy of the active life over the contemplative life. Now Dante does exactly the opposite, whence his interpreters for the most part conclude that, in one or the other of the two cases, Dante does not really believe what he says. I think this is a mistake, the fatal mistake that all will commit who try to interpret Dante's thought by identifying it simply with one of the doctrinal positions taken up by other philosophers and already familiar to us. In fact, after what we have seen it is impossible to doubt that Dante did in truth place ethics at the summit of the hierarchy of the sciences; but we shall shortly see that he no less certainly affirmed the superiority of the contemplative life to the active life. To understand the meaning of his doctrine we must therefore find a position of which each of the two theses necessarily forms part, the one balancing and complementing

the other. We must above all make sure that this position was
in fact his. That is perhaps not easy, but it is certainly the goal
at which we must aim.

For reasons which we shall later have to elucidate, Dante
chose to remain faithful, in this particular as in so many others,
to the teaching of the authorities competent to speak on the
matter. Here, in point of fact, they are all in agreement. Theology teaches us that the only perfect beatitude to which man
should aspire is the vision of God face to face in eternity. This
vision is by the nature of the term a form of contemplation. The
ultimate triumph of the contemplative life over the active life
is therefore certain, and this alone would be enough to establish
the inferiority of action in comparison with contemplation. But
that which faith ordains that we should believe is also in the
teaching of philosophy. Aristotle explicitly says, in Book X
of the *Ethica ad Nicomachum*, that the highest felicity to which
man may aspire is that which is sometimes experienced, even if
only for brief moments, in the practice of the contemplative life.[1]
Finally, Jesus Christ Himself teaches, in St. Luke's Gospel, that
the better part has been chosen not by Martha, the symbol of
the active life, but by Mary, the symbol of the contemplative
life. Dante therefore concludes without hesitation: "In truth,
we must know that we may obtain in this life two kinds of
felicity, by following the two roads, one being good, the other
excellent, which lead to them: one is the active life, the other
the contemplative. Now although we obtain a good kind of
felicity through the active life, as has been said,[2] the contemplative life leads us to a felicity and a beatitude that are excellent,
as the Philosopher proves in the Tenth Book of the *Ethics*. And
this is affirmed from the lips of Christ Himself, in Luke's Gospel,
when He is speaking to Martha and answering her: 'Martha,
Martha, thou art anxious and troubled about many things: of
a surety one thing is needful', that is to say, what thou doest.
But He adds: 'Mary hath chosen the better part, which shall not
be taken away from her.' Now Mary (as is written before these
words in the Gospel), seated at Christ's feet, showed no interest

---

[1] ARISTOTLE, *Eth. Nic.*, X, 7, 1177 a 12–18.

[2] Cf. DANTE, *Convivio*, IV, 17: "E queste [vertudi] sono quelle che fanno l'uomo
beato, o vero felice, ne la loro operazione, sì come dice lo Filosofo nel primo de l'Etica
quando diffinisce la Felicitade, dicendo che: Felicitade è operazione secondo vertude in
vita perfetta." Cf. ARISTOTLE, *Eth. Nic.*, I, 6, 1098 a 15–18.

in the service of the house, but listened only to the words of the Saviour. If we wish to explain this in the moral sense, Our Lord intended to show by it that, good though the active life is, the contemplative life is excellent. That is evident to any who will ponder well the words of the Gospel."[1] Nothing, it is clear, could be more in accordance with tradition than this conclusion.

It is true that we may wonder—and Dante himself raises the objection—how what he maintains here, in the Fourth Treatise of the *Banquet*, accords with what he has said earlier about the pre-eminence of the moral virtues. In other words, why, then, did he begin by promising as the aim and the fruit of wisdom that felicity which the active life offers? To which Dante replies without hesitation: "In all teaching it is necessary to take into account the capacity of the pupil, in order to lead him along the path that is easiest for him. Now the moral virtues appear to be, and indeed are, more prevalent, better known, more sought after than the others, and more useful from the outward point of view; it was therefore more advantageous and more convenient to follow this road rather than the other. All the same, one would come more surely to know bees by their fruit if one started from the honey than if one started from the wax, although each comes from them" (IV, 17). Thus Dante has thought first of the honest folk engaged in the active life whom the *Banquet* was to win over to philosophy. He has therefore suggested to them as an aim their beatitude, in other words the kind of felicity which may normally reward the kind of life they lead. Dante has no need to take back what he has said, for if Mary's part is better, Martha's is good; but, conversely, the fact that such people are lawfully engaged in the active life and are entitled to expect from it the special happiness that crowns it does not authorize them to believe that their part is the better. Who knows even whether they may aspire to the other? We shall see that there are reasons for doubting it.

Whatever the truth on this point, it is impossible to suppose that Dante does not here cleave with the utmost sincerity to the thesis which he propounds. Moreover, he returns to it later on with a wealth of detail that leaves no room for any doubt.

---

[1] DANTE, *Convivio*, IV, 17. Cf. ST. LUKE, X, 38 *seq*. The passages from St. Thomas and the Fathers assembled at this point by G. Busnelli and G. Vandelli (*op. cit.*, Vol. II, p. 219, note 3) are entirely appropriate and excellently chosen.

Of our two intellects, he says, one, the speculative, *è più pieno di beatitudine che l'altro*. Not only does philosophy teach this, but the allegorical meaning of the Gospel proves it. The three saintly women whom St. Mark's Gospel reveals to us arriving first at the tomb—Mary Magdalene, Mary the mother of James and Mary Salome—represent the three philosophic schools of the active life, namely the Aristotelians, the Stoics and the Epicureans. They go to the tomb, that is to say to this world, the repository of corruptible things. They ask for the Saviour, in other words beatitude, and they do not find Him, but they find an angel clad in white, in other words that nobility, derived from God, which speaks through our reason and says to each of these three sects, in other words to all who seek beatitude in the active life: It is not here; go and tell those who seek it here that the Saviour will go before them into Galilee, in other words that beatitude will go before us into the realm of speculation. The Angel says "will go before", for God, our supreme beatitude, always goes before us along the way of contemplation: "It thus becomes apparent that our beatitude (that felicity which is here in question) is to be found first as it were in an imperfect form in the active life, that is to say in the functions of the moral virtues; then as it were in a perfect form in the functions of the intellectual virtues, these two classes of function being the easy and direct way to the attainment of supreme beatitude, which, moreover, cannot be enjoyed on earth, as is evident from what we have said" (IV, 22).

If we summarize these conclusions in tabular form, we obtain the following diagram of the Dantesque beatitudes:

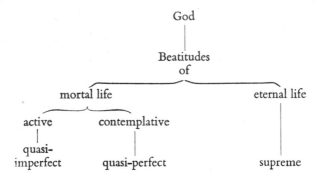

Nothing could be more conventional or more intelligible than this table, but the premises that justify it, if they are equally intelligible, are not always as conventional. It has doubtless been noticed how, in contrasting the ideal of the active life with that of the contemplative life, Dante has ranged on one side, as representing the former, the Epicureans, the Stoics *and Aristotle*, whereas the latter is represented solely by the Saviour, Who is God. If we remember what we have said of the limits imposed by Dante on metaphysics, we shall see everything beginning to grow clearer. There are indeed three kinds of beatitude: two belong to this life and the other to the future one. Of the two kinds of beatitude that belong to this life, however, only one is peculiar to it and capable of reaching its height in it. This is the beatitude of the active life. As to that of the contemplative life, it is present only as the beginning of a line of which the end is in the beyond. To put Aristotle, philosophy and the active life on one side, and the Saviour and the contemplative life on the other, is to indicate clearly enough that contemplative beatitude depends less on philosophy than on theology. The felicity of the active life is quasi-imperfect, that is to say it is perfect so far as we are concerned, because it is the felicity to which man may aspire in this life, merely through the natural resources of philosophy, but it appears imperfect if we compare it to other sorts which, though less accessible to us, are superior to it in themselves. The felicity of the contemplative life is on earth quasi-perfect, that is to say it is perfect in itself, since, like supreme felicity, it is a form of contemplation, but so far as we are concerned it is only quasi-perfect, because it lies in the contemplation of objects which, on earth, elude our grasp. As to the felicity of eternal life, it is perfect and superior, since it consists in the contemplation of its object finally encountered face to face.

Thus the intrinsic and essential superiority of the contemplative life is in no way disputed by Dante. On the contrary, he affirms it in so many words. Nor can it be doubted that Dante admits the possibility of a beginning of speculative beatitude in this life: quite the contrary, he has spoken often, and with enthusiasm, of the joys awaiting the reader of the *De consolatione philosophiae* of Boëthius, whose contemplative Platonism served his purpose admirably; or again the *Liber de causis*,[1] and the *De Intellectu* of Albertus Magnus, a book crammed with examples of the neo-Platonic and Arabic influences, the philosophical doctrine of which is animated with the most intense religious feeling. But such contemplation never seemed to him to find its limit in itself. To him it was not the contemplation of a man, but rather that of an angel. The man who gives himself up to it, he says explicitly, is *di sì alta condizione, che quasi non sia altro che angelo . . . E questi cotali chiama Aristotile, nel settimo de l'Etica, divini*.[2] We may therefore rise above ethics, and we are already doing so if we rise to metaphysics, but we only do so if we rise above man. Thus, far from refuting the primacy of ethics, the transcendency of contemplation establishes it, for we do not regard ethics, for its part, as transcendent. When Dante writes *ogni vertù*, he is thinking first of the moral virtues referred to in the *Ethica ad Nicomachum*,[3] because, he says in a dictum to which

---

[1] See in this connection B. NARDI, *Saggi di filosofia dantesca: V. Le citazioni dantesche del Liber de Causis*, Milan, Società anonima editrice Dante Alighieri, 1939–VIII, pp. 91–119; and M. BAUMGARTNER, *Dantes Stellung zur Philosophie*, pp. 64–67, with bibliographical indications, p. 64, note 3.

[2] DANTE, *Convivio*, III, 7. Cf. ARISTOTLE, *Eth. Nic.*, VII, 1, 1145 a 23–25. Aristotle does indeed refer in this passage to a virtue that is "above us" (1145 a 9), a "heroic and divine" virtue (1145 a 20), so that, through excess of this very virtue, those who possess it "change from men to gods" (1145 a 23).

[3] The ethics of the *Convivio* are visibly inspired by the fundamental ideas of the *Ethica ad Nicomachum*. In Aristotle's eyes, the objective of the city is to ensure the felicity of the citizens. This felicity, or sovereign good, is an absolutely ultimate aim (*Eth.*, I, 7, 1907 a 33); Dante was therefore only repeating Aristotle's dictum when he made happiness in this life an *ultimum*. Moreover, according to Aristotle, there are two classes of men, capable of pursuing a single aim in two different ways, *viz.* by means of moral virtue or intellectual virtue (*Eth.*, I, 13, 1103 a 3–10). In the sphere of action, the perfect moral virtue is Justice (*Eth.*, V, 1, 1129 b 31), because he who possesses it can exercise virtue not only towards himself, but towards his neighbour (1129 b 32–33). In this sense Justice is not a part of virtue: it is actually co-extensive with virtue (1130 a 9). The state of perfection to which the virtuous man of action rises is prudence (φρόνησις), that is to say practical wisdom, or, as Aristotle often says, πολιτική (*Eth.*, I, 1, 1094 a 27). In effect, prudence and *political* virtue are precisely the same virtue, viewed in the light of whether it governs religiously the practical activity of the individual or that of the city (*Eth.*, VI, 8, 1141 b 23–30). Above the felicity which is conferred on man by prudence and the practical wisdom resulting from it is the felicity of the contemplative life. We obtain it through the exercise of the intellect, which is our most divine attribute. This, says Aristotle, is where we find perfect happiness, ἡ τελεία εὐδαιμονία (*Eth.*, X, 7, 1177 a 17)—an expression which (as we have seen) Dante, in order to vindicate the claims of the beatific vision, watered down to *beatitudine quasi perfetta* (see above, p. 210). The happiness of the contemplative man is therefore different in kind from that of the statesman (*Eth.*, X, 7, 1177 b 14–15) and far exceeds it because it is the happiness of the divine element in man. In fact, it is a superhuman and literally divine form of happiness (1177 b 24–28). The happiness of the moral life, which is essentially a human form of life, will therefore be placed in the second rank (*Eth.*, X, 8, 1178 a 9–14). The philosophers, then, are versed in the rules that guide men to the two forms of human beatitude, but as men are a prey to their passions, the Legislator must force them through civil law to observe the moral laws (*Eth.*, X, 9, 1180 a 5–12). It is evident that what is here presented to us is the entire ideological framework of Dante's doctrine: affirmation

we are constantly obliged to return, "it should be known that the fruits by which above all we are known are the moral virtues, because in all respects they are within our reach" (IV, 17).

This fundamental point, on which Dante has displayed such firmness, was inevitably destined to become one of those on which the aptitude of certain of his commentators for "agreeing" him with St. Thomas would be exercised with special partiality. In spite of the passages which they accumulate in their notes, these interpreters are absolutely compelled to recognize that, so far as St. Thomas Aquinas is concerned, the intellectual virtues are no less the prerogative of man than are the moral virtues.[1] Now if Dante does not agree on this point with St. Thomas Aquinas he agrees entirely with Aristotle, and even with the interpretation of Aristotle offered by St. Thomas in his commentary on the *Ethica ad Nicomachum*. According to Aristotle, says St. Thomas, "both moral virtue and prudence are related to the compound: the virtues of the compound are the peculiarly human virtues in so far as man is compounded of a soul and a body. That is why life lived in accordance with these virtues is human, and this is what is called the active life. And consequently the felicity that consists in this life is human felicity. But speculative life and felicity, which are the prerogative of the intellect, are divine".[2]

Dante's attitude to this question is therefore identical with that of Aristotle, both as he is and as St. Thomas interprets him. But precisely because it is the attitude of Aristotle, and although he reproduces the identical terms, it is perhaps not quite that of St. Thomas. St. Thomas's commentary rests in effect on the hypothesis, which is certainly tenable and has even been maintained by many modern expositors, though it has not been proved, that Aristotle's "active intellect", although in a sense divine, and independent of the body in its activities, is a part of

---

of a temporal beatitude postulated as the final aim of man; distinction between the two forms of beatitude—active or political, contemplative or intellectual; superiority of the second; natural divinization of man through intellectual contemplation; invocation of the Chief of State in order to ensure, with the aid of the civil laws, respect for morality. One need only admit that Dante has taken the doctrine of the *Ethica ad Nicomachum* literally in order to explain the general position of the *Convivio* with regard to philosophy.

[1] ST. THOMAS AQUINAS, *Sum. theol.*, Pars Ia IIae, qu. 58, art. 3, Resp. Cf. G. BUSNELLI and G. VANDELLI, *ed. cit.*, Vol. II, p. 206, note on p. 205.

[2] ST. THOMAS AQUINAS, *In X libros Ethic. Nic.*, lib. X, lect. 12, ed. Pirotta, No. 2115.

man's soul.[1] If that is true, we may very well explain from this point of view all the passages from Aristotle in which perfect felicity is located by the philosopher in speculative activity,[2] but it becomes extremely difficult to explain the opposition introduced by Aristotle between the essentially human character of the moral virtues of the compound and of the felicity that they bring, and the essentially divine character of intellectual contemplation and of the felicity that it brings. If the intellect is really a part of man's soul, which is itself part of the compound, contemplation remains a human activity, the contemplative life a human life and the felicity that it brings a human felicity. So true is this that the authentic thought of Aristotle breaks through St. Thomas's commentary on it as though of its own accord: "So then it is apparent that speculative felicity triumphs over active felicity as completely as something individual and divine triumphs over what is composite and human."[3]

To convince oneself of his divergence on this point from Aristotle it is enough to listen to St. Thomas when, freed from the actual text of the *Ethics*, he expresses himself freely. We have just seen him explain, following the text of Aristotle, that the moral virtues of the active life are the human virtues *par excellence*, because they are those of the compound; but when he speaks in his own name St. Thomas categorically reverses the attitude of Aristotle by maintaining that the contemplation of divine things through the intellect is the most characteristically human activity that there is: *Et quia unusquisque videtur esse id quod est optimum in eo, ut dicitur in 9 Ethic. (cap. 4 et 8) et 10 (cap. 7 ad fin.), ideo talis operatio est maxime propria homini.* ("And because every man is seen to be what is most excellent in him, as is stated in *Ethics*, IX (Chapters 4 and 8) and X (Chapters 7 to the end), therefore this activity is above all things the property of man.")[4] St. Thomas may well invoke an Aristotelian premise here, but Aristotle

---

[1] "Quidam enim posuerunt intellectum humanum esse aliquid sempiternum et separatum. Et secundum hoc ipse intellectus esset quoddam divinum. Dicimus enim res divinas esse quae sunt sempiternae et separatae. Alii vero intellectum patrem animae posuerunt, sicut Aristoteles. Et secundum hoc intellectus non est simpliciter quoddam divinum, sed est divinissimum inter omnia quae sunt in nobis, propter majorem convenientiam quam habet cum substantiis separatis, secundum quod ejus operatio est sine organo corporeo" (ST. THOMAS AQUINAS, *In X libros Ethic. Nic.*, lib. X, lect. 10, ed. Pirotta, No. 2084).

[2] For example, *Eth. Nic.*, X, 8, 1178 b 7–8.

[3] ST. THOMAS AQUINAS, *In X lib. Ethic. Nic.*, lib. X, lect. 12, ed. Pirotta, No. 2116.

[4] ST. THOMAS AQUINAS, *Sum. theol.*, Pars Ia IIae, qu. 3, art. 5, Resp.

never inferred this consequence from it. In his eyes, to live as a man—τὸ ἀνθρωπεύεσθαι—means in fact to practise the moral virtues in social life;[1] as to contemplative beatitude, not only is it inaccessible to man in a perfect form, but even if man partakes of it "he will live on such a plane not as man, but in so far as he has within him something divine. For such a life differs as much from that of the compound as its functioning differs from that of the other virtues. If, therefore, the intellect is something divine when related to man, life lived under the sway of the intellect is a divine form of life when related to human life".[2] Such is the authentic thought of Aristotle, and it is very difficult to read into it, with St. Thomas, that pure intellectual knowledge is *maxime propria homini* ("above all things the property of man").

To place Dante in his proper relationship to St. Thomas one need only compare what he says with what the Angelic Doctor had written, in the *Summa theologica*, about the classification of the various forms of beatitude: "The ultimate and perfect [*perfecta;* Dante says *somma*] beatitude anticipated in the future life consists entirely in contemplation as in its principle; as to imperfect beatitude [Dante says *perfetta quasi*], in the form in which it may be enjoyed on earth, it consists, in truth, primarily and principally in contemplation, but secondarily in the activity of the practical intellect as a regulator of actions and passions, as is stated in Book X of the *Ethics*, Chapters 7 and 8."[3] The stamp of Aristotle is here impressed on the most authentically Thomistic of creeds, just as, in the *Banquet*, it is impressed on the creed of Dante, which is not exactly that of either Aristotle or St. Thomas Aquinas.

With St. Thomas, and like the good Christian that he is, Dante admits a third scale in which the different forms of beatitude are considered according to their absolute hierarchical order, with the beatitude of the active life at the foot, that of the contemplative life in this world above, and that of the beatific vision at the top. On the other hand, and this time in opposition to St. Thomas, Dante maintains with the authentic Aristotle, whose text served his ends far better than did the Thomistic commentary,

[1] ARISTOTLE, *Eth. Nic.*, X, 8, 1178 b 5–7.
[2] ARISTOTLE, *Eth. Nic.*, X, 7, 1177 b 26–31.
[3] ST. THOMAS AQUINAS, *Sum. theol.*, Pars Ia IIae, qu. 3, art. 5, Resp.

that the only one of these three forms of beatitude that is strictly
the prerogative of man *qua* man is also the lowest of all—namely
that of the active life of the human compound, activity that
accords with virtue. The reason for this return on Dante's part
to the real Aristotle is not, however, that he has accepted the
Averroistic interpretation which makes the active intellect a
single and independent substance. Like St. Thomas Aquinas,
Dante is convinced that, according to Aristotle and in fact, every
human being possesses his own personal active intellect, which
is a part of his soul and similarly immortal;[1] but he also thinks
that, without the help of Christian Revelation, the speculative
intellect attains its special end only very imperfectly, whereas
our practical intellect has no need of Revelation in order to attain
its end. It may therefore be said that, in Dante as in Aristotle,
what goes beyond the plane of the moral order also goes beyond
the plane of the human order to reach that of the divine order;
but, in Aristotle, the divine order which transcends the moral
order is that of contemplation, because the intellect that actually
contemplates does not belong to man *qua* man, and anything
that contemplates, in so far as it contemplates, is a god; in Dante,
on the contrary, the intellect of the contemplative man is indeed
his intellect, but it is an intellect too feeble to attain its object
without the divine light of a Revelation that transcends it. That
is why, in Dante as in Aristotle, the contemplative life is less
human than divine, but for a reason quite different from that
which forms the basis of Aristotle's thesis. What "super-
humanizes" the contemplative life in Dante is not the fact that
the intellect which guides it is not our own; it is the fact that,
even for the very precarious success that it may hope for in this
life, our speculative intellect requires a divine Revelation, so
that in the long run the success of this intellect, which is wholly
ours, is not itself wholly ours. On the other hand, intrinsically
inferior though it is to that of metaphysical contemplation, faith
and the beatific vision, or rather by very reason of its inferiority,
the practical department of the moral life enjoys complete
self-sufficiency, since it consists in pursuing, by those purely
natural and human means which are the moral virtues, that
purely natural and human end which is happiness in this life

---

[1] Cf. THOMAS AQUINAS, *Tract. de Unitate intellectus contra Averroistas*, ed. L. W. Keeler,
Rome, 1936, cap. I, 15, pp. 11–12; and DANTE, *Purg.*, XXV, 62–66.

in a society regulated by the most human of the virtues—justice.[1]

We are now coming to what was undoubtedly the most personal of Dante's thoughts—I would gladly say "the most secret" if this term did not suggest that he wished to conceal the thing which, on the contrary, he never ceases to tell us, but which we do not always desire to hear because this thought makes him unclassifiable and, as historians, we all have a desire to classify him. Dante has, however, expressed it in a passage from the *Banquet* which leaves no room for doubt, because the thesis is there presented in what is at once its extreme and its purest form, based on the very principle which we have just assigned to it: the natural incompleteness of a knowledge of the intelligible possessed by an intellect whose human character compels it to feed on sensible notions.

After postulating the existence of the Empyrean as required and taught by faith, Dante tackles the problem of the pure Intelligences, which the people call the angels—*le quali la volgare gente chiamano angeli*—but which Plato called Ideas, and which the heathen worshipped under the names of Vulcan, Juno, Pallas and Ceres, as if they were so many gods or goddesses. Dante undertakes to prove that their number far exceeds anything that we can imagine. Indeed, we only know of their existence by the effects which they produce. Now the only Intelligences that produce effects perceptible by our senses are those charged with governing the world, that is to say pure Intelligences engaged in the active life; but since even men may lead two distinct lives and thereby attain two distinct forms of beatitude—active and contemplative—it is quite certain that in addition to the active Intelligences of whose existence we know by their effects, there are contemplative Intelligences whose existence escapes our notice because they exercise no influence here below. That is an obvious fact which no one doubts, be he a philosopher, heathen, Jew, Christian or an adherent of any religion whatever. The number of these pure Intelligences is therefore incalculable.

Thus the whole of Dante's proof rests on the principle that an active pure Intelligence cannot at the same time be contemplative

---

[1] DANTE, *Convivio*, I, 12: "E quanto ella è più propria, tanto ancora è più amabile; onde, avvegna che ciascuna vertù sia amabile ne l'uomo, quella è più amabile in esso che è più umana, è questa è la giustizia, la quale è solamente ne la parte razionale o vero intellettuale, cioè ne la volontade."

—otherwise there would be no guarantee that in addition to those which act, and of which we may know by their effects, there are others which contemplate and which, because they do not act, escape our observation. This is indeed what Dante explicitly affirms when he bases his thesis on the absolute principle that one cannot enjoy two distinct forms of beatitude at once: *come quella [Intelligenza] che ha la beatitudine del governare non possa l'altra avere;* whence it follows that, while certain Intelligences govern the world, there must be others, *fuori di questo ministerio, che solamente vivano speculando* (II, 4).

Everything, then, accords with the supposition that, as soon as he came to the Empyrean, Dante enforced in the world of the Angels a distinction between contemplation and action, in other words between theology and the Empire. He who contemplates does not govern, he who governs does not contemplate. To each his beatitude. Now—let us note—the whole of this proof is an *a fortiori* argument, based on the supposition that what is already true of man must be even truer of the Angels. It is because, on earth, "humanity enjoys not merely one form of beatitude, but two, namely that of civil life and that of the contemplative life",[1] that it would be contrary to reason to think anything else of the Angels. Thus the two forms of beatitude are not merely distinct, they are mutually exclusive. Nowhere is the Dantesque breach of the classic relationship between the hierarchies of dignity and the hierarchies of authority more apparent than here, for Dante clearly affirms that the contemplative Intelligences are more divine and more beloved of God than the active Intelligences, but precisely because they are higher, they do not govern. Thus, and as an immediate consequence, the active Intelligences are not subject in their action to Intelligences whose contemplative beatitude, like that of the unblemished dove Theology, is too pure to condescend to disturb its repose by stooping to govern. It is typical of Dante to base the autonomy of an inferior order on its very inferiority in this way, and I would say that we shall encounter the same principle at work again when the question arises of assuring the independence of the Empire in relation to the Church, if this were not

---

[1] "Onde, con ciò sia cosa chè quella che e qui l'umana natura non pur una beatitudine abbia, ma due, sì come è quella della vita civile, e quella de la contemplativa . . ." (DANTE, *Convivio,* II, 4).

precisely the function that it had just discharged here before our eyes. In contrast to that of St. Thomas Aquinas, Dante's universe is of such a kind that the hierarchy of dignities never gives rise to any jurisdictional hierarchy within it, but rather to their mutual independence.

Dante has elaborated this cardinal point of his whole doctrine with such thoroughness that he has clearly discerned the most formidable objection by which its balance is threatened. It is, in fact, not enough, in order to make man seek and find happiness in the practice of the moral and political virtues, to say that the characteristically human beatitude is not that of the contemplative life. For after all, Aristotle has indeed taught that man finds his beatitude on earth in wisdom. Now, how can wisdom make man happy, if he is obliged to content himself with the active life precisely because he knows that knowledge in its loftiest form eludes his grasp? A practical felicity of this kind would strongly resemble a last resort—not so much beatitude as resignation. Dante has found an answer to the objection: "One may reply clearly to this by saying that in everything natural desire is proportioned to the capacity of the thing that desires; otherwise this desire would be divided against itself, which is impossible, and Nature would have created it in vain, which is equally impossible. It would be divided against itself since, desiring its perfection, it would desire its imperfection, in this respect at least, that it would desire to desire always without ever satisfying its desire. . . . And Nature would have created it in vain, since it would not be directed towards any goal. Therefore human desire is proportioned in this life to the knowledge which it is possible to acquire on earth and it only extends beyond that point in consequence of an error which is foreign to Nature's intention. . . . That is why, since it is naturally impossible for us to know the essential nature of God or of other such things, we naturally do not desire to know it. And this is the answer to the objection" (III, 15. Cf. IV, 13).

As may be seen, Dante dismisses the problem, so much debated to-day, of the "natural desire for God" in a manner as radical as it is unexpected. But let us not ascribe to him any such ambitious theological designs. Dante has simply been caught in an impasse from which it is absolutely essential for him to escape, and he escapes from it by the shortest route. The personal idea to which he desires to bring us back is that very one which animates the whole of the *Convivio*: philosophic reason suffices to give us the almost perfect beatitude to which our human nature is susceptible. Dante knows that it is not the supreme beatitude, but it is ours; it is therefore also that with which he occupies himself in this work. And so, following the logical line of his argument, which was to celebrate philosophy in the image of the merciful *donna gentile*, he began by placing ethics at the highest point of the scale of wisdom; but as soon as he remembered the superiority of contemplation to action, Dante felt that if man is to find complete happiness in the active life he must be delivered from the misfortune which the desire for a knowledge and a contemplative beatitude situated beyond his grasp would entail for him. He therefore simply and solely laid down that man should not desire to know on earth what he is in fact incapable of knowing there. Once cut off from every unrealizable contemplative ambition, man no longer desires to know anything save what he can know and, without any lurking thought, can enjoy the beatitude of action. So he is satisfied, and what is the satisfaction of every desire if not beatitude? The *donna gentile* whom God Himself has charged with ensuring our temporal happiness is therefore equal to her task, which it was required to prove.

VI. The Philosopher and the Emperor

In the Fourth Treatise of the *Banquet*, Dante approaches the supremely delicate problem of the origin, nature and extent of the Imperial authority. The problem that he here engages to discuss is therefore, in fact, the very one to which his *Monarchy* will be devoted. However, he does not yet approach it for its own sake, nor does he do so directly. The starting-point of his discussion is in fact the problem of nobility and of its true definition; but it happens that the Emperor Frederick II of Swabia, questioned as to the nature of nobility (*nobilitade* or *gentilezza*), has not been afraid to dismiss the question with the reply that nobility resides in the long standing of prosperity and in fine manners: *antica ricchezza e belli costumi* (IV, 3). At first sight this definition is wholly innocuous; but Dante thinks

otherwise, first of all because to the majority of men nobility is
even less: for them wealth is enough without manners—and
Aristotle teaches that the opinion of the greatest number cannot
be entirely wrong; then because we here find ourselves faced
with this extraordinary phenomenon: an Emperor who arrogates
to himself the authority of the philosopher. It is this second
point especially that is serious, for the Emperor is a very high
authority, but is he so in the matter of philosophy? That is the
question.

In order to elucidate it we must delve to the root of the
Imperial authority. Man is an animal which lives in society,
because his nature is such that, if he lived in isolation, he could
not meet his needs or attain his complete development. The
aim of political society is therefore to ensure the happiness of
men. Unfortunately, the human soul is such that it does not
know how to limit its desires. The man who possesses a certain
amount of land is eager to have more—hence the spreading of
war and strife from kingdom to kingdom, the seeds of disturb-
ances in cities, then in villages, later in families and finally among
individuals, whose happiness is thereby compromised. Accordingly, in order that this cause of disturbance may be eliminated,
it is necessary that there should be a single monarch, in other
words that one prince, one authority, should reign over the
whole earth. Since he possesses everything, this universal monarch
can desire nothing more; he will therefore be able to keep kings
within the frontiers of their kingdoms, in other words to ensure
peace between states, concord in towns, love in the bosom of
families and that satisfaction of his needs which confers on man
the happiness for which he has been born. In fact, wherever
there is a head, there is order; in a word, the command of the
Empire is the highest of all commands; the Emperor is he who
commands all those who command, prescribes their laws and,
being obeyed by all, confers on all other sovereignties vigour and
authority (IV, 4). Let the Emperor be elected in accordance with
the counsel of God, as God Himself once elected the people of
Rome to that office, and it will be clear to all that God is the
ultimate root of the Imperial authority. But who possesses the
philosophic authority? And what is its root?

The word "authority", says Dante, signifies "act of an author",
and the word "author" itself comes from the Greek root *autentin*,

which means "act of faith and obedience";[1] therefore Aristotle, whose words are so worthy of faith and obedience, is a man whose words possess a very high, a supreme authority. There follows the proof, which, to be sure, adds nothing to our knowledge of the Middle Ages, though its tone and gradations do not fail to provide some interest. In the first place, the actual terms of the thesis to be proved give forth an unwonted sound: *che Aristotile sia dignissimo di fede e d'obedienza*. That Aristotle was among philosophers the worthiest of faith very few in the Middle Ages would have disputed, but that we owe him obedience is an arbitrary rule far more rarely formulated. To tell the truth, if there are other instances of it before Dante, I have not come across them. Dante does not hesitate on this point: All human activities have one aim, consisting in human life, to which man is destined in so far as he is man; if there is a master and an expert capable of knowing and demonstrating what appertains to this aim, he is eminently entitled to our faith and our obedience. Now this master is Aristotle—*questi è Aristotile: dunque esso è dignissimo di fede e d'obedienza*. Dante's intention is therefore clear: Aristotle is a master who, by virtue of his learning, is a guide: *Aristotile è maestro e duca de la ragione umana, in quanto intende a la sua finale operazione*. Most certainly, there were other philosophers, e.g. Zeno, Cato, Epicurus, Socrates, Plato, Speusippus; but by reason "of the superior and almost divine genius that nature had implanted in Aristotle" it was he who brought ethics to its perfection: *la perfezione di questa moralitade per Aristotile terminata fue*. So we see that his disciples, the Peripatetics, to-day dominate the world of learning: *tiene questa gente oggi lo reggimento del mondo in dottrina per tutte parti, e puotesi appellare quasi cattolica oppinione*. From this it may be seen that Aristotle is the guide and leader of the human race towards its human goal.[2]

From such expressions it is easy to perceive the nature of

---

[1] Cf. ". . . auctor, quando αὐθέντην significat, commune est . . ." (PRISCIAN, *Institutionum Grammaticarum, lib. XVIII*, lib. V, 20; ed. M. Hertz, Leipzig, Teubner, 1855, Vol. I, p. 154). This etymology is also found in various grammarians, e.g. Pierre Hélie (twelfth century), in the *Doctrinale* of Alexandre de Villedieu and in the *Grecismus* of Evrard de Béthune (thirteenth century). See on this point C. THUROT, *Notices et extraits de divers manuscrits latins pour servir à l'histoire grammaticale du moyen âge*, Paris, 1868, p. 103, note 2. Cf. G. BUSNELLI and G. VANDELLI, *op. cit.*, p. 59, note 2.

[2] *Convivio*, IV, 6. Cf. "lo maestro de l'umana ragione . . .", IV, 2; "lo maestro de la nostra vita, Aristotile . . .", IV, 23.

Dante's Aristotle: the moralist who holds in the philosophical order the same rank as does the Emperor in the political order. The one, like the other, is alone in his rank. He is a monarch obeyed by numerous princes, and reigns with no superior over a clearly defined section of the human order. This is the very precise sense in which the great shade that holds sway in Limbo is entitled to the homage of all, even of Socrates and Plato, who are merely closer to him than the rest:

> Vidi il maestro di color che sanno
> seder tra filosofica famiglia.
> Tutti lo miran; tutti onor gli fanno.
> (*Inf.*, IV, 131–133.)

It is therefore not enough to say: To Dante, as to almost all the thinkers of his time, Aristotle is the highest philosophical authority: it is necessary, with him, to regard that authority as a right to the exercise of a command. God and nature have subjected ethics to Aristotle as they have the Empire to the Emperor.[1] The authority of this supreme philosopher is *piena di tutto vigore*, so much so that before reconciling the authority of the Emperor with that of the Pope, it is necessary to reconcile the authority of the Emperor with that of Aristotle. Happily, this is easy, for these two authorities stand in need of each other. Without the authority of the Philosopher that of the Emperor is in danger of aberration; without the authority of the Emperor that of the Philosopher is almost powerless. And let us take careful note of this "almost", for Dante is so afraid of letting it be thought that the powerlessness from which in fact philosophy was at the time suffering derogates in any way from the perfect autonomy of Aristotle's Empire that he immediately comments: *E' quasi debile, non per se, ma per la disordinanza de la gente.* Consequently, far from opposing each other, the authority of Aristotle and that of the Emperor should unite. Moreover, what do we

---

[1] Dante seems convinced that in many cases it would be possible to reduce the apparently divergent opinions of the philosophers to a certain unity, but as this unity would be obtained by making them coincide with the doctrine of Aristotle, the simplest course is to adopt the latter straight away. Thus, as a means to determine the origin of the hierarchy of souls we have at our disposal the various opinions of Pythagoras, Plato, Algazel and Avicenna, "and if each of them were there to defend his opinion, it would perhaps be seen that the truth is present in them all; but as, at first sight, they seem to diverge slightly from the truth, we must conform not to these opinions, but to that of Aristotle and the Peripatetics" (*Convivio*, IV, 21).

read in the *Book of Wisdom?* "Love the light of Wisdom, all ye
who hold sway over the peoples" (*Wisdom*, VI, 23)—in other
words, let the philosophical authority unite with the Imperial.
Unhappy are the kings of this age, and unhappier still their
subjects, when, for the government of their peoples, princes
do not draw their inspiration from Aristotle either by studying
his works or by following his counsel! And here is the motif:
I say unto you, King Charles and King Frederick, and unto you
other tyrants and princes, *meglio sarebbe a voi come rondine volare
basso, che come nibbio altissime rote fare sopra le cose vilissime.*[1]

Let us now picture what could and should have been Dante's
attitude towards an Aristotle whom he himself had dressed in
this supreme authority. Unless he openly contradicted himself,
Dante was debarred from according himself the right to dispute
a single one of Aristotle's theses in the field of philosophy, any
more than to dispute a single one of the Emperor's laws in the
field of politics. This, moreover, is what he himself suggests
again and again when he protests at one and the same time, in
the same sentence, his obedience to the Philosopher and to the
Emperor: *Per che io volendo, con tutta reverenza e a lo Principe e al
Filosofo portando . . .; nè contra l'imperiale maiestade nè contra lo
Filosofo si ragiona inreverentemente. . . . E prima mostrerò me non
presummere contra l'autorità del Filosofo; poi mostrerò me non presummere contra la maiestade imperiale.*[2] From this we see first of
what assistance the great poets—those visionaries of reality—may
be to history. We said without hesitation that the Middle Ages
are personified by the Pope and the Emperor; prompted by Dante,
let us say henceforth "by the Pope, the Emperor and Aristotle".
But that is not all, for this tripartite division of mediaeval reality
suggests a conclusion whose importance will soon become quite
evident—namely, that these three Monarchs represent three
principles of authority whose independence is complete in the
particular sphere in which each is supreme. To confine ourselves
to the case under discussion, it is clear that if a philosopher is not
entitled as such to exercise any authority in the political field,

---

[1] ". . . it were better for you to fly low like the swallows than, like the kite, to wheel
in the sky above what is most vile" (DANTE, *Convivio*, IV, 6).

[2] "That is why I wish, in all reverence towards both the Prince and the Philosopher
. . .; men do not talk disrespectfully about either the majesty of the Emperor or Philosophy. . . . And first I shall show that I do not defy the authority of the Philosopher,
then I shall show that I do not defy the majesty of the Emperor" (DANTE, *Convivio*,
IV, 8).

the Emperor is not entitled as such to exercise any philosophical authority. The authority of the Emperor affects everything that ensures the perfection of human life; it therefore extends to every branch of our *voluntary activities*; it governs them through the law and controls them so completely that it may be said of him that he is "the rider of the human will";[1] but this authority cannot go outside its own sphere in order to govern philosophy, by which it should, on the contrary, govern its own policy. On that point Dante is as firm as may be desired: *Per tanto oltre quanto le nostre operazioni si stendono, tanto la maiestade imperiale ha giurisdizione, e fuori di quelli termini non si sciampia.*[2] All those activities which, because they depend on the human will, may be good or bad, just or unjust, and which are defined and prescribed by the written law, are therefore subject to the authority of the Emperor; it is he who determines that formulated reason which is the law and ensures respect for it, but he has no say outside the clearly defined sphere within which his jurisdiction is exercised: *A questa |ragione scritta] scrivere, mostrare e comandare, è questo officiale posto di cui si parla, cioè lo Imperadore, al quale tanto quanto le nostre operazioni proprie . . . si stendono, siamo subietti; e più oltre no.*[3]

It follows, then, from the passages that have just been analysed (1) that the *Convivio* does not propound the problem of the re-lationship between Pope and Emperor; (2) that it propounds, in a general way, the problem of the justification of *authority*; (3) that the forms of authority whose justification it examines are two in number: Aristotle's and the Emperor's; (4) that the justification of the Imperial authority is in God, Whose boundless wisdom has entrusted the Empire to the Roman Emperor; (5) that the justification of Aristotle's authority comes from the fact, recognized by all scholars, that he is the only person to have indicated the true goal of human life, which the other sages have sought in vain; (6) that each of these two forms of authority is unique and sovereign in its own sphere: Aristotle's in Philo-sophy, the Emperor's in the political life of the peoples; (7) that

---

[1] DANTE, *Convivio*, IV, 9.

[2] "As far as our activities extend, thus far extends the jurisdiction of the Emperor's majesty, and it does not extend beyond these limits."

[3] "It is with a view to the formulation of this written law, its promulgation and its enactment that this dignitary of whom I speak is installed—namely the Emperor, to whom, as far as our individual activities extend . . ., we are subject; but farther than that we are not" (DANTE, *Convivio*, IV, 9).

neither of these forms of authority is competent outside its own sphere; (8) that nevertheless, far from obstructing each other, they need each other, Philosophy needing the Empire in order that it may modify manners effectively, the Empire needing Philosophy in order that it may know how to modify manners in accordance with truth and justice.

If this summary is accurate, it cannot be said that the *Convivio* has examined for their own sake the relations of Church and Empire, but it should be said that it has determined in advance the doctrine which the *De Monarchia* was to expound on this subject. Unless he repudiated his own principles, Dante now was no longer free to say anything but what he was going to say, so much so that we may regard it as practically certain that the author of the *Banquet* already believed what the author of the *De Monarchia* was to write. Indeed, if we arrange the elements which constitute the thesis of the *Banquet*, the thesis of the *De Monarchia* seems to occupy automatically the empty place whose outline the dialectic of the *Banquet* has already traced. There are two authorities, Aristotle and the Emperor, radically distinct in their functions, radically independent but closely associated for the purpose of leading the peoples to the natural goal of man. Nowhere does the *Convivio* say or suggest that either of these two authorities is not fully independent in its own sphere. On the contrary, everything in it excludes such a hypothesis. The reason owes fidelity and obedience to Aristotle only in Philosophy, but, in this sphere, in which he is supreme, it owes them only to him—the *sommo Filosofo*. The will owes fidelity and obedience to the Emperor only in the political sphere, but, in this sphere, the Emperor—that "rider of the human will"—is totally independent.[1] Above each, in his respective sphere, there is only God, the supreme Emperor, Whose daughter is Philosophy, directly subject to His power, as the Pope and the Emperor are subject to it, sovereign though each and all are in their own province.[2]

Thus, there is nothing which authorizes us to suppose that the author of the *Banquet* thought for a single moment of subordinating the Philosopher and the Emperor to another ruler who,

---

[1] "Sì che quasi dire si può de lo Imperadore, volendo lo suo officio figurare con una imagine, che elli sia lo cavalcatore de la umana volontade" (DANTE, *Convivio*, IV, 9).

[2] With regard to the theory of the Empire in *Convivio*, IV, consult F. ERCOLE, *Il pensiero politico di Dante*, Vol. II, pp. 303–310.

deriving his authority from God, would control and restrict their own. On the contrary, in that work Dante strongly insists on this fact, that God, Who has imposed a limit on His own power, has imposed on the human will the limit which the Emperor prescribes to it: *Sì come ciascuna arte e officio umano da lo imperiale è a certi termini limitato, così questo da Dio a certo termine è finito.* As to this authority which God has relinquished to the Emperor's advantage, how can we suppose that He wishes to regain possession of it through the agency of the Pope? Since God, Who has subjected the realm of nature to laws, has chosen, by inserting within it the realm of the human will, to subject that will to the Emperor, He has certainly not meant that it should afterwards be taken over by someone else, even in His name: *Dunque la giurisdizione de la natura universale è a certo termine finita, e per consequente la particulare; e anche di costei è limitatore Colui che da nullo è limitato, cioè la prima bontade, che è Dio, che solo con la infinita capacitade infinito comprende.*[1]

If we ask ourselves how far the immediate jurisdiction of the Pope extends in this composition, the positive elements are lacking for the formulation of a confident reply. All that we know amounts to this: *Quello che è di Dio sia renduto a Dio.*[2] Yet although Dante does not explicitly fix the bounds of the Pontifical authority,

---

[1] "Just as every art and every human function is seen to be restricted within fixed limits by those of the Emperor, so those of the Emperor are restricted by God within a fixed limit. . . . Therefore the jurisdiction of universal nature is restricted within a fixed limit, and in consequence this particular jurisdiction is likewise so restricted; and it too is restricted by Him Who knows no restriction, namely the first Goodness, which is God, Who alone understands the infinite through His infinite comprehension" (DANTE, *Convivio*, IV, 9). The Emperor therefore has no authority over theology, the sciences or handicrafts, for although it depends on our will whether we apply ourselves to them or not, their actual make-up is independent of our will. We cannot make bodies rise naturally in defiance of the force of gravity, nor can we make a syllogism whose premises are false yield a true conclusion. On the contrary, it depends on us "whether we help others or harm them, whether we stand fast or shun combat, whether we are chaste or lewd, and all these activities are subject to our will; it is therefore they which determine whether we are called good or culpable, because they are peculiarly and wholly ours, since the potential range of our will constitutes the range of our activities. Now, as in all these voluntary activities there is a certain equity to be preserved and a certain iniquity to be shunned, and as that equity may be lost for two reasons, either because we do not know in what it consists, or because we do not wish to conform to it, man has invented the written Law (*ragione scritta*), with the object both of promulgating it and of compelling its observance" (DANTE, *Convivio*, IV, 9). No mention is here made of the possible rôle of grace, because grace comes to the aid of ethics in order to promote supernatural felicity, and for no other reason. The written law, formulated, promulgated and enforced by the Emperor, comes to the aid of ethics in order to promote the natural felicity of the political animal that is man, and for no other reason.

[2] "Let what is God's be rendered unto God" (DANTE, *Convivio*, IV, 9). Cf. *Matt.*, XXII, 21.

we know that there are two domains to which it does not extend. And we know it with complete certainty, because the supreme authority in these domains has already been entrusted by God to others than the Sovereign Pontiff. I refer to the domain of natural reason, which He has subjected to Aristotle, and to that of the human will, which He has subjected to the Emperor. Now taken together, Philosophy and the Empire govern the entirety of human life in the realm of nature, and against them there is no appeal. Within this sphere nothing evades their suzerainty, since Aristotle shows men what is their natural aim, while the Emperor subjects their wills to it. Once the principles which the *Banquet* propounds have been admitted, *there remains no element of the natural life of man over which the Pope can claim any authority*. After writing this work, Dante could no longer help confining the authority of the Pope within the realm of the supernatural life or declaring it invalid. Not for a single moment did he envisage the second reply; it is hard to see how he can have written the *Trattato Quarto* of the *Banquet* without thinking of the first one, for all that he there says makes this reply inevitable and seems to be elicited by it as by one of those final causes which operate without revealing themselves.

It is commonly admitted that the *Banquet* was drafted between 1300 and 1308. The four Treatises to which it is limited represent only a little more than a quarter of the work which Dante had conceived, since he intended to speak of justice in the Fourteenth Treatise, which was to be the last but one of his book. We therefore cannot know if he proposed to speak of the spiritual power in one of the subsequent books, and it is even dangerous to attempt to expound a "philosophy of Dante" on the evidence of a work that is so far from being complete. At least it may be said with certainty that it supposes a clearly defined idea of the nature of philosophical knowledge in general. Wisdom is presented throughout as a possession of natural man using his natural resources, and the whole treatise seems to turn upon the following fundamental ideas: The natural aim of man is the happiness which he can secure on earth through the exercise of the moral and political virtues as defined by Aristotle in the *Ethica ad Nicomachum*. Therefore, if it is a question of knowing what these virtues are and how man must live in order to be happy, it is Aristotle who possesses the supreme authority to decide. But men's wickedness is such that they will not live in accordance with virtue unless they are obliged to do so. If it is a question of knowing what laws must govern the peoples in order that ethics may command their respect, and who has the authority necessary to impose on all human wills a respect for justice, it is to the Emperor that we should turn. As to metaphysics, although it may give us a foretaste of contemplative beatitude, it cannot fully achieve its end in this life. Although higher and more perfect in itself, the felicity that it gives is less complete. Only theology can finally lead us to perfect contemplative beatitude, but it cannot do so in this life. This is also the reason why, holding as it already does undivided sway in the Empyrean of souls, the truth of this science is not of this world. Only in the next will it lead us to that vision of God face to face of which it is the instrument.

VII. The Spirit of the *Banquet*

The general position taken up by Dante in the *Banquet* is therefore composed of ·multiple elements, all of them traditional, though he has modified and improved them with the object of balancing them in a manner that is his alone.

That is why all efforts to classify his doctrine by identifying it with any one of the attitudes already known to and described by historians was destined inevitably to end in failure. Scholars have referred to the "rationalism" of Dante in the *Banquet*, but, as Signor Michele Barbi has justly pointed out, this is a label whose exact signification can never be known.[1] Thus, reference is made to the "Christian rationalism" of St. Anselm, but it is equally easy to demonstrate that, if his rationalism is Christian, it is not a form of rationalism, or that, if it really is a form of rationalism, it cannot be Christian. It has also been said that Dante, reversing the Anselmian formula *credo ut intelligam* ("I believe that I may understand"), had replaced it with *intelligo ut credam* ("I understand that I may believe").[2] We should thus have an Anselmian Beatrice and a rationalist *donna gentile*. This

[1] M. Barbi, *Razionalismo e misticismo in Dante,* pp. 20–21.
[2] *Vita Nuova,* with a commentary by T. Casini; 3rd ed., revised by L. Pietrobono, pp. 149–150.

is a picturesque contrast; but is it a historical fact? Not only—
and none disputes the fact—has Dante never referred to a formula
intelligo ut credam, but he has definitely affirmed that, if he
believes, he does so precisely where he does not quite succeed
in understanding. It is not because he perceives the immortality
of the soul perfectly clearly that he believes in it; he believes in
it, on the contrary, because he does not perceive it perfectly
clearly. Let us, for example, refer to the famous passage in the
Banquet, Treatise IV, 21, where Dante confronts himself with the
intricate problem of the origin of the soul—a problem to which
St. Augustine, who never ceased to ponder it all his life, finally
confessed that he did not know the solution: *Nec tunc sciebam, nec
adhuc scio.* ("I did not know then, nor do I know even yet").[1]
What does Dante think? He too thinks that he knows nothing.
That is precisely the reason why we find him announcing that
he will first proceed *per modo naturale, e poi per modo teologico,
cioè divino e spirituale.* Taking the first point of view, that of
natural knowledge, we discover a variety of opinions regarding
the origin of the soul; probably they are reconcilable; but why give
oneself the trouble of reconciling them, since we have only to
follow Aristotle? So here we have him following Aristotle, that
is to say what he takes to be Aristotle's doctrine, after which he
observes: "Let no man be astonished if the manner in which I
speak seems hard to understand; for I myself think it astonishing
that one should be able to see and to infer the existence of a
creation of this kind through the intellect . . ."[2] Whereupon,
passing a little farther along the theological road, Dante confines
himself strictly to considerations of a supernatural order, none
of which, whether viewed closely or from a distance, could be
justified by the resources of reason. Dante's attitude in the
Banquet is therefore not a form of rationalism which, supposing

---

[1] St. Augustine, *Retractationes,* lib. I, cap. 1, no. 3; Pat. lat., Vol. 32, col. 687.

[2] Dante, *Convivio,* IV, 21. There is in Dante's eyes a twofold difficulty: that of speaking
of these things in the vulgar tongue, and that of speaking of a subject which is so difficult in itself. The only thing in this passage that we are bearing in mind at this point
is the observation regarding the inadequacy of philosophy in such a matter, a sentiment that is so well expressed by its conclusion: "E quasi questo è tutto ciò che per via
naturale dicere si puote." With regard to the problem, which does not arise directly
from our study, of whether Dante faithfully follows St. Thomas (*Cont. Gent.,* II, 89)
on the question of the infusion of the soul, or whether he rather draws his inspiration
from another doctrine, the reader should refer to the commentary of Busnelli and
Vandelli, in their edition of the *Convivio, ad loc.,* and the objections of Bruno Nardi in
Note critiche di filosofia dantesca, Florence, L. S. Olschki, 1938–XVI, pp. 15–28.

that the formula has a meaning, bases faith on reason; not only does he admit that reason has its limits, but he distinguishes them never more clearly than when dealing with the numerous questions in the case of which they are shown to him by the Christian Revelation. In order to find room for reason in a ready-made classification we must therefore turn elsewhere.

Why should we not try to identify his position with that of Thomism? Certain scholars have not failed to do so, but the point is not an easy one to make. The distinction between the two forms of beatitude understood according to the explanation of Dante himself absolutely forbids such an identification. Nothing, I think, could be clearer than this point will be when we come to the *Monarchy*, but it is already sufficiently so in the *Banquet*. If we consider only the hierarchy of dignity which Dante accepts as existing among the three forms of beatitude— active life, contemplative life, beatific vision—his accord with St. Thomas is virtually perfect; but we have already pointed out that, in St. Thomas, a hierarchy of dignity is at the same time invariably a hierarchy of jurisdiction, whereas, except when God is involved, Dante never regards a hierarchy of dignity as a hierarchy of jurisdiction. Thus, to him, philosophic certainty is assuredly less complete than that of theology, but these are kinds of certainty existing in different spheres and prescribed for different ends. This is why Dante subjects philosophy to the authority of Aristotle without accepting any limit to that authority. If he makes use of St. Thomas so readily, even in matters of philosophy, it is because he is absolutely convinced that in matters of philosophy St. Thomas, like himself, is just a perfect and always submissive disciple of Aristotle. Where, on the contrary, he catches St. Thomas in the act of contradicting Aristotle *in matters of philosophy*, Dante gives him the slip and follows Aristotle faithfully. That is precisely what he does as regards the different forms of beatitude. In Dante's eyes, the human felicity which man may obtain in this life through the exercise of the political virtues is an end in itself, completely distinct from that higher end which is heavenly beatitude and which is accessible through means completely distinct from those which may lead to the felicity of the next world. Completely distinct from each other, these two categories are therefore no less completely independent. In short, Dante's ethic has in view an end as distinct from that of the supernatural ethic, and pursues it by means as completely alien from those of the Christian religion as are the end and the means of Aristotle's ethic from those of the Gospel. Moreover, this fundamental opposition between Dante and St. Thomas paves the way for their no less fundamental opposition with regard to the relations between Church and Empire. Hence, according as we probe into one or the other of these two doctrines, we enter two different worlds, not that the elements of which they are made up are not the same, but because, according as they go to the making of one or the other of these two worlds, they do not obey the same laws.[1]

Such, moreover, is the fundamental reason why it will always be fruitless to classify Dante not merely in terms of some previously defined idea, but even in terms of the authorities which he invokes, cites and follows. Distinction between the orders is indeed carried so far in his work that, from the fact that he regards an author as the authority *par excellence* as regards a certain order, we may conclude with certainty that he will not be so as regards the remainder as well. If it is a question of classifying the heavens, the problem is one of astronomy; Dante will therefore follow Ptolemy, who is the competent authority in the matter; but the authority of Ptolemy becomes invalid in the Crystalline, where astronomy ends and theology begins. Consequently, having reached this point we shall have to describe the supernatural heaven *secondo che la Santa Chiesa vuole, che non può dire menzogna* (II, 3), for if the question is one of the supernatural, it is no longer science that is competent to discuss it, but Revelation.

---

[1] F. ERCOLE (*Il pensiero politico di Dante*, Vol. II, pp. 299–300), contradicting B. Nardi, denies that Dante professed a rationalism bent on invading the domain of theology itself. I think that he is right, but that he exaggerates in the opposite direction when he defines the spirit of the *Banquet* as "purely Thomistic" (*op. cit.*, p. 300, note 3). Similarly, L. Pietrobono seems to me to be right, if not in all his assumptions, at all events in principle, when he contradicts Michele Barbi (*Razionalismo e misticismo in Dante*, p. 30), according to whom, while "St. Thomas entirely subordinates the present life to the future life, Dante wishes to endow the earthly life with an end of its own, although he too regards it as *quodammodo* subordinate to the heavenly life. In principle they are less widely separated than it appears". In fact, Dante has used this *quodammodo* only in *Monarchia*, III, *sub. fin.*, in a passage to which we shall return later on (Chapter III). Furthermore, even there Dante has spoken not of subordination but of destination ("quum mortalis ista felicitas quodammodo ad immortalem felicitatem ordinetur"). Here, as elsewhere, Dante has in view a hierarchy of orders that entails no kind of subordination.

More than this, Dante does not like to contradict Aristotle in the matter of philosophy and I know of no instance in which he has done so with full knowledge of the case, but he has no scruples at all about contradicting him in the matter of astronomy, because if Aristotle is the Philosopher, the Astronomer is Ptolemy. Moreover, that is what Aristotle himself did, for he recognized, in Book XII of his *Metaphysics*, "that he had simply followed the opinion of another where he had had to speak of astronomy" (II, 3). If, on the contrary, it is a question of the number of the independent Intelligences, philosophers and theologians are not in agreement, but it is certainly the theologians who are right, because in these matters the philosophers are no more than partially competent. The Ancients erred on this point, with which natural reason declares itself incapable of dealing, *per difetto d'ammaestramento*—for want of instruction by the proper authority. The Jewish people were better informed in the matter. Because Angels were involved, and because on that subject their Prophets were capable of enlightening them at least in part, Israel was *in parte da li suoi profeti ammaestrato*. As for us, as Christians we are in this matter the pupils of Christ, sons of the Emperor of the world, Who is God: *Noi semo di ciò ammaestrati da colui che venne da quello, da colui che le fece, da colui che le conserva, cioè de lo Imperadore de l'Universo, che è Cristo* (II, 5). He Who created the Angels and preserves them probably knows how many of them there are. Now it is He Who instructs us as to their number; consequently, we are completely enlightened on this subject.

This constant need of an *ammaestramento* received each time from the most competent authority is one of the most characteristic traits of Dante's thought. It is this same trait which will later imbue him with the desire to provide himself with guides and will advise him in the remarkably judicious choice of them that he will make: Virgil as far as the Earthly Paradise, then Beatrice, finally St. Bernard of Clairvaux. For each separate order, a separate competency; for each separate competency, a separate authority. In Limbo the philosophers spontaneously group themselves around Aristotle even as the poets do honour to Virgil; St. Thomas Aquinas presides over speculative theology as St. Bonaventure does over affective theology, each in his turn speaking as a master where he really is the master and exercising

authority where he really has authority. And where, it will be
said, are those who wish to exercise it where they do not have it?
They are in Hell. And it may indeed be said that they alone
have put themselves there by their violation of the holy law of
divine Justice which is not only the supreme creator of the
constitutive orders of nature and supernature, but also the
inexorable protector of the authorities which it has wisely
placed at their head. There is no greater crime than to betray
the divine order, and it is betraying it to refuse to follow Aristotle
in the matter of philosophy, because philosophy is the daughter
of God and it was God Himself Who desired that it should be
taught to us by Aristotle. But it is no less a crime for a Franciscan
to betray St. Francis, for a Dominican to betray St. Dominic,
for a subject to betray the Emperor, for a Christian to betray the
Gospel, and the worst crime of all, the one which in this world
gives rise to disorders, abuses, wars and miseries without number,
is to betray all forms of authority at once through a desire to
install one of them, which is competent in its sphere, in the
place of those which are equally so in theirs, for each form of
authority is master in its own house and even the humblest of
all is directly responsible to God alone.

Hence the indignation that we have witnessed when Dante
came to define *gentilezza*, that is to say, practically, personal
nobility. For this is a philosophical question, and yet here we
have Frederick of Swabia taking a hand in its solution. The
Emperor wishes to legislate in matters of philosophy! An
extremely grave difficulty, and the very prototype of what may
be called the *Aporia Dantesca*, because it expresses a conflict
between different forms of jurisdiction and authority. Here, the
whole question turns upon this point: *l'autoritade de la diffinizione
de lo imperadore* (IV, 3). Once the question has been propounded,
Dante cannot but settle it completely: origin of human society,
its nature, its aim; origin of the Empire, nature of the Empire,
aim of the Empire—until at last the conclusion leaps to the eye:
The philosophical authority of the Emperor, *qua* Emperor, is
non-existent. Aristotle is the Emperor in matters of philosophy,
and if the masters of this world submitted as completely as they
should to his authority, their government of the Empire would
only be the better for it! "It is therefore manifest that to define
gentilezza is not a function of the art of governing the Empire;

if that is not one of its functions, we are not subject to the Emperor when we discuss this question; if we are not subject to him, we do not owe him any consideration in the matter. This is what I intended to prove." Whereupon Dante declares war on the Emperor: "That is why henceforth we must, with a complete lack of inhibition and complete mental freedom, fly in the face of the accepted opinions, casting this one aside, in order that, thanks to my victory, the rightful opinion may prevail in the minds of those in whom this light shines with some strength" (IV, 9).

If we re-read the *Banquet* from beginning to end, we shall have many an opportunity to notice this attitude and, so far as I know at any rate, we shall find nothing which contradicts it. Here, then, is the necessary starting-point for a correct appreciation of Dante's position with regard to these questions. Is it an Averroistic position? Not if by Averroism we mean the position of Averroes himself, who regards philosophical learning as the prototype of perfect knowledge, to which faith only bears a useful but crude resemblance. Nothing was likely to be more repugnant to Dante's mind than such a confusion of forms of jurisdiction, which would make Beatrice his guide through Hell and the Earthly Paradise, where she would be relieved by Aristotle, relieved in his turn by the Prophet on the summit of Paradise.[1] Not only did Dante never claim that theology is subordinate to philosophy, but we may say that such a thesis is the negation of his whole doctrine, or that his whole doctrine is the radical negation of such a thesis, as we prefer.

If the author of the *Banquet* is not an Averroist after the fashion of Averroes, is he one after the fashion of the Latin disciples of Averroes—Siger of Brabant and Boethius of Dacia, for instance? To give weight to such a theory, we should have to be able to cite one or more cases in which Dante has maintained in opposition two contradictory theses, the one propounded as being necessary for the satisfaction of reason, the other as being consonant with the demands of faith. So far as I know, the *Banquet* does not furnish a single case of this kind, and I do not believe that he who looks for one there has the slightest

---

[1] Regarding the place of the Prophet in the doctrine of Averroes, see L. GAUTHIER, *Accord de la religion et de la philosophie. Traité d'Ibn Rochd (Averroès) traduit et annoté* Algiers, P. Fontana, 1905, pp. 48–49.

chance of finding it. But he will find many an example of the contrary case, in which Dante expresses his joy at establishing a perfect accord between philosophy and theology, between reason and faith. We have quoted the majority of these passages. But there remains at least one, and it is not the least fine. The envoy of the *Canzone Terza* which precedes the Fourth Treatise of the *Banquet* begins with the line *Contra-li-erranti mia, tu te n'andrai*, which it would not be wholly inaccurate to translate: "Go, my *Contra Gentiles*." As Dante himself says in his commentary on this line, "this *Contra-li-erranti* forms but a single word, and it is the name of this *Canzone*—a name suggested by the example of the good friar Thomas Aquinas, who bestowed on the book he wrote in order to confound all who deviate from our faith the title of *Contra li Gentili*". Why this title? Dante then asks himself. Because, he answers, just when the good work-man is on the point of taking leave of his work he touches it up and embellishes it to the best of his powers in order that it may leave his hands more glorious and more precious. *Contra-li-erranti*, like *Contra li Gentili*, is the most beautiful title that Dante could find. The man who wrote those lines certainly never admitted the existence of any cleavage between his reason and his faith.

We should be reduced by this to accepting the hypothesis of a Thomistic Dante if the philosophical doctrines expounded in the *Banquet*, which are certainly reconcilable with those of St. Thomas Aquinas, did not so often testify to the presence of other influences,[1] like, for example, that of the *De Intellectu* of Albertus Magnus (III, 7), and above all if, even where he is in complete

---

[1] The influence of Albertus Magnus on Dante has often been noticed (PAGET TOYNBEE, *Some Obligations of Dante to Albertus Magnus*, in *Dante Studies and Researches*, Methuen, London, 1902, pp. 38–55; BRUNO NARDI, *Raffronti fra alcuni luoghi di Alberto Magno e di Dante*, in *Studi di filosofia dantesca*, p. 69). For his part, E. Krebs connects Dante in this matter with the Dominican group of Albertus Magnus, Ulrich of Strasburg, Dietrich of Vrieberg and Berchthold of Mosburg, in *Scritti vari . . . in occasione del sesto centenario della morte di Dante Alighieri*, Milan, 1921: *Contributo della Scolastica alla relazione di alcuni problemi danteschi*, pp. 86–90.

I do not believe that Dante adhered to any definite philosophical school, nor even that he distinguished such schools with the rigour with which we strive to approach these studies. To follow Albertus Magnus on any point undoubtedly did not signify to him parting company with St. Thomas. As Signor Bruno Nardi has rightly said, "egli [*sc.* l'Alighieri] non è averroista e neppure tomista; non esclusivamente aristotelico, nè soltanto neoplatonico, o agostiniano puro" (B. NARDI, *Sigieri di Brabante nella Divina Commedia e le Fonti della Filosofia di Dante*, from the *Rivista di Filosofia Neo-Scolastica* (April and October, 1911, February and April, 1912), published by the Author, Spianate (Pescia), 1912, p. 69). Cf. M. BAUMGARTNER, *Dantes Stellung zur Philosophie*, p. 71.

accord with him, Dante did not differ from St. Thomas by virtue of a most important peculiarity. We have solid reasons for believing that after the death of Beatrice the author of the *Banquet* went through a crisis of philosophism; and when we began these analyses we wondered if he was still involved in that crisis at the period at which he wrote the work, or if he had emerged from it without preserving the marks of it, or—a third hypothesis—if he had emerged from it, but in such a way that the *Banquet* retained visible traces of it. To the first of these questions we may reply with certainty that if Dante really experienced a crisis of pure philosophism, that crisis was over when he wrote the *Banquet*. Theology pervades this work, like an Empyrean that envelops the world and, if it does not move it, nevertheless sheds its supernatural light over it. The *Banquet* is hallowed from its outset by the memory of a heavenly Beatrice who, although she is not yet what she will become in the *Divine Comedy*, is none the less already one of the blessed and, to Dante himself, a summons from the next world.

To the second of these questions the reply should likewise be in the negative, for if Dante has recovered a sense of theological and supernatural exigencies, he seems in the *Banquet* to profess not a philosophical rationalism directed against theology, but a doctrine of the autonomy and the adequacy of the aims of philosophy viewed in its proper setting—a doctrine which, if he really did pass through a crisis of philosophism, may be regarded as the lasting imprint with which this crisis marked his thought.[1] If it is true that, while affirming the transcendency of theology, while allowing himself to be deeply imbued with the Christian spirit and even while stressing time and again the perfect accord between his philosophy and his faith,[2] Dante

---

[1] Such is our interpretation of the *scuola* of *Purg.*, XXXIII, 85. It is, of course, a hypothesis, but I see none that is more immediately suggested by the letter of the text. It has been supposed that here Beatrice is, on the contrary, reproaching Dante for having once followed the Guelfist and Curialist school, according to which the Empire, the instrument of *jus humanum*, is not derived from God, but from sin. See PARODI, *L'albero dell'Impero*, in *Poesia e storia nella Divina Commedia*, Milan, Perrella, 1921, p. 257 *et seq.*, summarized and in principle approved by F. ERCOLE, *Il pensiero politico di Dante*, Vol. II, pp. 295–296. This Guelfist phase in Dante's thought seems to me purely hypothetical, whereas Dante's moral and political secularism is a fact.

[2] See with regard to this point the passages which Signor MICHELE BARBI has done a service in collecting (*Razionalismo e misticismo in Dante*, in *Studi Danteschi*, Vol. XXI (1937), pp. 6–9). We may, moreover, concede to the same interpreter that Dante's philosophy is at once human "and Christian" (p. 11), for it would certainly not be what it is if its author had not been a Christian philosopher; but it is a philosophy that

carried the Thomistic distinction between theology and philosophy
to the point of separation in order to pave the way for a second
distinction—between the Priesthood and the Empire—it becomes
extremely difficult to qualify his position with the epithet
"Thomistic". Clearly, in this field Dante is engaged in a wholly
personal enterprise, and there is nothing in the work of St.
Thomas that can have suggested it to him. We may even wonder
if Dante's readiness to concede to the theologians the whole
essence of their theology and to leave them in peace with the
philosophy which they claimed to be the true one does not betray
the secret hope that, once assured of possessing what they had
set their hearts on, theologians and philosophers would more
readily consent to withdraw to their respective domains. When
one has all that one wished to have, what more can one desire?

It will perhaps be objected that it was quite futile to claim for
philosophy an independence of which it was to make no use.
But that is equivalent to returning once more to the position of
a professional theologian or philosopher. When an Averroist
proclaims the independence of philosophy, he does so in order to
protect his own against a theology with which he knows it to
be at variance. When a theologian declares that theology "treats
the other sciences as inferiors and servants", the truth is that he
is according theology the right to control the other sciences and
to regard as false everything about them that contradicts it.[1]
Having asserted once and for all that philosophy and theology
are in harmony, Dante has neither a personal philosophy to
protect nor a personal theology to defend, but he needs to ensure
the independence of philosophy if he is to ensure that of the
Empire. Now Dante clearly saw—and we may say that the
certainty of the fact never ceased to haunt him—that these three
forms of independence are inextricably linked and that the
existence of each is bound up with that of the other two. The
purity of each of the orders involved is therefore the necessary
condition both of their common independence and of their

---

requires to be autonomous in its end as in its means, because the Christian God wills
it so. A philosophy that is separate because it is Christian is certainly not the usual type
of Christian philosophy.

[1] Cf. St. Thomas Aquinas, *Sum. theol.*, Pars I, qu. 1, art. 5, ad 2m: "Non enim accipit
[sacra doctrina] sua principia ab aliis scientiis, sed immediate a Deo per revelationem.
Et ideo non accipit ab aliis scientiis tanquam a superioribus, sed utitur eis tanquam
inferioribus et ancillis: sicut architectonicae utuntur administrantibus ut civilis militari."

individual adequacy. His personal discovery of the merciful *donna gentile* and the profound sense of gratitude which he harbours towards her for having saved him from despair certainly lie at the root of the *Banquet*, but if he is there defending a personal thesis, it is that of the adequacy of philosophy to confer beatitude on men. The temporal happiness of the individual through human wisdom—this, then, is the lesson that the *Banquet* teaches. The temporal salvation of humanity through the Empire—such will be the conclusion of the *Monarchy*. The eternal salvation of men through the Church—this will be the ultimate teaching of the *Divine Comedy*. But since this threefold work is knit together in all its parts, Dante was never able to uphold one of these theses without preparing, formulating or even defending the other two. That is why, just as we have seen him vindicate the claims of the Empire and maintain the transcendency of theology in the *Banquet,* we shall now see him affirm the autonomy of philosophy and that of theology in the *Monarchy*, pending the supreme appeal to the *Veltro* launched in the *Divine Comedy* and the solemn beatification of the pure philosopher in the person of Siger of Brabant.

III

Philosophy in the *Monarchy*

WHATEVER his reason for interrupting his work, the author of the *Banquet* was certainly not sustained by the lasting philosophic enthusiasm which alone would have led him to finish it. The author of the *De Monarchia*, of which the exact date is unknown,[1] though it is certainly later than the *Banquet*, was sustained to the last by his solemn passion for the Empire, the sole guarantee that he could imagine of justice, peace and felicity for the whole of mankind. The importance of the work which this passion inspired in Dante is quite different from that which would have probably been attached to the work that he left unfinished, even in its complete form. He himself was conscious of this, and a simple observation of the difference in tone at the beginning of the two treatises leaves no doubt on the matter.[2]

[1] With regard to the probable date of the treatise see C. FOLIGNO, *The Date of the "De Monarchia,"* in *Dante. Essays in Commemoration*, London, University Press, 1921. The author decides in favour of the approximate date of 1313 (*op. cit.*, p. 150). But many other dates have been suggested. Witte puts it before 1300; Steiner between 1300 and 1303; Traversi as late as 1306; others, reverting to Boccaccio's belief, link its composition with the descent of Henry VII, and consequently with the year 1313 or thereabouts. The most recent study on this question is that of E. J. J. KOCKEN, *Ter Dateering van Dante's Monarchia*, included among the publications of the *Instituut voor Middeleeuwische Geschiedenis der Keizer Karel Universiteit te Nijmegen*, No. 1, 1927.

[2] With regard to the general lines of the doctrine contained in the treatise and the current controversies on the matter see specially F. ERCOLE, *Sulla filosofia politica di Dante* and *Le tre fasi del pensiero politico di Dante*, in *Il pensiero politico di Dante*, Vol. II, pp. 231–407; there is a copious bibliography in Vol. I, pp. 38–40. For an examination of these disquisitions see B. NARDI, *Il concetto dell'Impero nello svolgimento del pensiero dantesco*, and *Tre pretese fasi del pensiero politico di Dante*, in *Saggi di filosofia dantesca*, pp. 241–305 and pp. 309–345. I am in full agreement with the dualistic interpretation offered by Signor B. Nardi. It seems to me only necessary to define a little more accurately what is called the "Averroism" of Dante; here it remains to make some distinctions. In addition, it is regrettable that such an excellent historian had allowed himself to be induced by Signor G. Gentile to make some hazardous generalizations. Where does it become evident to him that the audacity of the *De Monarchia* cuts across the mediaeval plan of the *Divine Comedy* (*op. cit.*, p. 285)? If one of these plans is mediaeval, so is the other, for they are the same. In the eyes of Signor B. Nardi they are different because, as G. Gentile had written in a seemingly admirable formula, "the Virgil of the *Monarchy* does not expect any Beatrice" (*op. cit.*, p. 304). How should he do so, seeing that there is no Virgil in the *Monarchy*? Besides, even in the *Comedy*, it is not Virgil who expects Beatrice, but Dante. Such a formula is literally devoid of meaning. It is true that

Nothing remains in the *Monarchy* of the timidities, characteristic of the apprentice philosopher and almost of the amateur, that find expression at the commencement of the *Banquet*. Here Dante no longer presents himself as the poor man sitting at the feet of the princes of wisdom to gather the crumbs that fall from their table. This time he speaks as a creator who knows himself to be such: "I desire to bear fruit and to show forth truths yet unessayed by others." What would be the good of once more proving some theorem of Euclid? Who would want to waste his time in rediscovering the nature of happiness, which Aristotle has already discovered, or in vindicating old age, which Cicero has so well defended? Nothing can result from that but tediousness. What Dante condemns in these terms so closely resembles what the *Banquet* had proposed to do that one cannot but wonder if his chief reason for not completing this work was not that he found it tedious. The question is, after all, of little importance, for what Dante immediately adds is much more deserving of our attention. In fact, we there see his passion for the cause of the Empire nourished by the personal ambition of a thinker and author—an ambition of which he makes no secret. Among all the truths, still hidden but useful, which remain to be discovered, that which is at once the most safely hidden and the most useful is the truth about monarchy. The obscurity of the question, the few immediate benefits that may be expected from the study of it, sufficiently explain the fact that no one has yet broached it. The question, Dante states explicitly, remains *ab omnibus intemptata* ("unapproached by any man"); he therefore aspires to the glory of carrying off this palm and even to

---

Signor B. Nardi, still following G. Gentile, concludes that the *Monarchy* is the first act of rebellion against "scholastic transcendency" (*op. cit.*, p. 284). In doing so he forgets that the independence attributed by Dante to the Empire results exclusively from the Emperor's direct responsibility to a transcendent God. The reason why the Emperor does not derive his power from the Pope is that he is directly subject to this God. Signor B. Nardi does not seem to suspect that as a historian he is far superior to G. Gentile, whose immanentism is the scourge of this contemporary Italian scholarship with its abundance of learning and ingenuity.

With regard to the text, see C. WITTE, *Dantis Alighieri De Monarchia lib. III*, 2nd ed., Braumüller, Vindobonae, 1874. French translation of the treatise: B. LANDRY, *Dante. De la Monarchie*, F. Alcan, Paris, 1933. On the historical background of the treatise consult M. BARBI, *L'ordinamento della Repubblica fiorentina e la vita politica di Dante*, in *Problemi di Critica dantesca*, 1st Series, Sansoni, Florence, 1934–XII, pp. 141–155; and B. BARBADORO, *La condanna di Dante e le fazioni politiche del suo tempo*, in *Studi Danteschi*, Vol. II (1920), pp. 5–74. We shall cite the *De Monarchia* in the edition of R. Allulli, C. Signorelli, Milan, 1926.

that of being the first to win it: *Ut palmam tanti bravii primus in meam gloriam adipiscar* (I, 1).

It does indeed seem that Dante has spoken the truth,[1] not only because no one before him had attempted the theoretical justification of a universal Empire of mankind united and pacified under the authority of a single individual, but because in effect the very way in which he justified such an Empire for the first time set up, above the Christian ideal of a universal Church, the human ideal of a single universal temporal order with the Emperor playing the part which the Pope fills in the Church. What Dante calls the "universal community of the human race" (*universalis civilitas humani generis*), or simply "the human community" (*humana civilitas*), was bound to enter into competition with the ideal of the Church, as would a universal community ruled by a single head with another universal community likewise ruled by a single head.[2] Moreover, the state of mind of Dante himself while he was composing this work was not quite the same as that of the author of the *Banquet*. In the *Banquet* Dante was trying to persuade the Emperor not to meddle in philosophy, unless his intention was to submit to the authority of Aristotle, and he hoped to convince the philosophers themselves that their special mission was to teach mankind moral virtue, itself the foundation of political virtue, without which there can be no justice, peace or felicity on earth. In spite of the philosophical pretensions of Frederick II, it might be hoped

---

[1] See the just remarks of F. Ercole, *Il pensiero politico di Dante*, Vol. II, pp. 25–30, and especially pp. 289–292.

[2] Dante was the first to offer a philosophical justification of the Empire so conceived; but there were at the time other justifications of an Empire differently conceived. It would be interesting to know whether or not the *Monarchy* is of an earlier date than the treatise of Engelbert (elected Abbot of Admont in 1297): Engelberti . . . Admontensis, *De ortu et fine Romani imperii liber*, Basileae. Joannes Operinus, 1553. Engelbert teaches "omnia regna et omnes reges subesse uni imperio et imperatori christiano" (*op. cit.*, cap. XVIII, p. 98), but to him it is rather a question of a Christendom united by faith than a humanity united by reason, and that is why his Emperor seems to be first and foremost the soldier of the Church. There is only one divine right, only one faith, "et per consequens, una sola respublica totius populi Christiani. Ergo de necessitate erit et unus solus princeps et rex illius Reipublicae, statutus et stabilitus ad ipsius fidei et populi christiani dilatationem et defensionem" (*op. cit.*, cap. XV, p. 78). Here, in short, the Empire derives its firm basis "ab unitate corporis Ecclesiae et totius christianae reipublicae" (*op. cit.*, cap. XVIII, p. 99), which fact makes it possible to ensure the unified command in case of war of "tota Christianitas contra totum paganismum" (cap. XVIII, p. 101). This Emperor who is under the wing of the Church ("cum . . . extra Ecclesiam non sit nec possit esse imperium," cap. XXIII, p. 131), and whose goal is subordinated to that of the Church, accords less with Dante's ideal than with Roger Bacon's. We find the same analogy and the same difference between Dante's version of the doctrine of twofold beatitude and that of Engelbert of Admont (see below, p. 193, note 1).

that few Emperors would wish to assail the authority of the
Philosopher, and Dante was too much convinced of the limitations
of our metaphysic not to hope that the philosophers would one
day consent to come to an understanding with the theologians.
Theologians like "the good friar Thomas" were, moreover,
there to facilitate the understanding. Where, then, does Thomas
Aquinas find philosophy, if not in the works of Aristotle? He
reads it, studies it, comments on it and explains it to others, as
we see him do in that admirable exposition of the *Ethica ad
Nicomachum* which Dante studied with such care. All the philosophical concessions demanded of the theologians have already
been made to him by St. Thomas. It is understandable, then,
that Dante loves him and that he expects to be able to come to
an understanding with theology on ground so well prepared.
There is no sacrifice which he himself has to consent to in the
matter. We do not know what he may have thought at the
time of the philosophical crisis which he seems to have experienced,
but it is now over and I do not believe that it is possible to find
in his works a single definite Averroistic thesis of which he
undoubtedly maintained the truth. So far as he is concerned
philosophy is Aristotle, and as his Aristotle is, in the main, the
Aristotle of Albertus Magnus and of St. Thomas Aquinas, the
understanding between philosophers and theologians seems to
him easy to bring about. In fact, thanks to these great theologians
themselves, it exists, and even those who shut their eyes to it
will certainly accept it in the end. But to establish a concordat
between the Emperors and the Popes was quite another matter,
and anyone who tried to base it on the previous accord between
the theologians and the philosophers ran a great risk of aggra-
vating the situation in both domains. Yet that is what Dante
tried to do. He had at his disposal only the philosophical ideal
defined in the *Banquet* for the foundation of his "universal
community of the human race", comparable to a natural church
of moralists in face of the supernatural church of the theologians.
How is one to persuade the theologians that, for the very reason
that makes them abandon philosophy to Aristotle, they should
abandon the Empire to the Emperor? Such is the problem whose
solution Dante's *Monarchy* offered to the world.

The idea of this universal temporal community, so new in his
age—he seems, indeed, to have been its first advocate—took

shape in Dante's mind in a very curious way. The only universal community of which the idea existed at the time was a community essentially supernatural and religious: the Church, or, if one prefers, Christendom. Not only had the Church never thought that there should or could exist a Humanity unified for the purpose of pursuing a temporal happiness regarded as its special goal, but it had, since Augustine's *City of God,* discountenanced the ideal of a unification of all mankind through the common acceptance of the Christian faith and under the supreme government of the Pope. In order, then, to conceive of the possibility of a universal temporal community, it was necessary to borrow from the Church its ideal of a universal Christendom and to secularize it. On the other hand, it was impossible to secularize this ideal without establishing philosophy as the basis of the universal community of all mankind, subject to the same monarch and pursuing the same form of happiness in obedience to the same laws. The man who advised the Emperor Alexander to treat the Greeks as free men and the barbarians as slaves assuredly had not thought that all mankind was capable of seeking, through the same channels, one and the same goal. In order, then, to justify his idea Dante had to seek in the philosophy of Aristotle a certain natural aim whose complete realization—although Aristotle himself had never dreamed of such a thing—demanded the collaboration of a completely unified human race.

I. THE GOAL OF THE HUMAN RACE

For the solution of this problem Dante has made very skilful use of the genuinely Aristotelian and Thomistic principle that, if man is a social animal, it is because the life of the city, with the co-operation which it permits, is absolutely essential if he is to be able to attain his full development. Dante's starting-point was all the better chosen in that St. Thomas, having strongly insisted on the obligation incumbent on every man to place the resources of his individual reason at the disposal of the community, had come to the conclusion that the best political régime is government by a single person. St. Thomas was nevertheless so far from thinking of a universal monarchy that he ended his exposition thus: "It follows from what precedes that the king is he who governs the people of a city or of a province with a view to the common good; hence the saying of Solomon in *Eccl.*, V, 9: *Universae terrae rex imperat servienti* ("The king of all the earth governs him who is his subject").[1] Even if the words *universa terra* ("all the earth") merely bring to St. Thomas's mind the whole territory of a city or province, the fact remains that the collaboration of reason of which he is thinking in this passage has the primary object—and the context proves it—of providing men with the material comfort of which they stand in need. Dante goes much further than these *necessaria vitae* ("essentials of life"),[2] which, in his time at all events, did not demand the universal co-operation of the modern mechanical arts, which are themselves based on the universality of the sciences. To find in Aristotle a demand for universality he had to turn to the sphere of the human intellect.

A universal human community does indeed appear necessary if it is absolutely essential in order that man may attain his ultimate goal. Now man is distinguished from all other creatures by the fact that he is endowed with *reason*, in other words with that discursive faculty which enables him to acquire new forms of intelligible knowledge beginning from the intellection of the first principles of knowledge. Man possesses what is called a "possible" intellect, which is the faculty of progressively acquiring forms of intelligible knowledge by the light of the active intellect. In other words, man is neither a pure active intellect, like the angels, nor a mere animal sensibility, like the beasts, but he is distinguished from the beasts by this possible intellect which raises him to the plane of rational knowledge, and he is distinguished from the angels by this same possible intellect without which he could not acquire it. If it may be said that man's possible intellect raises him above the beasts and places him below the angels, it is assuredly this same faculty which distinguishes man as a reasonable animal and circumscribes him within his own species, between the unreasoning animals and the angelic Intelligences.

---

[1] St. Thomas Aquinas, *De regimine principum*, I, 1, end.
[2] "Ex quo manifeste ostenditur quod de ratione regis est quod sit unus qui praesit, et quod sit pastor commune multitudinis bonum et non suum commodum quaerens. Cum autem homini competat in multitudine vivere, quia sibi non sufficit ad necessaria vitae, si solitarius maneat, oportet quod tanto sit perfectior multitudinis societas, quanto magis per se sufficiens erit ad necessaria vitae" (St. Thomas Aquinas, *op. cit.*, I, 1).

Granting this, let us picture these human individuals, each endowed with his possible intellect. Each of them endeavours to acquire a certain amount of knowledge by the use of his reason, but what he can acquire in the way of intelligible knowledge represents but a minute part of the total intelligible knowledge which is accessible to the human species. This total knowledge cannot be realized all at once by any individual, or even by any particular group of human beings. Only the human species taken in its entirety is entitled to lay claim to it, but it may aspire to such an achievement only on condition that it exists as a universal community, endowed with a kind of existence of its own, and having this as its special function: *propria operatio humanae universitatis, ad quam ipsa universitas hominum in tanta multitudine ordinatur.*[1] The specific goal of this function of the human race taken as a whole is such that no individual, family, commune, city or kingdom can attain it, for it is a question of organizing things in such a way that at every moment of its existence the human race, thanks to the great number of the individual intellects of which it is made up, is continually realizing the total power of the possible intellect: *proprium opus humani generis totaliter accepti est actuare semper totam potentiam intellectus possibilis.*[2]

As early as the fourteenth century the Dominican Guido Vernani thought he could accuse Dante of upholding here an Averroistic thesis. Even if he was mistaken, it must be acknowledged that everything encouraged him to do so, and I am not sure, moreover, that Guido Vernani did not give proof of real sagacity on this delicate point. In the first place, Dante himself incited him to make the error by openly quoting Averroes as his authority on this point: *Et huic sententiae concordat Averrois in Commento super hiis quae de Anima* ("And with this opinion Averroes agrees in his commentary on what has been written *de Anima*"). Taken literally, this sentence would mean that Dante is in agreement on this point with the doctrine of the unity of the possible intellect, in other words with the doctrine that recognizes but a single possible intellect for the entire human race, as taught by Averroes in his commentary on the *De Anima*. This is exactly how Vernani understood Dante's sentence, and it may indeed be said that he did not seek to understand it otherwise, but not that he made it say anything other than what,

---

[1] DANTE, *De Monarchia*, I, 3.   [2] DANTE, *De Monarchia*, I, 4.

ut littera sonat, it actually does say: "If one speaks in this way, it manifestly follows that there is but a single intellect in all mankind; now to say and to think this is the gravest error, and its author and inventor is that Averroes whom he cites."[1]

We must go further besides. Dante would not quote Averroes in support of his thesis if he were not thinking of him at the very moment of writing and if the idea which he was then expounding were in no way connected with the Averroistic doctrine of the possible intellect.[2] It is, indeed, connected with it so closely that one cannot visualize any other doctrine by which it may have been suggested. Averroes conceived the possible intellect as a single entity, an intellectual substance wholly independent of the body—in short, what Christians call an angel—and he taught that, to an individual man, knowing means simply sharing in some part or other of the knowledge possessed by this intellect. Thus conceived, then, the possible intellect of Averroes presented Dante with a kind of individual human race whose unity would always be realized in a concrete way, while at every moment of its duration it would actualize the whole of the knowledge accessible to man. If to know is man's goal, it may be said that in this independent possible intellect the human race would have its goal eternally and permanently within its grasp. In order, then, to construct his own doctrine, Dante has transposed the thesis of Averroes by taking the human race, in other words the individuals existing at all times on earth regarded collectively, as an equivalent of the single possible intellect of Averroes. If he here refers us to Averroes, the reason is that in fact he finds his starting-point in Averroism, but this does not mean that he has adopted it.

Let us note, indeed, that the two theses are essentially different. What Averroes desires in order to realize the possible intellect completely is a being; what Dante requires in order to obtain

---

[1] GUIDO VERNANI, *De reprobatione Monarchiae*, ed. Jarro (G. Piccini), Florence, Bemporad, 1906, pp. 4 and 6, and pp. 8 and 10.

[2] The works of Averroes are not very easy to find, but extensive and well chosen fragments may be read in G. THÉRY, *Autour du décret de 1210, II: Alexandre d'Aphrodise* (Bibl. thomiste, VII), Paris, J. Vrin, 1926, pp. 58–61. As regards Dante himself and the meaning of the passage in question, see B. NARDI, *Saggi di filosofia dantesca*, pp. 261–264. Here the reader will find the passages from Averroes to which Dante refers him. I have not thought it my duty to reproduce this admirably executed analysis, the precision of which is such that one cannot summarize it without doing it less than justice. Its conclusions seem to me beyond discussion and all I am doing here is merely to confirm them with an argument actually derived from the philosophical essence of the theses in question.

the same result is a community, that universal community of all
individual possible intellects which is constituted by the human
race. If Dante had accepted Averroism in this particular his own
doctrine would have had no justification, since, with or without
a universal community, the goal of humanity would be ever-
lastingly attained in the permanence of the independent possible
intellect.   When Dante speaks of realizing the intellectual
potentialities of the whole of humanity (*potentia totius humanitatis*),
it is certainly those of all mankind (*universitas hominum*) which
must be understood. In short, to him what is involved is a
multitudo, that very multitude of individuals which the universal
human community will render capable of attaining its goal by
imposing on it the unity which is essential to the independent
possible intellect of Averroes, though humanity as conceived by
Dante does not yet possess it and will, moreover, enjoy it only
if it accepts the unifying hegemony of the Emperor.

It is therefore quite impossible to maintain, as has been done,
that Dante is here clinging to the doctrine of Averroes, but is
is still true that Dante transposes it with an originality that is,
incidentally, striking and truly creative. He does not, like
Averroes, speak as a metaphysician taking note of a *de facto* unity
based on the actual structure of the universe; he speaks as a
political and social reformer, as the herald of a community
which has to be created and which he conceives as a temporal
duplicate of that universal religious community which is the
Church. It is through this human community that humanity
will be able to attain its special goal. Dante asserts as much at
the beginning of his work; he propounds this fundamental idea
as the key which unlocks its meaning: "From the things which
have just been explained there emerges clearly the means by which
the human race may better, or rather best, accomplish its special
task. That is why this very thing has seemed to be the most
direct means to the attainment of that purpose to whose fulfil-
ment all our activities are directed as to their final goal, to wit,
universal peace, which will therefore be regarded as the principle
of the arguments that follow." This is what Dante propounds
as his starting-point. No universal human community, no peace;
no peace, no opportunity for man to develop to the highest
pitch his aptitude for discovering truth or, consequently, to
attain his goal. That is the fixed point, the cardinal fact to

which all that Dante proves in the *Monarchy* amounts and on which it is based.[1] Here his philosophy will be essentially that of a reformer: "Since, therefore, the matter under discussion is political, or rather the source and principle of all correct politics, and since everything political is subject to our power, it is evident that the matter under discussion is not concerned in the first place with speculation, but with action."[2]

It would therefore be an error—one that is invariably committed in interpreting Dante—to seize on a philosophical attitude which is with him a passing phase, and which he takes up in order to go beyond it, as if he were really adopting it as his own. Most certainly he does owe something here to the philosophy of Averroes. To be precise, he owes to him the idea, which is, moreover, a splendid one, of a unity of the human race in which the whole of humanity would at all times realize its special aim, namely to possess the entire intellectual knowledge which it is capable of assimilating. But we need not go back from this idea to what it implies in Averroes; rather must we look from it towards what it betokens in Dante: a community that man must create that he may secure a peace which does not yet exist, with a view to attaining an object which humanity has not yet secured, because before it can be secured it must first exist. Dante is to be identified with the authorities he invokes only to the extent to which they suggest, fashion or confirm his own doctrine regarding the best way to ensure that universal peace without which the human race cannot attain its goal.

II. NECESSITY OF THE MONARCHY

If we admit that such is indeed the goal of the human race, it remains for us to seek the means to attain it. This is one of the questions on which Dante is most readily compared to St. Thomas Aquinas. Nevertheless, the first fact to be noted—and

[1] "Ex hiis ergo quae declarata sunt patet per quod melius, immo per quod optime genus humanum pertingit ad opus proprium; et per consequens visum est propinquissimum medium per quod itur in illud ad quod, velut in ultimum finem, omnia nostra opera ordinantur, quod est pax universalis, quae pro principio rationum subsequentium supponatur. Quod erat necessarium, ut dictum fuit, velut signum praefixum in quod quidquid probandum est resolvatur, tanquam in manifestam veritatem" (DANTE, *De Monarchia*, I, 4).

[2] DANTE, *De Monarchia*, I, 2.

it is probably not without some significance—is that St. Thomas never propounded the problem of the relationship of the Empire to the Papacy. So far as I know, he never once went so far as to write the word *imperator*. This theologian, then, views everything as if the Emperor did not exist. Those of whom he always speaks in his writings are the "princes", that is to say chiefs of States, varying in extent, men who themselves hold different titles—kings, dukes, princes, etc.—the sole qualification being that they should possess supreme temporal authority in their respective countries. The fact is accounted for by two things of which the historians tell us. First, the majority of theologians defend the supreme authority of the Pope in temporal matters against the Emperor; they are therefore the natural allies of the local temporal powers over which the Emperor claims to have authority.[1] Consequently, it was not in the interest of the theologians to attribute to the Emperor a theoretical importance greater than his real importance. A sole spiritual head could more easily exercise his rights over a sprinkling of petty States and petty princes than over a sole universal Empire which set up in opposition to the Pope a temporal sovereign having a jurisdiction co-extensive with his own. Even if there were an Emperor it would be better to act as if there were none. In fact—and this is the second reason—we may say that in practice there was none. "The humiliation of the Empire is so profound," wrote H. Pirenne of these times, "that for a moment after 1250 it may have seemed on the point of disappearing."[2] Moreover, this is the very thing that makes Dante's attitude such a great one. Writing in an age when there is no longer an Emperor of any kind, he does not fight for a man, but for an idea. One understands the fact that St. Thomas did not think it his duty to galvanize this corpse or to join battle with a phantom authority when it was in the Church's interest that it should remain so.

In examining St. Thomas's doctrine we must therefore confine ourselves to what he says of the relations between the prince of a specific country and the Pope who presides over the universal Church. Now Dante differs from him here in the emphasis of his demonstration that the existence of a universal monarch,

---

[1] See the remarks of H. Pirenne, in L. HALPHEN and P. SAGNAC, *La fin du moyen âge* (*Peuples et Civilisations*, Vol. VII, 1), Paris, F. Alcan, 1931, pp. 6-7.
[2] H. PIRENNE, *op. cit.*, p. 7.

supreme temporal sovereign of all mankind, is absolutely essential in the name of philosophical principles which are themselves universal and necessary. As it is here a question of Dante's most original personal contribution to the history of political philosophy, this primary difference cannot be regarded as negligible. Moreover, one gravely suspects that it will have consequences. St. Thomas, who cannot imagine a Church without a Pope, makes do admirably with a world without an Emperor, but Dante can no more accept a world without an Emperor than a Church without a Pope, precisely because he desires that, when a Pope takes a hand in the affairs of Florence,[1] he should find himself faced with someone to whom he may speak. Florence alone against the Pope faces defeat, but Florence represented by a universal Emperor against the Pope finds the chances once more in her favour. It was with the object of assuring all States of this protector and supreme temporal arbiter that Dante invoked all the principles of Aristotle and produced from them this universal monarchy which even the tutor of Alexander of Macedon certainly never dreamed of.

In this matter, therefore, Dante's achievement consisted in reviving the principal arguments which St. Thomas and Aristotle had used, in order to prove that a single head is required in every political community, these arguments being applied, however, to that universal political community for the existence of which he craved—a human fellowship. Since there exists a *propria operatio humanae universitatis* ("an activity characteristic of all humanity"), this universal community must also exist for the purpose of leading men to that goal. Now let us note carefully that here Dante is thinking particularly of the question of ensuring the complete actualization of the human intellect in the sphere of action. Not that he regards the practical function of reason as superior to its speculative function. As I have said, Dante never called in question the hierarchies of dignity established by Aristotle and confirmed by St. Thomas. Speculation is nobler than action and the practical arts, the moral order of action and the technical order of creation are subordinate to the theoretical

---

[1] It is impossible to explain Dante in terms of the history of Florence, for many other Florentines have lived that history, and yet there is only one Dante; but the events of which he was a witness were certainly the origin of the course which he adopted and of which his doctrine is professedly a universally valid justification. Cf. F. ERCOLE, *Il pensiero politico di Dante*, Vol. II, pp. 274-296.

order of knowledge, and contemplation remains the supreme
goal assigned by the supreme Good to the human race. That is
even the reason, notes Dante in this connection, why Aristotle
says in his *Politics* "that those who prevail by virtue of understanding naturally have authority over others".[1] Only, ethics
and politics, though mere concomitants of contemplation, are its
essential concomitants. No peace, no philosophy. Therefore
universal peace, if not our beatitude, is at any rate the loftiest
of its concomitants. In other words it is supreme and transcendent in the sphere of ways and means. That is why we should
regard this universal peace, which was heralded by the Angels
on the birth of Christ, as the best means whereby the human
race may accomplish its special task. Looked upon in this way,
universal peace should therefore be regarded as the first essential
for the attainment of the goal assigned by God to humanity.[2]
Now if there is no universal monarch there will be no peace.
Therefore a universal monarch is necessary for the existence,
order and peace of a politically organized human race.

However interesting they may be in themselves, the arguments
which Dante uses to justify his thesis concern rather the content
of his philosophy than his general attitude towards philosophy.
Let us, then, merely recall that, supported by the "venerable
authority" of Aristotle as voiced in his *Politics*, Dante lays down
as a principle that "when several things are directed towards a
single goal, it is imperative for one of them to control or rule,
and for the others to be controlled and ruled".[3] Not only does
the authority of Aristotle prescribe this law, but inductive
reasoning establishes it. In the individual, everything must be
subject to the intellect if he desires to be happy. In a family,
everything must be subject to the father of the family if it is
desired that its members should attain the object of family life,
which is readiness to live a good life. Similarly, in a village,
a city, a kingdom, there must be a single head if it is not desired
that the word of the Infallible Truth should prove correct:
"Every kingdom divided against itself is brought to desolation"
(*Matt.*, XII, 25). If, then, the entire human race is directed

---

[1] DANTE, *De Monarchia*, I, 3, end. Cf. ARISTOTLE, *Pol.*, I, 2, 1252 a 31–32; but Dante
is inclined to follow ST. THOMAS AQUINAS, *In XII lib. Metaph. Aristot.*, Prooemium.
[2] DANTE, *De Monarchia*, I, 4.
[3] DANTE, *De Monarchia*, I, 5. Cf. ARISTOTLE, *Pol.*, I, 5, 1254 a 28–32; or better ST.
THOMAS AQUINAS, *In XII libros Metaph. Aristot.*, Incipit.

towards a single goal, it is essential to the well-being of the world that there should exist a Monarchy, in other words a sole command—that of the Emperor.[1]

Of the numerous arguments of this kind which Dante piles up seemingly at random in order to establish his thesis, there is one which should be examined with particular attention, for it is bound up with what is deepest and most personal in the poet's thought—his ideal of justice. Wishing to praise the era which he saw taking shape in his day, Virgil had already sung in his *Bucolics*: *Iam redit et Virgo, redeunt Saturnia regna.* ("Already too the Virgin returns, and the days of Saturn's dominion.")[2]

By the word *Virgo* ("Virgin") we must understand Justice; by *Saturnia regna* (Saturn's dominion") Virgil signified that age of excellence which was also called the "golden age". But the world is in its most perfect state only when justice reigns, and justice reigns without question only under the authority of a single Monarch; thus the world can only be in its most perfect state under a Monarchy or Empire. What is justice in fact? Considered in itself and with respect to its special character, it is a certain rectitude, or standard, which rules out everything that deviates from righteousness. It is analogous to those forms which, according to Gilbert de la Porrée, consist of simple and unvarying essences—abstract whiteness, for instance—and which, being in themselves incapable of increase or decrease, grow or diminish only in terms of the entities that embody them. Thus, considered in itself, justice is an absolute, but there may be varying degrees of it in the world, and it is when the minimum of injustice

---

[1] DANTE, *De Monarchia*, I, 6. Dante next proves that the unity of command which obtains in the parts of the human race should, *a fortiori*, obtain in the human race as a whole (I, 6); that, as the parts of which it is the whole are joined to it by single heads, the human race should be joined by a single head to the whole of which it forms part, viz. the universe, of which God is the Monarch (I. 7); that the human race, of which God is the cause, should tend to become assimilated in the highest degree possible to its cause: it should therefore be one, as God is one (I, 8); that the son should follow in his father's footsteps; now the human race traces its origin, partially at least, to heaven, which is moved by a single Monarch (I, 9); that wherever conflict is possible there should be a judge; now there may be conflict among princes; consequently there should be an Emperor to decide between them (I, 10). It is at this point in his argumentation that Dante comes to his decisive proof, which is derived from the idea of justice.

[2] VIRGIL, *Buc.*, IV, 6. The reader will notice in the passage one of those frequently recurring indications which enable us to understand in what sense Dante was able to regard Virgil as a "sage". It was no slight praise, especially coming from Dante, to represent him as the prophet of Justice in a world pacified by the Emperor Augustus. With regard to the mediaeval conceptions of Virgil, see D. COMPARETTI, *Virgilio nel Medio Evo*, La Nuova Italia, Florence, 1937-XV; as to the idea which Dante himself formed of him, see in particular two excellent pages, Chap. XV, pp. 274-275.

goes to its making and its mode of operation that the maximum of justice is to be found in the world. When it shines forth in the world, we may indeed say, with the Philosopher, that "neither in Hesperus nor in Lucifer is there anything so admirable".[1] What prevents men's wills from being imbued with a sense of justice is "greed", which is its antithesis; what prevents the just will from acting in accordance with justice is lack of power, or of strength: what is the use of wishing to assign to every man his due, if one cannot do so? "The more powerful the just man is, the more amply will his justice be able to express itself in deeds." In order, therefore, that the world's state may be of the best, justice must reside in it in a supremely active and supremely powerful will. There is none that can be more so than that of a single monarch; it is only, then, if justice resides in such a monarch, or Emperor, that it will reach its highest point in the world and the world will be supremely well ordered (I, 11).

The most important point in this proof is undoubtedly the definition which Dante offers of the antithesis of justice: "Where the will is not free from all greed, even if justice is in it, it is nevertheless not present in the full splendour of its purity: it is, in fact, present in an entity which, however little, in some measure resists it" (I, 11). This *cupiditas* ("greed"), of which the She-wolf of the *Divine Comedy* is most certainly a symbol,[2] does not at first appear in Dante as a religious and Christian notion. He borrows it from the Philosopher, or at any rate the Philosopher suggests it to him: *Justitiae maxime contrariatur cupiditas, ut innuit Aristoteles in quinto ad Nicomachum.* ("The greatest enemy of justice is greed, as Aristotle indicates in the fifth book of the *Ethica ad Nicomachum*.")[3] Eliminate greed, and there remains nothing in opposition to justice. Now it happens that the only

---

[1] ARISTOTLE, *Eth. Nic.*, V, 3, 1129 b 28–29. Cf. THOMAS AQUINAS, *In X lib. Ethic.*, lib. V., lect. 2, ed. Pirotta, No. 906.

[2] Cf. M. BARBI, *Nuovi problemi di critica dantesca*, in *Studi Danteschi*, 1938–XVII, p. 29.

[3] DANTE, *De Monarchia*, I, 11. Aristotle in fact distinguishes legal justice, which is not a particular virtue, but virtue in its entirety, and of which the antithesis is injustice (*Eth. Nic.*, V. 3, 1130 a 9–10), from justice regarded as a particular virtue, the antithesis of which is that particular form of injustice which is called "avarice". (Regarding πλεονεξία, see V, 2, 1129 b 9.) The notions of greed and avarice are, moreover, closely related; but Dante seems to have preferred that of greed, because, as is clearly indicated by what is to follow, the evil of which he is thinking is specifically the active avarice of princes who covet for themselves the territories of others. Let us note, moreover, that *cupiditas* translates better than *avaritia* the fundamental meaning of πλεονεξία :

way to procure a man free from all greed is to install in power one who, possessing all, can no longer covet anything.

Such, to be exact, would be the single Monarch of Dante's dreams: a sovereign whose jurisdiction ends only at the edge of the ocean, that is to say—since in Dante's time fleets count for hardly anything—a sovereign whose jurisdiction is limitless. The universal Monarch exercises an authority that knows no frontiers: there is therefore no frontier for him to violate. The universal Monarch can have no feeling of greed: he therefore has feelings only of love and charity. Now just as the slightest trace of greed is enough to obscure justice, so too charity, that is to say integrity in love (*recta dilectio*), refines and clarifies justice. It is therefore certain that under a Monarch free from all greed justice must reign without constraint. Expressing himself with rare vigour, Dante notes that greed consists essentially of scorn for the unique dignity of each man and covets everything else, whereas charity scorns everything else, seeking only God and man, and consequently the good of man. Now the most precious good within the reach of all men is to live in peace. Justice alone can enable them to enjoy it, and the charity, unmarred by covetousness, which a universal Monarch alone can reveal for all men is the necessary condition of the reign of justice. The world therefore needs a single Emperor, who shall stand in relation to the entire universe as a kind of universal cause. The nearer such a cause approaches to universality, the more truly will it be a cause, and the more truly it is a cause, the more pregnant will it be with love. That such a Monarch would be eminently disposed to act in accordance with justice who can doubt, unless he is ignorant of the meaning of the word "monarch"? If he is truly Monarch, he can have no enemies (I, 12).

Having reached this point, Dante will now hurl himself into the thick of the fray, for the moment has come for him to reveal

the desire to have more than others, avidity, greedy desire, the tendency to usurp. Cf. in this connection the work of ALLAN H. GILBERT, *Dante's Conception of Justice*, Duke University Press, Durham (North Carolina), 1925. This book has the merit not only of dealing with what is truly a fundamental point in Dante's doctrine, but also of having, by an obligatory reference to St. Thomas's commentary on the *Ethica ad Nicomachum*, shed light on the exact meaning of the notions of justice and avarice (or greed) in the works of Dante. Even if, as is natural, we do not regard as justified all the parallels between the *Banquet* and St. Thomas's commentary which the author suggests, enough of them remain established for the thesis of Mr. A. H. Gilbert to be considered proven. Consult especially Chap. I, *The Materials for Dante's Treatise on Justice: St. Thomas' Commentary on Ethics V*, 1–9, pp. 3–66.

to the world the very foundation of that freedom to which greed
of any kind is a menace. Men say that this foundation is free
will and that free will is free judgment as to what one should
desire. And what they say is true; but, adds Dante, people repeat
these formulas without understanding what they are saying
any more than do our logicians when they cram their logic with
mathematical examples—for instance, that the three angles of a
triangle are equal to two right angles. What it is important
to understand here is that a judgment is free in so far as it
comes near to being purely rational, i.e. in so far as it approaches
complete emancipation from the appetite and the desires. Freedom is the possession of the rational judgment which actuates
the appetite and which is in no way actuated by it. Now this
capacity for making up our minds through reason is the greatest
good with which God has endowed human nature, since it alone
enables us to be happy on earth as men and to be so as gods in
the after-life. Only the Monarch of the human race can desire
the good of the human race—namely, that all men, existing
each for his own sake, should be as good as it is possible for
them to be. Such is not the goal that single States have in view.
Whether democracies, oligarchies, or tyrannies are involved,
each pursues some particular interest to which it subjects men,
although this goal is not theirs. That, moreover, is why Aristotle
in his *Politics* says that "in a perverted community the honest
man is a bad citizen, whereas, in a righteous community, the
honest man and the good citizen are one and the same". Thus,
good communities are those which understand freedom aright,
that is to say those which desire that men should exist for their
own sakes, not for that of the State of which they form part.
The authority of a single Monarch is therefore absolutely essential
if it is desired that men should be governed with a view to their
own good instead of being exploited for particular ends which
are not their own.[1]

These are only a few of the philosophical arguments accumu-
lated by Dante, with a vigour and a richness of invention that
are remarkable, to justify the necessity of a universal monarchy,
and we cannot even consider the historical and juridical arguments of which Book II of the *Monarchy* is entirely composed.

---

[1] DANTE, *De Monarchia*, I, 12. Cf. ARISTOTLE, *Pol.*, III, 2, 1276 b 40–1277 a 1, or
better ST. THOMAS AQUINAS, *In X lib. Ethic. Aristotelis*, lib. V, lect. 3, ed. Pirotta, No. 926.

The essential thing is, indeed, for us to notice the profound gulf that separates the actual nature of the problem propounded by Dante from the apparently similar problem in St. Thomas Aquinas to which it is often compared. Sometimes, indeed, scholars argue as if the Thomistic question of the relationship between princes and Popes were identical with the Dantesque question of the relationship between the Emperor and the Pope. It is not entirely so. Not only does St. Thomas never speak of an Emperor of any kind, but, even if he did, the head of the Romano-Germanic Empire of whom he might be thinking would only be in a general sense comparable to this supreme master of the human race for whom Dante clamours. By a curious paradox, Dante was able to raise up a universal Monarch vis-à-vis to the universal Pope only by imagining this Monarch himself as a kind of Pope.[1] To be sure, a temporal Pope, but nevertheless the head of a kind of natural Catholic community deriving its dogma from the ethics of Aristotle and guided towards its specific goal by the authority of a single pastor. If the *genus humanum* ("human race") of Dante is really the first known expression of the modern idea of Humanity, we may say that the conception of Humanity first presented itself to the European consciousness merely as a secularized imitation of the religious notion of a Church. This, moreover, is why Dante portrays his Monarch as a temporal father compelled by his position and his functions to practise charity and justice no less absolutely than the Pope, the spiritual father of mankind, is compelled by his function and his position—if, that is, he respects them—to practise spiritual fatherhood and sanctity. Like the head of an immense religious community, Dante's Monarch, precisely because he is responsible for subjecting others to the laws which

---

[1] So true is this that theologians were able to accept Dante's attitude without any modification, provided only that the Pope was substituted for the Emperor. That is what was done by the Franciscan François de Mayronnes in the writings in which he dealt exclusively with this problem, expecially in his *Tractatus de Principatu Temporali,* Bib. Nat., Fonds latin, 3655 and 14195. It is true to say that François de Mayronnes, like Dante, believed that "in universo nostro est dare unum monarcham qui ita praesit omnibus temporaliter, quod nulli in temporalibus sit subjectus" (*op. cit.,* MS. 3655, fol. 44 vo.), although in his eyes this universal temporal Monarch is the Pope; if it is insisted that he should be the Emperor, it is better to do without him: "In universo, secundum optimam dispositionem sui, non est dare, secundum rectam rationem, aliquem monarcham sui principem, videlicet in temporalibus, quando ille subsit temporaliter et etiam in temporalibus principe spirituali, ut puta Papae" (*op. cit.,* Explicit). An edition of this treatise and of the chief passages in François de Mayronnes dealing with this problem has just been prepared by M. Pierre de Lapparent.

lead them to their goal, is in reality merely their servant: *Monarcha, qui minister omnium habemus est* ("The Monarch, who must be regarded as the servant of all") (I, 12). This Emperor is therefore a minister, almost as St. Bonaventure had been a minister of the Franciscan Order, and this indeed is what will shortly invest the problem with an entirely new urgency, a scope quite different from that which it had in the *De regimine principum* of St. Thomas Aquinas, not only because of the formidable power that this leader of Humanity will wield in the presence of the leader of Christendom, but especially because of the right that he too will henceforth have to speak as one invested with supreme moral authority in his sphere and charged with leading to a clearly defined goal the entirety of mankind, which God has entrusted to him. In thus investing temporal society with all the attributes of the Church Dante was transposing the classic controversy between the Priesthood and the Empire into a new key. Any comparison between Dante's doctrine and those of his predecessors or contemporaries must necessarily take this fact into account; otherwise it is bound to fall into errors of perspective which themselves suggest doctrinal pseudo-similarities and misinterpretations.

III. INDEPENDENCE OF THE EMPIRE

It follows from Book II of the *Monarchy* that the Roman Empire, in the form in which it survives in the Middle Ages, is a lawful power, the existence of which is desired by God with a view to the happiness of mankind. Now the Papacy likewise claims to be a universal authority of divine origin. The question, consequently, is how to reconcile the authority of "those two great luminaries, the Roman Pontiff and the Roman Prince". And first of all "we ask whether the authority of the Roman Monarch, who is by right the Monarch of the world, as the Second Book has proved, is directly subject to God's will or whether it is subject to that of some vicar or minister of God, by which I mean the successor of Peter, who is in truth the key-bearer of the Kingdom of Heaven".[1] It is, I think,

---

[1] DANTE, *De Monarchia*, III, 1. Several other equivalent formulas occur in the same treatise: "Isti vero ad quos erit tota disputatio sequens, asserentes auctoritatem Imperii ab auctoritate Ecclesiae dependere, velut artifex inferior dependet ab architecto . . ." (III, 4). Cf. "Quod autem auctoritas Ecclesiae . . ." (III, 13).

unnecessary to stress the word *directly*. That the authority of the Emperor of the world is in the long run subject to the will of God goes without saying; the only question is whether it is subject to it directly or through the Pope, but it is a very important question.

In approaching the matter, it is of some interest to note that the Third Book of the *Monarchy* begins with a quotation from the Scriptures, with which Dante in a sense covers himself as with a shield, because it places him under the protection of justice: *Conclusit ora leonum, et non nocuerunt mihi; quia coram eo justitia inventum est in me* ("My God . . . hath shut the lions' mouths, and they have not hurt me: forasmuch as before him justice was found in me") (*Dan.*, VI, 22). If collected, the sentences in which Dante stresses this virtue would form a very long list, but they would lose their meaning. In his work justice resembles, indeed, a kind of theme, or *leit-motiv*, which is never long in reappearing, sometimes in the least expected forms. If he wishes to base his argument on natural reason, Dante has recourse to the *Ethica ad Nicomachum*, Book V, where the two kinds of justice, legal and personal, receive such unreserved homage. If he is thinking of that definite form of human justice whose reign is associated with the supremacy of the Roman Empire, Dante has recourse to Virgil, the prophet of the golden age in which felicity will reign in peace under the authority of Rome;[1] if only as the singer of Roman justice realized in the triumph of law, Virgil would already have amply deserved the honour of suggesting, as a theme of Dante's thought, the glory of the sage in addition to that of the poet. But if he wishes to reveal the religious, sacred and truly divine character of the virtue of justice, Dante turns to the Scriptures, and not only to its text, but to its heroes and sages. As a counter to the presumptuous Popes, Dante disposes in paradise of an ally whose holiness renders him immune to their attacks and whose justice judges them: the most wise King Solomon, in whose behalf David had entreated God: "Give to the king thy judgments, and thy justice unto the king's son."[2] Every form of justice—

---

[1] DANTE, *De Monarchia*, II, 3; note that King Aeneas is here mentioned as the father of the sovereign people on account of his justice: "Quo justior alter nec pietate fuit . . ." Cf. *op. cit.*, II, 6, for Rome's natural capacity for government: "Tu regere imperio populos, Romane, memento", and II, 8: "Certe hinc Romanos olim volventibus annis hinc fore ductores . . ." Cf. *Epist.* to the Emperor Henry, on the justice of Augustus.

[2] DANTE, *De Monarchia*, I, 13, quoting Psalm LXXI, 1-3: "Deus judicium tuum regi da, et justitiam tuam filio regis;—judicare populum tuum in justitia, et pauperes

the philosophical, the poetic and the Christian—is here brought into operation in the service of the Emperor.

The fundamental principle propounded by Dante as the basis of all his reasoning is that *God does not desire that which contradicts the intention of nature* (III, 2); for it was God Himself Who desired the existence of nature; if, then, God, desiring the existence of nature, did not desire that which is necessarily desired by nature, one, would have to say that God does not desire that which He does desire. Furthermore, Dante does not think there is any real uncertainty as to the correct answer to be given to this question. At heart all know what they should think; if there is any argument on the point, ignorance is not the cause of it, but rather it is the cause of ignorance. Passions and feelings of all kinds here come between truth and the light of reason, inciting against it three main adversaries:

1. The Sovereign Pontiff, vicar of Our Lord Jesus Christ and successor of Peter, to whom we owe, not all that is due to Christ, but all that is due to Peter, and who perhaps allows himself to be led astray by his zeal for the power of the keys. Let us place in the same category certain Christian pastors who do not gainsay the truth out of pride, but only out of zeal for the Church.

2. There are others, on the contrary, in whom an inveterate greed has extinguished the light of reason; true sons of the devil, these self-styled sons of the Church do not content themselves with sowing on earth universal discord; to such a degree do they abhor even the thrice sacred name of the Imperial Principate that they do not hesitate shamelessly to deny the very principles on which it rests.

3. Last come the Decretalists, folk whose ignorance of theology, as of philosophy, is complete; these know nothing but their famous Decretals. To be sure, no one denies that the latter are venerable, but they count on their ultimate victory and take their stand on them in order to belittle the Empire.

Of these three kinds of adversary Dante begins by eliminating

---

tuos in judicio.—Suscipiant montes pacem populo, et colles justitiam." Solomon is again quoted in support of justice (with Daniel, David and St. Paul) in *De Monarchia*, III, pending the time when Dante will crown him in heaven, with detailed introductory notes of the greatest possible clarity on the symbolism assigned to him, in the *Divine Comedy, Par.*, X, 109–114. With regard to the meaning and implication of this last passage, see below, Chap. IV, pp. 253–257.

the last, for it is not on the Decretals, but on the Scriptures, that he for his part intends to rely in order to find the truth of the Church. He likewise eliminates, as being impervious to persuasion, those who are blinded by greed. The only enemies remaining to him are therefore the Pope and those prelates who, led astray by their very zeal for our mother the Church, do not know the truth in question (III, 3). But even as Dante thus defines his adversary he dismisses his claims in advance. No doubt the reader has noticed the skilful formula which the poet uses in the passage in order to limit, even while he proclaims it, the extent of his obedience to the Pope: All that he owes not to Christ, but to Peter. To propound this article as something beyond discussion was equivalent to regarding the question as settled in advance, for it was an affirmation that there are privileges belonging to Christ which neither Peter nor his successors have inherited. More precisely still, it was tantamount to excluding privileges belonging to Christ which Peter and his successors have inherited—that very temporal primacy which Dante was making ready to refuse to them. The simplest way to convince oneself of the importance of the issue at stake is to collate the two formulas in which Dante and St. Thomas have expressed the essence of their positions:

DANTE	THOMAS AQUINAS
De Monarchia (III, 3)	*De regimine principum* (I, 14)
"Summus namque Pontifex, Domini nostri Jesu Christi vicarius et Petri successor, cui non quicquid Christo sed quicquid Petro debemus."	". . . summo Sacerdoti successor Petri, Christi vicario, Romano Pontifici, cui omnes reges populi christiani oportet esse subditos, sicut ipsi Domino nostro Jesu Christo."
"For the Sovereign Pontiff, vicar of Our Lord Jesus Christ and Peter's successor, to whom we owe what is the due, not of Christ, but of Peter."	". . . the Sovereign Priest Peter's successor, the Vicar of Christ, the Roman Pontiff, to whom all the kings of the Christian people owe submission, as to Our Lord Jesus Christ Himself."

The whole problem is there, concentrated in those two sentences, the almost word-for-word opposition between which is so striking that one cannot help wondering whether, when he wrote his, Dante was not recalling St. Thomas's. Whatever the truth may be in this matter, the theses which these two formulas define flagrantly contradict each other. Undoubtedly both admit without question the supremacy of the temporal power of Christ; but St. Thomas teaches that Christ bequeathed His twofold kingship, spiritual and temporal, to Peter and to all the successors of Peter, to whom all the kings of the Christian people should consequently be subject as to Jesus Christ Himself; in Dante's eyes, on the contrary, if Jesus Christ possessed, like God, a temporal sovereignty which, as it happens, He never used, that temporal authority returned to heaven with Him. The Popes have not inherited it. Between St. Thomas's Pope, *qui utriusque potestatis apicem tenet* ("who holds the supreme authority in either sphere"), and Dante's Pope, who is entirely without control of the temporal power, a choice must be made: they cannot be reconciled.[1]

Dante's doctrine touching the relations between the Priesthood and the Empire has been interpreted in almost every conceivable way. Some conceive it as teaching the total isolation of the two powers: each is competent in its own sphere and owes absolutely nothing to the other. Others maintain that, whatever he may seem to say, Dante recognizes the subordination of the Emperor to the Pope. Others maintain, on the contrary, that Dante subordinates the Pope to the Emperor. Finally, some, disturbed

---

[1] With regard to the problem of the temporal power of the Popes, and that we may confine ourselves strictly to introductions to the study of it, see the mainly doctrinal work of CHARLES JOURNET, *La juridiction de l'Eglise sur la Cité*, Paris, Desclée de Brouwer, 1931 (especially two most excellent pages, pp. 117–118), and the mainly historical work of M. GRABMANN, *Studien über den Einfluss der aristotelischen Philosophie auf die mittelalterlichen Theorien über das Verhältnis von Kirche und Staat*, Munich, 1934. If I do not here undertake to interpret the Thomistic doctrine for its own sake, it is not that I disclaim interest in it; rather is it that, even if to St. Thomas it is only a question of an "indirect power", essentially spiritual, exercised by the Popes over temporal things, I think that Dante is at variance with him *on this point*. For the thesis here upheld to be affected by it, one of the following two propositions would have to be maintained: 1. that St. Thomas did not recognize any Papal authority, indirect or direct, in temporal things, whatever the pretext; 2. that Dante recognized some sort of temporal Papal authority direct or indirect, over the Emperor, whatever the pretext. No one, I think, would to-day uphold the first of these two theses; the second still has its champions, but we shall see that it is difficult to uphold it in the precise sense of a jurisdiction which, whatever its nature and its cause, implies some kind of limitation of the universal, exclusive and absolute temporal authority that belongs by divine right to the Emperor. If I have made a mistake, it concerns this last point, and if I have made it, the reason is that I do not see how one can agree with St. Thomas while denying the Pope a temporal authority that one concedes to Jesus Christ. St. Thomas's doctrine rests in fact on this principle— that Peter and his successors have inherited the whole power of Christ. See the passage in the *Contra errores Graecorum* (in *Opuscula*, ed. P. Mandonnet, Vol. III, p. 324) where St. Thomas bases this thesis on the authority of the Pseudo-Cyril, quoting his *Liber Thesaurorum*: "Cui [*sc.* Petro] omnes jure divino caput inclinant et primates mundi tanquam ipsi domino Jesu obediunt."

at all these contradictions, come to the conclusion that the
historians would agree more wholeheartedly if *Dante* had not
contradicted himself.[1] Before resigning ourselves to this des-
pairing solution, we must ascertain the exact nature of the
apparently discordant theses which it is sought to reconcile.

In fact, Dante has several times asserted that the Emperor is
subject to the influence of the Pope and even that he needs to
come under it because of the beneficial effects that it produces
on him. The care which Dante exercises in stressing this point
as clearly as possible whenever he seems to force the contrary
viewpoint to its extreme limit is a very sure guarantee that the
co-existence of these two apparently contradictory theses does
not result from any negligence on his part. It is because he
wishes to uphold them as being simultaneously valid that Dante
simultaneously affirms them. For instance, when in the *Monarchy*
he discusses the classic comparison of the two powers with the
two great luminaries created by God on the fourth day (*Gen.*,
I, 15–16), Dante does not deny that one may, in a certain sense,
liken the Empire to the moon and the Papacy to the sun; he
therefore does not deny either that, in a certain sense, the Empire
benefits by the action exerted on it by the Papacy, as the moon
profits by the illuminative action of the sun. On the contrary,
Dante expressly affirms it: "The moon receives from the sun the
means to function better and more strongly (*virtuosius*), to wit,
an abundant light through which it functions with greater
intensity after receiving it; so, too, the temporal government
. . . receives from the spiritual the means to function more
strongly, through the light of grace which God, in heaven, and,
on earth, the blessing of the Sovereign Pontiff, infuse into it"
(III, 4). This, moreover, is the sense in which we must interpret
the famous final article of the *Monarchy*, which scholars have
already discussed at such great length without reaching agreement: "The truth with regard to this last question should not be
taken in the strict sense that the Roman Prince is not subject
in any respect to the Roman Pontiff, since this mortal felicity is
somehow designed as a means to immortal felicity. Let Caesar
therefore show for Peter that reverence which a first-born shows
for his father, in order that, illuminated by the light of paternal

[1] HANS KELSEN, *Die Staatslehre des Dante Alighieri* (Wiener Staatswissenschaftliche
Studien, VI Bd., 3 Heft), Vienna and Leipzig, F. Deuticke, 1905, Chap. VIII, pp. 97–98.

grace, he may shine forth more strongly (*virtuosius*) upon the terrestrial orb, of which he has been appointed ruler by Him alone Who orders all things, both spiritual and temporal" (III, 16, end).

This last sentence shows us at the same time the other aspect of Dante's thought. In the first place, God is absolutely without peer as sovereign both of the spiritual and of the temporal worlds; we may therefore be sure that neither the Emperor nor the Pope may aspire to the exercise of this twofold authority. Furthermore, Dante is careful to make it clear, in this final sentence of his work, and at the very moment when he is recalling Caesar to a feeling of filial respect for Peter, that the Emperor derives his universal authority from God alone: *Orbem terrae . . . , cui ab* Illo solo *praefectus est, qui est omnium spiritualium et temporalium gubernator* ("The earth . . ., of which he has been put in command by *Him alone*, Who is the Lord of all things, both spiritual and temporal") (III, 16, end). If we go back from this to the first of the two sentences which have just been quoted, we shall see that together they form a perfect whole.

Indeed, even if we leave aside the skilful exegesis with which Dante disposes of the Biblical argument of the two "great luminaries" created by God on the fourth day, we should note that he argues at the end as if this allegorical reasoning were valid. Now, even if we admit that it is so, the thesis that Dante wishes to prove remains unaffected. In the first place, the moon does not owe its existence to the sun: *Quantum est ad esse, nullo modo luna dependet a sole.* ("As regards its existence, the moon is in no wise dependent on the sun"). It follows clearly from this that the Imperial power likewise does not owe its existence to the Pope, but to God alone, Who created these two powers unaided, as He created the moon unaided to be an accompaniment to the sun. Moreover, speaking generally, the moon is likewise independent of the sun so far as its own energy and functioning are concerned: it owes its movement to its own driving force (which is not the sun's), and the influence which it exerts proceeds from its own rays (not from the solar rays), for it possesses a certain luminosity of its own, as may be seen whenever it is in eclipse: *Habet enim aliquam lucem ex se* (III, 4). Dante's intention is therefore clear: he desires an Imperial authority which owes its existence directly to God, not to the Pope; which wields a power whose course is in itself, not in the authority of the Pope, and which, finally, is capable of moving and acting of itself, by itself, of its own volition, without borrowing from the Pontifical authority the mainspring of its resolutions. In short—and this is the decisive point—the influence exerted by the Pope over the Emperor is analogous to that of a blessing, i.e. of a form of grace: *Lucem gratiae, quam in coelo Deus et in terra benedictio summi Pontificis infundit illi* ("The light of grace, which in heaven God, and on earth the blessing of the Sovereign Pontiff, shed upon him") (III, 4).

There are, then, two errors to be avoided in interpreting Dante's doctrine. One might at first think that, if the Pope's influence over the Emperor extends no further, it amounts to very little. This would be a grave error. Dante's Christianity was certainly somewhat personal; this son of the Church liked to reason with his mother about the conditions of his obedience, but he was not an indifferent Christian any more than our own Charles Péguy. Such men desire to know the exact nature of that to which they bow the knee, but, the decision once taken, their genuflexions are complete. For a Pope who is faithful to his office and who acts only as the spiritual father of mankind Dante's respect and love are boundless. The proof is that, unyielding though he is in these matters, he made a point of explicitly pardoning those among them whom "zeal of the keys", not greed, so unfortunately led astray. And not only them, but those of their fellow crusaders against the temporal power whom the same zeal had deluded: the "good friar Thomas" seems indeed to have profited by this indulgence in Dante's heart, and Dante must have loved him greatly to have forgiven him on this point. But this is not all. By reducing the problem of the two powers to a particular case of the general problem of nature and grace Dante was, incontestably, locating it in its true sphere. He knew, having derived the notion from St. Thomas, whose fundamental thesis it is, that the peculiar effect of grace is not to vindicate nature or to suppress it, but to perfect it. He knew also that in the eyes of that same St. Thomas the temporal order exists as a natural order created by God as such, endowed with special powers for the purpose of attaining its special goal, and that the Church is not there to destroy it by taking its place, but to give it new vigour and consolation, and to guide it to its ultimate supernatural goal through grace. In imagining that the work of grace thus conceived was in Dante's eyes a superfluous work we cannot be attributing to him his true conception of it. To walk in Dante's world as a pagan is to walk as a stranger. Conversely, to live in it as a Thomist is, if not to live as a stranger, at all events to propagate a misapprehension, for the special achievement of Dante's thought is to have eliminated the hierarchical gradations essential to Thomism and replaced them merely with a system of equal authorities. In St. Thomas, the actual distinction between the orders justifies and necessitates their gradation; in Dante, it excludes it. Here, then, we are faced not with a Christian world and a pagan world, but with two different dispositions of the Christian world and even with two dispositions which clash only by virtue of an identical principle: Grace presupposes nature; hence, without rendering itself purposeless, it cannot suppress nature.

In order to understand the structure of the Christian world as Dante understood it, we must return once more to his doctrine whereby the world is divided into three orders, unequal in dignity but mutually independent in their respective spheres—namely, the human order, the political order, the order of the Church. Dante and the hierocrats are agreed as to the absolute validity of the fundamental principle implicit in the philosophy of Aristotle, viz. that everything which falls within a given genus is reduced to a single term, the measure of everything which falls within that genus: *Omnia quae sunt unius generis reducuntur ad unum, quod est mensura omnium quae sub illo genere sunt.* The antagonism between Dante and the hierocrats arises from the fact that they do not agree as to the number and nature of the genera which should be thus reduced to uniformity.

Whenever Dante has to settle a conflict of authorities, his first care is to define the *genus* of the authorities in question. Indeed, in his eyes the independence and the autonomy of the genera constitute an invariable rule. Let us, for instance, suppose we are seeking that which possesses authority over man; we shall have to propound the question in terms of man *qua* man, *and in no other sense.* Man is what he is *qua* man by virtue of his substantial form, which places him in a genus (animal), in a species of that genus (reasonable), and makes him a substance. He who has authority in the genus "man" is therefore the unit of measure

by which the worth of those substances which we call men is
estimated. For all men fall within one and the same genus; they
are therefore reduced to a single term which is their measure.
What is this term? It is the perfect man, the Idea of man, if
one may so put it; in other words, it is the pattern of the virtuous
man as described in the final books of the *Ethica ad Nicomachum.*
If, therefore, we wish to know who has authority to say how man
should live *qua man*, it is fitting that we should turn to him who
most perfectly realizes in himself human nature, the substance
"man". The rule has no exceptions and applies to every man,
including Popes and Emperors: *Nam, prout sunt homines, habent
reduci ad optimum hominem, qui est mensura omnium aliorum et ydea,
ut dicam, quisquis ille sit, ad existentem maxime unum in genere
suo: ut haberi potest ex ultimis Ethica ad Nicomachum* ("For, in so
far as they are men, their standard must be the most excellent
man (whoever he may be) who is the measure and ideal of all
others, so to say—he who is in the highest degree one in his own
kind, as may be inferred from the end of the *Ethica ad Nicomachum*") (III, 12).

It inevitably follows from this that if, *qua* men, the Pope and
the Emperor ought to be reduced to uniformity, both are
amenable to a principle and a measure other than the Papacy
and the Empire. Both should in that case be judged by the
norm of Aristotle's virtuous man, whose human perfection
measures and judges their degree of human excellence. It is quite
another matter in the case of the two distinct genera which they
themselves represent. To be Emperor, or to be Pope, is not the
same as to be a man. To be an Emperor, *as such*, is to be a master;
to be a Pope, *as such*, is to be a spiritual father. Now, just as a
man is a man by virtue of the substantial form which causes him
to be such, he is a master, or he is a father, by virtue of the
incidental forms which cause a specific human being to be also
a master or a father. In other words, one is a man and is judged
as such in the category of substance, but one is a master, or a
father, and is judged as such, in the category of relationship.
Thus, the Pope regarded as a Pope is such by virtue of the
incidental form of Papacy, which confers on him the relationship, incidental to the human substance, of spiritual fatherhood.
The Emperor, regarded as an Emperor, is such by virtue of the
incidental form of the Imperial authority (*imperiatum*), which

confers on him the relationship, incidental to the substance "man", of sovereign lordship of men's wills. If, therefore, one wishes to reduce the two genera to uniformity, it is useless to seek a measure common to them both, for it does not exist; one can hope to find a principle of uniformity and of measure only in each of these two orders of relationship taken separately: *Altera sub ambitu paternitatis et altera sub ambitu dominationis* ("The one in the sphere of fatherhood and the other in the sphere of authority") (III, 12). Hence three distinct orders, whose independence is in Dante such that one can never generalize from one to another: All men are governed and measured by the ideal man of Aristotle; all spiritual sons are governed and measured by the supreme father, who is the Pope; all subordinates are governed and measured by the supreme sovereign, who is the Emperor. The fatal error which it is important not to commit would be to wish to subordinate one of these principles to another, as if it were possible for them to fall within a single genus or a single species. Dante is categorical on this point, for his whole doctrine is bound up with it: *Non potest dici quod alterum subalternetur alteri* ("It cannot be said that the one is subordinate to the other") (III, 12). Thus, just as the Pope has no superior *qua* Pope, the Emperor has no superior *qua* Emperor, nor the wise man *qua* man.

None—let us be clear—in this world. For God is the measure and the supreme authority that governs, measures and judges all substances and all relationships. If we assemble these notions, we obtain the following scheme, which summarizes the disposition of the authorities in the Dantesque universe:

Deus
(God)

Substantia humanae naturae (Substance of human nature)	Relatio dominationis (Relationship of authority)	Relatio paternitatis (Relationship of fatherhood)
Optimus homo (The most excellent man)	Imperator (Emperor)	Papa (Pope)

This is how the tripartite scheme of authorities which the *Banquet* suggests is reconstituted and completed in the *Monarchy*. So that it may be justified completely, it remains to be proved that, like the Pope's, the Emperor's authority is *directly* subject to the will of God alone.

IV. THE TWO FORMS OF BEATITUDE

In order to establish his thesis on an unshakable foundation, Dante chose to base it on the actual structure of the human entity. Alone of all creatures man occupies the middle point between the corruptible beings and the incorruptible beings; that is why the philosophers compare him, with good reason, to a horizon, the common limit of two hemispheres.[1] Indeed, man is composed of two essential parts, soul and body. He is corruptible in terms of one of these parts—the body; in terms of the other, which is the soul, he is incorruptible. As Aristotle says in Book III of his *De Anima*, referring to the incorruptibility of the soul: "And this alone may be separated, as being everlasting, from what is corruptible."[2] If, therefore, man occupies the middle point between the wholly incorruptible natures (the independent substances) and the wholly corruptible natures (the unreasoning animals), he must also, like any middle term, partake of the nature of the two extremes. Man must therefore have something of the nature both of corruptible beings and of incorruptible beings. Now the nature of anything is designed in view of a specific ultimate goal. If, then, man's nature is twofold, his goal must also be twofold. It will no doubt be objected that this is a unique case; but man, in fact, is a unique case in the universe, since he alone is thus placed at the frontier of two worlds: "Hence, just as, alone of all beings, he partakes of incorruptibility and of corruptibility, so too, alone of all beings, he is designed in view of two final goals (*in duo ultima*), of which one is his goal in so far as he is corruptible, the other, on the contrary, in so far as he is incorruptible" (III, 16). In other words, man has one final goal in so far as he comprises a mortal body,

[1] DANTE, *De Monarchia*, III, 16. Cf. ST. THOMAS AQUINAS, *Quaest. disp. de Anima*, art. I, Resp.

[2] ST. THOMAS AQUINAS, *In Aristotelis librum de Anima*, lib. III, lect. 10, ed. Pirotta, No. 473.

and another final goal in so far as he comprises an immortal soul, which amounts to saying that man has two final goals, the one to be attained in this life before death, the other to be attained in the future life after death.[1]

These *duo ultima*, which correspond in the fullest sense to the *duo beatitudini* of the *Banquet*,[2] have a strange sound to ears accustomed to the language of St. Thomas Aquinas. One of the principal theses of the latter's *De regimine principum* is, on the contrary, that man has but one final goal: the eternal beatitude to which he is summoned by God and which he can attain only through that Church without which there is no salvation. That precisely is the reason why the princes of this world are subject to the Pope, as to Jesus Christ Himself, Whose vicar he is. The connection between the two pairs of theses is here fully apparent, as is the irreducible character of their opposition. Dante maintains that man has two final goals; if both are final, neither can be subordinate to the other; if they cannot be graduated, neither can the two authorities that preside over each of these two orders. St. Thomas certainly does not deny that natural man has a natural

---

[1] Dante here uses a formula which was transparent in his time, but which may mislead his modern readers: "Nam homo, si consideratur secundum utramque partem essentialem, scilicet animam et corpus, corruptibilis est si consideretur tantum secundum unam, scilicet corpus; si vero secundum alteram, scilicet animam, incorruptibilis est" (*De Monarchia*, III, 16). This mode of expression, which is wholly classical, consists actually in contrasting the "human compound", including the soul, as the animating force of the body, with the soul considered by itself and in its own substantiality. It is even possible that Dante was here recalling a famous passage: "Duae quippe vitae sunt: una terrena, altera coelestis; altera corporea, altera spiritualis. Una qua corpus vivit ex anima, altera qua anima vivit ex Deo. Utraque bonum suum habet quo vegetatur et nutritur ut possit subsistere. Vita terrena bonis terrenis alitur, vita spiritualis bonis spiritualibus nutritur. Ad vitam terrenam pertinent omnia quae terrena sunt. Ad vitam spiritualem quae spiritualia sunt bona omnia. . . . Propterea in utroque populo secundum utramque vitam distributo, potestates sunt constitutae. In laicis . . . potestas est terrena. In clericis autem . . . potestas est divina. Illa igitur potestas saecularis dicitur, ista spiritualis nominatur. . . . Terrena potestas caput habet regem. Spiritualis potestas habet summum pontificem. Ad potestatem regis pertinent quae terrena sunt, et ad terrenam vitam facta omnia. Ad potestatem summi pontificis pertinent quae spiritualia sunt, et vitae spirituali attributa universa" (HUGH OF SAINT VICTOR, *De Sacramentis*, Lib. II, P. 2, cap. 4; Pat. lat., Vol. 176, col. 417-418). The parallelism of the two doctrines is evident, but their meaning is different. Not only does Hugh of Saint Victor say nothing of the universal Monarch who is actually the subject of Dante's treatise, but he imagines these two tribes as the two walls of the Church (*loc. cit.*, cap. 3, col. 417B), in the unity of which the whole temporal order is thus included. It is therefore natural that Hugh not only affirmed the superiority of the pontifical dignity to the royal dignity, which Dante himself will not dispute, but attributed to the Sovereign Pontiff the power of conferring the kingship (*loc. cit.*, cap. 4, col. 418D), which Dante categorically denies him (*De Monarchia*, III, 6). Regarding this part of Dante's reasoning, consult B. NARDI, *Saggi di filosofia dantesca*, pp. 272-284.

[2] See above, Chap. II, pp. 129-142.

goal to seek and attain in this life. Rather ought it to be said that, of all the theologians of the Middle Ages, none did more than he to establish this thesis. It is inseparable from his differentiation between nature and grace, which pervades his work like a principle infinitely productive of unity in the sphere of life. On the other hand, differentiation between the orders is accompanied by unity in the Thomistic doctrine only because here differentiation between the orders entails their gradation. Consequently St. Thomas never admitted that man's natural goal in this life was man's final goal in this life, for man experiences this life only with a view to the after-life, and his goal in this life is to be sought only with a view to the goal of the after-life. With an utter inflexibility that excludes in advance Dante's thesis considered in its proper form, St. Thomas declares that the final goal of the body of society is not to live in accordance with virtue, but, through a virtuous life, to come to the enjoyment of God: *Non est ergo ultimus finis multitudinis congregatae vivere secundum virtutem, sed per virtuosam vitam pervenire ad fruitionem divinam.* Once the goals have been thus graduated, those who are charged with leading men to them are inevitably graduated as well, for those who are charged with the care of the preliminary goals must be subject to whoever is in charge of the final goal, and must be guided by his orders: *Sic enim ei ad quem finis ultimi cura pertinet, subdi debent illi ad quos pertinet cura antecedentium finium et ejus imperio dirigi.*

Hence, there is in genuine Thomism a supreme head, who controls all other heads, for the simple reason that "he who is in charge of the final goal always finds himself in command of [*imperare*] those who labour at the means prescribed for the attainment of the final goal".[1] Such, in St. Thomas's eyes, is the Roman Pontiff, mankind's supreme guide to the beatific vision, the sole end of man, beyond which there is no other and in comparison with which all the rest are only a means. Since he conceded to St. Thomas, and in the first place to Aristotle, that the head is he who prescribes the means with a view to the end, Dante could only avoid St. Thomas's conclusion if he refused to subordinate the end envisaged by the Emperor to the

---

[1] ST. THOMAS AQUINAS, *De regimine principum*, I, 14. It will be profitable to compare the analogous doctrine of twofold beatitude, in ENGELBERTI . . . ADMONTENSIS, *De ortu et fine Romani Imperii*, Basileae, J. Oporinus, 1553, cap. XVII, pp. 92-98.

end envisaged by the Pope. That is why, as we have just seen, he exalted the goal of political life to the dignity of a final goal, thus making of the Imperial power a supreme authority in its own sphere, an authority "in charge of a final goal", like the Roman Pontiff.

We do not know if Dante had in mind the doctrine of St. Thomas Aquinas when he wrote these pages, but it is a fact that the *De Monarchia, III*, 16 is in such direct opposition to the *De regimine principum, I*, 13 that it could not have been more so if Dante had written his chapter with the intention of refuting that of St. Thomas. Furthermore, it is noteworthy that, as he here opposes St. Thomas, he elsewhere opposes his continuator Tolomeo di Lucca, with such frequency that it can scarcely be doubted that he had before his eyes the *De regimine principum* as completed by Tolomeo, that is to say as we know it to-day. This fact does not constitute a proof, for there are many arguments which are employed by all defenders of the subordination of the State to the Church, but the analogies between the two treatises seem too numerous to be attributed to mere chance.[1] Whatever the truth of the matter, the doctrinal opposition between Dante and St. Thomas remains a fact in itself, and one that certainly seems undeniable.[2]

---

[1] See THEODORE SILVERSTEIN, *On the Genesis of "De Monarchia, II, 5"*, in *Speculum*, July, 1938 (Vol. XIII, No. 3), pp. 326–349. The object of this work is to establish that, as regards the passage in question, the *De Monarchia* draws its inspiration from, what time it opposes, the *Determinatio compendiosa de Iurisdictione imperii*, ascribed to Tolomeo di Lucca (ed. Marius Krammer, Hanover and Leipzig, Hahn, 1909), and the *De regimine principum*, Tolomeo's continuation.

[2] It is quite true that St. Thomas regards the determination of man's natural goal as the task of natural reason (cf. G. MANACORDA, *Storicismo attualista: seconda puntata*, in *Sofia*, Vol. II, January–June, 1934–XII, p. 153). It should even be conceded to this author that St. Thomas proves by reason alone that man's final goal is the sight of God (*Sum. theol.*, Ia IIæ, qu. II, art. 8, and qu. III, art. 1 and 8). What we have not succeeded in finding in St. Thomas is that man has another *ultimum* besides the beatific vision. The question here is not whether reason alone is equal to discovering what this *ultimum* is, but whether, in the Thomistic doctrine, man has one *ultimum*, or two *ultima*. Now not only—so far as we know—did St. Thomas never speak of *duo ultima*, nor, in this sense, of *duplex finis*, but his doctrine excludes even the possibility of their existence. When he speaks of Aristotle, a pure philosopher, St. Thomas tells us "quod opinio Aristotelis fuit quod ultima felicitas quam homo in vita ista acquirere potest, sit cognitio de rebus divinis qualis per scientias speculativas haberi potest" (*Cont. Gent.*, III, 44, *sub fin.*); but instead of deducing from this that Christians have two final goals, St. Thomas comes to the conclusion "quod ultima hominis felicitas non sit in hac vita" (*Cont. Gent.*, III, 48). And here it is certainly a question of the final goal naturally desired by man: "Felicitas autem est ultimus finis, quem homo naturaliter desiderat. Est igitur hominis desiderium naturale ad hoc quod in felicitate stabiliatur. . . . In vita autem ista non est aliqua certa stabilitas. . . . Non est igitur possibile in hac vita esse ultimam hominis felicitatem" (*loc. cit.*). If there is any natural felicity in this life, far from constituting a

Starting from this point, indeed, Dante will now make the principle of finality yield consequences quite contrary to those which St. Thomas Aquinas had inferred from it. Providence, we said, has offered man two final goals: happiness in this life, which consists in the practice of characteristically human virtue, and the happiness of eternal life, which consists in the enjoyment of the sight of God and which man cannot attain through his natural powers unaided by grace. Now, points out Dante, just as we must have different middle terms in order to reach different conclusions, we must use different means to attain different ends. We shall therefore reach our natural final goal by following the teachings of the philosophers, that is to say by regulating our actions in accordance with the law of the intellectual and moral virtues. We shall reach our supernatural final goal thanks to spiritual teachings, which transcend human reason, provided that we obey them by acting in accordance with the theological virtues—faith, hope and charity (III, 16).

This is the exact point at which Dante will epitomize his whole doctrine in a wonderfully compact sentence in which every word tells and every member assigns its special function to each of the three authorities which share control of the Dantesque universe: "Although these conclusions and means have been shown to us, some by human reason, which has been explained to us in its entirety[1] by the philosophers, others thanks to the

---

goal distinct from the final goal, it is merely a stepping-stone to it. Such, says St. Thomas, seems to have been the thought of Aristotle (*loc. cit*, *Potest autem aliquis . . .*), who, unaware that the beatific vision was possible, "posuit hominem non consequi felicitatem perfectam, sed suo modo" (*ibid., Propter has autem . . .*). It therefore seems wrong to put into St. Thomas's mouth, in order to bring Dante closer to him, such expressions as "la salute puramente terrena" (G. MANACORDA, *op. cit.*, p. 153), not only because St. Thomas does not make use of them, but because all his energies are bent on proving that man's final goal, as conceived by natural reason, is prescribed as a stepping-stone, and is subordinate, to that goal of whose attainment Revelation shows us the possibility. Dante's dualism, and the *temporal final goal* which it implies, are excluded in advance by St. Thomas. B. Nardi, with great shrewdness, has seen and pointed out that there is disagreement here between Dante and St. Thomas, and that this difference implies another, regarding the nature of philosophy itself (*Saggi di filosofia dantesca*, p. 282 and pp. 304–305). I am convinced that he is entirely right on this point, and even that what he says is an incontestable and obvious historical fact. On the other hand, the reflections with which he accompanies his conclusions (pp. 282–283) seem to me of most doubtful quality. There are feelings at work behind the writings of Dante, as there are behind those of St. Thomas, but the two compositions are governed by a perfect logic, which unfolds its consequences starting from different principles.

[1] Dante here uses some very strong expressions: "Has igitur conclusiones et media, licet ostensa sint nobis, haec ab humana ratione quae per philosophos *tota* nobis innotuit . . ." (*De Monarchia*, III, 16). In the *Defensor pacis*, even the Averroists Marsilius of Padua and Jean de Jandun will not dare to go so far ("Has etenim [disciplinas] *quasi*

Holy Spirit which has revealed to us the supernatural truth essential to man through the Prophets, the sacred writers, the co-eternal Son of God, Jesus Christ, and His disciples, human greed would none the less turn its back on them if men, like horses which in their brutishness run wild, were not curbed by the bridle and the bit" (III, 16). Nothing could be clearer than the distinction between these three authorities: philosophy, which teaches us the *whole* truth about the natural goal of man; theology, which alone leads us to our supernatural goal; finally, political power, which, holding human greed in check, constrains men, by the force of the law, to respect the natural truth of the philosophers and the supernatural truth of the theologians.

If, then, we arrange these ideas, we obtain the following scheme (shown on opposite page), in which the two forms of beatitude are seen to be as distinct from and as independent of each other as are the means to their attainment and the two supreme authorities by which men are led to them.

If this is correct, the special function of the Priesthood and the Empire stands clearly revealed, and the radical distinction between their goals is the most complete guarantee of their independence that could be desired. On the one hand, the Pope, who leads the human race to eternal life through revelation; on the other hand, the Emperor, who leads the human race to temporal happiness through philosophy. Thus is newly affirmed the alliance between Philosophy and the Empire already proclaimed in the *Banquet: Propter quod opus fuit homini duplici directivo secundum duplicem finem: scilicet summo Pontifice, qui secundum revelata humanum genus perduceret ad vitam eternam, et Imperatore, qui*

---

omnes habemus ex traditione admirabilis Philosophi et reliquorum gloriosorum virorum. . . ."—*Defensor pacis*, I, 6, 9, ed. Previté-Orton, Cambridge U.P., 1928, p. 25). It seems, however, that it would be a waste of time to try to extract from this passage an answer to the question: Is Dante a complete rationalist? His words are important only for the problem they propound. Dante is certainly thinking here of Aristotle and his *Ethica ad Nicomachum*; what he means to say is that natural human reason, alone and unaided by faith, is equal to discovering *all the moral truth necessary for the good management of the Empire*. The rest does not interest him here. When, like L. Pietrobono, one tries to make him say more, one provokes a reply that makes him say less, like that of M. Barbi (*Razionalismo e misticismo* . . . , IV, in *Studi Danteschi*, Vol. XVII (1933), pp. 5–44, especially pp. 29–31). In both cases he is made to say something different from what he did say. Dante explicitly taught that faith surpasses reason in all that concerns heavenly things, such as the independent Intelligences or God Himself. That is why he repeats that our intellect does not attain perfection in this life; but Dante never said that our intellect was not fully equal to leading us to *the natural final goal of earthly life*. He even says the opposite in the passage from the *De Monarchia*, III, 16, which we are commenting upon here and in those from the *Convivio* which we have already studied (pp. 105–112).

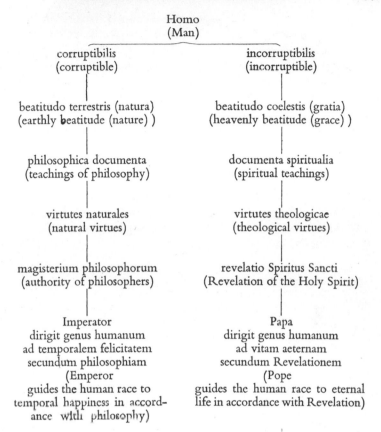

Homo
(Man)

corruptibilis   incorruptibilis
(corruptible)   (incorruptible)

beatitudo terrestris (natura)   beatitudo coelestis (gratia)
(earthly beatitude (nature))   (heavenly beatitude (grace))

philosophica documenta   documenta spiritualia
(teachings of philosophy)   (spiritual teachings)

virtutes naturales   virtutes theologicae
(natural virtues)   (theological virtues)

magisterium philosophorum   revelatio Spiritus Sancti
(authority of philosophers)   (Revelation of the Holy Spirit)

Imperator   Papa
dirigit genus humanum   dirigit genus humanum
ad temporalem felicitatem   ad vitam aeternam
secundum philosophiam   secundum Revelationem
(Emperor   (Pope
guides the human race to   guides the human race to eternal
temporal happiness in accord-   life in accordance with Revelation)
ance with philosophy)

secundum philosophica documenta genus humanum ad temporalem felicitatem dirigeret ("Wherefore man needed a twofold authority, in accordance with his twofold goal—namely the Sovereign Pontiff, to lead the human race in accordance with Revelation on to eternal life, and the Emperor, to guide the human race in accordance with the teachings of philosophy to temporal felicity"). Only the Emperor can ensure to human communities the order and peace without which neither of these two goals can be attained. Such is the special function which God has assigned to him; such, too, is the authority which he owes to God alone, and to no one else. It is therefore obvious that the temporal authority of the Emperor descends to him directly, *sine ullo medio* ("through no intermediary"), from the divine and unique source whence all forms of authority are derived. Most certainly, as Dante opportunely recalls in the last lines of his treatise, the happiness of this mortal life is prescribed, in a certain way—in a way which he does not, as it happens, specify—with a view to immortal beatitude. The Roman Emperor is therefore subject to the Pope in something—something which this time he will specify: the supremacy of the Pope is the supremacy of Fatherhood: "Let Caesar therefore show for Peter that respect which an eldest son should show for his father. Thus, lightened by paternal *grace*, he will the more efficaciously lighten this terrestrial orb, of which he has been appointed ruler by *Him alone* Who orders all things, both temporal and spiritual."[1]

Some have tried to find in these last lines a belated repudiation of the entire treatise.[2] To do so is to misread them badly, for their last words would then be a repudiation of the repudiation

---

[1] "Quae quidem veritas ultimae quaestionis non sic stricte recipienda est, ut Romanus Princeps in aliquo Romano Pontifici non subjaceat, cum mortalis ista felicitas quodam modo ad immortalem felicitatem ordinetur. Illa igitur reverentia Caesar utatur ad Petrum qua primogenitus filius debet uti ad patrem: ut luce paternae gratiae illustratus virtuosius orbem terrae irradiet, cui ab Illo solo praefectus est, qui est omnium spiritualium et temporalium gubernator" (DANTE, *De Monarchia*, III, 16). The expression *quodam modo* is vague. It is therefore dangerous to try to define its meaning. Nevertheless, the comparison between earthly felicity and the Earthly Paradise on the one hand, and heavenly felicity and the Heavenly Paradise on the other (*De Monarchia*, III, 16), suggests a possible interpretation. If earthly felicity is to heavenly felicity as the Earthly Paradise is to the Heavenly Paradise, we may say that it is designed with a view to it in the same way as a prefiguration is designed with a view to that which it prefigures. I give this interpretation, however, merely as a hypothesis; there is no passage in Dante that warrants it. It is possible, as B. NARDI would have it (*Saggi di filosofia dantesca*, p. 285), that this conclusion is an addition made by Dante after the completion of the treatise. Yet this is by no means certain, for in it Dante retracts nothing of what he has said. On the other hand, the sentence certainly betrays his desire to conclude on as conciliatory a note as possible, by going as far to meet his opponents as his doctrine permits him to go.

[2] The conclusion of the *De Monarchia* is the chief argument of those who seek to make Dante conform to the absolute authority of the Church on this point. Thus, among many others, J. RIVIÈRE, *Le problème de l'Eglise et de l'Etat au temps de Philippe le Bel*, Paris, 1926, p. 338. Bellarmin is largely responsible for this movement of reconciliation (cf. P. RONZY, *Bellarmin et Dante*, in *Mélanges sur Dante*, ed. P. Mignon, *Nouvelle Revue d'Italie*, Rome, 1931, pp. 93–108; especially pp. 106–107). More recently, G. Manacorda has returned to this passage in opposition to G. Gentile (G. MANACORDA, *Storicismo attualista: seconda puntata*, in *Sofia*, Vol. II, January–June, 1934–XII, p. 152). In doing so he forgets that if the Emperor receives from the Pope the grace which enables him the better to exercise his authority, he by no means receives that authority from him. To G. Gentile, who opposes to the orthodox doctrine the Dantesque idea of a "purely human State", G. Manacorda retorts: "And where, then, is the *purely human* State, if the State derives its authority from God?" If it comes to that, how can nature exist, if it is created by God? In Dante's eyes, the Emperor does not derive his authority from the Pope for the very reason that he derives it from God. On the other hand, some entirely objective conclusions will be found in F. KERN, *Humana civilitas*, p. 27, note 1, and in N. ZINGARELLI, *La vita, i tempi e le opere di Dante*, Vallardi, Milan, 1931, Parte IIa, p. 701.

itself—*cui ab Illo solo praefectus est* ("of which he has been put in command by Him alone"), says Dante explicitly. To the end, therefore, the Emperor remains independent of the Pope in the field of the Imperial authority. From him he only receives grace; he therefore owes him only the son's respect for a father whose goal is nobler than that which falls within his own competence, *but on whom he is dependent only in the specifically separate field of spiritual fatherhood*. Let us, moreover, remember who are Dante's chief opponents throughout this Third Book: *Isti vero ad quos erit tota disputatio sequens, asserentes auctoritatem Imperii ab auctoritate Ecclesiae dependere velut artifex inferior dependet ab architecto . . .* ("Now those to whom the whole of the following disputation will be directed, inasmuch as they assert that the authority of the Empire is subordinate to the authority of the Church just as the junior artisan is subordinate to the architect . . .") (III, 4). Whether he knows it or not, what he is rejecting is certainly St. Thomas's thesis. If we are to find in these last lines a repudiation of the entire work, which would in itself be rather strange, we must once more forget that the graduation of the orders in the matter of *absolute dignity* does not confer on the superior orders any *authority* over the inferior ones. In Dante, the orders of jurisdiction are closed systems, which meet only in God.

The *De Monarchia*, then, is a perfect complement to the *Banquet*, each work settling the specific problem with which it deals, and dovetailing into the other. Henceforth we see Dante's world as a system of relationships of authority and obedience. In this world philosophy rules over reason, but the wills of philosophers owe obedience to the Emperor and their faith owes allegiance to the Pope. The Emperor rules alone over men's wills, but his reason owes obedience to the Philosopher and his faith to the Pope. The Pope rules without peer over men's souls, but his reason owes obedience to the Philosopher and his will to the Emperor. All three, however, owe obedience and the tribute of faith to Him from Whom each immediately derives the supreme authority which he exercises in his own sphere—to God, the sovereign Emperor of the terrestrial world as well as of the celestial world, in Whose unity all irreconcilables meet.

In order, therefore, to obtain a comprehensive scheme of the human *ultima* and of the authorities that preside over them we should have to place at the top God, as being the sovereign Love and the supreme Mover Who draws the universal human fellowship to Himself through the following twofold *ultimum*:[1]

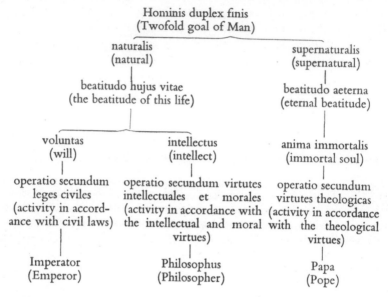

Hominis duplex finis
(Twofold goal of Man)

naturalis
(natural)

supernaturalis
(supernatural)

beatitudo hujus vitae
(the beatitude of this life)

beatitudo aeterna
(eternal beatitude)

voluntas
(will)

intellectus
(intellect)

anima immortalis
(immortal soul)

operatio secundum
leges civiles
(activity in accordance with civil laws)

operatio secundum virtutes
intellectuales et morales
(activity in accordance with the intellectual and moral virtues)

operatio secundum
virtutes theologicas
(activity in accordance with the theological virtues)

Imperator
(Emperor)

Philosophus
(Philosopher)

Papa
(Pope)

To convince oneself of the gulf that here separates Dante from St. Thomas, it is enough to refer to the passage in which the Dominican Guido Vernani takes his stand against the thesis of "twofold beatitude" propounded in the *Monarchy*. "This man," says Vernani of Dante, "did not need to discern a twofold beatitude resulting from a twofold nature, corruptible and incorruptible, for in corruptible nature there can, strictly speaking, be neither virtue nor beatitude. He says, moreover, that man is predestined to these two goals by God. Whereupon I say that man is not predestined by God to temporal beatitude as to a final goal, because such beatitude has never been capable of ending

---

[1] This scheme deals with the different forms of jurisdiction, not with those of dignity. The noblest goal is the Pope's, then the Philosopher's, finally the Emperor's, but this does not mean that the Pope as such has any authority over the Philosopher or over the Emperor as such. That is why, in Dante, one order may be designed with a view to another as if the latter were its goal without, however, being subordinate to it in the matter of authority. Thus, it is true to say that the goal of political peace is to make possible the contemplative life (cf. F. KERN, *Humana civilitas*, pp. 17–22 and pp. 127 *seq.*), but it in no way follows from this—nor, for that matter, does Kern maintain that it does —that political authority is dependent on the authority of the philosopher or on that of the theologian.

and satisfying man's hunger. Even philosophically speaking, the
action of such virtues [*sc.* the moral virtues] is designed with a
view to the contemplative life, in order that through those
virtues man, all his passions having been quelled, may more
calmly and freely contemplate eternal things. . . . Man is
therefore predestined to eternal felicity as to his final goal, and
should organize and employ all his assets—natural, moral and
supernatural—with a view to securing it."[1] There is not one
original word in this criticism of Dante, but that is the very
reason why it interests us. Guido Vernani's firm opposition to
Dante is nothing but the opposition of the Thomistic universe
to one of the gravest dangers that have ever threatened it.

V. Dante's Place in History

The most laborious, but the surest and most profitable, way
to estimate correctly the meaning and importance of Dante's
political philosophy, particularly as regards the idea of philosophy
implicit in it, is to place it in its proper historical and doctrinal
perspective. It would be something of merely local importance,
were it possible to conceive of a political philosophy which did
not depend on any general philosophy. Such is not the case, and
we shall shortly see that Dante's attitude to these problems
involved him in a certain number of other questions, the exact
determination of which is important for the understanding of
his work.

It may be postulated as a historically verifiable philosophical
law that *the manner in which one conceives the relationship of the
State to the Church, that in which one conceives the relationship of
philosophy to theology and that in which one conceives the relationship
of nature to grace, are necessarily correlated.* Considered from this
point of view, the political doctrines of the Middle Ages may be
divided, roughly at least, into three main types. There can be
no question of identifying any one of them with one of these
types: the facts of history do not in their diversity permit themselves to be identified with pure doctrinal essences any more

[1] Guido Vernani, *De reprobatione Monarchiae*, ed. Jarro (G. Piccini), Bemporad,
Florence, 1906, pp. 42 and 45. As regards this treatise and its author's writings, see M.
Grabmann, *Studien über den Einfluss der aristotelischen Philosophie auf die mittelalterlichen
Theorien über das Verhältnis von Kirche und Staat*, Munich, 1934, pp. 76–100.

than individuals permit themselves to be identified with the
essential type of their species. One may, however, relate particular doctrines to certain types, of which they are distinct
individual realizations, and classify them according as the resemblance which they bear to one or another of them is more or
less striking.

The first of these types is characterized by a dominating
tendency to integrate the order of nature with the order of
grace in the highest degree possible. Doctrines of this type
may be recognized by the fact that in them the distinction
between grace and nature tends to merge into the distinction
between good and evil. The reason for this is obvious. These are
essentially religious doctrines. Centring on the problem of
healing fallen nature, these doctrines take into account only
that part of nature which needs to be healed through grace,
that is to say the wounds that have been inflicted on it by sin—
in short, its corruption. If one is to appraise this attitude correctly,
it is essential not to transform it into a philosophical doctrine.
To do so would be tantamount to making those who adopt it
say that nature is essentially evil. As Christians, they know, on
the contrary, that all that is, in so far as it is, is good. When
they speak of nature, they do so not as philosophers whose
purpose is to define its essence, but as doctors who regard it as
a patient to be cured, or rather as priests who regard it as a
creature to be saved. The *opus creationis* ("work of creation")
interests the philosopher directly, but the *opus recreationis* ("work
of re-creation") is the direct concern of the priest. The attitude
to nature which we are describing is essentially a "priestly"
attitude. As such, it is characterized by three features, whose
permanence in history is remarkable: it tends to integrate the
order of nature with the order of grace in the highest degree
possible, to integrate the order of reason with that of faith in the
highest degree possible, and to integrate the order of the State
with that of the Church in the highest degree possible.

Since it is this third aspect of the problem that particularly
engages our attention here, it will be enough to go back as far
as St. Augustine to find its prototype. If there is anything that
corresponds to the formula "political Augustinism", it should
be said that, when it penetrates into political problems, Augustinism tends to integrate the State with the Church, by virtue of

an internal logic which nothing in it can keep from reaching its conclusion. The two communities which Augustine took a special delight in describing and which include all others are the City of God and the Earthly City. Now both are supernatural and religious cities, designated by two "mystic" names, of which one, Jerusalem, designates the community of all the elect, past, present and future, while the other, Babylon, designates the community formed by all the damned, past, present and future. Strictly speaking, no earthly community can be identified with one or the other of these mystic cities; indeed, it cannot be said that the Church harbours only the elect, or even that it harbours all the elect; yet the Church is the most exact approximation on earth to the City of God, because it is the city of God's intention; as for Babylon, it is the worldly city and the prototype of all pagan States, in so far as, in accordance with Pagan laws, their organization has in view ends that are not God's ends.[1]

In the form in which he left it, Augustine's doctrine contained an idea of capital importance: that of a universal religious city; but it said nothing of a universal temporal community of which. on the morrow of the sack of Rome by the Barbarians, the condition of the Roman Empire scarcely invited him to think. Augustine cannot, then, be represented as having absorbed the Empire into the Church. Undoubtedly he considers that a Christian Emperor can and should serve the Church, but the State itself, regarded as such, is in his eyes simply a variable quantity. If the State is essentially pagan, as had been the case with the old Roman Empire, it is essentially evil and may in fact be identified with Babylon, as the Church may be with Jerusalem. If the State is not exclusively pagan, but tolerates Christian citizens, or is even governed by a Christian ruler, its members will be divided between the two mystic cities to which they owe allegiance: "Just as there is only one holy city— Jerusalem—so there is only one city of iniquity—Babylon. All the wicked belong to Babylon just as all the godly belong to Jerusalem."[2] As for the States themselves, they are no longer

---

[1] For the sake of greater brevity, I venture at this point to refer the reader to my *Introduction à l'étude de saint Augustin*, Paris, J. Vrin, 1929, Chap. IV, §II: *La société chrétienne*, pp. 220–238.

[2] ST. AUGUSTINE, *Enarr. in Ps. 86, 6*; Pat. lat., Vol. 37, col. 1106. H. SCHOLZ (*Glaube und Unglaube in der Weltgeschichte. Ein Kommentar zu Augustins De Civitate Dei . . .*, Leipzig, J. C. Hinrich'sche Buchhandlung, 1921, p. 102) says that Augustine passed on

in either camp, for they can no longer be identified with Babylon and they have not yet become one with Jerusalem.

As soon as there was a Holy Roman Empire, its integration with the Church became, on the contrary, inevitable by virtue of the very principles which Augustine had laid down. If, in practice, a pagan State may be automatically identified with Babylon, a Christian State may be automatically identified with Jerusalem. After the reign of Charlemagne, during that of Louis the Pious, the integration of the State with the Church is an accomplished fact. Beginning from this time, indeed, we encounter with growing frequency examples of those distinctive formulas *in which the definition of the Church includes the State.* This is a new fact and one big with consequences. To tell the truth, from the very day that theologians and canonists first gave currency to a conception of the Church in which the temporal order was included as a matter of course, a reaction such as Dante's became inevitable. "The body of the Holy Church of God in its entirety divides to form principally two eminent persons," it was said as early as the ninth century, "the priestly and the royal." Likewise Jonas of Orleans: "All the faithful should know that the universal Church is the body of Christ, its head is this same Christ, and in it (*in ea*) we find, principally, two persons, to wit, the priestly and the royal, and the predominance of the priestly over the other is the greater inasmuch as it will have to render an account to God even of kings."[1]

---

temporal society "ein reguläres Todesurteil". In reality Augustine condemns the earthly, city, but not necessarily temporal society. In his eyes, what is evil is not temporality, but the "world". Conversely, the mediaeval conception of a universal theocracy has been called "political Augustinism" (H. X. ARQUILLIÈRE, *Sur la formation de la "Théocratie pontificale"*, in Mélanges Ferdinand Lot, Paris, E. Champion, 1925, and the same author's *L'Augustinisme politique*, Paris, J. Vrin, 1934). The formula has the advantage of emphasizing the part played by the thought of Augustine in the doctrinal justification of mediaeval theocracy; its drawback, very clearly seen and indicated by its author, is that it fosters the belief that St. Augustine himself thought of it. If he prepared it, he did so, in the words of H. X. Arquillière, "in spite of the fact that he was far from suspecting it". The formula is, in any case, of little importance; the essential thing is to remember that nothing like a "Pontifical theocracy" was ever advocated or even, apparently, imagined by St. Augustine.

[1] The first passage is taken from a Letter addressed by the bishops of the Empire in 829 (Council of Paris) to the Emperor Louis the Pious; see *Mon. Germ. historica*, Leg., sect. II, Vol. II, No. 196, quoted by R. W. CARLYLE in *A History of Mediaeval Political Theory in the West*, London, 1903, Vol. I, p. 254: "Principaliter itaque totius sanctae Dei ecclesiae corpus in duas eximias personas, in sacerdotalem videlicet et regalem, sicut a sanctis patribus traditum accepimus, divisum esse novimus, de qua re Gelasius Romanae sedis venerabilis episcopus . . . ," etc. It is true that Gelasius, Pope from 492 to 496, had

Beginning from the moment when the temporal order itself was thus integrated with the Church, there remained, to be sure, a Church to represent the City of God, but there no longer remained a pagan Empire to represent the Earthly City. Thus, as a consequence at once surprising and inevitable, Jerusalem alone remained and Babylon disappeared. This is what Otto of Freising explicitly says in his celebrated *De duabus civitatibus*. Finding himself further from events than Augustine, Otto dates the disappearance of Babylon from the accession of Constantine. "In view of the fact that not only all men, but even the Emperors, with a few exceptions, were Catholics, it seems to me that, beginning from this time, I have written the history, not of two cities, but, so to speak, of only one, which I call the Church. For although the elect and the damned occupy a single dwelling, I can no longer call these cities two, as I have done above: I ought to say that they are really only one, although it is composite, for in it the grain is mixed with the tares."[1]

Thus, through identifying the City of God with the Church and the Earthly City with the State, men have gradually come to integrate the State with the Church, whose universality will henceforth embrace the temporal and spiritual domains alike. It is this same fundamental attitude that recurs in the thirteenth century—but this time enhanced and enriched by all the contributions made to it by contemporary philosophy and theology— in the doctrinal synthesis of Roger Bacon. Never has the priestly conception of the world been more clearly or more completely expressed than in the work of this Franciscan,[2] who may be said to be in this matter the arch-adversary of Dante. The

---

made a clear distinction between the two orders, but he did not regard them both as being inherent in the unity of the Church (see the passages quoted and analysed in CARLYLE, *op. cit.*, Vol. I, pp. 190–191. Cf. ROBERT HULL, *Mediaeval Theories of Papacy*, London, 1934, pp. 13–28). For the passage from JONAS OF ORLEANS, *De. Instit. regia*, cap. I, see CARLYLE, *op. cit.*, Vol. I, p. 254, and J. REVIRON, *Les idées politico-religieuses d'un évêque du IXe siècle. Jonas d'Orléans et son "De institutione regia"*, Paris, J. Vrin, 1930, p. 134.

[1] OTTO OF FREISING, *Chronicon*, lib. V, Prol.; lib. VII, Prol.; lib. VIII, Prol.; in *Monumenta Germaniae Historica*, Scriptorum, Vol. XX, pp. 214, 247 and 248. On the work of Otto, see J. SPÖRL, *Grundformen hochmittelalterlichen Geschichtsanschauung*, Munich, 1935, Chap. II, pp. 32–50, and the excellent Introduction by CHARLES CHRISTOPHER MIEROW to his translation of Otto, *The Two Cities. A Chronicle of Universal History to the Year 1146 A.D. by Otto Bishop of Freising*, New York, Columbia University Press, 1928 (Introduction, pp. 1–79; Bibliography, pp. 81–84).

[2] Consult on this point the penetrating work by R. CARTON, *La synthèse doctrinale de Roger Bacon*, Paris, J. Vrin, 1924, Chap. III, *Le Savoir et la Cité Chrétienne*, pp. 82–106.

Baconian universe presupposes a dovetailing of the orders, wherein that which we call nature, or natural, finds sustenance and justification only through being integrated with the super-natural and the religious. All wisdom is contained in the Holy Scriptures as the open hand is contained in the closed fist. What is called Philosophy, or Law, is merely an explanation, and, as it were, the development of what is implicit in the Scriptures. In other words, all that is valid and cogent in Philosophy or Law is virtually what may be gleaned from the Bible. Thus under-stood Christian Revelation is Wisdom itself, and it is this Wisdom, proclaimed, dispensed and applied by the Pope, that ensures the unity of the Church, governs the community of faithful peoples, ensures the conversion of infidel peoples and the destruction of those which cannot be converted.[1] In short, since the treasure of Revelation, the law of the world, is in the Pope's power, so also is the world: *Habetis ecclesiam Dei in potestate vestra, et mundum totum habetis dirigere* ("You have the Church of God in your power, and you have the task of governing the entire world").[2]

We are therefore faced here with a unitary system of Wisdom, in which each science derives its principles from the science above it, while all alike derive their principles from Revelation, which contains them. In a corresponding, or rather an identical sense, we are faced with a unitary system as regards the social order, in which all Christian temporal communities, which together form the *respublica fidelium* ("republic of the faithful"), are included in the spiritual community that is the Church, just as the sciences are included in the Wisdom to which the Pope, custodian of the treasure of Revelation, holds the key. One Wisdom, one world, one goal.

Let us now imagine a doctrine like that of St. Thomas, in which the order of nature is really distinct from that of grace,

[1] ROGER BACON, *Opus Tertium*, cap. XXIV, ed. Brewer, p. 81. Reference to this passage will serve to establish the cardinal fact that the only Law that is in Bacon's eyes completely valid is not Civil Law, but Canon Law. This single fact, which entails the complete subordination of the State to the Church, is enough to place his doctrine at the opposite extreme to Dante's. As Bacon says elsewhere (*Compendium studii theologiae*, cap. IV, ed. Brewer, p. 418), the abuse of Civil Law "non solum destruit studium sapientiae [since wisdom is the Bible, the foundation of Canon Law], sed ecclesiam Dei et omnia regna".

[2] ROGER BACON, *Opus Tertium*, cap. XXIV, ed. Brewer, p. 87. Cf.: ". . . quoniam ejus potentia coelos penetrat, purgatorium solvit, inferna conculcat, mundum com-primit universum" (*op. cit.*, cap. I, p. 8).

but subordinate to it. In such a doctrine we ought to expect to find, together with a real distinction between natural wisdom and revealed wisdom, a real distinction between the temporal order and the spiritual order, between the State and the Church. However, since we have a hierarchical system entailing the subordination of nature to grace, there will certainly have to be also a hierarchical system entailing the subordination of the temporal domain to the spiritual and of the State to the Church. Containing distinctions of a far more flexible kind and enjoying opportunities of agreement denied to that of Bacon, the Thomistic doctrine will not on that account be any the less antagonistic, in its ultimate conclusions, to that of Dante. Instead of the dovetailing and, so to speak, the telescoping of all the natural orders into the religious order, we shall have in St. Thomas's doctrine a linear hierarchy of the orders, based on a linear hierarchy of the *ultima*, which are all subordinate to the final goal of man. Now since this goal is the beatific vision, it is essentially religious. In Thomism, therefore, the Church will necessarily have direct authority over the State.

The tendency to-day, however, is to admit that St. Thomas, if he did not preach the doctrine of the "indirect" subordination of the temporal power to the spiritual, at any rate laid its foundations.[1] It is easy to see why this expression has finally gained currency. Certain mediaeval theologians did in fact attribute to the Pope an absolute and universal power, which he, according to their theory, freely delegates to princes, and which the latter, since they derive it from him, only exercise under his supervision and by virtue of his authority.[2] In such doctrines, therefore, the Pope, as a temporal sovereign, has direct temporal authority

---

[1] See especially the valuable and suggestive work by M. GRABMANN, *Studien über den Einfluss der aristotelischen Philosophie auf die mittelalterlichen Theorien über das Verhältnis von Kirche und Staat.* Munich, 1934, pp. 8–18. See also C. JOURNET, *La juridiction de l'Eglise sur la Cité,* Desclée de Brouwer, Paris, 1933, pp. 138 *seq.*

[2] Mgr. Grabmann (*op. cit.,* pp. 72–76) quotes, as being typical of this attitude, a number of passages from Dominicus de Sancto Severino (fifteenth century). They are, indeed, very interesting. Their conclusions are as follows: 1. That which is the cause and fountain-head of spiritual things is also the cause and fountain-head of temporal things; 2. The vicar of Christ, Peter's successor, is the cause and fountain-head of spiritual things, and therefore of temporal things; 3. If we refuse to identify the temporal authority of princes with that of the Pope, we shall have to admit either (*a*) that the temporal power of the Popes and that of princes do not form any design, which is impossible, since all God's works are part of a design, or (*b*) that the Pope has only spiritual power and the prince only temporal power, which is virtually the misapprehension of Mani, who maintained that the Church militant has two fountain-heads; 4. That the prince is the ruler of the

over all other temporal sovereigns. Now that is certainly not the
teaching of St. Thomas, in whose eyes even the temporal authority
of the Popes is essentially spiritual in origin as in purpose. Indeed,
the Pope's duty and right of intervention in temporal matters
is always bound up with a spiritual purpose, and is due to the fact
that that purpose falls within his competence. The expression
"indirect power" is therefore justified in so far as it indicates
the important fact that, even in temporal matters, the Pope
remains a spiritual sovereign. King and priest, it is because he is
a priest that he is a king.

This expression has, however, the disadvantage of fostering
the belief that, because the temporal power of the Popes over
princes is essentially spiritual, it is merely an advisory or cor-
rective power, exercising no direct influence over the temporal
authority of the prince as such—a power whose scope is strictly
delimited by the celebrated formula *ratione peccati*.[1] In order to

temporal world, but a subordinate ruler: *Erit caput sub capite*; 5. That, consequently, not
only is the temporal power of princes derived (*derivari*) from that of the vicar of Christ,
but even their laws and statutes are valid only in so far as they are approved and confirmed
by the Pope. It seems clear that, in its general tone and its actual principles, such a
doctrine differs from that of St. Thomas Aquinas.

[1] This tendency to minimize the temporal authority of the Pope in St. Thomas's
teaching makes itself felt even in the historical interpretation of his works. Indeed,
scholars always quote the following passages: 1. St. Thomas said that "in his autem quae
ad bonum civile pertinent, est magis obediendum potestati saeculari quam spirituali,
secundum illud Matth. XVII, 21: *Reddite quae sunt Caesaris Caesari*." But they often
forget to add the sequel, save when the Pope is involved: "Nisi forte potestati spirituali
etiam saecularis potestas conjungatur, sicut in papa, qui utriusque potestatis apicem
tenet, scilicet spiritualis et saecularis, hoc Illo disponente qui est sacerdos et rex: sacerdos
in aeternum secundum ordinem Melchisedech, rex regum et dominus dominantium,
cujus potestas non auferetur et regnum non corrumpetur in saecula saeculorum. Amen"
(*In II^m Sent.*, dist. 44, expos. text, ad 4^m, last sentence of Book II). Thus the Pope is
the supreme custodian *utriusque potestatis* and, even in temporal matters, must be obeyed
rather than the secular power; 2. Scholars also quote the famous sentence: "Jus autem
divinum, quod est ex gratia, non tollit jus humanum, quod est ex naturali ratione."
But St. Thomas employs it when answering the question: *Utrum infideles possunt habere
praelationem vel dominium supra fideles?* And this answer is that an unbeliever should
not be permitted to establish his authority over believers; that believers already under
the authority of an unbeliever have no right to evade it on their own initiative—this
by virtue of the principle defined in the formula quoted; but that, not being himself
subject to any prince, the Pope has the right to deprive this pagan prince of the authority
which he exercises over Christians. This right the Pope may use or not as he deems
expedient, just as Christ once chose to pay Caesar a tribute which he did not owe him:
ad scandalum vitandum (*Sum. theol.*, IIa IIæ, qu. 10, art. 10, Resp.). Any affirmation of
the autonomy of the temporal world in St. Thomas's teaching therefore confirms the
Pope's supremacy, for the simple reason that, as the successor and vicar of Christ, the
Pope is the supreme custodian of the two powers, the temporal and the spiritual alike.
The distinction between the "direct" power and the "indirect" power is theoretically
important; in practice, his deposition by the Pope is always the same thing so far as the
prince is concerned: whether deposed directly or indirectly, he is none the less deposed.

see how foreign such a conception is to St. Thomas it is only necessary to reconsider the particular problem against its general background, which consists in the relations between nature and grace. It is because St. Thomas always makes a real distinction between the orders that, thus distinguished, they are directly subject to graduation on a hierarchical principle. Hence, the Pope, by reason of his eminence and his supreme spiritual authority, has temporal authority over princes. How far does this authority extend? To all of the prince's activities which, in any way and in any degree, concern man's final goal, which falls within the competence of the Pope. Thus, because the goal of the political order is designed with a view to the religious and supernatural goal of the Church, the ruler of the Church as such is the ruler of princes, even in temporal matters. It would, however, be a waste of time to try to determine *a priori*, by some general formula, when, why, how and to what extent the Pope has the right of intervention in the life of the State. It rests with the Pope alone to judge. He it is who speaks or does not speak and, according to the particular circumstances, exercises or does not exercise his right to intervene in temporal matters in order to ensure to men the attainment of the final goal which God has promised them, and to which, as the vicar of Jesus Christ on earth, he leads them.

Nothing could be more lucid in this connection than the comparison that St. Thomas himself has drawn between the pagan order, the Jewish order and the Christian order. It indicates with the utmost clarity the question which dominates the whole problem. Is man's final goal temporal or spiritual? If it is temporal, priests are subordinate to princes; if it is spiritual, princes are subordinate to priests. There is absolutely no question in all this of direct or indirect power; it is a question of the hierarchical subordination of the means to the end. That is why, in Christianity, and in Christianity alone, princes are subject to the priesthood in that the Pope, *qua* Pope, has supreme authority over princes *qua* princes. Here, incidentally, is a comparative table of these relations as it emerges from the *De regimine principum* of St. Thomas, Book I, Chapter 14:

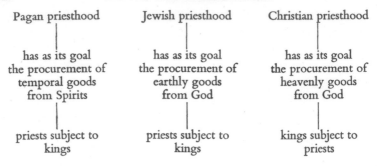

Pagan priesthood	Jewish priesthood	Christian priesthood
has as its goal the procurement of temporal goods from Spirits	has as its goal the procurement of earthly goods from God	has as its goal the procurement of heavenly goods from God
priests subject to kings	priests subject to kings	kings subject to priests

Such, then, in their nakedness, are St. Thomas's principle and its consequence. The principle: *Ei ad quem finis ultimi cura pertinet, subdi debent illi ad quos pertinet cura antecedentium finium et ejus imperio dirigi* ("Those who are in charge of the subordinate goals must submit to him who is in charge of the final goal, and they must be governed by his authority"); the consequence: *In lege Christi reges debent sacerdotibus esse subjecti* ("In the law of Christ kings must be subject to the priesthood"). Now, as St. Thomas repeated in Book I, Chapter 15, "the goal of life, which enables us to live righteously in this world, is heavenly beatitude; it is therefore an essential part of the king's function to organize the life of his people in a way that makes it easier for it to secure heavenly beatitude. The king should therefore prescribe that course which leads to heavenly beatitude, and forbid the contrary as far as possible". And how will the king get to know all this? By learning the divine law which priests are charged with teaching. There is, then, no break in the hierarchy of these powers: *Tanto est regimen sublimius, quanto ad finem ulteriorem ordinatur* ("The more remote the goal to which government is directed, the more sublime that same government"). Now man's final goal is the enjoyment of God; to lead man to this goal there must be a king who is himself not only man, but God—i.e. Jesus Christ or his successor, the Roman Pontiff, "to whom all the kings of the Christian people should be subject, as to our Lord Jesus Christ Himself". From whatever angle one regards this doctrine, one cannot make it say, as Dante says, that the Pope exercises no temporal authority over the Empire. Indeed, it says precisely the opposite, and not all the skill that is expended to bring the two doctrines into line can have the effect of reconciling them.

If this is correct, the doctrinal gulf that divides the champions of the Pope's temporal supremacy and their opponents is not fixed between Roger Bacon and Thomas Aquinas, but between Thomas Aquinas and Dante. Under the pressure of Dante's political passion, the unity of mediaeval Christendom, with its subservience to the Popes, has now been abruptly and utterly shattered. The emperor may henceforth pursue his special aim without looking to the head of the Church for anything but his blessing. Everywhere expelled from the temporal order, the authority of the Roman Pontiff finds itself confined exclusively to the order of grace. This Dantesque Pope who no longer deposes princes is therefore very different from the Pope of St. Thomas Aquinas.[1] The most remarkable thing about Dante's attitude, however, is that he understood, with a profundity of thought for which he must be commended, that *one cannot entirely withdraw the temporal world from the jurisdiction of the spiritual world without entirely withdrawing philosophy from the jurisdiction of theology.* It is because he clearly saw this fact and plainly indicated it that Dante occupies a cardinal position in the history of mediaeval political philosophy. For after all, if philosophic reason, by which the Emperor is guided,[2] were

---

[1] By the very fact that he restricts the authority of the Church to the purely spiritual domain Dante is seen to be naturally in sympathy with all who have in any sense striven to detemporalize the Church—as, for example, St. Bernard (see the excellent study by E. JORDAN, *Dante et saint Bernard*, in the *Bulletin du Comité français catholique pour la célébration du sixième centenaire de la mort de Dante Alighieri*, Oct., 1921, No. 4, pp. 267–330). Yet his attitude need not be identical with theirs, for the Spiritualists are concerned above all with the purity of the Church, whereas Dante is concerned at least as much with the independence of the Empire. To bring these two attitudes into line one would have to establish that St. Bernard refused Pope Eugenius III all right of intervention in temporal affairs, which, so far as I am aware, he never did. That is why it will not readily be conceded that Dante contented himself with repeating more or less what had already been said by St. Bernard (E. JORDAN, *Dante et l'idée de "Virtu"*, in *Mélanges sur Dante*, ed. P. Mignon, Rome, *Nouvelle Revue d'Italie*, 1931, p. 92), or, especially, that Dante forgot "the distinction between the natural and the supernatural" (*op. cit.*, p. 91). On the contrary, he speaks of nothing else. On the other hand, it will be conceded to P. FOURNIER (*Le De Monarchia de Dante et l'opinion française*, in the *Bulletin du Comité français catholique* . . . , No. 3, July, 1921, pp. 155–158), that the absolutism of Boniface VIII and of certain hierocrats partly explains Dante's reaction. Yet this movement does not entirely explain it : in his eyes, any power which the Pope may have over the temporal world is excessive by its very nature. For it is true, as E. Jordan says in the article quoted above (p. 316, note 10), that Dante's doctrine does, after all, advocate a "theocracy", but it excludes any trace of "presbyterocracy", thereby differing not only from doctrines that proclaim the absolute temporal power of the Popes, but even from that of St. Thomas Aquinas.

[2] It has been said that Dante here was unwittingly returning to the famous utopia of Plato: the State governed by the philosophers (FRITZ KERN, *Humana Civilitas. Staat Kirche und Kultur; eine Dante-Untersuchung*, Koehler, Leipzig, 1913, p. 5). That is not

to remain in the smallest degree subject to the authority of the theologians, the Pope would through their agency recover the authority over the Emperor which it is desired to take from him. By the very fact that he controlled reason, he would control the will that is guided by reason. Thus, the separation of Church and Empire necessarily presupposes the separation of theology and philosophy, and that is why, just as he split mediaeval Christendom into two camps, Dante also completely shatters the unity of Christian wisdom, the unifying principle and the bond of Christendom. In each of these vital matters this alleged Thomist struck a mortal blow at the doctrine of St. Thomas Aquinas.[1]

Faced with these indisputable facts, one appreciates why some interpreters of Dante have resolutely taxed him with Averroism.[2] And we are this time nearer the mark—but what is the Averroism in question? Is it that of Averroes himself? A primary reason for doubting it is that the principal passages in Averroes dealing with the place of religion in the State seem to have remained unknown to Dante and his contemporaries, owing to the fact that they had not been translated from the Arabic into Latin. Moreover, it is only necessary to refer to his treatise on the *Reconciliation of Religion and Philosophy* or to that part of the *Destructio destructionum* which deals with these problems to find oneself transported to a universe as different from Dante's as was his from those of Roger Bacon and St. Thomas Aquinas. It is a known fact that Averroes recognized no absolute truth apart from pure philo-

---

quite accurate. Dante expressly declares that the philosophers are incapable of governing the State; this, moreover, is the reason why he calls for an Emperor who shall rule all men—even the philosophers. The fact that Dante urges the Emperor to rule philosophically does not mean that the philosophers are the rulers. Essentially, Dante's attitude, which a sort of traditional conspiracy persists invariably in identifying with some other one, denies the Imperial authority as such access to philosophy and excludes the philosopher as such from the government of the State. Even when a philosopher-Emperor rules philosophically, he derives his authority over the human wills that are subject to him not from his wisdom, but from God alone.

[1] Considerable importance would attach to the publication of the text of Guido Vernani's unpublished commentary on the *Ethica ad Nicomachum* (in *Cod. Vat. lat.* 1172, fol. 1 r-90 r; referred to by Mgr. M. GRABMANN, *Studien über den Einfluss* . . . , p. 79), in which Guido seems to have put his finger on the sensitive spot with some shrewdness. In Lib. I, dist. 2, cap. 3, he does indeed speak *De opinione loquentium moraliter de felicitate*, but, in dist. 4, he speaks *De felicitate secundum veritatem*. Indeed, political doctrines agree or differ with regard to the Priesthood and the Empire in so far as they agree or differ with regard to this moral distinction.

[2] "A philosopher imbued with Averroism as deeply as a Christian can be—such is what Dante appears to be in his *De Monarchia* (B. LANDRY, *Dante: De la Monarchie*, Paris, F. Alcan, undated, p. 52).

sophical truth, discovered by means of the irrefutable demonstrations of reason. Below the extremely limited class of the philosophers, who alone are capable of aspiring to knowledge of this kind, Averroes placed the more numerous class of the theologians, folk who seize eagerly upon the probabilities indicated by dialectics, but are as incapable of irrefutable demonstrations as they are disinclined to aspire to them. Lower still comes the host of ordinary people, as blind to dialectical probability as to rational certainty, susceptible only to the persuasion of rhetoric and the artifices of orators with the ability to excite their imaginations and passions.[1] In a doctrine of this kind, which has with reason been termed "the most profound commentary that has ever been forthcoming on that celebrated formula: *The people must have a religion*", there can be no question for one moment of in any sense subordinating philosophy to religion. On the contrary, it is rather, indeed, religion that is subordinated to philosophy.[2] The special rôle which then devolves upon religion—and in which there is no possible substitute for it, not even philosophy—consists in teaching the people myths capable of inducing them, by their implications of punishments or pleasures in store, to live orderly and virtuous lives. An example is the doctrine of the future life, with its chastisements or its rewards—a doctrine whose prevalence among so many different religious sects must have a profound significance. That significance is as follows. The philosophers may indeed prove by reason the necessity for men to live virtuous lives, but what effect will their proofs have on the immense host of people who cannot even understand them? Only religion can perform the miracle of teaching the mass of mankind just as much as they can understand of truth, and in the exact form required in order that they may be convinced of it. Accordingly, let the people be given full knowledge of the resurrection of the body, the pains and chastisements of the life to come, prayers, sacrifices and all

---

[1] On this question consult first L. GAUTHIER, *Accord de la religion et de la philosophie. Traité d'Ibn Rochd (Averroès)*, P. Fontana, Algiers, 1905, and AVERROES, *Destructio destructionum*, Disputatio Quarta, in ARISTOTELES, *Opera omnia*, Venetiis, apud Juntas, 1550, Vol. IX, fol. 63. By far the most complete and most happily balanced study on the question is that of L. GAUTHIER, *La théorie d'Ibn Rochd (Averroès) sur le rapport de la religion et de la philosophie*, Paris, Leroux, 1909. For a more concise introduction see E. GILSON, *Reason and Revelation in the Middle Ages*, C. Scribner's, New York, 1938, Chap. II, pp. 38–53.
[2] For these formulas, see L. GAUTHIER, *La théorie d'Ibn Rochd . . .* , p. 11.

that will be deemed necessary for their moral education,[1] for that is the special function of religious doctrines—to enable the State to be well ordered by spreading enlightenment among its citizens.

That such a doctrine is completely unacceptable to a Christian is obvious, and that is why, even if he had been or was acquainted with it, Dante could not have accepted it. All his convictions rebelled against it—even his separatism. Nothing was capable of more deeply wounding his passionate feeling of respect for the complete independence of the orders than this Averroistic doctrine whereby the religious order was subordinated to the philosophical order and subjected to moral or political aims. Dante does not for one moment doubt that the noblest of human aims is to enjoy the beatific vision in a blessed eternity, or that the Church, whose sole head is the Pope, exists to lead us to it. No more than the author of the *Divine Comedy* does the author of the *Monarchy* regard the immortality of the soul, the resurrection of the body, Hell and Paradise as so many myths that help to further the ends pursued by politics and ethics. In short, there is in Dante's eyes a distinct supernatural order, existing in its own right, and all men, philosophers included, are equally bound by its special conditions, which are a means to its special end.

If there is any Averroism in Dante, and if it is not the Averroism of Averroes himself, is it not an attitude imitated from that of the Latin Averroists of the thirteenth century, such as Boethius of Dacia or Siger of Brabant? It is extremely difficult to answer "Yes" or "No" to the question so put, for the simple reason that, if Dante preached some sort of political Averroism, his *Monarchy* must be regarded, in the present state of our knowledge, as the first and perhaps the most perfect evidence of the existence of such a movement. No treatise on politics written by an Averroist and at present known to us is of earlier date than the *Monarchy*. This fact assuredly does not prove that Dante does not here draw his inspiration from Averroism. In the first place, it may be that Averroistic political writings of earlier date than his work will one day be discovered. Nor is it impossible that conversations, or even a teaching-campaign of which no written traces survive, may have exerted on Dante an influence of which

[1] AVERROES, *Destructio destructionum, loc. cit.*

the *Monarchy* is in this respect the fruit. In fact, in a passage that
has often been quoted, Pierre Dubois informs us that Siger of
Brabant had publicly debated in Paris a question taken from the
Politics of Aristotle.[1] Since we are ignorant of the duration, scope
and content of this teaching, and since, moreover, we do not
know if and how Dante may have been affected by it, nothing
that we might say on this subject would be more than mere
conjecture. Since our ignorance is complete, it is better to refrain
from discussing the matter.

It is, on the other hand, legitimate to wonder whether, by
virtue of the principles from which it draws its inspiration and
the use to which it puts them, Dante's *Monarchy* is not itself in
some way, and even, perhaps, in a very original way, one of
the expressions of mediaeval Latin Averroism. In answering this
question we must first of all remember that, in its very essence,
Latin Averroism was confirmation of an actual disagreement
between certain conclusions of philosophy, regarded as rationally
necessary, and certain teachings of Christian Revelation, regarded
as true on the authority of the word of God. Now we do not
find in the *Monarchy*, any more than in the *Banquet*, proof that
Dante ever accepted as rationally necessary a single philosophical
conclusion that is at variance with Christian dogma. Not only
did he never preach the eternity of the world and the unity of
the active intellect, or deny the immortality of the soul and the
penalties of the life to come, but he always maintained that the
conclusions of philosophy, in so far, that is, as philosophy is
competent in these matters, tend in the same direction as the
teachings of Christian Revelation. Let us, moreover, note carefully that Dante could not have thought differently without
destroying the balance of his own doctrine, since it rests entirely
on the absolute certainty that all forms of authority, being
equally derived from God, have only to develop in accordance
with their respective natures in order to be assured of agreement.
In fact, there is no more conflict between the faith and reason

---

[1] PIERRE DUBOIS, *De recuperatione Terre Sancte*, ed. Ch.-V. Langlois, pp. 121–122
(quoted by P. MANDONNET, *Siger de Brabant*, Vol. I, p. 141, note 6). The passage from
P. Dubois is as follows: "Ad hec facit id quod super Polytica Aristotelis determinavit
precellentissimus doctor philosophie, cujus eram tunc discipulus, magister Segerus
de Brabantia, videlicet quod: *Longe melius est civitatem regi legibus rectis quam probis
viris;* quoniam non sunt nec esse possunt aliqui viri tam probi quin possibile sit eos
corrumpi passionibus ire, odii, amoris, timoris, concupiscentie." Cf. ARISTOTLE, *Pol.*,
I, III, 16, 1287 a 18–20.

of Dante than between the faith and reason of St.Thomas Aquinas. Dante has less confidence than St. Thomas in the capacity of reason for furnishing proofs in matters of natural theology. He appeals to faith a little more readily than the theologian, but he does so in order to confirm or round off the conclusions of philosophy, never in order to deny them. If, then, the conflict commonly referred to as that of "twofold truth" is co-essential with Averroism, it is scarcely possible to call the doctrine of the *De Monarchia* Averroistic.

Why, then, in spite of everything, can we not re-read the final chapters of this treatise without thinking of the Latin Averroists? Undoubtedly because of the separatism of the orders which is there so vehemently affirmed and which, indeed, constitutes one of the characteristic features of Averroism. Yet, so far as Dante is concerned, what is involved is a form of separatism which is not only free from conflict, but which entails and assists the harmony of the orders thus separated. The influence exerted by Averroes was so vast, so profound and so multiform that we cannot say with certainty that Dante escaped it. History here clashes with psychology, which is one of its bounds. If one remembers the crisis of philosophism which the poet seems at one time to have experienced, and thinks of the place that later, in the *Divine Comedy*, he reserved for Siger of Brabant, one's inclination is to regard the formal separatism, unmarked by any opposition between its components, which Dante preached as a mild and very much attenuated form of the material separatism, abounding in conflicts, which was professed by the Latin Averroists of his time. Let us say, then, if it is desired, that Dante's attitude towards philosophy naturally finds a place in the history of mediaeval Aristotelianism between St. Thomas Aquinas and the Averroism condemned in 1277, in which, for personal reasons, the separatism of the orders is to his liking; but let us be careful to make it clear that if, in this precise particular, Dante was able to regard Averroism as an ally, his attitude is derived neither from the doctrine of Averroes nor from that of any of the Latin Averroists known to us.

In the first place, this Averroistic philosophy was not accepted by Dante. Again, if Dante's separatism was inspired by politico-philosophical motives, no known Averroist seems to have gone before him along this road—indeed, none, to my knowledge, seems to have followed him along it.[1] There is nothing surprising in this. Since Dante's position necessarily implies that the philosophy of Averroes is false in so far as it contradicts the Christian faith, it is not clear how the influence of Averroes could have given rise to a political philosophy like Dante's. The same remark applies to Latin Averroism. The only reason for the excellent harmony existing between Church and Empire in Dante's thought is that the philosophy on which the Emperor bases his laws is in harmony with the theology which the Pope teaches. Since philosophy and theology do not harmonize in Latin Averroism, the unity of the Dantesque world can find neither foundation nor even acceptance in it.

We cannot, then, rule out the hypothesis that, having set himself a personal problem of political philosophy, Dante himself evolved its solution with the help of the materials placed at his disposal by Aristotle. The hypothesis commends itself to our notice all the more as Dante's attitude towards philosophy does not admit of identification with any other. Whatever the influences of which it bears the stamp, his doctrine is no more a second-hand doctrine than his answer to the problem of the

[1] If, as is generally admitted, Marsilius of Padua was influenced by Averroism, a comparison of his *Defensor pacis* with the *Monarchy* enables us to see how greatly Dante differs from the political Averroists. In the first place, although he regards the problem of the universal monarchy as foreign to his subject, Marsilius, while he avoids it, makes such a point of enumerating the objections to it that his hostility to the idea can hardly be doubted (*Defensor pacis*, dict. I, cap. 17, part 10, ed. C. W. Previté-Orton, Cambridge, 1928, p.94). Marsilius agrees with Dante in distinguishing the order of the State (governed by philosophy alone) from that of the Church (governed by Revelation alone) (*op. cit.*, dict. I, cap. 4, part. 3, p. 12), but, in the first place, he regards the necessity of the priesthood as undemonstrable; furthermore, although he is sometimes prudent enough to recall briefly that religion is useful in its bearing on the after-life (which is, moreover, quite outside the competence of philosophy), the whole force of his argument is derived from the Averroistic thesis that religious doctrines have been invented (*finxerunt*) by philosophers and Legislators to make men better and to ensure peace in the city. See the long and clear exposition which includes this pronouncement: "Cessabantque propter haec in communitatibus multae contentiones et injuriae. Unde pax etiam seu tranquillitas civitatum sufficiens pro statu praesentis saeculi difficile minus servabatur, quod expositione talium legum sive sectarum sapientes illi finaliter intendebant" (*Defensor pacis*, dict. I, cap. 5, part. 11, pp. 19–20). This is pure Marsilius: religious doctrines promote peace among States in this world—hence he cannot be reproached with forgetting that there is another world; but this was the ultimate goal that the legislators had in view when they proclaimed these doctrines—hence their goal cannot be to open to mankind the way to another world. In every critical particular Marsilius's pronouncement takes back what it has seemed to give. Never did Dante uphold the genuinely Averroistic thesis that the goal of religion is a temporal goal; on the contrary, that is the perversion of religion against which he never ceased to fight. Regarding the political doctrine of Marsilius, see C. W. PREVITÉ-ORTON, *Marsilius of Padua*, in *Proceedings of the British Academy*, Vol. XXI, London, 1935 (bibliographical particulars, p. 35, note 1)

Priesthood and the Empire is a second-hand answer. Now it is quite true that Aristotle could in no way help the author of the *Monarchy* to solve a problem which could not arise in a Greek civilization. Even if Dante read Aristotle's *Politics*, which is not certain,[1] it cannot have dictated his answer to the problem he set himself. The same observation would, moreover, apply to the *Ethica ad Nicomachum*, which to our certain knowledge Dante read and meditated, together with the commentary provided by St. Thomas Aquinas. Yet the enthusiasm with which his reading of this work filled him is probably responsible for Dante's conception of his ideal of a temporal order independent of the Church and seeking its own final goal under the guidance of reason alone. Since Aristotle envisaged the possibility of temporal felicity secured through the natural virtue of justice, why should not this final goal of the Greek city still be, even in the fourteenth century, that of the Empire?

Now Dante was not only acquainted with the *Ethica ad Nicomachum*, but he treasured it.[2] He was himself so conscious of this predilection that in the *Divine Comedy* he made Virgil say to him: *la tua Etica* (*Inf.*, XI, 80). If, as all his work attests, Dante was animated by an ardent desire for justice and peace in the temporal sphere, it is understandable that this altogether admirable book, in which, even through St. Thomas's commentary with its Christian inspiration, the ideal of human temporal felicity secured entirely through the practice of the natural virtues was so clearly visible, was to him in a sense the Bible of the Lawgiver. What promises did Dante not hear echoing in the pregnant phrases in which St. Thomas summarized the authentic thought of Aristotle! *Finis politicae est humanum bonum, idest optimus in rebus humanis;*[3] . . . *unde ad ipsam [artem civilem]*

---

[1] Cf. A. H. GILBERT, *Had Dante Read the "Politics" Of Aristotle?* (in *Publications of the Modern Language Association of America*, Vol. XLIII, No. 3 (Sept., 1928), pp. 602–613). The author does not, incidentally, claim to establish that Dante did not read the *Politics*, but that his quotations from it may be explained away as excerpts from Egidio Colonna and Thomas Aquinas. Though I do not wish to make light of the problem, and am even inclined to agree with the conclusion of this very useful work, I would point out that the author did not find all Dante's quotations from the *Politics* in the sources which he regards as possible (*op. cit.*, pp. 610–611). The question therefore remains open pending further inquiry. Quotations from the *Politics* occur in the following passages of the *Monarchy*: I, 3, 5, 12; II, 3, 7, 8; the *Ethics* is cited in I, 3, 11, 13, 14, 15; II, 2, 3, 8, 12; III, 10, 12.

[2] See above, Chap. II, p. 134, note 3.

[3] ST. THOMAS AQUINAS, *In I Ethic. Nic.*, lect. II, ed. Pirotta, No. 29.

maxime pertinet considerare finem ultimum humanae vitae, tanquam ad principalissimam.[1] ("The goal of politics is the good of humanity, in other words it is the loftiest goal in the realm of human affairs; . . . hence, the supreme function of this same [civic art], as the chief of all arts, is the consideration of the final goal of human life"). Is this not precisely that "final goal of human life", final although temporal, whose realization the *Monarchy* appeals to politics to ensure? Now what science lays the foundations of politics, if not ethics? And in what book do we find ethics, if not in the *Ethica ad Nicomachum?* Aristotle's thought is so clear that even the Christian amendments of St. Thomas never prevent it from emerging: "But we must know that Aristotle calls politics the very first of the sciences, not in an absolute sense, but in the category of the active sciences, dealing with human affairs, of which politics considers the final goal. For if the final goal of the whole universe is in question, it is the divine science that considers it, and *this* is the very first of all the sciences. But he says that it is the concern of politics to consider the final goal of human life, and if he defines the nature of that goal in this book [*on ethics*], the truth is that the teaching of this book contains the primary elements of political science."[2]

St. Thomas's conscientiousness is admirable, for, while his duty as a theologian compels him to recall in good time that the supreme science can only be that of the supreme Goal, and hence theology, he nevertheless does not forget to conclude, like the objective commentator he is: *Dicit autem ad politicam pertinere considerationem ultimi finis humanae vitae* ("Moreover, he says that the function of politics is the consideration of the final goal of human life"). Dante needed nothing more for the composition of his work. The rights of theology could wait their turn, in the certainty that they would be respected, so long as it was granted that of attributing to human life a final goal accessible by means of natural ethics and politics alone. Did St. Thomas's remarkable discretion as a commentator on Aristotle lead Dante to believe that even the Angel of the Schools acknowledged the existence of a "final goal" to human life attainable in this world through political and moral justice? Psychologically it is not impossible, but we shall never know. If we were to accept the theory, Dante's admiration for a St. Thomas thus

[1] *Op. cit.*, lib. I, lect. II, No. 30.   [2] *Op. cit.*, lib. I, lect. II, No. 31.

interpreted would merely be the easier to explain. There is, however, no need to accept it. Even if he clearly saw what modifications St. Thomas effected in Aristotle's doctrine, Dante none the less found Aristotle's doctrine in this commentary, which is incomparably more luminous than the obscure Latin translation with which it deals, and it was this doctrine that he seized upon—neglecting the rest—as though it were a prize that was his by right.

If we admit the reality of this influence exerted by Aristotle's *Ethics* on the formation of Dante's political philosophy,[1] its essential characteristics are easily explained. The striking external resemblance of Dante's attitude to that of the Latin Averroists is perhaps only one of those cases, like that of Erasmus and Luther, in which two adversaries agree in practice on a common attitude against a common foe, but for very different reasons. Such working agreements sometimes conceal profound dissensions, and these are not lacking between Dante and Averroism. We do not find, in the propositions condemned in 1227 by Etienne Tempier, any political thesis properly so called, but they contain more than two hundred physical, metaphysical and moral theses. Of these it cannot be said that Dante ever accepted a single one, but he explicitly rejected a certain number of them, and several were the very negation of his doctrine. Let us take, for example, Proposition 167: "Felicity is secured in this life, and not in another"; or Proposition 177: "There are no possible virtues apart from acquired or innate virtues"; or again, Proposition 157: "When a man is sufficiently disciplined in mind and feeling by the intellectual and moral virtues of which the Philosopher speaks in his *Ethics*, he is sufficiently prepared for eternal felicity." What such propositions express could in Dante's eyes

---

[1] Some considerations of a different nature, but reconcilable with ours, will be found in M. GRABMANN, *Studien über den Einfluss der aristotelischen Philosophie auf die mittelalterlichen Theorien über das Verhältnis von Kirche und Staat*, Munich, 1934. The author discerns three conceptions of the relationship of the Church to the State, corresponding to three attitudes widely adopted by mediaeval scholasticism towards the philosophy of Aristotle: 1. Conception of Albertus Magnus and Thomas Aquinas: individuality and independence of the philosophical order, save where it is a question of the doctrine of faith and the Christian conception of the world; in politics this leads to the doctrine attributing indirect power to the Pope in temporal affairs; 2. Latin Averroism: complete mutual independence of philosophy and theology, which leads, in politics, to the complete mutual independence of the two powers; 3. Complete subordination of philosophy to theology, which leads to the complete subordination of the State to the Church (*op. cit.*, pp. 6–7). It is only important to add that, *from Dante's point of view*, the first attitude is in practice identical with the third.

only be a most horrible confusion of the orders. If these Averroistic propositions are true, Dante's whole doctrine is false. Moreover, if the dictum that the conclusions of philosophy are *always* in agreement with theology is called in question, the structure of the Dantesque world totters on its foundations, because peace, consisting in the spontaneous harmony of the three autonomous powers that govern it, is thereby made impossible.

The simplest course would therefore be to regard Dante's attitude not as a particular case of Latin Averroism but as an effort to base his political separatism on the moral philosophy of Aristotle.[1] In this way we should understand why, instead of separating theology from philosophy in order to create opposition between them, Dante separated them in order to reconcile and unite them. Dante's universe remains thereby typically Christian, but it is so after his own fashion, and it does not admit of identification with any other known type of mediaeval Christian universe. Grace does not absorb nature, as in Roger Bacon, for example; it does not penetrate the inner nature, as in St. Thomas Aquinas; it is not eliminated to the advantage of nature, as in Averroes; it does not oppose nature, as in the Latin Averroists of the type of Siger of Brabant; indeed, one would say rather that it ranks above nature in dignity and beside it in authority, sure of a perfect harmony which nothing can disturb so long as grace and nature respect the limits set by God Himself to their domains.[2] Dante's Emperor possesses the key to the Earthly Paradise, but the Pope alone holds the key that opens to men the

---

[1] Perhaps I ought to make it clear that I do not offer this solution as being the most flattering to the imagination, but as the one that best explains Dante's writings. The ubiquity of the *Ethica ad Nicomachum* in those writings assures this solution of an objective basis. In general, anything that we may assume regarding whether Dante was an adherent of some specific Averroistic doctrine, a pupil of some particular Averroistic doctor, influenced by some Averroistic interpretation of the *Ethics* or the *Politics* of Aristotle, is certainly not impossible, or even unlikely; but at present it is neither possible to prove it nor necessary to assume it. Hence, without denying any of these hypotheses, considered as hypotheses, I am content with the minimum of assumptions necessary to explain Dante's personal attitude, considered in all its complexity.

[2] Perhaps this is what has suggested the strange idea that in the *Monarchy* and the *Paradiso*, "Dante innova e compendia in due opere distinte e diverse per lingua e per stile il *De civitate Dei* di S. Agostino, rianimando la filosofia cristiana della storia" (N. VIANELLO, *Il trattato della Monarchia di Dante Alighieri*, Genova, 1921, p. 51). If it may, stretching a point, be said that Dante, in eliminating its temporal aspect, reduces the Church to the state of an Augustinian City of God, there is no trace of Augustinianism to be found in the elevation of temporal political felicity to the status of a final goal. That is a thesis which St. Augustine would have rejected in horror.

Kingdom of Heaven. Even in this world the Pope's authority is no longer of this world: he dominates it without playing an active part in it.

Thus conceived, Dante's doctrine has the uniform flow of original thought, and we feel the presence of a personal initiative behind each of the theses of which it is composed. That, indeed, is why, properly speaking, it cannot be classified. The ideal of a universal monarchy, a universal philosophy and a universal faith, all three completely independent in their respective spheres, yet exhibiting perfect concord solely through the spontaneity of their individual action, has no parallel in the Middle Ages, or, for that matter, in any other epoch of history. It would be easy to find advocates to plead that there is concord among these three orders in the subordination of two of them to the third, but Dante desires that there should be a concord among them arising from their independence. One could also easily find subscribers to the belief that the three orders enjoy independence by virtue of the incompatibility of their conclusions and even of their principles, but Dante desires that they should enjoy an independence arising from their concord. That is why the notion of justice is, as it were, the mainspring of his work, for such a social organization cannot survive for one moment unless each of the interested parties is firmly resolved to show scrupulous respect for the various forms of authority by which its own authority is restricted. Hence, what characterizes Dante's ideal is his deep faith that the works of God will harmonize provided that they remain true to their nature. And so we see his desire for justice unceasingly accompanied by a boundless exaltation of freedom. In his eyes freedom is essentially the right of every being to act in accordance with his own nature, under the aegis of the beneficent authorities which protect him and enable him to attain his goal. For our will must be subject to that of the Emperor in order to be free from tyrants and Popes, just as our faith must be subject to the authority of the Pope in order to be free from that of tyrants and Emperors.

The singular character of Dante's doctrine is well indicated by the paradoxical interpretation that he has offered of the famous passage in Genesis, I, 16: *Fecitque Deus duo luminaria magna, luminare majus, ut praeesset diei; et luminare minus, ut praeesset nocti* ("And God made two great lights: the greater light to rule the day, and the lesser light to rule the night"). None could doubt that the reference there was to the sun and the moon, and there might well have been discussion aimed at discovering who was the sun—the Pope or the Emperor; but no one had ever thought of saying that God had created two suns —one to lighten the way of this world, the other to show us the way of God. Yet this is what the justly famous lines in *Purg.*, XVI, 106–108 say:

> Soleva Roma, che il buon mondo feo,
> due Soli aver, che l'una e l'altra strada
> facean vedere, e del mondo e di Deo.

These lines, which summarize exactly the separatism preached by Dante in the *Monarchy*,[1] admirably express his doctrine's divergences from the recognized standpoints. The distinction between the road of the world and the road of God, each lightened by its own sun, is a faithful reflection of the distinction between the two final goals to which the Pope and the Emperor lead humanity in the *Monarchy*. We cannot, then, accuse Guido Vernani of having made a mistake about the doctrinal implications of the work when, at the end of his *De reprobatione Monarchiae*, he denounced its peculiar character. With a clumsiness that is only too noticeable, but with a proper sense of the crucial features of the doctrine, Guido accused Dante of assigning a separate form of beatitude to corruptible man, who can have neither virtue nor beatitude properly so called; with regarding man, in consequence, as being destined by God for this beatitude, conceived as a final goal distinct from heavenly beatitude; and with inferring that the Empire is not subject to the Papacy from the fact that both are directly subject to the will of God.[2] It is surprising that such theses, of which the last two at any rate are so obviously antagonistic to Thomism, can to-day be regarded as hardly different from those which St. Thomas propounded. Not only did the Dominican Guido Vernani and the Franciscan Guglielmo di Sarzana judge of them otherwise, but Pope John XXII condemned the *De Monarchia* to the flames in 1329 and the

---

[1] The audacity of this deliberate modification of a commonly accepted Scriptural symbol has been well indicated by ALESSANDRO D'ANCONA, *Scritti Danteschi*, G. C. Sansoni, Florence (undated), pp. 325–326.

[2] GUIDO VERNANI, *De reprobatione Monarchiae*, ed. Jarro, passage quoted above, pp. 200–201.

book was put on the Index in 1554. Although it was withdrawn during the course of the nineteenth century,[1] it is hard to believe that the character of its doctrine changed between the sixteenth and the nineteenth centuries. Undoubtedly it was simply considered that political conditions had altered sufficiently for the doctrine to have lost much of its virulence, but it does not need a great effort of imagination to conceive of conditions under which it might recover it.

Yet however antagonistic Dante's political philosophy may be to Thomism, it does not seem to have been marshalled against it from abstract motives, whether religious or metaphysical. To seek the inspiration of the *Monarchy* along these lines is probably to steer clear of the one quarter in which one has any chance of finding it. Indeed, Dante here is rather carrying out his special mission as a political reformer and a righter of wrongs.[2] What he desires first and foremost is to abolish that monstrous injustice which in his eyes is constituted by the Papacy's usurpation of the Empire. Already, in the "covetous" and the Decretalists attacked in the *Monarchy*, we have those whom the *Divine Comedy* is presently to situate in Hell, for these men betray not only the authority on which they encroach, but even that which they represent. Like the tyrant who puts power to a personal use, the cleric who puts Revelation to a temporal use commits a crime; he even commits the supreme crime—the betrayal of the Holy Spirit: *O summum facinus, etiamsi contingat in somniis, aeterni Spiritus intentione abuti!* ("O most heinous of crimes (even if it be committed in dreams)—abuse of the eternal Spirit's intentions!")[3] Dante's conception of the nature and rôle of philosophy was such a personal one precisely because it was required for the solution of the essentially personal problem that he set himself in the *Monarchy*. It should therefore be interpreted not in terms of Averroes' or St. Thomas's doctrine, but in terms of his ideal of a universal Empire.

[1] Regarding these facts considered as a whole, consult N. ZINGARELLI, *La vita, i tempi e le opere di Dante*, Chap. XXV, Vol. II, pp. 680–681. As to the part played by Italian Protestants in the dissemination of the work, see PIERO CHIMINELLI, *La fortuna di Dante nella Cristianità reformata*, Bilychnis, Rome, 1921, pp. 62–73.

[2] It is this judicial function that unifies the multifarious elements of which Dante's thought is composed, and prevents it from being divided against itself. The complexity of Dante's position, apart from his principle of unity, is strongly emphasized by B. LANDRY, *L'idée de chrétienté chez les scolastiques du XIIIᵉ siècle*, F. Alcan, Paris, 1929, pp. 193–195.

[3] DANTE, *De Monarchia*, III, 4.

IV

Philosophy in the *Divine Comedy*

THE STUDY of Dante's attitude towards philosophy in the *Divine Comedy* inevitably brings one up against the problem that is raised by the presence in Paradise of the Averroistic philosopher Siger of Brabant. One might easily devote a large volume to a critical examination of the answers already suggested. It would take a very gifted writer, however, to make such a book readable; while it requires considerable temerity to re-open a question that has been debated so often, and with so little profit.

Indeed, strictly speaking, the problem does not admit of solution. Its principal data are two unknowns, and historians spend their time reproaching one another with arbitrarily determining the value of one in terms of the supposed value which they ascribe to the other. In other words, if we were sure, on the one hand of Dante's thought, on the other of Siger of Brabant's, it would be easy enough to discover what Dante may have thought of Siger. But we are not. It may therefore be proved with equal ease either that Dante was an Averroist, since he put a notorious Averroist in Paradise, or that Siger was no longer an Averroist when Dante put him in Paradise, since Dante was not an Averroist and yet put him there. Thus every historian will accuse his neighbour either of choosing the Siger he needs to justify his Dante, or of inventing the Dante he needs to justify his Siger. By itself this would still mean nothing. Every historian will undertake to prove that all his opponents make that mistake which he alone has avoided. In that case, it will be said, why refer again to a question which cannot even be formulated? And my answer will be: Because it is unfortunately inevitable once we seek to define Dante's attitude towards philosophy, which we *must* do if we wish to ascribe a precise meaning to the *Monarchy* and the *Banquet*. That is why, having defined the mistakes made by the majority of my predecessors, I am about to offer you my own.

I. Dante's Thomism

On the threshold of this new problem we encounter once again, and more inevitably than ever, the weighty Dantesque synthesis of Father Mandonnet. What makes it here singularly interesting is the fact that, unlike his fellows, this excellent historian has not begun by loading the dice. Hence, equally certain that Dante was a Thomist and Siger an Averroist, he has come up against the problem in the uncompromising form of a paradox, which, as it stands, would seem to be insoluble. This is not to deny that Dante's general philosophical attitude in the *Divine Comedy* is known, for it amounts to an admission that his attitude in that work was, on the whole, that of a Thomist, and that Dante's approval of Siger cannot be attributed to sympathy with his Averroism.

This makes it necessary to deal—finally, directly and for its own sake—with the proof of Dante's Thomism which has repeatedly been furnished by Father Mandonnet. Now this proof is in his writings bound up with, embedded in, a regular system of symbolical interpretation. If Dante is to be a Thomist there must be only three principal actors in the *Divine Comedy*; if there are to be only three of these actors their number must be determined by the symbolism of the Trinity; if their number is to be so determined this symbolism must dominate the *Divine Comedy* down to the last detail. Now no one dreams of disputing that Dante many a time had recourse to symbolism. Not only does he himself say that he did so, but it is obvious.[1] It will not even be disputed that, like all who have recourse to symbolism, Dante is capable of representing anything by any symbol. We have already come across notable examples of this, and it would be possible to add others. If, then, I am to discuss the cases of symbolism alleged by Father Mandonnet, the truth is not that I consider them unlikely in themselves, for, in this field, nothing is unlikely; nor is it that Dante seems to me incapable of them, for, in this field, he was capable of anything. The true aim of this discussion is to show that we are not entitled, just because all symbolism is arbitrary, to ascribe to Dante symbolist arguments for which we are not sure that he was in fact responsible.

[1] DANTE, *Epist.*, *XVII*, to Can Grande, Sect. 7, in *Tutte le opere . . .* , *ed. cit.*, p. 437.

We may reckon with his arbitrary symbolism whenever we are certain that it exists, but to his let us not add our own. Above all, let us not attribute to him precisely the arbitrary symbolism needed to justify the personal interpretation of his thought whose accuracy we are seeking to verify. Once having started along this road, we should be lost. To free oneself from the spell of Father Mandonnet's symbolist dialectics, one is absolutely bound to examine the data on which his arguments rest and to estimate their exact value. A doubly thankless task, in truth. Since no symbolism is impossible, we shall never prove that Dante did not accept, or would not have accepted, those forms of symbolism which are attributed to him. What I shall attempt, therefore, is to show that, instead of basing his thesis on the symbolism which he has found in Dante, Father Mandonnet has too often found in Dante the symbolism needed to prove his thesis.

A. The Number of Beatrice

As we have already seen in connection with the *Vita Nuova*, Father Mandonnet regards it as certain that Beatrice was "formed on the pattern of the Three-in-One".[1] To which our exegete adds: "Dantologists have pointed out some very curious cases of the appearance of the number three; however, they do not pay sufficient attention to its permanent correlation with unity. Thus, in Canto XXX (3 x 10) of the *Purgatorio*, Dante for the first time meets Beatrice, who reveals herself to him in the Earthly Paradise, in that impressive scene in which she says to him: 'Regard me *well*, it is *indeed* I, I am *indeed* Beatrice' (*Guardami ben: ben son, ben son Beatrice!*). Beatrice, the expression *par excellence* of the Trinity, since this mystery is the prime element in the Christian Revelation—Beatrice thrice utters the word *ben*, to indicate that she is the miracle of the Trinity, as is stated in the *Vita Nuova*."[2]

How are we to know if such was indeed Dante's intention in this passage? In thrice uttering the word *ben* in *Purg.*, XXX, 73, Dante, perhaps, was simply using the common device which consists in saying something and then twice repeating what has been said, for greater emphasis. It is the "No, no, no" formula.

[1] P. MANDONNET, *Dante le théologien; Introduction à l'intelligence de la vie, des oeuvres et de l'art de Dante Alighieri*, Desclée De Brouwer, Paris, 1935, p. 221.
[2] P. MANDONNET, *op. cit.*, pp. 198–199.

We find an example of it in this same Canto XXX of the *Purgatorio*, lines 49–51:

> Ma *Virgilio* n'avea lasciati scemi
> di se, *Virgilio*, dolcissimo padre,
> *Virgilio* a cui per mia salute die' mi.

Are we to say that this threefold mention of the name of Virgil is another symbol of the Trinity? If not, why should we say so of the word *ben*? Perhaps there is no symbolism in this repetition. Father Mandonnet does not stop there, for he claims that what is true of the numbers one and three is also true of their multiples. Consequently, 10 and 100 "are a phenomenon belonging to the same category as unity, and nine and 27 are of the same nature as three. This follows from the ideas which the Ancients had about the properties of numbers. Dante was, moreover, induced to employ this extension of the three-in-one by the requirements of his subjects. The possibilities offered by the numbers one and three were too limited to satisfy the artistic and doctrinal requirements of his work. The multiples of these numbers gave him more scope, and he made free use of it".[1]

Father Mandonnet has made even freer use of it. Thus he says: "Beatrice is mentioned 21 times in the *Vita Nuova*, i.e. seven times three. She is mentioned 63 times in the *Comedy*, i.e. three times as often as in the *Vita Nuova*, and seven times nine. It is only necessary to remember the symbolism of these figures and their relationship to Beatrice to appreciate their eloquence."[2] Yes, but there is no more mendacious eloquence than that of figures, especially when they are false. Beatrice is not mentioned 21 times in the *Vita Nuova*; her name occurs 23 times in its full form and once in the diminutive form of Bice. Neither 23 nor 24 is a third of 63.[3] Even if they were we should be no better off, for there

---

[1] P. MANDONNET, *op. cit.*, p. 195.

[2] P. MANDONNET, *op. cit.*, p. 189.

[3] If one is in a hurry, the quickest way to verify these figures is to re-read the whole of the *Vita Nuova* oneself, noting every mention of the name of Beatrice. This is what I have done. Those who have plenty of time may try to find the same number by making use of E. S. SHELDON and A. C. WHITE's *Concordanza delle Opere italiane in prosa e del Canzoniere di Dante Alighieri*, Oxford University Press, 1905. In view of the time it takes to make use of this learned concordance, one dare not contemplate how long it took to compile it. This is my own reckoning: *Vita Nuova*, II, V (twice), XII, XIV, XXII (twice), XXIII (three times), XXIV (four times), XXVIII, XXXI (four times), XXXIX (twice), XL, XLI, XLII.

would be nothing to prove that this proportion was not a result of chance. As a matter of fact, Father Mandonnet only singles out those numbers which, accurate or not, seem to conform to his thesis. Why say nothing of the others? If it is conceded that the former support the thesis, the others should be considered likely to weaken it. For instance, Father Mandonnet thought he had found a significant ratio between the frequency of the name "Beatrice" in the *Vita Nuova* and its frequency in the *Divine Comedy*. This ratio does not exist; but even if it did, what would it prove? Why choose these two works? Why should he not confine himself to the three parts of the *Divine Comedy*, for instance, as we shall see him do in the case of the words that follow? Simply because then the numbers would no longer suggest any ratio. Yet if there is a work in which the frequency of the name "Beatrice" ought to tell us something about the *Divine Comedy*, it is certainly the *Divine Comedy* itself. Unhappily, chance this time shows no benevolence: the name occurs twice in the *Inferno,* 17 times in the *Purgatorio* and 44 times in the *Paradiso*;[1] 2, 17, 44—there is nothing one can do with such numbers. Thus all this fine arithmetico-theological dialectic is baseless. We owe it not to the creative imagination of Dante, but to that of Father Mandonnet.

We might, moreover, have suspected as much from the first, on seeing how Father Mandonnet chooses the various expressions whose symbolism he seeks to compute. Why these and not others which ought to lend themselves no less readily to computation? Why should he not exercise his sagacity on a word like *Amore*, for instance? Simply because it refuses to enter into any numerical combination. *Amore* often recurs in the *Inferno*, even as a synonym for God: *la somma Sapienza e il primo Amore* (*Inf.*, III, 6); now, according to the arguments which we shall presently see applied to the word "will", the word "love" ought not to appear in the *Inferno*. Likewise, the expressions *luce, natura, sustanza, fede, ragione, operanza, bontade*, and many others besides, should at least have been tested before any conclusion on matters of this kind was formulated. Indeed, it seems reasonable to think that, even if apparently significant numerical proportions in the use of certain words may be found, the

---

[1] For these numbers see G. A. SCARTAZZINI, *Concordanza della Divina Commedia di Dante Alighieri*, Brockhaus, Leipzig, 1901, art. *Beatrice*, p. 17.

problem remains as to whether such things are due to chance or whether they express a premeditated design on the part of the poet. The only way of solving it would be to apply a similar test to other words, comparable to the former in meaning and in the importance of the part they play in the *Divine Comedy*. Nothing of the kind has been done here. Hence, in the cases which we are about to mention, the impression of arbitrariness that is left by the choice of expressions and the arguments advanced with a view to finding a symbolical value for the number of cases in which Dante has used them.

B. *The Verb "To Smile"*

Dante, says Father Mandonnet, "uses the verb 'to smile' sixteen times in the *Comedy*. He does so once in the *Inferno*—the occasion is a reminder that, in the natural order symbolized by the figure 1, laughter is the peculiar attribute of man. In the *Purgatorio* the supernatural order is still only in an imperfect state: the verb 'to smile' is used six times. It is used nine times in the *Paradiso*: the symbol is very transparent".[1]

It is true that the verb "to smile" is used only once in the *Inferno* (IV, 99); six times in the *Purgatorio* (II, 83; III, 112; XII, 136; XXI, 109; XXVII, 44; XXXIII, 95); nine times in the *Paradiso* (I, 95; II, 52; III, 24, 25, 67; XI, 17; XXII, 135; XXXI, 92; XXXIII, 49). Even when the numbers have been verified, the question of their meaning, and even more perhaps of whether they have one, remains untouched upon. Father Mandonnet seems to have been fascinated by the ratio 6 : 9, which may indeed seem satisfactory so far as the *Purgatorio* and the *Paradiso* are concerned; but the single smile in the *Inferno* must have caused him great embarrassment. The most natural explanation is that, if the word is encountered only once in this part of the *Comedy*, and in Limbo at that, it is because Hell is a place where opportunities to smile are somewhat rare. But there would be no symbolism in such a prosaic reason. Father Mandonnet therefore prefers to think that the number 1 is here a reminder of the natural order, and that this was the time to recall it to mind, since laughter is the peculiar attribute of man. To which we

---

[1] P. MANDONNET, *Dante le théologien*, p. 189.

shall object first that Hell was not created by God to harbour the peculiar attribute of man, but also that smiling is not laughing. If what Dante meant to symbolize by his peculiar attribute was human nature, the word whose appearances should have been reckoned up was not *sorridere* but *ridere*. Now although *riso* is encountered in an immortal passage (*Inf.*, V, 131), *ridere* does not appear in the *Inferno*. If it is objected that the two words are in practice synonymous, they will have to be reckoned together in the *Purgatorio*. Now I have noted nine cases of their use (*Purg.*, I, 20; VI, 48; XI, 82; XX, 108; XXI, 122, 127; XXV, 103; XXVIII, 67, 76); there may be others, but in that case, whatever their number, the ratio 1 : 6 : 9 ceases to exist. The only way of avoiding this consequence is to do what Father Mandonnet has done—to admit that "to smile" means "to laugh" in Limbo, but that "to laugh" does not mean "to smile" in Purgatory or in Paradise. What a lot of complications, and very arbitrary ones, to secure such a meagre result!

C. The Symbolism of Intelletto

Dante, adds Father Mandonnet, "also in the *Comedy*, uses the word *intelletto* 30 times: six times in the *Inferno*, 12 in the *Purgatorio*, 12 in the *Paradiso*. The reason is that the understanding of the damned is deprived of the *ben dell'intelletto*. On the other hand 30, as we know, is the symbol of Philosophy; now the sciences are the property and the appanage of the human understanding: hence the number of mentions."[1]

Once more, Father Mandonnet gives no references. Now Scartazzini's Concordance notes only 28 examples of the use of *intelletto* in the *Divine Comedy*:[2] five in the *Inferno*, 12 in the *Purgatorio* and 11 in the *Paradiso*. Let us assume, however, that Father Mandonnet's figures are accurate; how shall we explain Dante's decision to symbolize the fact that the understanding of the damned is deprived of the sight of God by the number 6, a multiple of the perfect number, which is 3? At a pinch we might have understood his using *intelletto* once in Hell to symbolize the intellect in its natural state. Even better should we have

---

[1] P. MANDONNET, *Dante le théologien*, p. 189.
[2] G. A. SCARTAZZINI, *Concordanza della Divina Commedia*, p. 74.

understood his not using the word at all, as is the case with "will";
but there is here no conceivable significance implicit in the
number 6, and Father Mandonnet himself does not suggest
any. The same may be said of the number 12 which applies to
the *Purgatorio* and the *Paradiso* alike. Assuming that there is
any sense in naming the intellect six times in Hell in order to
indicate that it is there deprived of the sight of God, it is not clear
why it should be named 12 times in Purgatory, where it does
not yet enjoy that sight, and, again, why it should once more
be named 12 times in Paradise, where it enjoys the sight of God.
A sequence such as 1, 6, 9 would have been understandable; the
sequence 6, 12, 12 is absolutely the reverse. If, as is probable,
the correct figures are Scartazzini's (5, 12, 11) the problem does
not even arise.

D. The Symbolism of "Will"

"Like a good Thomist," continues Father Mandonnet, "Dante
uses the word 'will' only ten times: that is to say one third as
many times; for the understanding is the dominating faculty.
The will is not mentioned in Hell, because the damned and the
devils no longer have the will to make for their goal. They
blaspheme God and do not desire Him, but hate Him. The
will is named once in Purgatory: it has not achieved its object.
It is named nine times in Paradise."[1]

This time the reader's perplexity is greater than ever, for
not only does Father Mandonnet give us no references, but he
does not even tell us what Italian word he translates by the
French *volonté*. We have, in fact, a choice of three forms:
volontà, volontade and *volontate*. Which is the relevant one?
We cannot be sure. Father Mandonnet simply tells us in a note
to look in SCARTAZZINI, *Enciclopedia dantesca*. We must conclude
from this that Scartazzini's Encyclopaedia is not at one with his
Concordance. If we refer to this latter work we find seven
examples of *volontà*, one of which is the variant *volontate*. If we
ignored the variants and totalled up the three forms, we should
obtain 13 examples, and not ten. If we totalled up the examples
of *volontà* and *volontade*, we should have two in the *Purgatorio*
and eight in the *Paradiso*, which is not one and nine. If we totalled

[1] P. MANDONNET, *Dante le théologien*, pp. 189-190.

up the examples of *volontade* and *volontate*, we should have one in the *Purgatorio* and five in the *Paradiso*: one and five are not one and nine.[1] However we go about it, we cannot arrive at Father Mandonnet's figures.

Once more, however, let us pretend to accept the figures that are given us. We wonder what they can really mean. *Sorridere* appears once in the *Inferno* because laughter is the peculiar attribute of man. *Intelletto* is used six times because in Hell the intellect is deprived of the sight of God. And now we are told that *will* is not used at all because the will of the damned is rooted in evil. Yet certainly the damned still have a will, otherwise they could not hate God. It should therefore be mentioned either once, like the "peculiar attribute of man", or six times, like the intellect. The same remark applies to the single mention of the will in Purgatory. True, it has not there achieved its object, but neither has the intellect of the souls in Purgatory; why, then, should the intellect be mentioned there six times and the will only once, seeing that these two faculties are in the same state? Of the sequence 0, 1, 9, as of the previous ones, it may be said that strictly it does not signify anything. The fact that Father Mandonnet's thesis triumphs whatever the figures entitles us to conclude that any number may symbolize anything.

E. The Actors in the Sacred Poem

These arguments would in any case be merely futile if Father Mandonnet had not extended the application of his method to the far more important problem of the actors in the *Divine Comedy*. This time it is no longer merely the structure of the written drama, but the underlying meaning of the work, that is queried. For the purpose of determining the number of the principal actors in the sacred poem and their functions, it would have been natural to proceed first to an objective analysis of the work and to extract from this the items of information it contains on the subject. Perhaps, indeed, Father Mandonnet himself thought he was proceeding along these lines. In fact, his unitrinism had settled the question for him in advance. The problem is, indeed, bound up in his mind with that of Dante's symbolism.

[1] G. A. SCARTAZZINI, *Concordanza della Divina Commedia*, p. 166.

The general unitrinism of the work required that it should contain three principal actors, each charged with three principal functions. It is all as clear to him as it is that $3 \times 3 = 9$, and he long ago confided to us the names of these three protagonists. No objection has ever been successful in obtaining from him even the smallest sign of attention, let alone any modification, however slight, of his views. Anything that may have been said on the subject by those around him has remained, so far as he is concerned, a dead letter. In the last of his works on Dante, therefore, he repeated literally what he had said in the early ones: "The actors of the first or second order, like the mere walkers-on, form a numerous body in the Dantesque theatre; but the importance of their rôle is established with consummate scenic skill. Between them there is a scale of values which may be called perfect. The stage is occupied by three principal characters —Dante, Virgil and Beatrice."[1] For the purpose of determining the scale of values which distinguishes these characters, Father Mandonnet applies the simple rule that led him to choose them. It will, moreover, be acknowledged that it is the very rule by which actors measure the importance of parts: their length. "Dante, however, is the protagonist, because the poetic element in the Comedy is conceived as an imaginary journey undertaken by Dante, and the Poet is on the stage from start to finish. Virgil only takes part in the journey through Hell and Purgatory, as far as the approaches to the Earthly Paradise. From that moment it is Beatrice who takes the place of Virgil and becomes Dante's guide."[2]

This criterion would be unassailable if employed by a dramatic critic; its use by a theologian who treats Dante himself as a theologian is rather surprising. It is, indeed, easy to see that the theological value of the part played by each of these actors is in inverse proportion to its theatrical value. Dante is the protagonist of the drama, but he is the most passive of its heroes, the guided of all the guides. Virgil only appears in 65 cantos, but he appears in them in the capacity of Dante's master and

---

[1] P. MANDONNET, Dante le théologien, p. 204. We find the same thesis in Dante théologien, an article published in Revue des Jeunes, May 25, 1921, p. 379 (cf. ibid., pp. 391–392), and in Theologus Dantes, in the Bulletin du Comité catholique français pour la célébration du VIᵉ centenaire de la mort de Dante, No. 5, January, 1922, p. 490.

[2] P. MANDONNET, Theologus Dantes, p. 490. The passage is reproduced in Dante le théologien, p. 204. See in this connection E. GILSON, La philosophie de saint Bonaventure, J. Vrin, Paris, 1924, Preface, p. 6.

guide. Beatrice only appears in 25 cantos, but she represents in them an infinitely loftier supernatural reality than do Dante and Virgil. If the characters in the *Comedy* are distinguished by "a scale of values which may be called perfect", explicit reservations should be made on the subject of a criterion that leads one to consider Dante's part four times as important as that of Beatrice. But, one suspects, Father Mandonnet had his reasons for reckoning thus, for if the importance of the parts is measured not by their length but by their theological value, there are no longer three protagonists, but four: Dante, Virgil, Beatrice and St. Bernard of Clairvaux. Now Father Mandonnet was unwilling either to admit that there are four protagonists, for the *unitrinism* of the *Divine Comedy* was at stake, or to reduce the number of these protagonists to the last three, for that would have been tanta-mount to limiting Dante's Thomism. He therefore had to stick to his first criterion, and that is what he did.

In doing so he was not only establishing among the characters of the *Comedy* a hierarchy in accordance with his taste; he was categorically eliminating one of them. It is a wholly arbitrary elimination, and one that may be explained but not justified, for it distorts the theological structure of the sacred poem. Of the principal actors in the drama that is played in it, we may first of all isolate Dante, a pilgrim from the other world, who is conducted by his various guides. Among these guides, first place must be given to Beatrice, for she is not only a guide, but the guide who appoints the other two. Lastly come the two guides appointed by Beatrice: Virgil at the beginning of the journey, St. Bernard at the end. It is easy to verify these various points. In the first place, it is certainly Beatrice who steers the bark, or rather the fleet; as Dante says, she is the admiral (*Purg.*, XXX, 58) who conducts the whole action; she has set Virgil on the move: *Io son Beatrice che ti faccio andare* (*Inf.*, II, 70), and she will send St. Bernard when the moment arrives: *A terminar lo tuo disiro, mosse Beatrice me del loco mio* (*Par.*, XXXI, 65–66). Next, it is clear that Dante has marked the principal stages of his journey through the next world by these peripeties which consist in the appearances or disappearances of his guides. Now there is an intentional analogy between these various episodes:
1. Appearance of Virgil (*Inf.*, I, 79): *Or se' tu quel Virgilio . . . ?*
2. Disappearance of Virgil at the moment when Beatrice makes

her appearance to take his place (*Purg.*, XXX, 31–57); 3. Disappearance of Beatrice at the moment when Bernard makes his appearance to take her place: *Credea veder Beatrice, e vidi un sene* (*Par.*, XXXI, 59). The lines in which Dante announces these changes of guide clearly indicate the analogy between them: *Volsimi alla sinistra col rispitto . . . per dicere a Virgilio* (*Purg.*, XXX, 43–46), and *Volgeami con voglia riaccesa per domandar la mia donna* (*Par.*, XXXI, 55–56). These events are interconnected and they only take on their full meaning in the light of the bond that unites them. What is this meaning?

As the reader no doubt remembers, Father Mandonnet is absolutely certain that Beatrice is a mere symbolical fiction.[1] The moment has come for us to examine more closely the significance he ascribes to her and to weigh the facts on which his interpretation of her rests. Outside Paradise, he tells us, Beatrice symbolizes faith, and Dante himself (he declares) has explicitly asserted as much in the passage from *Purg.*, XVIII, 48 in which we read that "Beatrice is a work of faith": *Beatrice ch'è opra di fede.*[2] "The poetical meaning," says the distinguished historian, "is that Beatrice is a creation of faith. . . . But the true meaning is that she is faith itself." That—I fear so at least—is a false meaning. *Ch'è opra di fede* does not seem to me to signify "who is a work of faith", but rather "because this is the task of faith". Scartazzini has correctly understood this passage in his Commentary: "I can speak to thee on this subject only in so far as reason is capable of understanding it; with regard to what goes beyond the limits of human reason, as a question of faith is involved put thy faith in Beatrice alone, who will explain it to thee." There is no question here of Beatrice's being a "creation of faith"; Dante merely says that she is its mouthpiece. Let us therefore say, with him, that she is here not the symbol but rather, indeed, the interpreter to Dante of faith in the divine Revelation, which guides man towards his final goal—the beatific vision.

Now in the *Divine Comedy* Beatrice is neither an absolutely fundamental cause nor an absolutely final goal. She has been sent to Dante as the representative of divine love: *Amor mi mosse, che mi fa parlare* (*Inf.*, II, 72), and she has to lead him, by way of the knowledge of God, to the love of God. In short, she comes

[1] P. MANDONNET, *Dante le théologien*, p. 219.
[2] P. MANDONNET, *Dante le théologien*, p. 211 and p. 219.

from love and returns to love. This, indeed, is why, with admirable skill, Dante has indicated in advance that, as soon as he begins to feel the first ardour of ecstatic love, he also begins to forget Beatrice. Far from being offended by this, Beatrice is actually amused, for, like faith, she has come only so that she may afterwards stand aside. This significant incident will be found in *Paradiso*, X, 52–60, where Beatrice urges the poet to thank God, the Sun of the Angels. Filled with religious zeal as he hears these words, Dante turns in spirit towards his Creator:

> E sì tutto mio amore in lui si mise
> chi Beatrice eclissò nell 'obblio.

Beatrice only laughs at him. Now this first eclipse of Beatrice by love clearly portends her final eclipse, which she herself will have intended and caused. She it is who sends St. Bernard to Dante's side to lead him to the final ecstasy, the culmination of his pilgrimage through the next world, the final goal of the sacred poem and a prefiguration of the final goal of man. The truth is, then, that she cannot herself lead Dante to the end of his journey. The poet's intention is perfectly clear, and Pietro Alighieri, when annotating his father's work, was not deceived as to the meaning of this passage: *Fingendo se relinqui a Beatrice. Figura est, quod per theologiam Deum videre et cognoscere non possumus, sed per gratiam et contemplationem. Ideo mediante sancto Bernardo, idest contemplatione, impetratur a Virgine gratiam videndi talia, quae per scripturas percipi non possunt*[1] ("He pretends that he is abandoned by Beatrice. The metaphor is that we cannot see and know God through theology, but through grace and contemplation. Hence, through St. Bernard, that is through contemplation, he obtains from the Virgin the privilege of seeing such things as cannot be apprehended through the written word"). Just as Beatrice caused Virgil to fill her rôle while faith was not yet necessary, taking Virgil's place at the point at which the light of nature became inadequate (*Purg.*, XXX, 73 *sq.*), she retires in her turn before St. Bernard at the moment when the work prepared by knowledge is due to be completed by love (*Par.*, XXXI, 192). For it is quite true that Dante, like St. Thomas, regards heavenly beatitude as

---

[1] P. ALLEGHERI, *Super Dantis ipsius genitoris Comoediam Commentarium*, G. Piatti, Florence, 1845, p. 729.

essentially a vision of God with love as its sequel;[1] yet love must first guide man towards beatitude. That is why, with his almost infallible sureness, Dante entrusts the conclusion of his poem to St. Bernard, the personification of the ecstasy caused by loving contemplation of God:

> Tal era io mirando la vivace
> carità di colui, che in questo mondo,
> contemplando, gustò di quella pace.
>   (*Par.*, XXXI, 109–111.)

It does not seem a good plan to search the commonest Dantesque formulas in an effort to find hypothetical symbols, while shutting one's eyes to facts as blatantly obvious as these. The length of the parts entrusted to the actors in the *Divine Comedy* is not everything. The general economy of the poem demands that charity should be added to faith, and be its consummation, just as faith is added to reason and enlightens it. Most certainly, St. Bernard's part is short, but it is decisive, since without it the poem would remain incomplete. Is it an exaggeration to count among the protagonists of the sacred poem this St. Bernard whom we cannot omit without truncating the poem? I do not think so; I even think that in Father Mandonnet's eyes St. Bernard's part would have assumed capital and unrivalled importance if Dante had entrusted it to St. Thomas Aquinas.

That is the whole question. The exegetical acrobatics of Father Mandonnet had no other motive than to demonstrate the fundamentally Thomistic character of Dante's theology. If there are but three principal actors in the *Divine Comedy*, it is clearly Dante's unitrinism that makes it necessary; but what makes it necessary that this unitrinism should be so implacably consistent and universal in its application is the fact that St. Bernard of Clairvaux must at all costs be eliminated. The moment there ceases to be any room for him Beatrice ceases to fear any rival, and she should have none, because with

---

[1] As regards this question Father Mandonnet is entirely right (*Dante le théologien*, p. 274, where the reader is referred to *Par.*, V, 7–9 and XXVIII, 109–111). Dante certainly decided in favour of the Thomistic and intellectualist conception of beatitude as against the Franciscan and affective conception. This is a definite, and important, case in which we may speak of Dante's Thomism. Yet even here, where he is wholly right, Father Mandonnet oversimplifies when he concludes that, in Dante's eyes, "the final beatitude appertains to the intellect". See above, Chap. I, p. 47.

the absolute triumph of Beatrice is bound up that of St. Thomas Aquinas.

St. Thomas and his theology clearly occupy a place of honour. Yet he is not the only theologian in the poem, for, to say nothing of St. Bernard, St. Bonaventure is on a par with the Dominican Doctor. Dante, then, has identified Thomistic theology with the *Divine Comedy*, but it cannot be maintained that he has identified the *Divine Comedy* with Thomistic theology. Now what Father Mandonnet desired to prove was clearly the opposite. In his eyes Dante "is a faithful disciple of Thomas Aquinas", a disciple whose principal work, the *Divine Comedy*, "is of a theological order as regards its aims, its subject matter and even its poetic form".[1] It is understandable that an interpreter of Dante in whom this idea amounted to a conviction should automatically have done what was necessary to eliminate the facts that would have compelled him to modify the terms of its expression. It is no less understandable that he should have magnified out of all proportion every fact that tended to confirm his thesis. Thus, we have just heard him say that, after Virgil, Beatrice becomes Dante's guide, which is true, but we have seen him ignore this other fact—that after Beatrice Dante's escort is St. Bernard. For the same reason, as we shall presently see, he will confuse St. Thomas with theology and Thomistic theology with Revelation itself. After that there will no longer be room in the *Divine Comedy* for any non-Thomistic element, whatever its origins, and this is what he is concerned with establishing.

F. The Voice of St. Thomas

Here, in fact, is one of Father Mandonnet's favourite arguments in support of the fundamental Thomism of Dante, and it at first appears quite decisive: "Finally, so that it may be impossible for any mistake to be made regarding the Poet's thought, which all these details have already made so clear, Dante informs us that the *speech of Thomas Aquinas is like that of Beatrice*:

---

[1] P. MANDONNET, *Dante le théologien*, pp. 277–278. With regard to the history of what has been justly called "la leggenda di Dante tomista" and the methods by which the attempt has been made to justify it, see B. NARDI, *Sigieri di Brabante nella Divina Commedia e le fonti della filosofia di Dante*, from the *Rivista di filosofia neo-scolastica*, published by the Author, Spianate (Pescia), 1912, pp. 11–12.

Per la similitudine che nacque
del suo parlare e di quel di Beatrice.''[1]

This argument would in fact be decisive if the translation of
Dante's text offered by Father Mandonnet were not so free.
Literally translated, the two lines from Dante mean: "Because of
the likeness that sprang from his speech and from that of Beatrice."
One readily admits that this is not clear, but in point of fact
no one, if he read only Father Mandonnet's translation, would
suspect that there was any obscurity here. Yet there is, and it is
an obscurity on which the sagacity of the commentators has been
exercised with some success.

In order that we may understand the sense of these two lines,
let us put them back in their context: "In a round vessel, the
water moves from the centre towards the circumference, and
also from the circumference towards the centre, according as
it is disturbed in the middle or at the edge. What I am saying
suddenly occurred to me at the moment when the glorious spirit
of St. Thomas fell silent, because of the like effect produced by
his speech and by that of Beatrice, who was pleased to begin
after him in this wise" (Par., XIV, 1–9). It is, in the first place,
the context that justifies this translation. If Dante meant that
"the speech of Thomas Aquinas is like that of Beatrice", it would
be incomprehensible that the resemblance between their two
voices could have made him think of water contained in a round
vessel, whose concentric waves flow from the centre to the circumference or from the circumference to the centre according
as one disturbs the water in the middle of the vessel or the vessel's
rim. This, on the contrary, is not hard to understand if the
characters are restored to the positions which Dante allotted to
them at the beginning of Par., XIV. Dante and Beatrice are
then in the centre of two concentric rings of the Blessed. Thomas
Aquinas stands on the circumference of one of these rings. He has
just spoken to them: his voice has therefore moved like a wave
that travels from the circumference of a vessel to its centre. No
sooner has Thomas completed his utterance than Beatrice begins
to speak in answer to him: her voice therefore moves in the
opposite direction, like a wave that travels from the centre of a

---

[1] Par., XIV, 7–8 (in P. MANDONNET, Dante le théologien, p. 267). Cf. Dante théologien,
in Revue des Jeunes, 1921, p. 395; Theologus Dantes, in Bulletin du Jubilé, No. 5, p. 521;
and Siger de Brabant et l'averroïsme latin, 2nd edit., Louvain, 1911, Vol. I, p. 299, note 1.

vessel towards its rim.[1] Hence, we must certainly translate *la
similitudine* as Scartazzini rightly does in his commentary—*per
il fatto simile, che avenne, del parlare di S. Tommaso e di
Beatrice*, i.e. "because of the similar [*viz.* to the afore-mentioned
one] phenomenon that resulted from the speech of St. Thomas
and from that of Beatrice".

This interpretation yields a sense consistent with the passage
as a whole; it is therefore preferable to Father Mandonnet's, which
is utterly irrelevant to the passage and even makes it incoherent.
If this point is conceded, we must conclude that Dante never said
St. Thomas's voice resembled that of Beatrice, but rather that
their two voices had produced the similar, and contrary, movements of the atmosphere which suggested to him the comparison
already described. Father Mandonnet was therefore building
on sand when he asserted, before quoting these lines: "Dante,
moreover, clearly indicates what is in his mind when, after
letting Thomas discourse at length, Beatrice begins to speak,
and the poet declares that there is a similarity between the
language of Thomas and Beatrice, in other words between the
theology of the great doctor and the Christian faith itself, so that
it is hard to distinguish the voice of the one from that of the
other."[2] Father Mandonnet now no longer rests content with
making Dante say that these two voices are similar; he insists that
the voice of Beatrice is that of Faith, that the voice of Thomas is
actually that of Theology, and that it has become hardly possible
to distinguish them—a formula, this time, which no jugglery
will ever extract from the text. This fantastic argument, aimed
at establishing that Dante considered Thomistic theology and
faith to be hardly distinguishable, is precisely the equal in merit
of the misinterpretation to which it owes its existence.

We need not here discuss afresh the nature of Dante's Thomism;
the only question that interests us is whether it has limits and,
above all, what is their nature. So far we have grounds for concluding that his Thomism was neither so complete nor so exclusive as has sometimes been supposed. We must now consider

---

[1] This is the meaning proposed by Pietro Alighieri: ". . . sicut percutiendo unum vas,
puta bacile plenum aqua, in suo centro, idest in medio, undatio vadit ad extrema; et
e contra percutiendo illud idem vas extra, undatio vadit ad dictum centrum, ut per
experientiam patet, ita locutio Beatricis, quae erat contra auctorem, ut centrum, in illis
choreis et rotis ivit, et responsio redivit, qualis dicit textus" (P. ALLEGHERI, *Super Dantis
ipsius genitoris Comoediam Commentarium*, G. Piatti, Florence, 1835, pp. 646–647).
[2] P. MANDONNET, *Siger de Brabant*, Vol. I, p. 299, note 1.

another set of facts, an examination of which will bring us appreciably closer to the heart of our problem and will directly pave the way for its solution.

II. DANTE'S CRITICISM OF THE MENDICANT ORDERS

The famous passage in *Par.*, XI, 124–139, in which Dante assumes the voice of St. Thomas in order to criticize certain tendencies in the Dominican Order that displeased him, is one of those that have given rise to the most varied interpretations. Father Mandonnet has adopted one of the oldest, though he is not certain that it is the right one. We in our turn must tackle the problem anew; this is all the more necessary in that, if we were to accept Father Mandonnet's interpretation of the relevant passages, we should at once be reduced either to eliminating the thesis which he himself has adopted or, like him, to regarding the passages so understood as null and void.

Let us take as our starting-point the passage in the *Comedy* in which Thomas Aquinas begins to speak and personally introduces himself to Dante: "I was numbered among the lambs of the sacred flock which Dominic leads along a road where they wax fat, if they do not stray" (*Par.*, X, 94–96). Scartazzini's commentary expounds this passage correctly: "I belong to the Order of Preachers, founded by St. Dominic with the establishment of a rule which, if duly observed, leads man to Christian perfection. . . . We advance in Christian perfection if we do not deviate from the right road laid out by the founder, pursuing the false goods of the world." The question which then arises concerns the exact nature of the reproach which Thomas levels against his Order, *u' ben s'impingua, se non si vaneggia*. Whether we translate *vaneggia* "strays", "pursues false goods", or "pursues the vanities of this world", the problem remains: What are the vanities in question?

Fortunately, it happens that Dante himself has enlightened us, for he attached great importance to this line, alluding to it for the first time in the following passage (*Par.*, XI, 22), and on a second occasion even reproducing it in full (*Par.*, XI, 139), in order to indicate clearly that what he had just then said explains it. In fact, this explanation commences right at the beginning of *Par.*, XI and completely fills the whole of that Canto, which ends designedly with a repetition of the line: *U' ben s'impingua, se non si vaneggia.* The general sense of the explanation is very clear, the whole of Canto XI leading up to this conclusion: The Dominicans betray their founder's ideal precisely in so far as they turn aside from the pursuit of spiritual ends so as to engage in temporal affairs, *whatever form they take.*

This theme is proclaimed in the first twelve lines of Canto XI. Still moved by his meeting with the distinguished Doctors whom Thomas Aquinas has just pointed out to him at the end of Canto X, Dante exclaims: "Mortals, with your senseless cares, how faulty are the judgments which make you fly so low! While one devoted himself to the Law, another to Medicine, and others yet forced their way into the priesthood, seeking to gain the upper hand by force or trickery, to steal, to succeed in commerce, plunging to the point of exhaustion into the pleasures of the flesh or giving themselves up to idleness, I, freed from all these things, received with Beatrice this glorious welcome in heaven above" (*Par.*, XI, 1–12). So we have been forewarned; Dante is going to speak henceforth as one who judges everything from the viewpoint of the Fourth Heaven: he intends to demand peremptorily absolute purity in the spiritual sphere.

So intent is Dante on this purpose that he immediately makes Thomas Aquinas say to him: I know what you are thinking at this moment. You have two doubts. First, you are wondering what I meant by these words: *U' ben s'impingua se non si vaneggia*; then, you would like to know how I could say of King Solomon that there was never another as great as he: *A veder tanto non surse il secondo* (*Par.*, XI, 19–27). So Thomas Aquinas will now clear up this twofold difficulty for Dante.

The Church is the mystical bride of Christ. To ensure the union of the Church with her divine bridegroom, God has sent her two guides—the one, St. Francis, burning with love like a seraph; the other, St. Dominic, shining with the light of wisdom like a cherub (*Par.*, XI, 37–39). Thomas will now undertake to recount the life of St. Francis, just as Bonaventure, in Canto XII, will recount that of St. Dominic. Moreover, observes Thomas, whichever of the two we praise, we praise the other (*Par.*, XI, 40–42). The observation is important, for it explains

how, after describing the Franciscan ideal, Thomas is able to use
it to find fault with certain Dominicans. From the point of view
that he adopts in this Canto, the two Orders are in practice·
interchangeable, because, in spite of the slight differences between
them, they envisage the same ideal. In point of fact, what
Thomas emphasizes especially in his eulogy of St. Francis is his
marriage with Poverty (*Par.*, XI, 55–75), that inscrutable and
abundant fount of richness, which his first disciples espouse
(*Par.*, XI, 76–87) and which, before he dies, he bids his sons serve
and love always (*Par.*, XI, 112–114).

Thus, the St. Francis of Thomas Aquinas is a perfect example
of total renunciation of temporal goods. Now, he adds immediately, think what a worthy companion St. Dominic was
for St. Francis, when they endeavoured to steer the bark of St.
Peter safe into port! "This [Dominic] was our patriarch, for
you can see with what a precious freight he loads his bark who
follows him as he desires to be followed. But his flock is become
so greedy for fresh sustenance that it cannot be prevented from
scattering through the ravines, and the more his wandering
sheep stray from him, the more often do they return to the fold
devoid of milk. There are, indeed, those which fear danger
and cling close to the shepherd, but they are so few that it takes
little cloth to make their copes. Now, if I have expressed myself
clearly, if you have listened to me attentively and if you recollect
what I have said, your desire will be partly satisfied, for you will
know what is the tree that loses its bark, and you will understand my reservation: 'Where they wax fat, if they do not
stray'" (*Par.*, XI, 121–139).

This final passage is one of those—there are many such in
Dante—which even an Italian reader is obliged to translate in
order to understand it. We have adopted the translation of the
last three lines for which Beccaria and Bertoldi have won recognition. We were tempted to accept it for two reasons. Firstly,
of the two obscure lines:

> E vedrai il corregger che argomenta,
> "U' ben s'impingua, se non si vaneggia"
> (ll. 138–139.)

the last, which is a quotation taken by Dante from his own
writings, must inevitably depend on one of the two words

corregger and *argomenta* in the previous line. In the translation that we propose, line 139 depends on *corregger*: "The reservation [or correction] '*if they do not stray*'." In the translation proposed by Father Mandonnet, to which we shall return, line 139 is left in the air and does not link up with the previous one. Our second reason for preferring this translation is that it is far less favourable than the other to the thesis which we are upholding. Let us keep it, then, just as it stands, and draw from it the conclusion that the general meaning of Canto XI is this: God gave St. Francis and St. Dominic to the Church with one and the same end in view—namely, that they should revive its respect for its spiritual nature and its contempt for worldly things.

In order to understand the translation of these two lines proposed by Father Mandonnet, we must substitute for the reading *corregger* ("correction") the equally well attested reading *corregiér*. Those who read this word, of which I do not believe there exists any other example in Italian, regard it as an abbreviation of a hypothetical *corregiéro*, itself formed on the model of *cordigliéro*. Just as *cordigliéro* means "cordelier", and hence "Franciscan", *corregiér(o)* would mean "the man with the strap", that is to say the Dominican. The meaning of the passage would then become as follows: "You know what trunk loses its bark, and you see the man with the strap who wastes his talents in sterile arguments [*e vedrai il corregiér che argomenta*]. It was because of this that I said: 'There they wax fat if they do not become ineffectual'."[1] And undoubtedly, if we were sure of the existence of the word *corregiér*, line 138 would merely be the easier to translate. "The Dominican who argues" gives a very satisfactory sense. But, in the first place, the existence of this word remains doubtful, which is disturbing enough,[2] and, most important of all, once line 138 has been translated thus the transition to line 139 becomes impossible. Literally translated, the passage then yields this meaning: "You will see the man with the strap who argues, where they wax fat, if they do not become ineffectual." Father Mandonnet could not help seeing

---

[1] *Op. cit.*, Vol. I, p. 296.

[2] Father Mandonnet rightly says (*op. cit.*, Vol. I, p. 297, note 2) that *corregiér* is merely a derivative of the Latin word *corrigerus* = *corrigiam gerens*, just as *cordelier* comes from *cordigerus* = *cordam gerens*; but we are sure that the French word *cordelier* exists, and the fact that it is possible to find an analogous etymology for the hypothetical Italian *corregiér* does not suffice to prove that this word really existed.

the difficulty, since he was translating the passage; he therefore evaded it by adding a clause to Dante's text: "You see the man with the strap who wastes his talent in sterile arguments. *It was because of this that I said:* There they wax fat if they do not become ineffectual." If a composition was necessary it could not have beeen effected with greater ingenuity, but the fact that the reading chosen by Father Mandonnet makes it inevitable is not in its favour.

Later on we shall analyse the reasons—very sound in themselves —which induced Father Mandonnet to follow this hypothetical reading, although it was fatal to his own thesis. For the moment let us leave the talking to him and follow him in the conclusions that he draws from it: "The end of this passage has been the bugbear of the commentators, who have not grasped the literal meaning of two lines, because of their failure to understand the precise meaning of the censure that Dante puts into the mouth of Thomas Aquinas.[1] The reproach which the great doctor levels against his Order, whose vocation is entirely doctrinal, is that many of its members are greedy for fresh sustenance, that is to say for profane learning and study. Instead of crowding round Dominic and confining themselves to the study of the Scriptures and to piety, they are wanderers in the pastures of philosophy and worldly sciences. You will see, says Thomas, that my words are intended as a reference to 'the strap-bearer who disputes', that is to say the inclination for argument and disputation carried to extremes. Thomas then concludes by repeating word for word the line on which the whole of this passage has been a commentary: 'There they wax fat if they do not become ineffectual,' in other words, in the Order of Dominic men wax fat on sound doctrine, or on sacred science, if they do not become ineffectual through immoderate study of the profane sciences which, if they are not ineffectual in themselves, at all events engender ineffectualness."[2]

However great our astonishment at the meaning that can be read into two lines, it is justifiable; but there is no certainty that Dante intended to convey it. Canto XI of the *Paradiso* is evidently

---

[1] Accordingly, Father Mandonnet himself proceeds from what he regards as the meaning of this censure to the meaning that he ascribes to these two lines. It is unnecessary to emphasize the danger of such a method, which is the reverse of the usual order of procedure.

[2] P. MANDONNET, *Siger de Brabant*, Vol. I, pp. 297–298.

linear in structure, and hence there is scarcely room for the introduction of this development. In effect, the arrangement of the ideas which the Canto embodies is as follows: 1. Dante feels that he has been freed through grace from his weakness for temporal things; 2. Thomas, who reads Dante's thoughts, announces that he is going to explain the meaning of the reservation with which he has himself qualified his eulogy of the Dominicans: *Se non si vaneggia*; 3. In order to explain it, he recalls that God has given to the Church St. Francis and St. Dominic; he, being a Dominican, will praise Francis, but praise of one is tantamount to praise of the other; 4. Eulogy of St. Francis, especially his ideal of poverty; 5. Censure of the Dominicans who, betraying their founder's ideal, go in pursuit of fresh sustenance; 6. Hence the reservation with which the eulogy of them is qualified: *Se non si vaneggia*. Nothing could be simpler than this arrangement, and what it suggests is that, after recalling that it is impossible to praise one without praising the other (*Par., XI, 40–41*), Thomas Aquinas censures the Dominicans in the name of the ideal of poverty. Father Mandonnet points out that the Dominican vocation is "entirely doctrinal"; it is indeed "doctrinal", but not "entirely". The Dominican Order professes poverty no less than the Franciscan Order. It is therefore possible that in his eulogy of St. Francis Thomas was trying to revive his brethren's respect for the Dominican ideal of poverty. This is all the more possible as Dante makes Thomas say of St. Dominic (*il nostro patriarca*) that he was a *degno collega* of St. Francis in the work of steering the bark of the Church safe into port (*Par., XI, 118–120*). Yet that is not the strongest piece of evidence; but as it is bound to occur to us when we analyse Canto XII, let us for the moment assume, *dato non concesso*, that Father Mandonnet's interpretation is the right one. How would it affect the problem before us?

It would affect it in this way—that Dante would be making Thomas reproach the Dominicans with devoting themselves excessively to the profane sciences. Coming from the author of numerous commentaries on Aristotle and from a theologian so well versed in philosophy, the reproach would be truly surprising. That, moreover, is what Father Mandonnet immediately remarks: "Here Dante is merely the echo of what is being said around him. . . . In this respect he shows himself neither very independent nor very judicious. It is this that leads him unwittingly to adopt inconsistent points of view. It is, indeed, contradictory to choose Thomas Aquinas, whom Dante regards as the ideal of right and sound theology, to find fault with a state of affairs that he himself brought about."[1] Once more, after introducing his own misconstruction into the work that he is studying, a historian blames Dante for it, accusing him of contradicting himself. In fact, Dante does not make Thomas say a single word against profane studies; their only detractor is this "strap-bearer who disputes", a mythical being introduced in line 138 of Canto XI owing to the unhappy choice of a bad reading. Dante is not to blame: let us, then, not accuse him of contradicting himself when he has not done so.

It would be all the more out of place to tax Dante with inconsistency as he handles this situation with consummate skill. It is, indeed, this skill that has deceived Father Mandonnet, and many other commentators with him. For it is true that Dante has reproached the Dominicans with excessive addiction to certain profane studies, but that was in Canto XII, and on that occasion he chose Bonaventure to be his mouthpiece. Having represented Francis and Dominic as collaborators in a single work, as indeed they were, Dante assigns to Thomas the task of recalling, in the name of St. Francis, that the Dominicans too are poor men, and to Bonaventure that of recalling, in the name of St. Dominic, that the Franciscans too are preachers of the faith. Such firmness of purpose, combined with sureness of method, is the very hallmark of genius. Let us first make sure that Dante has given proof of it.

Thomas has just stopped speaking. At the beginning of Canto XII the heavenly dance and chant recommence, then cease once more (*Par.*, XII, 1–21); a spirit from the second circle then

---

[1] P. Mandonnet, *Siger de Brabant et l'averroïsme latin au XIIIe siècle*, Vol. I, pp. 298–299. Scholars have likewise quoted, as a proof of Dante's opposition to speculative theology, the lines from *Par.*, V, 76–77: "You have as your guide the Old and the New Testaments, and the Church's shepherd: let this suffice to you for your salvation!" In fact, the entire context, which clearly indicates the sacred character of vows, proves that certain facilities accorded to the Jews (*Par.*, V, 49–51) are no longer conceded to Christians, because they are governed not merely by the Old Testament but also by the New, and by the authority of the Church. Moreover, Dante has heaped too many honours on speculative theology, in the persons of St. Thomas and St. Bonaventure, to have harboured any feelings of mistrust towards it. What he dreads, here as elsewhere, is *greed*, as we see in the line that immediately follows: "Se mala cupidigia altro vi grida" (*Par.*, V, 79).

begins to speak: it is that of Bonaventure, whom the divine love induces to speak in his turn *dell'altro duca*, in other words St. Dominic (*Par.*, XII, 32–33). In order to indicate his purpose more clearly, Dante now makes Bonaventure repeat what he has already made Thomas Aquinas say: "It is seemly that, when one is introduced, the other should be introduced also, in order that, just as they fought side by side (*sì che com' elli ad una militaro*), so they may shine together in glory" (*Par.*, XII, 34–36). It would be impossible to indicate more clearly that the two Orders are united in a common cause and that there is every justification for judging one from the point of view of the other: what is more, this is tantamount to judging it from one's own point of view, since they share one and the same ideal.

In point of fact, Bonaventure begins his eulogy of St. Dominic by recalling that, in order to save His tottering Church, God sent to the aid of His bride two champions who, by their deeds (*al cui fare* — St. Francis) and by their words (*al cui dire* — St. Dominic), were destined to rally an erring people (*Par.*, XII, 37–45). Then begins the eulogy of St. Dominic—a eulogy sprinkled with so many guide-marks that there is hardly any excuse for failure to recognize its meaning. The eulogy of St. Francis had exalted his love of poverty; that of St. Dominic exalts *his spirit of faith*. For us the question is not how some modern Dominican historian conceives the "doctrinal vocation" of his Order. What is important to us for our understanding of Dante is to know how he himself conceived the Dominican ideal. Now, in his eyes St. Dominic was above everything the ardent lover of the Christian Faith: *l'amoroso drudo della Fede cristiana* (*Par.*, XII, 55–56). From the day he was born the soul of this saintly athlete—tender to his own and harsh towards his enemies —was so filled with living faith that the mother who carried him in her womb prophesied the future. Just as St. Francis espoused Poverty, St. Dominic espoused Faith on the baptismal font, that virtue offering itself to him in order to save him, he offering himself to it in order to defend it (*Par.*, XII, 61–63). Born to till the field of the Lord, the child was prophetically named Dominic. In fact, the first love that he revealed was for the first counsel given by Christ. Many a time and oft, silent and wakeful, he was found by his nurse on the ground, as if he had said: "It is for this that I am come" (*Par.*, XII, 73–78).

The first counsel of Christ (*Matt.*, XIX, 21) is that men should seek poverty. Dante is visibly anxious to emphasize here, as strongly as possible that this champion of Faith was also the lover of poverty. That the two Orders share the same ideal is therefore firmly maintained by Dante in full view of the least attentive reader.

Nevertheless, it is still true to say that St. Francis and St. Dominic each had his own way of serving this ideal: Francis through love, Dominic through wisdom. Dante had already proclaimed the fact in Canto XI, in the justly famous lines:

> L'un fu tutto serafico in ardore;
> l'altro per sapienza in terra fue
> di cherubica luce uno splendore
> (ll. 37–39.)

From now on we know that this light of Wisdom which St. Dominic radiates is that of Faith. In order, therefore, to fulfil the mission with which he is entrusted by Dante, and which, moreover, suits him admirably,[1] Bonaventure will now render to the Dominicans the same service as Thomas Aquinas has just rendered to the Franciscans: that of inspiring them with a new respect for their own ideal. The sons of St. Dominic are proud, then, of their father's Wisdom? They have good reason to be! But it was not with an eye to the goods of that world which men serve to-day, nor by following in the footsteps of the canonist Henry of Susa,[2] but through his love of the heavenly manna that he became a great doctor in so short a time (*Par.*, XII, 82–85). The eulogy of St. Dominic therefore interweaves the two themes of his indifference to temporal things and of a Wisdom derived from the well-head of Faith alone: *Poi con dottrina e con volere, insieme, con l'officio apostolico si mosse* (*Par.*, XII, 97–98). It is in the name of this ideal that Bonaventure will now in his turn censure the Franciscans who, in quitting the footsteps of St. Francis, at the same time abandon those of St. Dominic. So,

[1] Regarding this point, see E. GILSON, *La philosophie de saint Bonaventure*, J. Vrin, Paris, 1924 (Chap. II: *La critique de la philosophie naturelle*).

[2] Dante says: "Non . . . diretro ad Ostiense ed a Taddeo" (*Par.*, XII, 83). *Ostiense* is the canonist Henry of Susa. As regards *Taddeo*, the commentators hesitate between identifying him with a Bolognese jurist and a Florentine doctor (see *La Divina Commedia*, Scartazzini's commentary, *ad loc.*). Whatever the facts, these two names symbolize the pursuit of worldly sciences with an eye to temporal possessions.

unhappily, do the Spiritualists and the disciples of Matteo d'Acquasparta, the former interpreting the Rule more strictly, while the latter put it out of mind. As for me, concludes the speaker, "I am the spirit of Bonaventure of Bagnorea; when I held great offices, I always made temporal preoccupations take second place" (*Par.*, XII, 127–129). There follows the presentation of the Doctors by whom he is surrounded, including Joachim of Fiori whose place in this band corresponds to that occupied by Siger of Brabant among the companions of Thomas Aquinas.

If they are taken as they stand, Cantos XI and XII of the *Paradiso* form in their symmetrical construction a single entity and are open to the same interpretation. The thesis in vindication of which Dante wrote them was not the primacy of spiritual things—that would have been trivial—but *the exclusively spiritual vocation of the Mendicant Orders, charged by God with reminding the Church of the exclusively spiritual character of its mission.* Not only was there nothing trivial in this second thesis, but it was associated in Dante's mind with his deepest interests and his liveliest passion. The general meaning it confers on the passages which the reader has just seen in the process of analysis explains its tenor. The two Great Orders should, indeed, both abstain completely from the pursuit of temporal ends—so much their common ideal requires; nevertheless, the type of apostolate entrusted by God to each of them entails special duties. For that reason Dante cites St. Francis when he makes a Dominican recall *in particular* the spirit of poverty in the pursuit of heavenly goods, and St. Dominic when he makes a Franciscan recall *in particular* the spirit of Wisdom in the pursuit of the truth that is revealed by Faith.

Once his writings have been made to yield what certainly seems to be their true meaning, Dante's presentation of the problem of Siger of Brabant is evidently quite different from Father Mandonnet's. The latter's preoccupation is to prove that the introduction of Siger into Paradise does not constitute "a satire on the Dominicans, or anything resembling it".[1] In order to establish this point he wished to demonstrate that Dante could not have desired to misrepresent an Order towards which, in fact, he

---

[1] P. MANDONNET, *Siger de Brabant*, Vol. I, p. 300. He is here arguing against the first thesis of Gaston Paris.

showed himself "very sympathetic". What greater honour could he do it than to identify the voice of St. Thomas with that of Beatrice? It is true that Dante seems to accuse the Order of forsaking revealed Wisdom in order to cultivate the profane sciences, but in that he is only contradicting himself, and this small inconsistency in no way lessens his admiration for the Dominicans. It is therefore not with the object of being objectionable to their Order that he makes Thomas Aquinas eulogize Siger of Brabant. And that is what had to be demonstrated.

It might have been demonstrated at less cost, for Dante would most certainly not have assumed such a responsibility for so paltry a reason. Yet this is not the gravest flaw in Father Mandonnet's reasoning. Rather is it his tacit admission that Dante cannot have entertained any hostile feeling towards the Dominicans apart from a desire to satirize them. Now the whole of the passage which has just been analysed clearly proves that the accusation which he had to bring against them was as grave as it was definite—namely, that they had betrayed the spiritual order by coveting worldly goods, and especially that they had betrayed the Wisdom of faith and devoted themselves to juridical studies.[1] Now we know to what use Dante accused them of putting Canon Law; he would not forgive them for occupying their time in proving by canonical arguments the Pope's superiority to the Emperor. Let these monks, then, busy themselves with their own affairs! Let them return to the doctrine of faith, for that is their business! That, and that alone, concerns them, and it concerns only them.

The assumption to which this leads us is that, in the whole of this controversy, Dante was concerned above everything with ensuring the complete independence of the temporal order in face of the encroachments of the spiritual. We have looked upon Cantos X–XIII of the *Paradiso* as forming a single entity, but this united whole itself has a Preface, of which we have said nothing, consisting in the conclusion of Canto IX. It is only necessary to read it in the light of the foregoing analysis to grasp its signifi-

---

[1] These, moreover, are the two main adversaries that Dante had had in mind in the *Monarchy*. Once those who may be deluded by a misguided zeal for the Church have been disposed of, there remain: 1. "Quidam alii quorum obstinata cupiditas lumen rationis extinxit"; 2. "Tertii, quos Decretalistas vocant, qui theologiae ac philosophiae cujusdam inscii . . . Imperio derogant" (*De Monarchia*, III, 3). Hence, the present discussion concerns neither philosophy nor theology—not even if they be false.

cance: "Your city [Florence], which was founded by him [the Devil] who first renounced his Creator and whose envy is the cause of so many tears, produces and disseminates the accursed flower [the golden florin], which has led astray the sheep and the lambs because it has changed their shepherd into a wolf. This is the reason why the Gospel and the great Doctors are forsaken, and men no longer study aught but the Decretals, as appears from their margins. It is with this that the Pope and the Cardinals busy themselves: their thoughts go not to Nazareth, whither Gabriel made his wingèd way. But the Vatican and the other places in Rome elect of God, which were the graveyard of the army that followed in Paul's footsteps, will soon be purged of this adultery" (*Par.*, IX, 127–142). This reminder of the prophecy with which the *Divine Comedy* opens (*Inf.*, I, 97–102) comes just in time to determine the general meaning of the three Cantos that follow it; and it is in the light of this reminder that we must interpret the various problems which these Cantos present, notably those connected with the presence in the heaven of the Doctors of King Solomon and the philosopher Siger of Brabant.

III. THE WISDOM OF SOLOMON

Our analysis of Cantos XI and XII of the *Paradiso* testifies to their unity. We must, however, resume this analysis at the point at which we interrupted it, for it is still incomplete. It will be remembered that at the beginning of Canto XI Thomas Aquinas, in reading Dante's secret thoughts, had discerned two questions: What is the meaning of the reservation—*se non si vaneggia*—with which the eulogy of the Dominicans is qualified, and why did Thomas say that there has never been another king as wise as Solomon—*non surse il secondo?* We have the answer to the first question, but we are still waiting for the answer to the second. It is certainly believed to be no accident that Dante raises these two problems and links them together. He was the architect of his own writing. If he left difficulties in it so that he should be forced to elucidate them, he was assuring himself of the means to elaborate ideas on which his heart was set even as he solved these riddles. The mere fact that he propounded the two questions simultaneously suggests that the answers to them found their way into his mind through some secret passage, which an analysis of Canto XIII will perhaps enable us to find.

After Bonaventure's speech the dance and the chant of the two circles of celestial beings recommence. This purely poetical interlude occupies the first thirty lines of Canto XIII. At this point Thomas Aquinas takes up the thread of his discourse, which had been interrupted by Canto XII and the intrusion of Bonaventure. With a continuity of purpose for which the full credit belongs to Dante himself, Thomas reminds the poet that it still remains for him to clear up one of the two questions that Dante has asked himself: "Now that I have threshed one ear of corn, and the grain from it has been garnered, sweet love invites me to thresh another" (*Par.*, XIII, 34–36). Dante is indeed astonished, when he thinks of the fullness of wisdom with which God endowed Adam and Mary, that Thomas has earlier been able to say that "the perfection contained in the fifth light [i.e. Solomon] has not been repeated" (*Par.*, XIII, 46–48). To which Thomas replies that all beings, whether mortal or immortal, are merely the splendour of the Word that was engendered by the Father and is inseparable from Him as from the Holy Spirit, the bond of love that unites Them. The perfection of this Trinity is reflected in the nine choirs of Angels, and then descends from them even to inferior and corruptible substances. The matter of which these substances are made and the mould that shapes it are not always the same. That is why the matter shines more or less brightly according to the degree of perfection of the mould in which it is cast. Thus, for example, two trees of the same species will yield fruit of varying excellence. So with men and their understanding: *E voi nascete con diverso ingego* (*Par.*, XIII, 72). If this wax that is matter were perfectly prepared, and the celestial efficacy were at its highest pitch, the light of the seal that is impressed on the wax would be fully visible. But nature is never perfect; she acts like an artist who is master of his art, but whose hand trembles. However, if Love (the Holy Spirit) happens to impress on the creature the pure idea (the Word) of the prime Efficacy (the Father), the being thus created attains its full perfection. In this way was created the clay which God was to endow with the full perfection of Adam when He produced him from it. In this way was made the Virgin, from

whom Jesus Christ was to spring: "I therefore applaud your
opinion that human nature never was and never will be what
it was in those two persons" (*Par.*, XIII, 85–87).

It will be said that such a minor point did not merit this wealth
of explanation. That is true. Moreover, it cannot be denied,
a priori, that Dante may have written this theological exposition,
which takes up fifty lines, merely for the pleasure of it. There is
an element of byplay in all poetry, and Dante's is full of it. But
he never forgets his subject, and we now see him return to it.
If, continues Thomas, I were to add nothing to what I have just
said, you might with good reason ask me: "How, then, can
Solomon have been without peer?" He forestalls this question,
which he expects, and answers it in advance: "In order that
what seems to you obscure may become clear, consider who
Solomon was, and what motive led him, when God said to him
'Ask', to ask for what he did" (*Par.*, XIII, 91–93). Interrupting
our analysis for a moment, let us refer to the Biblical scene
which these lines evoke: "In that night did God appear unto
Solomon, and said unto him, Ask what I shall give thee. And
Solomon said unto God, Thou hast showed great mercy unto
David my father, and hast made me to reign in his stead. Now,
O Lord God, let thy promise unto David my father be estab-
lished: for thou hast made me king over a people like the dust
of the earth in multitude. Give me now wisdom and knowledge,
that I may go out and come in before this people" (II *Para.*,
I, 7–10).

Perhaps we are beginning to discern the objective to which
Dante is leading us. It may aptly be said that in this case the
thorn is hidden beneath the flowers. What Dante urges us to
notice in the Biblical passage is these words: "Wisdom . . .
that I may go out and come in before this people." In other
words, he praises Solomon less for having asked for wisdom
than for the fact that, like the king he was, he asked only for
kingly wisdom. This is what Dante himself explains: "My
words were not so obscure that you could not see clearly that
it was a king who asked for wisdom so that he might be a king
capable of governing" (*Par.*, XIII, 94–96). Does Dante then
consider renunciation of philosophy to be as great a merit in a
king as in a Pope? It certainly seems so to judge from what we
read next. For Solomon did not ask for wisdom "in order that

he might know the number of the celestial Movers, or whether a necessary premise and a contingent premise ever yield a necessary conclusion, or *si est dare primum motum esse* ['whether we must concede that motion has an origin'], or whether it is possible to inscribe in a semicircle a triangle that does not contain a right angle. If, therefore, you mark what I said earlier and what I have just said, you will see that this peerless knowledge at which the shaft of my intention is aimed is kingly prudence. Lastly, if you cast a searching glance at the word *surse* [*non* surse *il secondo*], you will see that it concerned only kings (who are above their subjects), and they are many, but good kings are rare" (*Par.*, XIII, 94–108).

It seems clear, as Scartazzini's commentary points out, that Dante "is here praising Solomon because he asked for understanding so that he might judge and govern his people well, instead of asking for long life, or riches, or victory over his enemies. Dante praises him because he did not ask for the capacity to solve the problems arising from metaphysics, dialectics and geometry that were, in his time, the paradise of the schoolmen". Having said this, we are left to wonder why Dante thought fit to explain all this to us. For after all, to him Solomon is obviously only a symbol—a symbol of the truth that he desires to instil into us. And does not that truth simply amount to this: Just as I have asked monks to turn their minds to the wisdom of faith, I ask kings to rest content, in the matter of wisdom, with the kingly prudence which they need in order to govern their peoples well? In short, after asking the monks to leave the Empire to the Emperor and to busy themselves with theology, Dante urges the Emperor to leave learning to scholars and to content himself with the administration of justice. For Solomon had already been in Dante's mind in the *De Monarchia*, I, 13, where he praised him for addressing to God this prayer: *Deus, judicium tuum regi da et justitiam tuam filio regis* ("O God, give unto the king Thy judgment, and unto the king's son thy justice").

This conclusion is already inclining us towards a definite interpretation of the presence in Paradise of Siger of Brabant. Let us not, indeed, forget that he is included among those whom Thomas Aquinas there introduces to Dante. Of this little band, Thomas himself, Dionysius the Areopagite, Isidore of Seville,

Boëthius, Bede, Peter Lombard, Richard of St. Victor and Albertus Magnus symbolize Theology—not, to be sure, a Theology denuded of all learning, but one that is not subordinate to any temporal aim. A canonist, Gratian, is there as well, but there is reason for that, since, instead of wrongfully using Canon Law for the exploitation of the temporal order, "he came to the aid of both Codes" (*Par.*, X, 104–105). Hence, the author of the *Decretum* is in Paradise as a symbol of respect for Civil Law and Canon Law, expressed in differentiation between their spheres of action. There too is to be found the fifth light, that of Solomon, which Dante does not hesitate to describe as the most beautiful of all: *La quinta luce, ch'è tra noi più bella* (*Par.*, X, 109). By this time we know why. Now, after these doctors whose only goal is spiritual wisdom, this canonist who does not use Canon Law for temporal purposes, this wise king who confines himself strictly to his royal calling, there finally appears before us— easily last, but he is in heaven none the less, and on the same footing as the others—the enigmatical figure of Siger of Brabant, that philosopher who chose to confine himself exclusively to his philosophical calling. Will it be thought that Dante put him there by chance? And how can we help believing that he too is there so that he may symbolize the independence of a definite portion of the temporal order, that portion which we call *philosophy*? It is clear, at all events, that the whole of the context suggests as much, but before we accept this solution to the problem we must make sure that no other answer fits the known facts, either better or as well.

IV. The Symbolism of Siger of Brabant

The problem created by Dante's introduction of Siger of Brabant into Paradise and by the eulogy of him which he puts into the mouth of St. Thomas arises in the fourth heaven, or Heaven of the Sun, the abode of those who knew that they were wise with the wisdom their offices demanded. Thomas Aquinas is there; after telling Dante the names of the blessed beings who surround him, beginning with Albertus Magnus, who is on his right, he comes to the last, who is immediately to his left: "This figure, which your eyes encounter as they return towards me, is the light of a spirit who, wrapt in grave thoughts, found death slow in coming. This is the eternal light of Siger, who, when he taught in the Street of Straw, established unwelcome truths" (*Par.*, X, 133–138).[1]

The last line—*Sillogizzò invidiosi veri*—cannot be literally translated. Of the three words of which it is made up the only one whose meaning is clear is *veri*. "Siger taught truths"— *sillogizzò*—signifies that these truths were based on reasoning; they were consequently rational truths. *Invidiosi* has here retained one of the meanings which attached to the Latin *invidiosus*. *Dux invidiosus erat* means "the leader was unpopular, he was an object of hatred". I have chosen *unwelcome* because this word makes it possible to render *invidiosi* without periphrasis, but it must be understood in the sense that the truths which Siger taught were viewed with disfavour and drew upon him the hostility of his contemporaries. It matters little, however, which literal translation enlists our support, for the meaning of the phrase is obvious. Scartazzini and Vandelli have brought out its general meaning clearly in their commentary: "*Sillogizzò*: argued, established by his syllogisms *invidiosi veri*, i.e. odious truths which earned him envy and hatred." This interpretation will suffice us as a basis for discussion.

It would be tedious to examine the numerous explanations already offered of Siger's presence in heaven. Of the oldest it may be said without injustice that they belong to Dantesque archaeology. A summary and some very apposite criticisms of several of them will be found in Father Mandonnet's book. It is all the more unnecessary to resume this critical examination after him as the problem has presented itself in a somewhat different light since the publication of his book on Siger of Brabant. Thanks to him, indeed, we can now form a pretty accurate idea of this personage. If it is admitted that Dante in his mind must have ascribed a philosophical significance to the introduction of this philosopher into Paradise, the problem presents itself in a new light now that we can read certain writings

---

[1] P. MANDONNET, *Siger de Brabant*, Vol. I, pp. 289–295. To the earlier works by G. A. Scartazzini, C. Cipolla and C. Baeumker to which Father Mandonnet refers his readers must be added the more recent work by B. NARDI, *Sigieri di Brabante nella Divina Commedia e le fonti della Filosofia di Dante*, published by the author, Spianate (Pescia), 1912 (from the *Rivista di filosofia neo-scolastica*, April and October, 1911, February and April, 1912). An account will there be found (pp. 1–9) of several interpretations of Dante's two tercets on Siger of Brabant.

from the pen of Siger of Brabant. It is these writings, rather than the conclusions of historians who have never read them, that should henceforth be taken as a starting-point.

Leaving aside the work that has recently been published under his name, but of which it is not certain that Siger was the author,[1] to us the most interesting of his definitely authentic writings are his questions *De Anima*. A cursory examination of these is enough to assure one that Siger of Brabant belongs to the group called "Latin Averroists" and that he was probably one of its most intelligent representatives. In these Questions, in which he reveals remarkable gifts as a philosopher, Siger professes to discuss and solve the problems with which he deals from the standpoint of reason alone. There is nothing of the extremist in Siger. He is not a rationalist in revolt against faith. He is not even a man who takes a delight in noting a dissension between his reason and his faith. He does not seek conflicts, he resigns himself to them. A Master of Arts in Paris University, he teaches philosophy and nothing else. When the conclusions to which he is led by the philosophy of Aristotle contradict the teaching of faith, Siger contents himself with propounding them *qua* the

---

[1] Cf. *Quaestiones in Libros Aristotelis de Anima*, in F. VAN STEENBERGHEN, *Siger de Brabant d'après ses oeuvres inédites*, Vol. I, Louvain, Institut supérieur de Philosophie, 1931 (pp. 121–156). This treatise settles the crucial problem of the unity of the intellect to the disadvantage of Averroes. The ascription of this treatise to Siger has been called in question by B. NARDI, *Il preteso tomismo di Sigieri di Brabante*, in *Giornale critico di Filosofia Italiana*, Vol. XVII (1936), pp. 26–35 and Vol. XVIII (1937), pp. 160–164. A new approach to the problem has since been made by F. VAN STEENBERGHEN in *Les oeuvres et la doctrine de Siger de Brabant*, Brussels, Palais des Académies, 1938. It would be premature to pretend to compose this dispute out of hand, for it turns on a question of fact and should be settled on its own merits, regardless of any other consideration. Consequently I can only wonder what becomes of my own conclusions according as B. Nardi's or F. Van Steenberghen's are regarded as correct. If B. Nardi is right, Siger of Brabant remains the Averroist described by Father Mandonnet and the Dante-Siger problem continues to present itself in the terms in which we have discussed it. If F. Van Steenberghen is right, Siger of Brabant finally abandoned the Averroistic thesis of the unity of the active intellect and, in the questions *De Anima* whose authenticity is at issue, came very close to the position of St. Thomas Aquinas (*op. cit.*, pp. 154–160). It is clear that, if this hypothesis were adopted, the entire Dante-Siger problem would present itself in a new light and the conclusions of my own work would be subject to reconsideration. The wisest course, therefore, is to await the end of the dispute and, meanwhile, to borrow F. Van Steenberghen's sage observation about the conclusions of history—to wit, that they are "provisional and subject to correction" (*op. cit.*, p. 40). It will, therefore, I hope, occasion no surprise that, after reading F. Van Steenberghen's latest book on Siger, we have in no way modified an interpretation which is wholly based on the assumption that the vexed questions *De Anima* are not authentic. As a matter of fact, all concede the authenticity of the passages on which our discussion rests; B. Nardi denies the authenticity of the questions that we do not take into account, and even F. Van Steenberghen, though he finds them convincing, does not regard their authenticity as absolutely certain. Cf. below, Eclaircissement V, pp. 317–327.

conclusions of philosophy, but he maintains at the same time that the teachings of faith are the true ones.[1]

Siger, then, does not pretend to discover in philosophy the last word on the nature of man or of God. He simply desires to try and find the relevant teaching of the philosophy of Aristotle,[2] i.e. of natural reason, it being clearly understood in advance that reason must often have erred when dealing with problems that are outside its scope, and that in the event of conflict between philosophy and Revelation the truth is that which God Himself has revealed to men. However, Siger's private intentions were one thing, and what they inevitably seemed to be from· his opponents' point of view was another. Philosophers or theologians whose rational conclusions were in harmony with the teachings of faith could not but disapprove of his attitude. There was no conflict in *their* minds, and to them the idea that rational conclusions might be at once necessary and false was incomprehensible. The *Prologue* to the list of propositions condemned by Etienne Tempier in 1277 explicitly declares that, *in fact*, the professors who represented their conclusions as being those of natural reason in the field of philosophy, accordingly represented them in their teaching as being correct. In adding that the conclusions of natural reason are not necessarily correct, they fell out of the frying-pan into the fire, for the necessary conclusions of reason are necessarily correct. From the point of view of his opponents, therefore, Siger's position obliged him,

[1] "Hoc dicimus sensisse Philosophum de unione animae intellectivae ad corpus; sententiam tamen sanctae fidei catholicae, si contraria huic sit sententiae Philosophi, praeferre volentes, sicut et in aliis quibuscumque" (*Quaest. de Anima Intellectiva*, III; P. MANDONNET, *Siger de Brabant*, Vol. II, pp. 156–157). Let us note, moreover, that Siger is of a very thoughtful turn of mind. So far as he is concerned the question "What was the teaching of Aristotle?" is not always identical with the other question, "What was the teaching of Averroes?" Cf. qu. VI, p. 162: "Dicendum est secundum expositionem Commentatoris *et forte intentionem Aristotelis* . . ."

[2] "Dicendum, sicut et a principio dictum est, quod nostra intentio principalis non est inquirere qualiter se habeat veritas de anima, sed quae fuit opinio Philosophi de ea" (*Quaest. de Anima*, VI; *op. cit.*, Vol. II, p. 163. Cf. *Prologus*: ". . . quid circa praedicta sentiendum sit, secundum documenta philosophorum probatorum, non aliquid ex nobis asserentes . . ." (Vol. II, p. 145). ". . . utrum anima intellectiva multiplicetur multiplicatione corporum humanorum diligenter considerandum est, quantum pertinet ad philosophum, et ut ratione humana et experientia comprehendi potest, quaerendo intentionem philosophorum in hoc magis quam veritatem, cum philosophice procedamus. Certum est enim secundum veritatem quae mentiri non potest, quod animae intellectivae multiplicantur multiplicatione corporum humanorum" (Qu. VII; Vol. II, p. 164. Cf. qu. III, Vol. II, pp. 153–154: "Quaerimus enim hic solum . . ."). Siger's formula, "secundum veritatem, quae mentiri non potest," may be compared with Dante's, "secondo che la santa Chiesa vuole, che non può dire menzogna" (*Convivio*, II, 4).

whether he liked it or not, to maintain that there are two contrary truths, that of reason and that of faith: *Dicunt enim ea esse vera secundum philosophiam sed non secundum fidem catholicam, quasi sint duae contrariae veritates* ("For they say that those things are true in the light of philosophy but not in the light of the Catholic faith, as if there were two contrary truths").[1]

Such is the origin of the so-called doctrine of "twofold truth", which, although commonly attributed to the Averroists, was not taught by them but was forced upon them by their opponents.[2] Whatever the truth in this matter, the important thing to us here is the fact that Siger of Brabant certainly passed in the eyes of all for an exponent of that doctrine which St. Thomas Aquinas abhorred. Hence the problem as to how and why Dante could compel St. Thomas to repudiate an essential element in his own doctrine by assigning him the task of glorifying Siger of Brabant. It is understandable that this problem has arrested the attention of Dantologists, for it involves the ultimate meaning of Dante's work.

When Father Mandonnet approached this difficulty in his turn, he did so with his mind already made up on two points, which in his eyes were to remain for the future the basic facts of the problem. On the one hand, he had himself been the first to prove that "Siger professed a pure, philosophical form of Averroism"; on the other hand, he regarded it as certain that "Dante condemned Averroism outright", so much so that "the whole of Dante's philosophy is the very antithesis of that of Averroes".[3] If, as we are entitled to do, we designate as "pure Averroism" that of the Latin Averroists (not that of Averroes), the first thesis is indisputably correct. The second, on the contrary, raises many difficulties. We shall examine them later. For the moment let us simply note that, in accepting these two theses, Father Mandonnet was engaging to explain how a poet

---

[1] *Chartul. Univ. Paris.*, Vol. I, p. 543. Cf. St. Thomas Aquinas, *De unitate intellectus contra Averroistas Parisienses*, the whole of the concluding part of the treatise, from *Est etiam majori admiratione . . .* (in *Opuscula omnia*, ed. P. Mandonnet, Vol. I, pp. 68–69).

[2] This conclusion has been simultaneously upheld by B. Nardi, *Intorno alle dottrine filosofiche di Pietro d'Abano* (from the *Nuova Rivista Storica*, V, 2–3, Milan, Albrighi Segati, 1921, pp. 34–35) and by myself in *La doctrine de la double vérité* (E. Gilson, *Etudes de philosophie médiévale*, Strasbourg, 1921, pp. 51–75). Cf. F. Sassen, *Siger de Brabant et la doctrine de la double vérité*, in *Revue Néo-Scolastique de Philosophie*, Vol. XXXIII (1931), pp. 170–179. As regards Siger's own position, see the subtly contrasted reflections in *op. cit.*, pp. 173–175.

[3] P. Mandonnet, *Siger de Brabant*, Vol. I, pp. 301–302.

who was a Thomist and an opponent of Averroism could cause
St. Thomas to glorify an Averroist like Siger of Brabant. If the
question is put in this form the only satisfactory answer is that,
"in all probability, Dante was not acquainted with the doctrines
of Siger of Brabant".[1]

On the whole, the theory is not impossible. It is arguable,
as it is arguable, on the contrary, that Dante knew Siger intimately through having been his pupil.[2] It is possible that Dante
was less well acquainted with the detail of Siger's doctrines
concerning the soul than was Father Mandonnet, or than we are,
thanks to him. It will even be granted that it is impossible to be
sure what Dante knew of those doctrines. And yet, even if it
were conceded—and this too is undemonstrable—that Dante
knew nothing of Siger's doctrine, the problem would remain
where it was. If we understand that it was possible for Dante
to put Siger in Paradise, it does not follow that we know why
he put him there. If Dante made a blunder in putting him there,
we want to know why he made it. That is the whole question.

---

[1] P MANDONNET, *op cit.*, Vol. I, p. 301.

[2] This hypothesis, which was formulated by E. RENAN (*Averroès et l'Averroïsme. Essai historique*, 9e édit., Paris, Calmann-Lévy, 1935, p. 272), has been newly adopted in a different form by SALOMON REINACH, *L'énigme de Siger*, in *Revue historique*, Vol. CLI (1926). This article is a reprint of a paper read to the Académie des Inscriptions et Belles-Lettres on September 4th, 1925. The author's principal conclusion is that Dante knew Siger personally in Italy, and that about 1282 the latter "met this handsome, thoughtful young man, scion of a Florentine family which was then very well-to-do, and gave him lessons for a living. He it was who introduced Dante to Albert and Thomas, to their common master Aristotle, to the great commentator Averroes," etc. Even if we grant that S. Reinach's story is likely, it is none the less a story, and history cannot be a catalogue of might-have-beens. On the other hand, S. Reinach has very aptly noted several facts to which it is important to pay heed. Here are the principal ones, formulated a little differently and completed: 1. Siger of Brabant regarded Albertus Magnus and Thomas Aquinas not merely as theologians but as the principal philo-sophers of his time: "Dicunt praecipui viri in philosophia Albertus et Thomas . . " (*De anima intellectiva*, III, in MANDONNET, *Siger de Brabant*, Vol. II, p. 152); 2. From the point of view of the Augustinian theologians, St. Thomas himself was compromised together with Averroes; in the condemnation of 1277, "a score of propositions . . . more or less directly attack the teaching of Thomas Aquinas" (MANDONNET, *op. cit.*, Vol. I, p. 231); 3. Siger and St. Thomas are at one in admitting that the philosopher *par excellence* is Aristotle; if they do not always agree as to how he should be interpreted, they very often agree, and in defiance of the same opponents; 4. Although St. Thomas does not admit that philosophy can justify conclusions that are contrary to faith, he insisted strongly on the specific distinction between philosophy and theology. Without wishing to draw from these facts more inferences than are implicit in them, we must none the less admit that, *from a certain point of view*, there did not formerly appear to be such a radical opposition between St. Thomas and Siger as our more scrupulous historio-graphy claims to detect. An opponent like John Peckham would have been delighted to see them thus associated (cf. MANDONNET, *Siger de Brabant*, Vol. I, p. 258); for the contrary reason, an opponent of theologism like Dante might have deemed it natural to reconcile them.

It might be assumed, for instance, that this blunder is simply the result of chance. Undoubtedly Dante does not ordinarily write down a proper name without having some reason for doing so, but the case of Siger might be an exception. What makes it hard to believe that Dante made this mistake fortuitously is the fact that he made the same mistake twice, and in circumstances so similar that one cannot help regarding them as indicative of deliberate intent. The facts, incidentally, are well known. In Canto XII of the *Paradiso* (ll. 139-141), Bonaventure, who is the counterpart of Thomas Aquinas, introduces in his turn the Doctors by whom he is surrounded. Among these Doctors is *il calavrese abate Gioacchino, di spirito profetico dotato."* This was a direct tilt at Thomas Aquinas, who expressly denied that Joachim of Fiori had the gift of Prophecy,[1] but it was an even more direct tilt at Bonaventure, who regarded Joachim as a justly condemned ignoramus, and who was accused by Angelo Clareno of having John of Parma, his predecessor as Minister General of the Order, tried and sent to prison because he professed Joachim's doctrine.[2] If we assume that Dante made two mistakes of this magnitude, and identical in kind, we are placing little reliance on his judgment.

It is, moreover, only necessary to read the relevant passages with a little attention to establish that in both cases Dante is very well aware of whom he is speaking. To represent Joachim as a prophet is to ascribe to him precisely the quality with which Friar Bonaventure and Friar Thomas, who saw in him only a false prophet, refused to credit him. As to Siger, the wealth of detail with which Dante describes him proves that he is not wrong about this actor in his drama. If he does not know his whole story, he at any rate knows that part of it which has led him to put him in Paradise. What Dante tells us about Siger amounts briefly to this: A professor of philosophy in the Faculty of Arts at Paris University, he was made to suffer for having taught certain truths and consequently looked forward to a death which was slow in coming. Leave aside the problem of the death of Siger of Brabant, which does not directly concern us,[3] and all the rest may be verified historically. Siger taught

[1] THOMAS AQUINAS, *In IV Sent.*, dist. 43, qu. 1, art. 3.

[2] E. GILSON, *La philosophie de saint Bonaventure*, J. Vrin, Paris, 1924, pp. 25-26.

[3] Regarding the story of Siger's last years, which has been reconstructed in a number of ways by different historians, see P. MANDONNET, *Siger de Brabant*, Vol. I, pp. 262-286, and

philosophy in Paris; we may still read several of his works; he was one of the philosophers against whom the condemnations of 1270 and 1277 were directed; he was summoned to appear before the tribunal of the Inquisitor of France, Simon du Val, on October 23rd, 1277,[1] and although by this time he had probably taken to flight, this summons would alone be enough to justify Dante's use of the word *invidiosi* in speaking of the *veri* taught by Siger. Whatever form the subsequent life and the death of this teacher may have taken, it is a fact that his university career was ruined by the condemnation of 1277. What Dante tells us about Siger is therefore historically accurate. To defend Father Mandonnet's thesis one is obliged to maintain that Dante, knowing that Siger was a philosopher and that this philosopher had been sentenced for certain of his philosophical opinions, has made himself responsible for the declaration that these condemned opinions reflected the truth without even knowing their content.[2]

Such a theory is improbable. And yet Father Mandonnet's historical accuracy led him to take up a position that is more improbable still. Dante's intention in writing the passage was so obviously to suggest that Siger occupies his seat as a philosopher that even Father Mandonnet could not fail to notice it. Since he saw it, his perfect honesty obliged him to point it out, and his eminent scholarship did not permit him to do so with anything but perfect clarity. But as he insisted that Dante was not acquainted with Siger's doctrine, Father Mandonnet found himself driven to maintain that Dante had put Siger in heaven *because* Siger was a philosopher, *although* Dante did not know precisely what the content of his philosophy was.[3]

S. REINACH, *L'énigme de Siger*, in *Revue historique*, Vol. 151 (1926) (passage on pp. 9–14). If scholars were agreed in regarding Dante as the author of the poem *Il Fiore*, the passage it contains on Siger's death would be of capital importance to us (*Il Fiore*, XCII, in DANTE, *Tutte le opere . . .*, *ed. cit.*, p. 200); but, since the authorship of the poem remains uncertain, we will not admit it as evidence.

[1] The text of the summons is reproduced in P. MANDONNET, *Siger de Brabant*, Vol. I, p. 255, note 1.

[2] This objection has already been raised against Father Mandonnet's thesis, and in such a way that there is nothing to add to it, by B. NARDI, *Sigieri di Brabante nella Divina Commedia e le fonti della filosofia di Dante*, in *Riv. di Filosofia neo-scolastica*, February-April, 1912 (pp. 65–66 printed separately).

[3] E. Gebhardt, on the other hand, thought of the right explanation, but rejected it as being improbable: "The explanation which is in that case held to account for Siger's presence, namely that his thought as a philosopher differed from his thought as a Christian, is not merely particularly absurd where a mediaeval conscience is involved, but would add further to these difficulties" (*L'Italie mystique*, Hachette, Paris, 5e édit., 1906, p. 328). Consequently, "there remains but one solution to the problem: the doctor's expiation,

Here the thesis is no longer merely improbable; it is contradictory. For if Dante has chosen Siger to represent philosophy, he has certainly done so, as Father Mandonnet himself shrewdly says, because he wants to place at the side of Thomas, the personification of learned theology, "a representative of the contemporary profane science, Aristotelism. That is why Dante puts Siger on the left hand of Thomas Aquinas, while Albert of Cologne, the latter's teacher and elementary instructor, stands on his right. In reality Siger is here as it were the vicar of Aristotle, who could not himself enter Paradise. It is so obvious that Dante wants to put a representative of the profane science near St. Thomas that he is careful to outline Siger's character clearly, lest it be thought that he is a theologian".[1]

Dante therefore knew at least this much about Siger—that he was one of the very few contemporary teachers who could be chosen to symbolize pure philosophy, that is to say an Aristotelianism undisturbed by any theological preoccupations. In other words, it is an essential article of Father Mandonnet's thesis, which here gives way to the facts revealed in our sources, that Siger symbolized a philosophical attitude which the theologian-philosopher Thomas Aquinas could not symbolize. Now such a distinction between theology and philosophy, here symbolized by Siger of Brabant, is at the very root of the indiscretions for which that philosopher had been sentenced in 1277. Accordingly we cannot, like Father Mandonnet, say that in exalting Siger Dante intended to glorify profane philosophy as distinct from theology, without tacitly admitting that Dante was acquainted with the philosophical-theological separatism which Siger taught. Hence, it seems that only one conclusion can be drawn. In any case, what Dante may not have known of Siger's philosophy cannot explain the fact that he introduced him into Paradise. The reason for his choice cannot have been something that he did not know about him; it must have been something that he did know about him. Now we are told, quite rightly, that Dante intended to make

---

that profound misery, attested by the *Fiore*, in which he had languished within the walls of bleak Orvieto, perhaps even the tortures or the acts of violence which cut short his life" (*op. cit.*, p. 328). The question of Siger's death is not part of our problem, since it is bound up with the interpretation of the text of the *Fiore*, to which others have now been added. Consult in this connection P. MANDONNET, *Siger de Brabant*, Vol. I, pp. 263–264 and 280–286, and S. REINACH, *L'énigme de Siger*, in *Revue historique*, Vol. 151 (1926) (passage on pp. 11–13).

[1] P. MANDONNET, *Siger de Brabant*, Vol. I, p. 307.

him represent a philosophy uncoloured by theology. The least, therefore, that Dante can have known about Siger is that that teacher had maintained a rigorous distinction between the philosophical and the theological orders; what he had said on that subject amounted to so many truths (*veri*); it was because he had upheld them that he had suffered (*invidiosi*);[1] but Dante at all events was anxious to glorify him for having maintained this radical distinction between the two orders, and it is because he had upheld it that he introduces Siger into Paradise.

Solutions which appear the most obvious to the mind that conceives them lose some of their weight as soon as they are formulated. Accordingly this one may in its turn be only one more false solution to be added to the long list which scholars have already offered to this problem. It has at any rate three merits: 1. It gives a positive reason for Dante's glorification of Siger; 2. It identifies that reason with Siger's symbolical function in the Dantesque Paradise; 3. It deduces the nature of that function from what Dante himself tells us of it. Surely no solution could go much further towards obtaining from Dante himself the answer to a question with which his work confronts us, and that is what appears to me to authorize this one.

In that case we may ask ourselves how it is that it has not yet been noticed. But the question is not fair, for, in fact, Father

---

[1] It is appropriate to note here that, contrary to the opinion of the Abbé F. Van Steenberghen (*Les oeuvres et la doctrine de Siger de Brabant*, p. 182), the hypothesis that Siger of Brabant was finally won over to Thomism would not readily explain St. Thomas's eulogy of him in this passage. If the fresh questions *De anima* which it is desired to ascribe to him are authentic the Dante-Siger problem will merely present itself in a new form, with the following as its main points: 1. Siger of Brabant, originally an adherent of Averroism, finally abjures that doctrine and, between 1275 and 1277, adopts the general attitude of St. Thomas, of whom he becomes an "admirer and even a disciple" (*op. cit.*, pp. 78–79 and p. 183); 2. Having abjured Averroism between 1275 and 1277, he is nevertheless sentenced for Averroism in 1277; 3. Summoned to appear before Simon du Val, Inquisitor of France, on November 23rd, 1277, Siger takes to flight instead of presenting himself and producing the authentic *Quaestiones* which prove conclusively that he rejects the doctrine of Averroes; 4. Sentenced in 1277 for his Averroism —though he has already renounced it—Siger of Brabant none the less ceases to write as from this time (*op. cit.*, p. 79): the silence of Siger of Brabant dates from the moment when he adopts an orthodox attitude and can freely say what he thinks; 5. Sentenced in 1277 for upholding doctrines which at this time he himself deemed false, Siger is praised in the Dantesque Paradise as a man who has formerly suffered for upholding doctrines which St. Thomas himself declares to be true (*invidiosi veri*). Thus, it is alleged that while the Siger of history was converted to Thomism, St. Thomas is converted in Dante's poem to the Averroism from which he himself had formerly alienated Siger of Brabant. I would not like to say that the problem put in this form is insoluble; I merely say that those who believe in Siger's conversion to Thomism will still have a few difficulties to surmount before they solve the problem, which they regard, a little prematurely, as solved already.

Mandonnet noticed it. What we must ask ourselves, therefore, is rather why, having noticed it, he did not accept it. The reason is probably to be found in the simplistic notion that is often formed of Dante's symbolism. The *Divine Comedy* contains as great a wealth of figurative meanings as the *Roman de la Rose*, but it expresses them differently. Instead of employing a system of frigid allegories and presenting us with personified abstractions, as Greed, Justice, Faith, Theology and Philosophy would have been, Dante employs a system of symbols, i.e. representative characters: Beatrice, Thomas Aquinas, Siger of Brabant, Bernard of Clairvaux. It was a prodigious artistic invention, a sheer stroke of genius, to people the poem in this way with a crowd of living beings, each having a spiritual signification as concrete and alive as the character that personifies it. The wonderful poetical triumph that is the *Divine Comedy* fully justifies this technique, and if it has often misled interpreters of Dante, he himself cannot be held responsible, since he did not write his work for future historians of Italian literature, but for the pleasure and instruction of his readers.

The dual nature of the characters in the *Divine Comedy* almost inevitably produces an optical illusion, against which interpreters of the work must be on their guard. Each is a historical personage chosen in view of the representative function which he or she is to perform. In order, therefore, to make a specific choice, Dante had first to take account of the part which the character in question had played in history. He could not allot symbolical meanings at random, and it is easy to see why the pagan Aristotle represents philosophy in Limbo while the Christian Siger represents it in Paradise, or why Thomas symbolizes speculative theology and Bernard of Clairvaux unitive mystical theology. In fact, Dante's choices are almost always justifiable historically; when they are not so historically, they can be justified on the basis of legend, and I do not remember coming across a single character whose presence did not accord with some definite plan. This said, the other aspect of the problem claims our attention no less urgently. *A character in the* Divine Comedy *conserves only as much of its historical reality as the representative function that Dante assigns to it requires.* Hence, to understand the poem properly we must remember that in it Virgil, Thomas Aquinas, Bonaventure and Bernard of Clairvaux each lead the particular existence—and no other—which justifies their presence in Dante's poetical universe. Most certainly, these characters remain closely associated with the historical reality of the personages whose names they bear, but they retain only as much of that reality as they themselves signify. Hence this second rule of interpretation, which it will be well to remember: *The historical reality of Dante's characters may influence their interpretation only in so far as it is essential to the representative function which Dante himself assigns to them and in view of which he has chosen them.*

As soon as we consider the matter, the necessity of this rule for Dante's own purposes becomes obvious. If he had adopted any other method his work would have been impossible. Those whose praises he causes to be sung by St. Thomas or St. Bonaventure are not the spiritual heroes whom the Thomas or the Bonaventure of history would spontaneously have chosen to celebrate, but those whom the Thomas or the Bonaventure of the *Divine Comedy* were bound to celebrate, granted the specific function with which Dante himself had entrusted them. It is this that enables the poet to pursue his judicial task without fear and, in the name of divine justice, to re-establish in heaven the scale of values which passions or human ignorance have overthrown on earth. His spokesmen have no function but that of conveying to us his own words—so much so that when the need arises Dante does not scruple to rehearse them. As another poet would say, Thomas and Bonaventure dwell in Paradise in the characters finally imposed on them by eternity. Henceforth their words will no longer be determined by themselves as they once were, but by their poetical function alone.

It is impossible to view these problems in any other light without encountering numerous serious improbabilities. In heaven Bonaventure, like a prophet inspired by God, celebrates that same Joachim against whom he fought so vigorously on earth. If we express the problem in terms of the actual historical character alone, we are bound to admit either that Dante was completely ignorant of the situation of the parties within the Franciscan Order, or else that he was aware of it and desired to amuse himself at the expense of the earthly Bonaventure by causing him to be publicly disowned by his celestial double. Now Dante was perfectly well aware of the internal situation of the Order; he defines St. Bonaventure's position in it to a nicety

when he makes him call for a new and strict observance of the
rule of St. Francis—a compromise between the austerity of
Ubaldino di Casale and the laxity of Matteo d'Acquasparta
(*Par.*, XII, 124–126). That Joachim's Franciscan supporters were
largely recruited from the Spiritualists of Ubaldino di Casale
was known to every cleric of the fourteenth century. To say
that Dante did not know it, and that he wrote on the subject
without acquiring the necessary information, would be tantamount to branding *Theologus Dantes* as an ignoramus and an
egregious blunderer. On the other hand, Dante not only rendered very deep homage to Friar Bonaventure in choosing him
as the herald of the affective theology of the Franciscans, but
rendered that theologian precisely the homage to which he had
a special right. I readily admit that Dante was not sorry to
teach him a mild lesson, but he cannot have intended to make
Joachim of Fiori counteract his deep homage even as he rendered
it.

We should eventually encounter the same difficulties if, on
the contrary, we supposed that Dante intended to make Bonaventure justify Joachim's entire doctrine. The two can live
together and play their parts in Dante's Paradise only because,
when they entered it, they left their earthly differences behind
them. That is not such a bad conception of heaven; yet it is not
an adequate one. Even to enter Dante's heaven positive cre-
dentials are needed. Joachim and Bonaventure can only be there
together because the functions which they perform are not
merely compatible, but related. Now the distinctive mark of
Dante's Bonaventure (*che ne' grandi offici sempre posposi la
sinistra cura*) is that in the highest offices of the Church he upheld
the primacy of the spiritual order If it was desired to place at his
side an extreme champion of the same cause, who was the one
to choose? A Franciscan "Spiritualist" like Ubaldino di Casale?
No, for Ubaldino was a Franciscan; St. Francis was therefore his
master and Dante's passion for loyalty made him detest the
attitude of a Franciscan who allowed himself to alter a Rule
which he had professed to uphold. It matters little, moreover,
what form the alteration took: *Uno la fugge ed altro la coarta,*
and so all are in the wrong. On the other hand, Joachim of Fiori
had not merely exalted the purity of the spiritual order; he had
been its prophet. Thus, to Dante's way of thinking Joachim

might in fact symbolize the same tendency as Bonaventure, but he symbolized it in a different way and one that is particularly interesting in view of his history. The author of the *Eternal Gospel*, who always ranked spiritual contemplation above action, was the herald of a third human era, an era of charity and freedom, in which the clerical order of the visible Church would be reabsorbed into the spiritual Church. Such a complete "detemporalization" of the Church was in strict accordance with Dante's political passions. This, then, is what Joachim will symbolize in Heaven, and he will symbolize nothing else. We shall therefore not be surprised to find him there, named last of all by Friar Bonaventure as is Siger by Thomas Aquinas. For it is certainly true that the Bonaventure of history would have strenuously refused to eulogize him; yet he has recast the prophecies of Joachim in orthodox terms—a certain sign of the hidden kinship between the two—and, most important of all, it is here Dante's Bonaventure who is speaking. This Bonaventure, who was a Cardinal and a Prince of the Church, continues after his arrival in heaven to bear witness to the primacy of the spiritual order; hence, whatever he may have thought of him while on earth, it is his duty to testify for all eternity in favour of Joachim, the prophet of a new age in which the complete spiritualization of the Church will be an accomplished fact.

The case of Siger is the counterpart of the case of Joachim. If we consider Thomas and Siger in all their concrete historical reality, we come up against a series of impossibilities. Siger was an Averroist, and Thomas fought Averroism as Bonaventure fought Joachimism. Siger assumed that reason is not always in harmony with faith; Thomas denied it. Siger assumed that philosophy believes in the unity of the possible intellect; Thomas rejected this thesis. The idea that the St. Thomas of history may have glorified the Siger of history conveys no determinable meaning, unless we see in it a blunder on Dante's part that is itself inexplicable, or admit that, in glorifying intellectualistic theology of the Thomistic brand, Dante intended to indicate by his eulogy of Siger that this theology which he exalts had become wholly discredited. It is no longer the same thing if we consider Thomas and Siger solely in the light of their poetical function. In the first place, St. Thomas is a perfect choice to signify Dominican intellectualistic theology. Furthermore, there is the same close affinity between him and Siger as there is between Bonaventure and Joachim: both distinguish philosophy from theology, both are intellectualists and admirers and expositors of Aristotle, and, although he attacked Averroism, St. Thomas owed enough to the work of Averroes for the attempt to be made to compromise him under the terms of that same sentence which in 1277 was passed on Siger of Brabant. Significant as they were, not all these historical affinities were even necessary. For Dante to be able to make Thomas Aquinas glorify Siger, it is both essential and sufficient that what Thomas Aquinas symbolizes in the *Divine Comedy* should be a vindication of what Siger of Brabant symbolizes in that poem. Such, in fact, is the case. A theology of the Thomistic brand is not merely reconcilable with a philosophy that derives its principles from natural reason alone; it requires such a philosophy, and since Dante also requires it for the personal reasons that have come to our notice, there is no doubt that he makes Thomas Aquinas eulogize the pure philosopher, Siger of Brabant, with full knowledge of the case.

Father Mandonnet therefore put his finger on the whole truth when he wrote in this connection: "Had Dante known Siger of Brabant better than we have supposed, I am inclined, in view of certain data that are seemingly quite decisive, to think that he would not on that account have given up the idea of making him the personification of philosophy."[1] To grasp this truth the moment it presents itself, it is only necessary to bow completely to the evidence of the text. If, without further ado, we add, with Father Mandonnet, that Dante entrusted this rôle to Siger despite the fact that that teacher was "given to spreading a fundamentally erroneous philosophical doctrine", either we make nonsense of the fact that he caused Siger to be praised for teaching *veri*, or else we come back to the hypothesis that Dante did not know the nature of Siger's doctrine; in any event there is a glaring inconsistency. Hence, if we are to take all the data

---

[1] P. MANDONNET, *Siger de Brabant et l'averroïsme latin*, Vol. I, p. 307. This passage is faultless, but Father Mandonnet ought to have left it at that. His next concern is to prove that, basically, the way in which Siger reconciles faith and reason was not "an insurmountable obstacle to the entry of Siger of Brabant into Paradise". That is not the real question, for, in the first place, we do not have to decide whether or not Siger of Brabant is in Paradise, but why he is in the *Paradiso* of Dante; moreover, it is not enough to establish that this doctrine did not prevent Dante from putting Siger in Paradise; we want to know whether it was not because of it that he put him there.

of the problem into account it is not enough to assume that Dante may have put Siger in Paradise despite what he had taught; we must go further, and say that he put him there *because he had taught certain truths which Dante held dear.* We are told that that would have been rather audacious, but it was also audacious to prepare a select place in hell for Pope Boniface VIII. And this audacity was not merely as great; it was identical. Boniface VIII has to appear in Dante's *Inferno* for the same reason as Siger has to appear in Dante's *Paradiso*, for the false belief that doomed the one to hell was the counterpart of the truth that the other represents in Paradise as by right. This was the belief that the spiritual order has power over the temporal order; the truth that theology, which is the spiritual wisdom of faith, has no authority over the temporal order through the medium of philosophy. Hence, of the truths which Dante praises Siger for having taught we know at least these two—that philosophy is a science of pure natural reason, and that theology, the wisdom of faith, has no authority over natural ethics or over politics, the foundations of which are laid by natural ethics. Being a martyr of pure philosophy, Siger of Brabant was in Dante's eyes qualified to represent it.

The objection will no doubt be raised that St. Thomas Aquinas would not have applauded the use which Siger had made of his philosophical independence.[1] That is true. Our analysis of the *Convivio* showed us that the use which Dante himself makes of

[1] It should be noted that, conversely, Siger would have felt no embarrassment at finding himself in the company of Thomas Aquinas and Albertus Magnus, whom he regarded as the best philosophers of his time—"praecipui viri in philosophia Albertus et Thomas" (*Quaest. de Anima*, in P. MANDONNET, *Siger de Brabant*, Vol. II, p. 152). Furthermore, Siger would have made no objection to the theology of St. Thomas, for he professed not to be a theologian and to accept the Christian faith as true without any reservation. Finally, even where his philosophy failed to accord with his faith, Siger was not always dogmatically certain of his philosophical conclusions. Thus, his conclusion on the capital problem of the unity of the possible intellect was as follows: "Et ideo dico propter difficultatem praemissorum et quorumdam aliorum, quod mihi dubium fuit a longo tempore, quid via rationis naturalis in praedicto problemate sit tenendum, et quid senserit Philosophus de dicta quaestione; et in tali dubio fidei adhaerendum est, quae omnem rationem superat" (*op. cit.*, Vol. II, p. 169). The problem would accordingly become very involved if one wished to discuss all the possible hypotheses. If, like Father Mandonnet, we assume that in the *Divine Comedy* Dante is speaking as a theologian, the fact that he denies the unity of the possible intellect would alone prove nothing, since, beyond all doubt, Siger himself regarded this thesis as deserving of condemnation from the theologian's point of view. As to the position of Siger touching this question, see the excellent work by W. J. DWYER, *L'Opuscule de Siger de Brabant* "*De aeternitate mundi*". *Introduction critique et texte*, Louvain, Editions de l'Institut supérieur de Philosophie, 1937. Cf.: "Haec autem dicimus secundum opinionem Philosophi, non ea asserendo tanquam vera", p. 42, 11, 5, 6.

his independence as a philosopher is far less characteristic of Siger than of St. Thomas Aquinas. But an examination of the *De Monarchia* will show us also that at least once during his life, and in what was to him a vital matter, Dante had to carry the distinction between philosophy and theology further than St. Thomas Aquinas had done. Now is the time to recall the rules of interpretation that we suggested and to deal with the inhabitants of the Dantesque world in accordance with the special laws which govern it. For it is quite true that the Thomas Aquinas of history would never have undertaken to eulogize Siger in the way in which Dante makes him eulogize him, but in refusing to do so he would automatically have acknowledged the authority of theology over ethics and, since they are inseparable, would have justified in advance all encroachments. of the spiritual order on the temporal order, including that of the Pope on the Empire. I do not for a moment question such an assessment of the Thomas Aquinas of history, but this was the part of his make-up which he had to leave at the gate of the *Paradiso* before he could enter. By refusing to carry the distinction between philosophy and theology to the point of upholding not the doctrine of the twofold truth, which even Siger never upheld, but the radical separatism that Dante had in mind, St. Thomas Aquinas would have forfeited the right to symbolize in the *Divine Comedy* the Dominican wisdom of faith, there would no longer have been any justification for his presence—in short, he would have been the cause of his own exclusion. This is not the only case in which Dante's symbolism is wholly out of keeping with the individual to whom it is applied. The closed world of the sacred poem is subject to internal compulsions which are not those of history; when the laws of these two worlds are in conflict it is the laws of history that have to give way.

If it is already not easy to appreciate exactly the relevance of a philosophical thesis, it is not even certain that a poem, though it be as full of ideas and theses of all kinds as the *Divine Comedy*, is intended to be understood philosophically. When the artist is labouring for a truth, he has his own way of serving it: he makes his appeal to feeling rather than to reason. When, therefore, we come to interpret the *Divine Comedy*, the artist's point of view has an indisputable priority over all others, not only where it is a question of determining the general meaning of the work, but also where problems relating to the means employed by Dante for its construction are involved. The characters that people the *Divine Comedy* are not exempt from his rule of interpretation. Since they are historical characters, we cannot disregard history if we are to discern the poet's intentions. The unbelievable wealth of erudition compressed into the notes of a good Italian edition of Dante is, to the majority of his readers—to the author of these lines, at all events—an invaluable source of help. Without these notes we should know only rarely or vaguely who or what was the subject of discussion. And yet if, broadly speaking, they help us to see or to guess why Dante has raised such and such a character to the dignity of a symbol, these historical indications subject us to a dangerous temptation—the temptation to explain Dante's symbolism in terms of history, instead of explaining his history in terms of his symbolism. In a work of art like the *Comedy*, even this symbolism is expressed by artistic means. When we think we have discerned some at least of the reasons that have led the poet to choose Thomas and Siger as symbols, and then to counterbalance them with Bonaventure and Joachim of Fiori, it is wise to leave it at that.

To be sure, it is easy to think of solutions to the problem that are much simpler, but it is perhaps not easy to find one that accords more readily with all the facts without running counter to the most obtrusive probabilities. Now, in view of what we know for certain we must admit at one and the same time that Dante knew of Siger's condemnation; that he made St. Thomas speak as though he knew of it; that he made St. Thomas praise Siger for having suffered in the cause of *veri*; that he placed him in that circle of heaven in which he praises Gratian and Solomon for having respected the distinction between the spiritual and the temporal orders; that he located this episode in a part of the *Divine Comedy* that is wholly devoted to the exaltation of the purity of the spiritual order and to its independence of the temporal order, and finally that Dante himself required the complete independence of philosophy as a necessary condition of the complete independence of the Empire in its relations with the Church. Such are the facts. It seems impossible to explain them all solely from the historical point of view. Neither St. Thomas, who beatifies Siger, nor Dante himself, who makes St.

Thomas beatify him, accepted the substance of the doctrine for the maintenance of which Siger was condemned in 1277. And yet Dante's two tercets certainly refer to a Siger who was subjected to censure and who suffered in the cause of truth. What principle is to be found in the doctrine of a Siger so condemned that may be praised as being true by St. Thomas without excessively straining our credulity[1] and regarded by Dante himself as an essential truth, and that may entitle him who upheld it to a place in heaven alongside Gratian and Solomon—all at the same time? The only thing that appears to fulfil these requirements is his doctrine of the mutual independence of reason and faith, of the temporal and the spiritual orders, and that is why we may very plausibly find the justification of the rôle with which Dante has entrusted him in that doctrine.

Let us therefore suggest, as an inference to be drawn from the text of the *Divine Comedy*, (1) that the problem raised by the beatification of Siger merges with the more general problem of the relationship between the spiritual and the temporal orders; (2) that Siger is introduced as representing not the substance of Averroism, but the doctrine of the mutual independence of philosophy and theology that was implicit in Latin Averroism; (3) that his own philosophical separatism was to Dante's way of thinking merely a corollary of the mutual independence of the

---

[1] Since this work was written, M. F. Van Steenberghen has gone much further in this direction. As I have said, the problem of literary history with which the thesis of Siger's ultimate conversion to Thomism is bound up cannot—in the main at least—be finally resolved here. In defending his interpretation of the evolution of Siger's doctrine against B. Nardi's objections, which remain very potent, M. F. Van Steenberghen has insisted on the fact that Siger was a rather hesitant Averroist—one who was no doubt influenced by Albertus Magnus and Thomas Aquinas, and who, even if we take into account only the works that are certainly authentic, progressively moderated his Averroism after 1270 (*Les oeuvres et la doctrine de Siger de Brabant*, pp. 171–176). Even if we disregard the questions *De Anima* that are involved—B. Nardi's objections have led the author to recognize that their authenticity is not beyond question, as Mgr. M. Grabmann had believed, but merely very probably and perhaps morally certain (*op. cit.*, pp. 24–25) —M. F. Van Steenberghen's observations (*op. cit.*, pp. 182–183) on the intellectual affinities and the community of doctrinal interests between St. Thomas and Siger seem to me quite just. As I have said, these things explain the fact that Dante was able to choose St. Thomas to beatify Siger of Brabant, whereas he could not in all seriousness have entrusted such a task to St. Bonaventure. And yet, unless we accept as certain Siger's final conversion to a species of Thomism, the fact remains that to the last Siger "placed the conclusions of philosophy and the affirmations of faith on a par" (*op. cit.*, p. 174). Although our conceptions of St. Thomas are not quite the same, I think that M. F. Van Steenberghen and I are at one in considering that this attitude is not Thomistic. Now it is precisely the attitude to which Dante himself has recourse, within the limits that we defined in our analysis of the text of the *Banquet*. See below, Eclaircissement V, pp. 317–327.

temporal and the spiritual orders, of the Church and the Empire, which he earnestly desired.

If such is indeed the case, we should be following an equally false trail if, as a means of deducing Dante's theoretical attitude towards philosophy, we assumed that he was a Thomist, or if, as a means of deducing his theoretical attitude towards theology, we assumed that he was an Averroist. Anyone who cares to glance through his work in the light of one of these hypotheses will encounter insuperable difficulties. The text of the *Divine Comedy* much rather suggests the idea that Dante is a moralist and reformer who arms himself with all the theses required for his work of reform and by his moral philosophy. We do not know who the *Veltro* was, and, if he was one destined to arise in the future, perhaps it is a little ingenuous to give a name to this Messiah. On the other hand we are certain, on the evidence of the text, that Dante heralds his coming at the very outset of his work, and we know the mission with which he entrusts him—the administration of justice. We even know for certain what his work of justice will be, viz. to put each of the human orders in its proper place by restoring temporal authority to the Empire and spiritual authority to the Church. The *Veltro*, the saviour of Italy, will be the destroyer of the She-Wolf, itself a symbol of the greed which is at the very root of injustice (*Inf.,* I, 100–111). When Dante reaches the heaven of Jupiter, which is the heaven of the wise and just princes, the formation which these blessed spirits adopt represents the sentence in the Scriptures: *Diligite justitiam, qui judicatis terram* ("Love justice, O ye who judge the earth") (*Wisdom,* I, 1). A little later, having first rearranged their ranks in the form of the letter M, which is the last letter of *terram*, they open out into a new formation, representing the Imperial Eagle, symbol of the Empire, which is to ensure the final triumph of justice (*Par.,* XVIII, 115–123). And over whom? Over greed and injustice. Again, over the greed and injustice of whom? Of that Pope John XXII who laid waste the vineyard of the Church, in whose cause the apostles Peter and Paul died (*Par.,* XVIII, 130–132). Let us make no mistake, the Imperial Eagle's discourse on Justice in this passage is an exact parallel to those that flowed from the lips of St. Thomas and St. Bonaventure on the spirituality of the Church's aims (*Par.,* XIX, 40–99). To each his order and his function.

The representative *par excellence* on earth of divine Justice is none other than the Emperor.

This burning passion for temporal justice, realized through the Empire, must undoubtedly be the basis of our renewed reflections on the use that Dante has made of philosophy and theology. The adversary that haunts his thoughts is the clergy that betrays its sacred mission and usurps that of the Emperor:

> Ahi, gente che dovresti esser devota
> e lasciar seder Cesare in la sella,
> se bene intendi ciò che Dio ti nota!
> (*Purg.*, VI, 91–93.)

Priests, monks or Popes—Dante hunted this detested breed with an anger that knew no pity. Just as he enlists saints in aid of his cause, the poet does not hesitate to make God the executor of his exalted purpose. Himself animated by an ardent desire to serve,[1] this herald of justice does not for one moment countenance failure to serve the divine authorities as he means that they should be served. As the creator and supreme lawgiver of his own universe, Dante assigns to each his place with an authority against which there is no appeal. We do not find Siger of Brabant and Joachim of Fiori where St. Thomas and St. Bonaventure put them on earth, but where they ought to put them in accordance with the conception of justice which, since it is Dante's conception, is necessarily God's as well.

This is a sufficient reason to deter us from systematizing the sacred poem around any thesis—even this one. Being the work

---

[1] We can understand how Dante's passion for authority is in keeping with the passionate independence of his attitude towards those who betray it only if we remember that in his eyes the greatness of the sovereign consists entirely in service. These seemingly contradictory reactions therefore spring from one and the same basic sentiment. Dante believes that the highest good is the liberty which makes us happy as men in this world and as gods in the next. If he desires the installation of an Emperor, the reason is that "existens sub Monarcha est potissime liberum". The universal Emperor in effect frees the individual from servitude in all its specific forms (democracy, oligarchy or tyranny). The special function of the Emperor is therefore to ensure individual liberties through the constant arbitration that his supreme authority enables him to exercise. The Emperor is thus lord of the means that lead to this end, but it is his duty to serve this end and all those whom he is responsible for guiding to it: "Hinc etiam patet, quod quamvis consul sive rex respectu viae sint domini aliorum, respectu autem termini aliorum ministri sunt, et maxime Monarcha, qui minister omnium procul dubio habendus est" (*De Monarchia*, I, 12). Dante therefore has the right to demand for every sovereign the full authority to which his function entitles him, and to condemn him in the name of that same function, with a ruthlessness proportionate to its exalted character, if he turns out to be unworthy of it.

of a poet, the *Divine Comedy* is infinitely mightier and more splendid than the political passions of its author.[1] Taken as a whole, it is an exaltation of all divine rights: that of the Emperor, most certainly, but equally those of the Philosopher and the Pope, since all rights are interdependent as being expressions of the living justice of God. The *Divine Comedy* accordingly appears as the projection, on the artistic plane, of the vision of that ideal world which Dante dreamed of—a world in which majesty would always be honoured according to its rank and every act of treason chastised as it deserved.[2] In short, it is the final judgment passed on the mediaeval world by a God Who will consult Dante before making His adjudications.

To be sure, the ideological framework of the *Divine Comedy* explains neither its origination nor its beauty, but it is there, and it alone enables us to understand the poem's contents. Virgil holds sway in Limbo over the poets and Aristotle over the philosophers, but Boniface VIII has a place all prepared for him in Hell, while Manfred, who died excommunicate, waits patiently in Purgatory for his daughter's prayers to shorten the

---

[1] I do not say, or think, that, as some have maintained, the chief inspiration of the *Divine Comedy* is political. That is true only of the *De Monarchia*. The poet's chief intention was aesthetic—to write a poem; the subject of the poem is theological—the final aims of man (*ultima regna*); the object that he had in view in treating this subject was moral—to inspire men with a new respect for justice, the mother of liberty. Given the subject that he had chosen, it was Dante's duty to miss no opportunity of lashing the kind of injustice from which he had suffered most and in which he saw the cause of so many evils—namely, the encroachment of the spiritual order on the temporal! That is why, if it is not the poem's main thesis, Dante's political thought is everywhere prominent in the *Divine Comedy*. Every time it comes to the surface we perceive the warmth of a genuine human passion; then Dante's superb tirades and the unjust though beautiful passages with which his polemic abounds find free expression.

[2] We thus find, not merely without having looked for it but without even having thought of it, the interpretation of the *Divine Comedy* offered by Dante himself in the *Epistola XVII* to Can Grande della Scala. After being acknowledged by laymen, the authenticity of this letter has been disputed, then once more acknowledged. It rests with Dante scholars to pass a final judgment. To me at all events it seems to express admirably the spirit and, as it were, the essence of the *Divine Comedy:* "Est ergo subjectum totius operis, literaliter tantum accepti, status animarum post mortem simpliciter sumptus. Nam de illo et circa illum totius operis versatur processus. Si vero accipiatur opus allegorice, subjectum est: homo, prout merendo et demerendo per arbitrii libertatem Justitiae praemianti aut punienti obnoxius est", (*Epist. XVII*, 8). From the philosophical point of view, he adds in section 16 of the same letter, it is a *moralistic* work, aimed not at speculation, but at action. Let us remember this useful admonition not to look upon Dante more as a metaphysician or a physician than as a moralist. Apart from a few opinions which are not quite watertight, we may regard as almost perfect the picture of Dante's political attitude painted by G. PAPINI, *Dante vivant* (French translation by Juliette Bertrand, Grasset, Paris, 1934; Book IV, Chap. XXXVI, *Les deux Soleils*, pp. 191-197). As to the view that Dante was above everything a moralist, see the excellent opinions expressed by FATHER MANDONNET in *Dante le Théologien*, p. 138, and pp. 143-145.

years that still stand between him and the sight of God. The fact is, as Villani said, that this Manfred was "an enemy of Holy Church, of clerics and of monks, seizing the churches as his father did before him". His crimes and those of Boniface VIII have no common measure: the one relieved the Church of possessions to which it had no right, and so he could be exonerated; but the other had attempted to violate the majesty of the Empire: hence it was impossible to save him. The same laws of the same Dantesque universe explain Siger's proximity to Thomas Aquinas, or rather they demand it, since Dante's allocation of authority makes it necessary. Everything encourages us to attribute to him the fundamental convictions that we have mentioned, for they are the convictions that animate the whole of his work. The *Convivio* having restored in its entirety the moral authority of the Philosopher over the Emperor, the *Monarchy* having restored in its entirety the political authority of the Emperor over the Popes, the *Divine Comedy* provides a fresh reminder of the rights and duties of all, but here Dante is no longer content, as in his previous works, with founding them in law on the absolute notion of divine justice; by the magic of his art he actually shows the movements of this Justice— the eternal custodian of the laws of the world, which it preserves in the form in which it created it. For it is certainly this Justice that beatifies the just with its love, as it crushes the unjust beneath its wrath. If it is only too true that in the poem it does not always seem to us equitable in its judgments the reason is that this divine Justice is, after all, merely Dante's conception of justice, but we are concerned rather with understanding the work and its author than with judging them.

If the essence of these conclusions should by right be regarded as true, Dante's general attitude towards philosophy would be less that of a philosopher anxious to cultivate it for its own sake than that of a judge desirous of rendering it its due, so as to obtain from it the contribution which ethics and politics are entitled to expect it to make to the great cause of temporal human happiness. Here, therefore, as in all his speculative work, Dante adopts the attitude of a defender of the public weal. His special function is not to promote philosophy, nor to teach theology, nor to demonstrate the working of the Empire, but to inspire these fundamental authorities once more with the

mutual respect which their divine origin exacts from them.
Whenever any one of them, out of greed, exceeds the limits
imposed by God on its domain, it enters a state of revolt against
an authority no less sacred than itself, an authority whose jurisdiction it usurps. This is the commonest and most pernicious
crime committed against justice, which is the most human and
the best loved of the virtues, even as injustice in all its forms—
treason, ingratitude, treachery, theft, fraud and peculation—is
the most inhuman and the most hateful.[1]

Understood in this sense, the virtue of Justice signifies in
Dante above all fidelity to the great authorities whose divine
origin renders them sacred, injustice, on the contrary, consisting
in every sort of betrayal of these authorities, which he himself
never mentioned save in tones of submission: philosophy and its
Philosopher, the Empire and its Emperor, the Church and its
Pope. When he attacks—and how harshly he does so!—one of
the representatives of these cardinal authorities, his sole object
is to shield one of them against what he regards as a transgression
on the part of its human representative. The savage freedom of
his invective against the leaders springs from his love for the
great spiritual realities which he accuses them of undermining
through failure to respect their limits, since each of these realities
destroys itself by usurping the power of another no less than it
destroys that power by usurping it. We may certainly argue
about the actual idea that Dante formed of these dominant
authorities and of their respective spheres of influence, but once
this idea has been accepted we are no longer justified in mistaking
the nature of the feeling by which he was actuated. Those who
accuse him of pride misinterpret his outbursts of invective, for his
violence is indicative of a passionate submission that demands
of others a like willingness to submit. His verdict descends on
the adversary not from a pinnacle of self-aggrandisement, but
from that pinnacle to which he raises his three great ideals. We
offend him only if we offend them. The torment of this great
spirit was to be ceaselessly in conflict with what he loved most
in the world in consequence of his very longing to serve it; his
enemies were Popes who betray the Church and Emperors who
betray the Empire. It is in response to this stimulus that Dante's
invective is unleashed to smite traitors, for in this universe in

[1] DANTE, *Convivio*, I, 12.

which the gravest of evils is injustice, the gravest injustice is treachery, and the gravest treachery of all is not betrayal of a benefactor, but betrayal of a leader. Every betrayal of this kind shakes the fabric of the world in that it shakes the authorities on which God Himself wills that it should be founded and which, together with order, ensure its unity and peace. The foulest denizen of the depths of Dante's hell is Lucifer, who has betrayed his Maker, and the three arch-criminals whose eternal chastisement Lucifer ensures are also the arch-traitors: Judas Iscariot, the betrayer of God, and Cassius and Brutus, the betrayers of Caesar. How can we mistake the implications of this terrible symbolism? It is most certainly a greater crime to betray the majesty of God than to betray the majesty of the Emperor, but it is the same class of offence, and in either case it is the crime of crimes: the betrayal of majesty.

In thus making sure what it is that Dante despises more than anything else in the world, we learn what he esteems above all things: loyalty to the powers established by God. This has been too often forgotten by expositors of his works, especially when their philosophical, theological and political content has been involved. It is idle to attempt to identify the single master whose disciple he is supposed to have been. Dante cannot be regarded as having less than three simultaneously. In fact, in a given sphere, he submits always to the supreme authority in that sphere: to Virgil in poetry, to Ptolemy in astronomy, to Aristotle in philosophy, to St. Dominic in speculative theology, to St. Francis in affective theology and to St. Bernard in mystical theology. Many others could be found answering to the description of guides. It matters little to him who the man is, provided that in every case he is sure of following the greatest. Such is the chosen system to which the only truly authentic Dante seems always to have adhered. If, as is asserted, a "unifying vision" of his work exists, it cannot be identified with any philosophy, or with a political cause, or even with a theology. We shall find it rather in his peculiarly personal conception of the virtue of justice and of the allegiances which that virtue exacts. Dante's work does not constitute a system, but is the dialectical and lyrical expression of all his loyalties.

Eclaircissements

I

Of Poets and their Muses

ONE WOULD not venture to broach a subject that will appear so frivolous in the body of a work that is apparently serious. Yet I believe that it lies at the very root of all the discussions that go on among scholars with regard to the reality or unreality of Beatrice. The sentiment which underlies the arguments of Father Mandonnet, O.P., is amazement at the fact that a sensible man, as Dante certainly was, could invent so many fables on account of a woman. This is not hard to understand. To an irreproachable churchman such as Father Mandonnet the significance of the clerical vocation was quite different from that of love. He therefore believed that in making Beatrice the object of a passion with which an intelligent man, in his right mind, could reasonably be inflamed he was merely explaining the *Vita Nuova*.

Father Mandonnet's case was an extreme one, but it is by no means unique. It is, indeed, far from being so. Almost all purely symbolical interpretations of the figure of Beatrice presuppose an attitude of the same kind, and other literary heroines besides her have aroused the same feeling of incredulity. How can one believe that a sensible man could go hot and cold, swoon, almost die on account of a young girl, then on account of a woman, who never gave him the slightest hope and to whom apparently he never even tried to speak? Beatrice dies, Dante loves her still and exalts her to a loftier plane than ever. Dante marries and becomes the father of a family, but he still loves Beatrice. Whereupon we all ask ourselves: Could *I* love a woman so intensely and so constantly in similar circumstances? The answer is "No". From which we at once conclude that Dante never loved any woman in this way either. It only remains to inquire what significance Dante can actually have attached to a woman's name which was not the name of a real woman. Then begins the review of the Beatrices who were not Beatrice: Dante's clerical vocation, faith, theology, grace, the Empire, the Franciscan spiritualism of the Joachimists, the light of glory, the heresy of the Albigenses and the active intellect.

But the improbability of the real existence of Beatrice implies another improbability, involving the general nature of the problem that she raises. Petrarch loved Laura. Whether the woman involved was Laura de Noves, or another woman who was or was not called Laura, is here of no importance. The thing which counts is that Petrarch was able to love the same woman for years on end, first when she was young and in the full radiance of her beauty, then when she was growing old, shrunken through illness and numerous confinements, and finally after she was dead—and this not only without obtaining anything from her, but even as he sought from substitutes who were easier of approach the consolations that she refused him. In each case we have the same lasting passion of a poet for the woman who is the subject of his song, the same absence of any carnal aftermath to that passion, and also, apparently, the same complicity on the part of the beloved woman in receiving an amorous eulogy which, had she really so desired, would undoubtedly have come to an abrupt end. Yet Laura certainly existed. Petrarch has given in his *Secretum* precise details concerning the nature of his feelings towards her which leave no room for doubt. He wooed her, but she rejected his courtship. One does not experience such rejections at the hands of a myth. Why should not Beatrice also have existed?

Is not the reason for these uncertainties simply that works of art, created by artists with artistic ends in view, inevitably end by becoming subjects of instruction, studied by professors with academic ends in view? The fact is obvious; its consequences are catastrophic. In the absence of a law making it an offence, punishable by a fine, to load the pages of masterpieces with footnotes for the use of schoolboys, or to make children learn summaries of *Berenice* by heart and turn the fables of the divine La Fontaine into prose, we must resign ourselves to seeing the whole of literature become an object of disgust to all. The evil, moreover, is merely growing, now that, at the instance of stupid writers, our pedagogy has appropriated modern writers in addition to the classics. Now that we teach Baudelaire and Verlaine, while Claudel and Valery await their turn, who will still have the courage to read them? Literature is now offered to us in a cup of which the lip is smeared with gall.

To avoid the distortions to which masterpieces are subjected by the professional outlook of so many historians and professors,[1] it would require the ability to draw one's inspiration from the psychology of the artist. Unfortunately, of all the parts of a most complex subject the psychology of the artist is not the least obscure. Few psychologists are artists, and artists who might be psychologists have better things to do than to analyse themselves. And yet we seem to discern here, in the cases of Dante and Petrarch, as it were a distinct variety of sentiment, in which love is identified with the creative activity of the artist to such a degree that it becomes scarcely possible to imagine the one without the other. Certainly the artist is a man. He can love as other men do, yield to the temptations of the most ordinary carnal desire, aspire to the order and peace that are lent to life by the mutual love of husband and wife, in short, be an artist and love as a man.[2] But he can also love as an artist, because he needs some sort of emotion or passion for the liberation of his creative power, and this kind of love is most certainly no more dissociated from the flesh than other kinds, but it does not always need to be accompanied by carnal satisfaction and its lasting properties are often enhanced if this is denied to it. Frau von Stein and Christiane Vulpius did not play the same part in the life of Goethe: she who was his Muse was not the woman he married. Heinrich Heine took Mathilde Mirat to wife, but Camille Selden, *The Fly*, inspired him with quite a different feeling. Richard Wagner certainly loved Minna Planer, and even more Cosima Liszt—each of whom he married—but not in quite the same way as he loved Mathilde Wesendonk, or even, perhaps, in a lesser degree, Judith Gautier. The perfect Muse gives to each of the men who love her what he expects of her:

[1] For an analogy in the field of the plastic arts and their technique, see the admirable pages in HENRI FOCILLON's *La vie des formes*, Paris, E. Leroux, pp. 53-55.

[2] Let us remember, in order that we may understand what follows, that Dante's contemporaries always represented him as being passionate and even licentious. In this great poet, we are told, in addition to all his learning and courage, "trovò ampissimo luogo la lussuria, e non solamente ne' giovani anni, ma ancora ne' maturi" (BOCCACCIO, *Della origine . . .* , ed. cit., Chap. 22, p. 51).

to Wagner, *Tristan* and *Die Meistersinger*, and to Wesendonk a child.

Being closer in time to men who are readier to tell their stories, we know these artists a little less vaguely than their predecessors. It is probable that the great creative artists resemble one another closely enough, in spite of the centuries that separate them, for us to be able to generalize from particular cases. Now Richard Wagner was speaking in quite a broad sense when he made the following observation: "My poetical conceptions have always preceded my practical experiences, so much so that I must regard my moral development as being conditioned entirely by them." It could hardly be more clearly stated that, so far from its being possible to ascribe Wagner's works to the circumstances of his life, the reverse is the case. If one put the idea in a more positive form, as is inevitable, one would say that the artist imagined situations which seemed to offer material for possible works and that, the better to create those works, he actually put himself in such situations. In fact, things are not so simple. Wagner the revolutionary accounts for *Rienzi* just as much as *Rienzi* accounts for Wagner the revolutionary. In order to curse the Rhine gold Wagner had no need to go to the trouble of ruining himself, and a decent middle-class competency inherited at the right time would probably have modified the symbolism of the Tetralogy. None the less it is still true to say that, in its application to the sentiment we are speaking of, what Wagner says seems to be right, and that it may to all intents and purposes be confirmed by reference to the case of *Tristan*.

We do in fact know, from indisputable evidence, that the composer conceived the plan of *Tristan* before he met the Wesendonks, but he did not write it. How is it, then, that we find him later in a situation corresponding exactly to that which obtains in his opera, trapped between an Isolde who loves him and is loved by him, and a King Marke to whom he is bound by ties of gratitude so strong that he can no longer love without being guilty of betrayal? As he himself says at this period: "You can easily guess the strange and unusual position in which I now find myself with respect to Tristan. I say frankly that never was an idea so completely translated into experience." We need not try, moreover, to put the case any more explicitly, for the artist immediately adds: "The question of the degree in which

idea and experience are in the first place actuated reciprocally is
so tricky and so complex that a superficial knowledge of it could
only yield an incomplete and altogether distorted conception of
it."[1] The very embarrassment to which the artist is subject in
this matter seems to guarantee the truth of the words just quoted.
In face of the inextricable bonds that unite his life as an artist
and his life as a man, Wagner forgoes an analysis which in any
case he would undoubtedly have found difficult to carry out
successfully.

Moreover, the problem would become even more complicated
if we were to supplement the study of the poet with that of his
Muse. In this case the documentary evidence is even rarer. It
is also more dangerous to handle, for Muses generally write their
memoirs only when they have ceased to be Muses. They sincerely believe then that they have written *The Disenchanted* or
Wisdom and Destiny. Vituperative Muses are terrible. And yet
the meannesses of mediocre ones do not entitle us to disregard
the part played by great ones—those who, joining in the game
at the start, can not only fall in with it, without always giving
themselves up to it, but can even control it, participating in it
just enough to bring to fruition the work which the artist carries
within him and of which only they can deliver him. Such,
apparently, was that Mathilde Wesendonk of whom it has with
perfect truth been said: "This shrewd woman knew that the
continuance of their love would only be assured at the cost of
her refusal—and that such, undoubtedly, must bethe price of
Tristan."[2] In fact, with the completion of *Tristan*, her love for
Wagner resigned itself to extinction as if, in the full meaning
of the term, it had itself attained its *end*.

It does not, then, seem idle to speak of a certain variety of the
passion of love which the artist identifies with the creation of
his work, and which, in respect to the conditions governing its
duration, in its rhythm and its actual life, is not altogether comparable with what is ordinarily called love. Of the very few
artists who have interested themselves in the problem we must

---

[1] These passages will be found collected under a single heading in *Wagner. Histoire
d'un artiste*, by Guy de Pourtalès (Paris, Gallimard, 1932, p. 244). This excellent book
fully justifies its title, for it is truly the story of Wagner the artist that its author has
related, and this is what makes it so instructive in its application to the problem which
we have propounded.

[2] Guy de Pourtalès, *Wagner*, p. 250.

place in the front rank Charles Morgan, whose *Sparkenbroke*, besides being a masterpiece, provides in this context ample matter for reflection. It has been said of Sparkenbroke that he was Byron and Shelley in one. Undoubtedly—but he is also Wagner, Charles Morgan and, broadly speaking, any artist who is conscious of the intimate relationship existing between art, love and death. Of these three forms of self-sacrifice death is the most complete and, as it were, the one which is adumbrated by the other two; it is even, beyond doubt, the richest and the most fruitful, but we see the result of the others more clearly and perhaps it is not so hard to understand why we so often find them associated in the artist's life. The Mary of Charles Morgan does not mean the same to George Hardy, whom she marries, as to Sparkenbroke, to whom she will never belong. Torn between the love that she bears her husband and the passion that unites her to Sparkenbroke, she feels herself to be an impostor, but she is above all a victim of the human misery experienced by those Muses who love and suffer in order that another may create. Is she not, moreover, protected from Sparkenbroke by the very genius of the man whom she inspires? If this inspiration is to flow, it is essential that she should be loved. As Sparkenbroke's wife, for how long would Mary liberate his creative inspiration? For a long time, no doubt; for ever, perhaps; but, more probably, for as long as was needed for Cosima Wagner to make way for Judith Gautier.

What does all this tell us about Dante and Beatrice? Absolutely nothing, I admit. Nothing, at any rate, which I can explain to those who cannot see it unaided. All the circumstances of these stories seemingly suggest that the measure of inspiration with which the princesses inspired the poets depended on their remoteness. One is inclined to say that, from the days of chivalrous love down to our own times, the creative instinct of poets has led them to choose inaccessible princesses in order to protect from themselves the sources of emotion that quicken their art. Most certainly, I do not think it is impossible for an artist's Muse to be purely the creature of his imagination.[1] Even when she

---

[1] An admirable exposition of this point of view will be found in MARIO CASELLA's essay, *Poesia e Storia*, in *Archivio storico italiano*, Vol. II, dispensa 3a e 4a del 1938–XVII. The author there discusses, zestfully and with sound judgment, the interpretations of the poetry of the Troubadours offered by philologists who pay too little heed to the essentially poetic character of the works which are the subject of their commentaries.

really exists it is still he who creates her in her character of a Muse. It is still true none the less that, at all times, and in particular, it seems, but not exclusively, among love-poets, there have been men who fostered, welcomed, cultivated the passions required for the origination of their work. Had they been less carnal these passions would have been less effectual; if satisfied, they would have subsided, and they have in effect subsided in cases in which the poet, having won his remote princess, has died. If, on the contrary, he has the good fortune, or the wisdom, to embrace only his emotion, the artist will engender his work, and also, if he has one, his Muse. Those who say that the world has never seen the like of Dante's Beatrice would be quite right if Dante and his work did not form part of the world, but that does not prove that the woman from whom Dante created Beatrice never existed. Those who say that a love like that of Dante for the heroine of the *Vita Nuova* and the *Divine Comedy* is hard to credit are quite right, but the *Vita Nuova* and the *Divine Comedy* were no less hard to credit before Dante wrote them; and yet they exist. Dante's love for Beatrice should normally appear to us just as likely as it would be for us to write the two masterpieces of which it was the inspiration.

II

Concerning Two Families of Dantesque Symbols

"HOW STRANGE is the case of Dante—an author whom we persist in reading and probing and never succeed in understanding!"[1] There is in this disillusioned remark much truth, but not all the responsibility for the state of affairs which it laments rests with Dante. The spirit in which we approach his work is also a contributory factor. Some credit him with an encyclopaedic knowledge of the speculative sciences, the moral sciences and the arts of his time. Centuries ago the chronicler Villani said of him: *Fue sommo poeta e filosofo e rettorico perfetto.*[2] I agree that his eloquence should be placed on a par with his poetry, but to describe him as a supreme poet and philosopher is tantamount to crediting him with the genius of Thomas Aquinas and Albertus Magnus in addition to that which he required in order to write his works. If we regard the *Divine Comedy* as such a fount of knowledge we in effect condemn ourselves to be drowned in it.

A second source of artificially created difficulties is the firm conviction, so prevalent among the poet's interpreters, that he used an "ultra-systematic" method in the composition of his poem. "Dante," writes Father Mandonnet, "carried the passion for system utterly beyond the limits of credibility."[3] Perhaps

[1] P. MANDONNET, *Dante le Théologien*, p. 15, note.

[2] G. VILLANI, *Cronica*, lib. IX, 136, in G. L. PASSERINI, *Le Vite di Dante*, Florence, G. C. Sansoni, p. 3. It must be added that Villani certainly does not pretend here to be speaking in a strict sense. Nor can we take literally the first two lines, so often quoted, of the epitaph composed by Giovanni del Virgilio for the poet's tomb:
> Theologus Dantes nullius dogmatis expers,
> Quod foveat claro philosophia sinu . . .
This eulogy, of which the complete text will be found in Boccaccio (*Vita di Dante*, 12, in G. L. PASSERINI, *op. cit.*, p. 192), and which has provided Father Mandonnet with the title and the epigraph of his book, is a poetical eulogy. Failure to credit Dante with an exhaustive knowledge of the theology and the philosophy of his time does not imply any belittlement of the mass of learning which he acquired.

[3] P. MANDONNET, *Dante le Théologien*, p. 14. Other interpreters, on the contrary, stress the changes of plan, cracks and faults which they think they find in the construction of the *Divine Comedy* (e.g. H. HAUVETTE, *Etudes sur la Divine Comédie*, Paris, H. Champion, 1922, pp. 1–64).

it ought to be considered that, if the passion for system that is ascribed to him is utterly beyond the limits of credibility, it is a strain on credulity to ascribe it to him. This, however, is not what happens. Hence the origination of those occultist and hermetic Dantes whose work is only intelligible to those who possess the key to it. Unfortunately, every initiate is sure that his key is the right one, and as no two have the same key their discussions on the *Divine Comedy* help not a little to obscure its meaning.

It is at this point that the confusion is increased still further by the interposition of the symbolist notion. Those who regard Dante's work not only as being admirably constructed, as it certainly is, but also—and this is quite a different matter—as submitting in its construction to the dictates of a system, owe it to themselves to find the consequences of that system on every page. There could be no more convenient way of attaining this end than to ascribe to it a symbolism with manifold ramifications, thanks to which it will always be possible to attribute to the text of Dante the meaning that it should yield according to the system attributed to it. This time, however, the mistake is not absurd, for there certainly is a great deal of symbolism in Dante, and it is not hard to understand that his interpreters do not always agree as to the meaning of his symbols, or even as to the parts of his work in which they occur; but even in this particular the difficulties seem to have been artificially multiplied without any need.

From the fact that Dante made use in his works of rhetorical formulas which every writer necessarily employs it has been inferred that he had studied, then applied, the table of "modes" of literary expression drawn up by St. Thomas in his commentaries on the Psalms and on the *Maxims* of Peter Lombard.[1] Similarly, in view of the fact that Dante admitted the distinction—classic in theological circles—between literal, allegorical or mystical,

---

[1] P. MANDONNET, *Dante le Théologien*, pp. 153–162. To prove this point Father Mandonnet shows that Dante made use in his work of the rhetorical "modes" enumerated by St. Thomas; but these modes were not devised by St. Thomas personally. Not only is it unnecessary to be familiar with his writings in order to employ the modes (controversial, deprecatory, laudatory, narratory, *etc.*), but Dante might have learnt them by a study of *Grammatica*. A large collection of these modes will be found in Cicero's *De Oratore*, or, more conveniently, in QUINTILIAN, *Oratoriae Institutionis*, lib. III, cap. 4. Cf. DANTE, *Epistola XVII* (to Can Grande), art. 9, in *Tutte le opere . . .*, Florence, G. Barbèra, 1919 (pp. 437–438).

moral and analogical meanings,[1] commentators have thought themselves entitled to seek an allegorical meaning everywhere, to the extent of stifling the literal meaning beneath the mass of symbols with which it is desired to encumber it. That there is symbolism in Dante, and in great abundance too, is obvious, but we shall understand its peculiar character much better if we work from his actual text than if we make the rules of Tyconius our starting-point. It is one thing to define the rules that enable the various meanings of the Bible to be explained, as the exegete does, but it is another thing to use those rules, as Dante did, for the construction of a poem which others will have to explain.

It is certain that Dante in his work applied the basic principle of the interpreters of the Bible. In the *Divine Comedy*, as in the Scriptures, even *things* have a significance. They may be inanimate things, animals, or men. Now it seems that the symbolical explanation should not be of the same character in these various cases, because the very things that are used as symbols differ in character. In more precise terms, the human beings who people the sacred poem, and who are designated by proper names, appear to be essentially different in their symbolical value from all other realities to which any kind of spiritual significance is attached.[2] If this is true, we ought not to use the same methods in order to determine their significance.

Let us take a few examples. Although interpreters of Dante

---

[1] DANTE, *Convivio*, II, 1. Cf. *Epistola XVII*, art. 7 (*ed. cit.*, p. 437).

[2] Dante treats even the mythological beings—romantic or poetic in origin—whom he mentions as real people, and, in some cases, it is hard to know to what extent he himself regarded them as such. The fact that a personage is called Minos, for example, does not prevent Dante from regarding him as an ancient king of Crete who became a judge in the pagan hell and has remained so in the Christian hell. Here as elsewhere, however, I am speaking only of the personages whom Dante says he has known, personally or through their works, and I must here recall that, if Beatrice is merely a fiction, there may be a second case of a similar kind, that of Matelda. The student will find her identified with the Wisdom of the Old Testament by L. PIETROBONO (*Matelda*, in *Il Giornale dantesco*, Vol. XXXIX, nuova serie, IX. Annuario dantesco 1936. Florence, L. Olschki, 1938, pp. 91–124). I take the liberty of confessing that this most ingenious demonstration does not convince me, but not without adding at once that, since I myself have not studied the question, my opinion on this point is valueless. I cannot overcome the odd impression with which I am left by lists of Dante's guides like those suggested to us, in which all but two are real people. If, for example, Virgil, Beatrice, Matelda, Cato, Statius, St. Bernard and the Virgin Mary are named, I always ask myself: Why five real persons and two mythical ones, or only one, according to taste? Seeing that Dante represents them to us as being so many real persons, and nearly all of them are, we should need some very strong evidence to the contrary before we agreed that he regarded two of them as nothing but fictions. Once again, I only give my impression here for what it is worth.

do not always agree as to the meaning of the "dark forest", the Lion, the Panther and the She-wolf, all admit by implication that the symbolism of these things or beings is of a simple kind. Whatever they may signify, they signify but one thing, which remains precisely the same however varied its modes of application may be. It is, moreover, worthy of note that in practice expositors of Dante agree much more readily about the symbolism in his work when it involves things than they do when it involves the characters. Thus, at the beginning of the *Divine Comedy*, the *selva oscura* certainly signifies the sinful life of man. Whether we say "sin", "vice" or "sinful life" is here unimportant, since the basic meaning remains the same. Nor is it important for our purpose whether we decide in favour of original sin or actual sin,[1] first of all because one does not exist without the other, but also because, once more, the thing symbolized is always essentially the same: sin.

The same remark would apply to the Hill, the Sun, the three beasts and, broadly speaking, to the innumerable symbols whose meaning may be understood without too much difficulty. Undoubtedly there are others about which agreement has never been reached, but the vast majority of expositors seem to admit that the Panther symbolizes lust, the Lion pride and the She-wolf greed or, in the technical and full sense of the word, avarice.[2] To be sure, lust, pride and greed are in their turn divided into species, but all these species belong to a single genus, and it is precisely their common genus that is designated by these symbols. Now their common characteristic is that they are pure fictions, or, if one prefers, simple images, to which Dante has decided

---

[1] ANTONIO SANTI, *L'ordinamento morale e l'allegoria della Divina Commedia. L'Allegoria*, Florence, Remo Sandron, 1924 (*La Selva*, pp. 11–15). The problem would, on the other hand, become one of capital importance if, having identified the "dark forest" with original sin, one wished to ascribe to Dante the statement that the mission of the Eagle, or Emperor, is to complete the liberation of men from the consequences of original sin, from which Christ's redemption has not wholly delivered them. This thesis has been amplified by Giovanni Pascoli in a series of works which to-day are famous. Chief among them are *Sotto il velame*, Messina, 1900, and *La Mirabele Visione*, Messina, 1902. G. Pascoli's thesis has been newly adopted and amplified by LUIGI VALLI, *L'allegoria di Dante secondo G. Pascoli*, Bologna, Zanchelli, 1922. These theses have been vehemently disputed by FRANCESCO ERCOLE, *A proposito di una recente interpretazione della "Divina Commedia"*, in *Il pensiero politico di Dante*, Milan, Alpes, 1927, Vol. I, pp. 213–266; and also *Il significato della Croce e dell'Aquila nella "Divina Commedia"*, in *op. cit.*, pp. 269–351. Another criticism of them will be found in MICHELE BARBI'S *Nuovi problemi della critica dantesca*, in *Studi Danteschi*, Florence, 1938–XVII, pp. 5–28.

[2] A bibliography of the symbolism of the three beasts will be found in ANTONIO SANTI, *op. cit.*, p. 32, note 2. He himself accepts this classic interpretation (*ibid.*, pp. 32–39).

to attach once and for all a certain significance. The forest and the She-wolf are poetical fancies; the poet represents them as such and asks us to accept them as such. To make things easier, let us assume that all symbols of this genus constitute a primary family. It will then be said that in Dante's writings symbolical fictions are generally possessed of a simple meaning, which no matter how varied the uses to which the poet may put it, remains univocal, and may consequently be indicated by a single word.

In a certain sense we may and should likewise regard the real people introduced by Dante into the *Divine Comedy* as being invested with a symbolical meaning. They are familiar types, signifying spiritual realities which often transcend their human character. And yet their case differs profoundly from the preceding one. Once it is understood that the Eagle symbolizes the Empire, this symbol can occasion no further surprise, for the simple reason that in its essence the eagle in question is virtually an image symbolizing the Empire. It is quite a different matter where Dante, Virgil and St. Bernard of Clairvaux are concerned. We are told that Dante symbolizes *homo viator*, man in his pilgrimage through human life. This is undoubtedly true, but he does so because, in reality, that is what he is. Behind the *Divine Comedy's* veil of poetical allegory we find a man telling his own story and his own human experience, which consists in his liberation from vice through divine grace:

> Tu m'hai di servo tratto a libertate
> (*Par.*, XXXI, 85.)
> Quinci su vo per non esser più cieco
> (*Purg.*, XXVI, 58.)

These lines, and countless others which we have quoted, or which might be added to them, point to the fundamental reality of the narrative and of the actors whom we meet in it. Now Virgil too behaves in the *Comedy* like a living man with whom Dante has established personal and concrete relations, and the same may be said of St. Bernard of Clairvaux. Hence the symbolical value of these characters is necessarily complex, as are they themselves, and, above all, the word "symbol" cannot now be applied to them in the same sense as when it was a question of pure fictions. Not only does the She-wolf signify greed, but nothing is left of it save an image if it is stripped of its symbolism. In such cases it is the meaning that creates the symbol. Where Virgil is concerned the contrary is true, so much so that we run a grave risk of misunderstanding the meaning of the *Divine Comedy* if we forget this point. For it is quite true that Dante chose Virgil and St. Bernard with the objective of making them representative types of spiritual realities, and the remark would apply quite as much to the cases of St. Bonaventure and St. Thomas Aquinas, King Solomon, Gratian, Joachim of Fiori, Siger of Brabant and countless others; yet here it is not the meaning that creates the symbolical being, but the symbolical being that creates its own symbol. In short, they are all primarily symbolical of what they are.

We should therefore be in danger of committing some grave errors of construction if we first asked ourselves what Virgil symbolizes, interpreting the text according to the symbolism which we decided to attribute to him. This method is legitimate in the case of the She-wolf, to which we should at once attach the unequivocal label of "greed" every time we come across it. But it is not legitimate in the case of Virgil because in the *Divine Comedy* that personage plays a complex part analogous to the one that he really played in Dante's life, and his reactions have the resilient, varied, often unpredictable unity of those of a concrete, living being.

It is because they have forgotten this that interpreters of Dante have so often looked behind the figure of Virgil for a simple and univocal symbolism like that of the She-wolf, the Panther or the Eagle. What theory has not been invented? Scholars have wanted to regard him as representing the Imperial authority, human reason, philosophy, the order of nature without grace, *etc.* Nothing would be easier than to think of many other interpretations besides, but it would be a waste of time, because Virgil is no more capable than any other real person of being accounted for in terms of some mere abstract symbol. His civil status and his birth-certificate are against it. Far from being the expression of a symbolical meaning, he is the origin of it. If our interpretation of the *Divine Comedy* is not to be utterly wrong, we should always proceed from what Virgil says and does to what he symbolizes, and not *vice versa*. In the *Comedy*, then, he is the supreme poet, but not Poetry; a wise man, but not Wisdom; an illustrious representative of the

natural virtues and of moral prudence, but not Philosophy. If
we seek to obtain a one-word answer, as we may expect to do
when mere poetical fictions are involved, we find that the
question "What does Virgil symbolize?" does not admit of any
answer. We may therefore provide a score of answers, each of
which will suggest itself as being the only one and as ruling out
all the rest; but by that very fact they will be contradictory.
Perhaps it would be wiser to forgo this sport, for Dante studies
stand to lose more than they gain by it.

We ought especially to forgo it in so far as Beatrice is concerned. I have criticized, more severely, perhaps, than was
necessary, several of the symbolical meanings that are attributed
to her, without myself suggesting any other. No doubt it will
be thought that this method is too simple. I am sorry, but no
man is beholden to the impossible. Those who lay it down as a
principle that Beatrice is merely a poetical fiction are right to
propound the problem of her symbolical meaning as if her
case were identical with that of the She-wolf or the Eagle. This,
moreover, is what they do when they seek a simple and univocal
connotation for her, as, for instance, Theology, Faith, Grace,
Revelation, the Theological Virtues, the Contemplative Life in its
pre-eminence over action, the Supernatural Life, *etc.* Even if we
confine ourselves to those which are most likely, these symbolical
meanings are numberless, but none of them accords with all the
data of the problem, and that is why those who suggest them all
hotly defend their own predilections, though none succeeds
either in accepting or in eliminating those of his colleagues.

What must we do to get out of the difficulty? We must return
to the golden rule laid down by Signor Michele Barbi: "The
most important thing of all is to understand Dante's poetry."
This rule has a natural corollary, *viz.*: "What lies outside the
poet's consciousness cannot concern us." In the present case,
what idea is in the poet's consciousness? This—that Beatrice is
the blessed spirit of a woman whom once he loved. In Dante's
eyes the immortality of the soul is an absolute certainty: the
actual existence of Beatrice is therefore, in his eyes, beyond
doubt. Nor is there any doubt in his mind that she is one of the
blessed, and consequently possessed of all the privileges and all
the spiritual virtues that befit her state. How can we be surprised
that she exercises on Dante's behalf the manifold functions that

he assigns to her? A woman elect of God, whose glory we know to be the subject of his meditations, may be the medium of his moral reform and of his religious salvation; she may be actively present to him, for the blessed in heaven know clearly all that happens on earth, they may intervene in our affairs in accordance with the requirements of divine justice,[1] and although they do not do so as a rule, they do so in certain exceptional circumstances;[2] she may intercede on his behalf with God, and her intercession will be as effectual as her charity is perfect; more, she may lawfully be the recipient of Dante's prayers, since she is a saint, and all the saints, *non solum superiores, sed etiam inferiores* ("not only the greater, but the lesser too"), should be the recipients of the prayers of mankind.[3] To quote St. Thomas Aquinas in support of these assertions is in no way necessary, save as a reminder that we are concerned here with genuinely Christian theses, for every Christian knows that this is how matters stand and, to know it, Dante did not need to be that *theologus Dantes* who has been the subject of some little misrepresentation.

If what has been said is true, we cannot understand the *Divine Comedy* in the sense in which he himself meant it unless we treat as fiction what was to him only fiction, and as reality what he himself conceived as reality. Those who do not share Dante's faith are not thereby absolved from the duty of reading his work on the assumption that it was written by a believer. Those who, while sharing his faith, do not feel that the dead are really present, in the way that enabled Dante to live in community of thought with them, are not on that account entitled to look upon Virgil and Cato as if they had signified to him only what they may signify to his expositors. In order, therefore, to avoid this error, we must avoid seeking a label indicative of Beatrice's symbolical meaning and equating her to the word which describes it. In the work from Dante's pen that we are trying to understand she is a person, not a thing—a being who is represented to us by Dante as a real individual, and who, because she has life, exhibits the complexity of life as well.[4]

---

[1] St. Thomas Aquinas, *Sum. theol.*, Pars I, qu. 89, art. 8, Resp.

[2] St. Thomas Aquinas, *Sum. theol.*, Pars I, qu. 108, art. 8, ad 2m.

[3] St. Thomas Aquinas, *Sum. theol.*, Pars IIa IIae, qu. 83, art. 11, Resp. et ad 4m.

[4] As a relief from the fantastic interpretations offered by so many historians, it will be a pleasure for the student to read the views expressed by Father Agostino Gemelli,

Here, indeed, we have one of the blessed, who enjoys the sight of God face to face, intercedes and prays for him who loves her, intervencs to set him up again after his fall and guides him towards his final goal. How could she bc so represented to us without conjuring up the ideas of heavenly beatitude, contemplation, theological virtues, faith, grace—in short, all those ideas which go to describe the Christian Life in its perfection? It is therefore right to mark them and to associate them with the figure of Beatrice, but we cannot, without being presumptuous, infer that she actually is the Light of Glory, or Theology, or the Contemplative Life, or, broadly speaking, any of these ideas. We have not even the right to infer that she is the Christian Life regarded as a whole. The sanctity of this member of the elect does not entitle us to equate her to this any more than that of St. Francis, St. Dominic and St. Bernard entitles us to identify them with similar abstractions.

O.F.M., in *Beatrice e Vergilio. A proposito dell'interpretazione filosofica del poema dantesco,* in *Scritti varî pubblicati in occasione del sesto centenario della morte di Dante Alighieri,* Milan, Vita e Pensiero, 1921, pp. 140–155. These pages are notable for their truth and for the wealth of Christian and human understanding which they reveal.

III

Concerning Dante's Political and Religious Ideal

THE BEST interpreters of Dante are at one in admitting that the problem of the relations between Church and Empire is the focal point of all Dante's political research, but they are not at one as to the character of these relations. This is especially the case with Signor Michele Barbi and Signor Bruno Nardi, two historians whose opinions in the matter must carry great weight with us and whose disagreement is for that very reason especially disturbing.

In order to account for their opposition we must first note its cause. It seems to me to lie not so much in their analyses of Dante's works, for here they are at one, as in certain personal inclinations which tempt them to stretch the meaning of those works in opposite directions. In the opinion of Signor Bruno Nardi the independence of the State in relation to the Church necessarily implies the autonomy of reason in relation to theology. For my part, I think that this excellent historian is entirely right on that point, for it seems to me impossible that the State should be absolutely independent of the Church if philosophy, from which the State takes its cue, is itself under the authority of the Church.[1]

But Signor Bruno Nardi goes further. Following the natural trend of his own thought, he adds that Dante came by such reasoning to accept "that form of political Averroism which was, by contrast, to be, a little more than ten years later, the starting-point of the political doctrines of Marsilius of Padua".[2] Consequently what we see here is, in his opinion, the shattering of the crust of mediaeval thought and the blossoming of Renaissance thought. Undoubtedly the *Divine Comedy* marked a

---

[1] See above, Chap. III, p. 212. Cf. B. NARDI, *Il concetto dell'Impero* . . . , in *Saggi di Filosofia Dantesca*, p. 284.

[2] B. NARDI, *ibid.*

return to the position which the problem had reached in the
Middle Ages, but the *Monarchy* at all events advanced beyond it.
In this work, therefore, Dante revolted, in the words of G.
Gentile, against "the transcendency of the schoolmen".

It seems clear, in the first place, that here Signor Bruno Nardi
goes far beyond what his most lucid analysis of the works of
Dante makes it possible to assert. I am deliberately leaving
aside the question that he raises of a return on the part of the
Divine Comedy to an earlier point than that reached in the
Monarchy, for the answer is bound up with the following problem:
Is the assertion that reason is independent of faith an implied
revolt against the "transcendency of the schoolmen"? The
answer to this is "Not necessarily", since one may acknowledge
the complete independence of reason in relation to theology
while acknowledging its complete dependence on God. Now this
is precisely the doctrine of Dante. Hence, the conclusion reached
by Signor G. Gentile and Signor B. Nardi does not follow.

Can it even be said that Dante comes to accept "a form of
political Averroism"? Here again we must eliminate the wholly
different problem as to whether this Averroism which Dante
comes to accept is that from which the Averroism of Marsilius of
Padua was to take its origin. I do not think it is, but that is
another question.[1] Whatever the truth with regard to this last
point, if it is a question of a "form" of Averroism, exactly what
is the form of Averroism involved? With a shrewdness and an
honesty that do him credit, Signor B. Nardi has noted that
Dante, "adopting an unusually bold line of thought, had infused
into his theological doctrine some purely Averroistic elements,
without being guilty of heresy; in this way he was able to use the
Averroistic theory to the advantage of his political thesis without
needing to subscribe to the thesis of the unity of the intellect
and the eternity of the human race".[2]

The position could not be more clearly stated, but it follows
that the form of Averroism embraced by Dante is a flat contradiction of the two Averroistic theses *par excellence*—the eternity
of the human race and the unity of the active intellect. What
peculiarly Averroistic element, then, does Dante's attitude still
incorporate? Is it the radical distinction between the twin aims
of man? Perhaps, but even this calls for a more precise definition.

[1] See above, Chap. III, p. 217, note 1.   [2] B. NARDI, *Saggi di Filosofia Dantesca*, p. 266.

Dante certainly did not accept Proposition 176—condemned in 1277—*quod felicitas habetur in ista vita, et non in alia* ("that felicity is enjoyed in this life, and not in the next"). He did not even admit—and we have insisted on this enough—that earthly beatitude is loftier and closer to perfection than heavenly beatitude. On the other hand, he certainly admitted the finality of each of these forms of beatitude in its own order, the distinction between and the radical independence of the reason that leads to the one and the faith that leads to the other, the corresponding independence of the Empire in relation to the Church, and finally the perfect harmony between these means and ends under the authority of the Christian God.

The question therefore amounts to this: Can a doctrine of this kind be styled Averroism? For my part, I have long been inclined so to term it. It is, indeed, certain that the doctrine of the separateness of the orders which Dante upheld is quite in accordance with the spirit of Averroism. And yet, when I have come to write on the question, I have certainly had to recognize that the perfect harmony between the orders thus separated by Dante is something without parallel in the history of Averroism. In short, this is a form of Averroism which does not embody a single one of the fundamental theses which were part of the teaching of Averroes and were upheld by the Latin Averroists as being philosophically necessary, even in opposition to the teachings of Christian theology and Revelation. Strictly confined in this way to the teaching inherent in the facts, Dante's Averroism is accordingly a "form of Averroism" that is purely formal and devoid of content. Is it worth while continuing to call it Averroism? I said that I did not think so; but Dante's doctrine may, if it is so desired, be referred to by that name, provided that advantage is not taken of the concession to ascribe to Dante Averroistic theses or Averroistic tendencies that are foreign to his work and to his mode of thought.

Faced with this Averroistic Dante raising a revolt against the transcendency of the schoolmen, Signor Michele Barbi could hardly do other than protest. He himself is far from denying the novel character of Dante's thesis, but he takes his stand, with full justification, against those who see behind the theses propounded in the *Monarchy* some sort of naturalism and rationalism typical of the Renaissance or of modern times and antagonistic to mediaeval Christianity: "When we speak of Dante's political thought . . . we should take good care not to dissociate it from his religious thought. Whenever such a dissociation has been effected, or attempted, the interpretation has obviously suffered as a result. In order to appreciate the obligation incumbent on us to preserve a sense of the indissolubility of these two elements, we need only reflect that the society for which Dante is writing is a *Christian* society, that his philosophy is Christian, and that even where purely worldly or secular interests are involved we are always dealing with a *Christian secularism* in the eyes of which the worldly goal can never be separated from the heavenly goal. Far from allowing this relationship ever to escape his attention, Dante is certainly to be included among those of his generation who are most aware of it!"[1]

There is in those lines enough material for two or three years of theological controversy. Is the philosophy of Dante a Christian philosophy? All theologians who regard the idea of Christian philosophy as being devoid of meaning will certainly deny it. Of those who concede that it has a meaning quite a number will hesitate to give it this title. And if it were a matter of securing agreement as to the possibility of a "Christian secularism", what a problem of perspective! But these theological complications most certainly do not enter into the thought of Signor M. Barbi. To appreciate this we assuredly need only acknowledge that Dante's philosophy is that of a Christian and that, if there is any question of secularism, Dante's secularism is that of a Christian. Now each of these points seems to me unassailable. As Signor M. Barbi justly observes, "the poet always distinguishes the human from the divine, and the truths which are essential to this life from those which have to do with God, His essence and His Providence, and which relate to the acquisition of eternal life. . . . In Dante reason and Revelation are always alike *distinct and indissoluble.* And if the State is *independent of the Church,* it is not on that account *independent of God:* on the contrary, it is *directly* dependent on Him and on His Providence, so much so that the electors of the Emperor are not regarded as in a strict sense electors, but as the *denuntiatores divinae providentiae: solus eligit Deus, solus ipse confirmat, cum superiorem non habeat*" ("officers of

[1] M. BARBI, *Nuovi problemi della critica dantesca,* in *Studi Danteschi,* Vol. XXIII, Florence, 1938,XVII, pp. 51–52.

divine Providence: God alone chooses, He alone confirms, since He has no superior").[1]

This second thesis seems no less solidly founded than the first, to which, however, it is in opposition; some misunderstanding must therefore exist between the authors of the two theses. Actually, what deters Signor Michele Barbi from going all the way with Signor Bruno Nardi is the fact that the latter's thesis seems to him to exaggerate the modernity of Dante at the expense of the traditional elements in his doctrine. We have seen that it is in fact possible to eliminate one conclusion which the exegeses of Signor Bruno Nardi do not warrant, and that in the process not only are they not weakened but, on the contrary, they are strengthened. Signor M. Barbi himself goes to work differently. His opposition is not restricted to the conclusion: it goes back to some of the grounds on which Signor B. Nardi claims to justify it. His first objection is that *"the independence of the Empire and the autonomy of reason and philosophy* are not quite the same thing. Having been created by Providence, the Church and the Empire are mutually independent, and they are both directly dependent on God. But acknowledgment of this fact does not constitute an admission of the alleged mutual autonomy of reason and faith". In what sense, Signor M. Barbi goes on, is this autonomy interpreted? Does it signify, in the case of reason, freedom of movement in its own domain? But there is nothing audacious in that. The theologians did not deny that politics and all questions relating to the aims, needs and duties of man as a citizen of the earthly city are a field in which human reason is entitled to move freely, because it is on its own ground. St. Thomas, following Aristotle, does not hesitate to enlarge on this earthly felicity *proportionata humanae naturae, ad quam scilicet homo pervenire potest per principia suae naturae.* On the other hand, Dante never ignored the fact that our knowledge has limits. He never hesitated to "withhold his confidence from reason in cases where it would lead to conclusions contrary to those of faith". How, then, could it have occurred to him "that to accept the principle of the independence of the Empire in relation to the Church was in a sense tantamount to denying a truth revealed by faith, and to resorting to the Averroistic

---

[1] M. BARBI, *op. cit.*, p. 69. The quotation from Dante at the end occurs in *De Monarchia*, III, 16.

quibble of twofold truth"? Let us therefore never forget that in
Dante's eyes all authority comes from God. As the conclusion
of the *Monarchy* clearly states, the aims of Church and Empire
are in no way separate; hence Dante cannot have conceived the
function of these two heads in terms of a clear-cut distinction;
rather must he have conceived it in terms of ceaseless co-
operation.[1]

Here again, what is certain and what is not? What is not
certain is that in insisting on a clear-cut distinction between faith
and reason Dante leaves himself no alternative but to resort to
the Averroistic quibble of twofold truth. In the first place,
Signor B. Nardi long since demonstrated that even the Averroists
never, in the strictest sense, gave currency to such a doctrine.
Whatever they themselves may have thought, they always said
that philosophy is *necessary*, but that faith alone reveals the
truth.[2] In subscribing to Averroism, therefore, Dante did not
force himself to uphold a doctrine of twofold truth. Moreover,
as Signor M. Barbi himself has observed, Signor B. Nardi does
not maintain that the drawing of a distinction between philosophy and theology implies, in Dante's mind, any contradiction
between their respective teachings. And the same thing might
be said of the distinction between Church and Empire. The
problem therefore amounts to this:[3] What meaning should we
ascribe to this "autonomy"—to use a modern term—which
philosophy and the Empire enjoy?

In this matter the poet's writings compel an interpretation
mid-way between those of our two Dantologists. In order to
find it we must first free our thoughts from any preoccupation
with Thomism or Averroism. We must concern ourselves only
with Dante, and with what he says and does. In essence, what

---

[1] M. BARBI, *op. cit.*, pp. 70–71.

[2] B. NARDI, *Intorno alle dottrine filosofiche di Pietro d'Abano*, from the *Nuova Rivista
Storica*, V, 2–3, Milan, Albrighi Segati, 1921, pp. 34–35; cf. likewise pp. 48–49. In
the very same year I for my part reached the same conclusion (cf. *La doctrine de la double
vérité*, in *Etudes de Philosophie Médiévale*, Strasbourg, 1921, pp. 51–75). Most of the
historians who have since then reopened the question have interpreted the position of
the Latin Averroists in the same way.

[3] I am assuming, of course, that no account will be taken of the overbold riders which
Signor B. Nardi adds to his admirable exegeses, with which they have no real connection.
To regard the Emperor as a primary redeemer of humanity, to speak of nature as
"seeking the remedy for its own wounds in itself", to call the Emperor the "first Messiah"
who prepares the way for the second Redeemer, Christ—this is a confusion of the
orders. Signor M. Barbi has, incidentally, provided an admirable exposition of all that
needs to be said on this point in *op. cit.*, pp. 71–72.

he does is to determine *functions* and *fields of jurisdiction*. When he speaks of philosophy Dante seeks far less to define its essence and its substance than to determine its object and its task. In his eyes its object and its task are to endow man with the earthly felicity which he is capable of enjoying in this life. The highest form of felicity is the felicity of the speculative life. In this particular, however, philosophy is not very successful. Too many problems —and they are precisely those which concern the loftiest subjects— transcend our reason for our natural desire for knowledge to be crowned with a wholly beatific success. True, faith comes to our aid wherever our reason fails us, but the privilege of believing is not the happiness of knowing. In short, reason can certainly endow us with an imperfect speculative felicity in this life, but not with a perfect speculative felicity.

It is quite a different matter in the practical sphere of life, and it is not hard to see why. If it is a question of organizing human life with a view to earthly happiness, reason does not come up against the insoluble problem of comprehending those pure intelligibles which consist in the soul, the Angelic Being and God; its only remaining concern is man—earthly man viewed against the background of his earthly life. Hence, since it is this time wholly adequate, it should be able to provide a satisfactory solution to the problem of the earthly felicity which man may find in the practical sphere of life. This, as we have seen, is what Dante in effect maintains. The essential postulate of his thesis, therefore, is simply this: *that natural reason is perfectly competent to confer on man earthly felicity in the sphere of action.* This sphere of action is the sphere of politics, together with its *sine qua non*, the sphere of ethics. I cannot see that Dante ever said anything else: he hardly stopped repeating this between the beginning of the *Banquet* and the *Divine Comedy*. Anything else that he is made to say, *including what I myself make him say,* is an interpretation of what he himself said. For Dante does not say that reason is "in revolt against transcendency", or that it is " distinct and indissoluble". What he does not say of reason he does not say of the Empire either. All these simple formulas are too restricted or too comprehensive to match his thought adequately. We should find agreement easier to secure if we honestly accepted this fact for a start. And if, in addition, we accepted this second fact—that even when he quotes Averroes or St. Thomas, Dante is responsible for Dante's thought alone—I verily believe that we should sooner or later discover the historical truth that we are seeking.

To me, at all events, this truth appears in the following light. To the very unequivocal and pertinent question put by Signor Michele Barbi the answer must be given that in Dante's eyes what we, merely for the sake of convenience, call the autonomy of reason in fact consists by no means in the right to adopt a line of thought that runs counter to the revelations of faith, and that the autonomy of the Empire by no means consists in the right to govern in a manner hostile to the Church. Not only does Dante demand nothing of the kind, but the mere possibility of such a state of affairs would be enough to ruin his entire system. Universal order, as conceived by Dante, *presupposes* and *requires* perfect and spontaneous harmony between reason and faith, between philosophy and theology, as a guarantee of the harmony which he aims to see established between the Empire and the Church. If, then, as is inevitable, we seek to understand his position by placing it in its historical relationship to others, it seems very difficult to connect it with that of the Averroists, whose doctrine was founded on the established fact that, on a certain number of important questions, the teachings of faith and of reason are not the same. If this is conceded to them, it must inevitably be asked who is in possession of the absolute truth on these questions. If the answer is "philosophy", then the Empire should rule the Church. If it is "theology", then the Church should rule the Empire. In both cases the structure erected by Dante falls to the ground. Accordingly, this cannot have been what he had in mind.

Thus, it seems that we are obliged to adopt the other hypothesis, namely that Dante held the same views on the subject as all the Christian theologians and philosophers of his time. And yet, just when we are on the point of reaching this conclusion, a serious difficulty holds us up. If Dante agreed with St. Thomas in his interpretation of philosophy's relationship to theology, how is it that he did not agree with him in his interpretation of the Empire's relationship to the Church? For no one disputes the fact that, in the minds of both, the two theses are connected. Starting from the same premises, they can only have reached different conclusions if one or the other was guilty of some paralogism. I confess that I do not see which of them it can have been. In point of fact, their premises are not the same. That Dante discovered ready to hand that perfect harmony between reason and faith which is to him an imperious necessity was due to the work of St. Thomas Aquinas. In his eyes philosophy lives in spontaneous harmony with theology because he identifies philosophy with Aristotle and the Aristotle of history with the Aristotle of St. Thomas Aquinas. In this sense, it is strictly true to say that Dante's attitude to philosophy actually presupposes the existence of Thomism. It is not, however, identical with it, because Dante claims the benefits of the work accomplished by St. Thomas while rejecting one of the essential conditions of their realization: that domination of philosophy by theology which inevitably entails domination of the Empire by the Church.

Heaven forbid that at this point I should once more re-open the never-ending controversy on "Christian philosophy"! No matter what views one may hold on the question, the twofold fact remains that, whatever the sense in which he meant it, St. Thomas formulated this dictum concerning theology: *Aliae scientiae dicuntur ancillae hujus* ("The other sciences are called the handmaids of this one"),[1] and that this dictum was never formulated by Dante. Indeed, we have seen that he replaced it with another, having a different meaning.[2] Hence, although harmony between reason and faith, as conceived by St. Thomas, may be spontaneous, it does not exclude that subordination of the first to the second which, in his doctrine, is the subordination of the natural order to the supernatural order. That is why, in St. Thomas's opinion, the moral and political order cannot be final: it is subordinate to the religious order as being the supreme order; earthly felicity cannot be final: it is subordinate to heavenly felicity as being the supreme goal; the moral and political order cannot be regarded as wholly self-sufficient in its own sphere, because, even to attain its goal *qua* nature, nature now stands in need of grace.[3] The whole of Thomistic nature is governed

---

[1] ST. THOMAS AQUINAS, *Sum. theol.*, Pars I, qu. 1, art. 5, *Sed Contra*.

[2] See above, Chap. II, pp. 114–120.

[3] The gulf that divides Dante's conclusion from St. Thomas's has been very well indicated by Signor Francesco ERCOLE, *Sulla filosofia politica di Dante*, in *Il pensiero politico di Dante*, Alpes, Milan, 1928, Vol. II, pp. 245–246. (This article is a critique of Sebastiano VENTO's work, *La filosofia politica di Dante nel* De Monarchia *studiata in se stessa e in relazione alla pubblicistica medievale da San Tommaso a Marsilio di Padova*, Turin,

from on high and is, as it were, moulded by the supernatural; the harmony between the two orders is therefore the result of true co-operation, not the consequence of a divine decree which ensures once and for all the pre-established concord between nature, regarded as self-sufficient in the natural sphere, and the supernatural, regarded as being confined within the supernatural sphere. In this matter Dante merely obeyed the tradition that requires an heir to accept his inheritance and to spurn the effort that has built it up. Seeing that harmony between faith and reason is henceforth assured, he seizes upon that harmony but rejects the jurisdictional hierarchy that has made it possible.

If in this Dante was wrong, he had many excuses for adopting such a course. In any case, the question here is not whether he was wrong in adopting it, but whether he did adopt it. From whatever angle I look at his writings, I fail to see how it could be doubted that he did so. When the Averroists separate the orders their purpose is to set them in opposition; when St. Thomas distinguishes and graduates the orders his purpose is to unite them; Dante separates the orders in the hope of recon-ciling them. Most certainly, God—the Christian God—is the keystone of Dante's system; hence, his thought is that of a Christian. And yet the Christian God of Dante is interested at least as much in protecting the Empire from the Church as in protecting the Church from the Empire. And I well know that justice would have it so! But He protects the Empire in the way that Dante prescribes. Whether this way is the right one or not it is not our task here to determine, but it is certainly not the way of either an Averroist or a disciple of St. Thomas Aquinas.

Bocca, 1921. I do not know this last-named book.) For a survey of Dante's political doctrine considered in itself and not simply, as in the present work, with respect to what it tells us of Dante's attitude to philosophy, the student will have to consult Signor F. Ercole's classic treatise, *Le tre fasi del pensiero politico di Dante*, in *op. cit.*, Vol. II, pp. 273–407. That Dante's political thought developed in the way the author describes has not been universally admitted; but, whatever opinion one may hold on this question, discussion of which must be left to Dantologists, the work is full of helpful views, which would still be helpful even to anyone who did not accept the general thesis upheld by its author.

IV

Concerning the Averroism of Siger of Brabant

WE ARE ignorant as to what Dante knew of Siger's doctrine, and as to how he construed what he may have known; and present-day historians are not agreed as to the meaning of that doctrine. Here, then, we are drifting in a sea of uncertainty. Nevertheless, as every slight variation in the view taken of Siger affects the explanation offered of the part that Dante makes him play, it is essential that we should take up a position of our own, if only to make our point of view more intelligible and to avoid laying ourselves open to the reproach that we are ignorant of certain difficulties although, *in petto*, we think we have taken them into account.

Scholars seem to be at one nowadays in admitting that Siger was both the object and the victim of the two adverse judgments pronounced on certain Averroistic theses by the Bishop of Paris, Étienne Tempier, in 1270 and 1277. It has likewise been admitted since the publication of the memorable articles by Father M. Chossat, S.J., that a work by Siger on Aristotle's *De Anima* must have existed, that it was written before the judgment of 1270, and that in it the philosopher gave unqualified expression to the doctrine that the human intellect is a separate substance, one and indivisible throughout the human race. It is also admitted, if we disregard a few minor disagreements, that this lost treatise is that, or one of those, which St. Thomas Aquinas was attacking when he wrote the treatise *De unitate intellectus* which was perhaps one of the grounds of the judgment of 1270. Finally, it is generally conceded that after this judgment, and as a reply to St. Thomas's treatise, Siger wrote the *Quaestiones de anima intellectiva* which were published by Father Mandonnet.[1]

---

[1] There was originally a Mandonnet-Baeumker controversy, which was heightened by the publication of F. BRUCKMÜLLER's book, *Untersuchungen über Sigers (von Brabant) Anima intellectiva*, Munich, 1908. Father Mandonnet finally saw here a conspiracy

It is here that our difficulties begin. One wonders, in fact, to what extent Siger modified his attitude in these *Quaestiones,* i.e. to what extent he qualified his Averroism in order to meet St. Thomas's objections and to trim his sails to the judgment of 1270. In publishing this work Father Mandonnet roundly declared that in it Siger was proclaiming the orthodox Averroistic doctrine of the unity of the intellective soul. However, to say nothing of the F. Bruckmüller episode, which belongs rather to the prehistory of the problem, Father Chossat points out with much subtlety that Father Mandonnet had over-simplified the attitude adopted by Siger in this work. Indeed, if we examine the crucial questions III and VII closely, we establish that, in the former, Siger does in fact uphold the doctrine of the separate intellective soul, but that, in the latter, he no longer expressly proclaims the doctrine of the unity of that soul. I believe, moreover, that Father Chossat's remarks are not only just but very suggestive, and that his articles will have to be regarded as marking the initiation of the inquiries, of which there are already signs, concerning the multiformity of thirteenth-century Latin Averroism.

Nevertheless, it still remains open to question whether Father Chossat in his turn has not over-simplified Siger's attitude. If he is to be believed, in these questions our philosopher finally "took his stand against the doctrine of the unity of the intellect".[1] Father Chossat's main argument in support of this thesis is that, at the end of question VII, Siger of Brabant formulated a certain number of objections, which he himself regarded as "insuperable", to the Averroistic doctrine of the unity of the human intellect.[2]

In reality, this is not quite how matters present themselves. In question VII Siger begins by maintaining that the human intellect is single and indivisible, as he had maintained even before 1270. It is true—and it is Father Chossat's great merit that he emphasized the point—that Siger modifies the terms of his doctrine in such a way that he is able to uphold this thesis without having to deny that the intellective soul is the mould

---

(*Siger de Brabant et l'averroïsme latin au XIIIe siècle,* Louvain, 1911, Vol. I, p. 180, note 6). The real discussion begins, however, with the admirable articles by Father M. CHOSSAT, S.J., *Saint Thomas d'Aquin et Siger de Brabant,* in *Revue de Philosophie,* Vol. XXIV (1914), pp. 553–575, and Vol. XXV (1914), pp. 25–42.
[1] M. CHOSSAT, *art. cit.,* p. 28, note 1.
[2] M. CHOSSAT, *art. cit.,* p. 42.

in which the individual is cast. In order to bring off this feat of legerdemain Siger declares that, although it is not a mould in the sense that it moulds man, the intellective soul may be described as a mould in so far as it operates within every man (*intrinsecus operans*). Having said this Siger adds that there remain objections to his thesis that are very hard to overcome and, after formulating them without replying to them, he concludes that in face of such a dilemma the best course is to place one's reliance on faith.

Such being the facts, there is some doubt as to the exact implication of Siger's attitude in these *Quaestiones*. One may regard the formulas that he uses as a trick to justify, at the cost of some verbal concessions, the doctrine of the unity of the intellect; this is what Father Mandonnet did; perhaps he was right, but there is no evidence that he was. One may regard them as the prudent disclaimer of an embarrassed professor who, without openly recanting, indicates to all with eyes to see that he has altered his opinion; this is what Father Chossat did; perhaps he was right, but there is no evidence that he was. Either interpretation is a presumption on the text. And I well know that we are bound to stretch its meaning in one way or another if we are to understand it, but I beg leave to observe that Father Chossat argues as if Father Mandonnet alone had presumed on the text, whereas he himself does the same thing.

First let us note that Siger's ultimate appeal to faith on this question, far from suggesting a *volte-face* on the philosopher's part, tempts one rather to think that at that time he was still in the characteristic position of the Latin Averroist, in which the teaching of philosophy in a certain matter is not in harmony with the teaching of faith. Siger might easily have said that, since faith rejected, or obliged a Christian to reject, the doctrine of the unity of the intellect, he himself regarded that thesis as *philosophically false*. We may suppose that he thought so, but we may not assert positively that he said so. All that is certain is that this man, who admittedly, in a work no longer extant, for a time proclaimed the doctrine of the unity of the intellect, and was condemned on this head in 1270, continues in the *Quaestiones* to proclaim that the intellect is a separate substance and to demonstrate that this substance is single and indivisible. It is likewise certain that, philosophically, the doctrine of the unity of the intellect now seems to him difficult to uphold in face of a number of objections which he leaves unanswered. But first of all he says that he has regarded the question as debatable *a longo tempore*; furthermore, even after the judgment of 1270 Siger does not, in the *Quaestiones* edited by Father Mandonnet, proclaim that the doctrine of the unity of the intellect is a philosophical error, or, consequently, that the plurality of intellects is philosophically certain. His hesitation, which is indisputable, leaves him still uncertain in this matter save as regards faith.

We ought therefore to concede to Father M. Chossat the point which, incidentally, constitutes the essence of his thesis, namely that the *Quaestiones* published by Father Mandonnet were written after, not before, the *De unitate intellectus* of St. Thomas Aquinas. We shall also recognize, as he does, that in this work Siger's Averroism proves to be more cautious and more hesitant than the formulas of Father Mandonnet, with their insufficiently subtle variations, might lead us to suppose.[1] These are important findings, and we are indebted for them to this excellent historian. And yet, just as he did not really take his stand against the doctrine of the unity of the active intellect, so Siger of Brabant did not represent his objections to it as "insuperable". He leaves them unanswered—that is a fact; he declares them to be *multum difficiles*—that is another fact; but that is all. A man who begins by expounding a doctrine for upholding which he has already been censured, and then formulates objections to it that are very hard to overcome, but does not overcome them, is certainly embarrassed, but he is not exactly faced with "insuperable" objections. If Siger had regarded them as insuperable he ought to have regarded his thesis as disproved, and he ought to have abandoned it; and yet, philosophically speaking, he did not do so. Let us once more recall the formula that he uses: *Et ideo dico propter difficultatem praemissorum et quorumdam aliorum, quod mihi dubium fuit a longo tempore, quid via rationis naturalis in praedicto problemate sit tenendum, et quid senserit Philosophus de dicta quaestione; et in tali dubio fidei adhaerendum est, quae omnem rationem humanam superat* ("And therefore I say, on account of the complexity of the premises and of certain other matters, that I had long been doubtful as to what should be regarded as the way of natural reason in the afore-mentioned problem, and as to what the Philosopher

[1] M. CHOSSAT, *art cit.*, p. 39.

felt with regard to the said question: and in face of such a doubt a man must adhere to faith, which utterly transcends human reason").[1] Did Siger believe he could overcome these objections, and is it possible that he refrained from doing so out of prudence? I do not know, for he has not told us. Did he, on the contrary, regard these objections as absolutely insuperable? No one is entitled to maintain that such was his opinion, for he did not say so.

If it is too much to assert, as Father Chossat does, that here Siger was "taking his stand against the doctrine of the unity of the intellect", it is also too much to maintain, at any rate on the evidence of these *Quaestiones*, that Siger steadfastly asserts "that philosophical theories are false in so far as they contradict the Christian Revelation . . ."[2] Like all Averroists, Siger does indeed say that he regards the teaching of faith as true, and that he does not speak in his own name, but in the name of the philosophers. He does not say, however, that, even where it contradicts the truth revealed by faith, the teaching of the philosophers is *false*. Even in the passage in Mandonnet, *op. cit.*, Vol. II, p. 163: *Quod si quis dicat hoc esse erroneum . . .* ("That if any man declare this to be false [*erroneum*] . . ."), Siger does not accept responsibility for the term *erroneum*; all that he says, here as elsewhere, is that he is concerned not with truth but with philosophy.

We ought therefore to make a careful distinction, if, that is, we wish to observe the letter of the text. In these *Quaestiones* Siger never represented as true a single philosophical conclusion that is in opposition to the teaching of faith; on the contrary, in cases of conflict, he regularly asserted that truth is on the side of faith; in this sense we may, in fact, say that in his eyes "faith and truth coincide". But Siger never, for that matter, gave it as his personal opinion that the teaching of philosophy is false, even where it is inconsistent with the revelations of faith. He was certainly able to say *quod nostra intentio principalis non est inquirere qualiter se habeat veritas de anima* ("that our chief intention is not to inquire as to the nature of the truth concerning

---

[1] P. MANDONNET, *Siger de Brabant et l'averroïsme latin au XIIIe siècle*, Vol. II, p. 169.

[2] F. VAN STEENBERGHEN, *Les oeuvres et la doctrine de Siger de Brabant*, Brussels, 1938, p. 72. The author, incidentally, regards the new set of *Quaestiones* attributed to Siger as authentic, and this fact naturally affects his view of Siger's work.

the soul"),[1] but he did not say, either in this work or in any
other that I know of, that the teaching of philosophy on this
subject was false. Nothing would have been easier for him than
to say this; let us note simply that he did not say it, and that all
the indications are that he avoided the formula.

The inevitable objection is that, whatever Siger may have
written, this nevertheless was what he thought. If faith reveals
the truth, how could philosophy be inconsistent with the revelations of faith without being false? I confess, indeed, that I do not
see how it could; but that is precisely the reason why I am not
an Averroist. And it is also the reason why, if I were in the
same position as Siger, I should openly propound the following
conclusions: The teaching of faith is true; therefore the teaching
of philosophy is false. Yet Siger does not argue along these lines,
but rather as follows: The teaching of faith is true; here the
teaching of philosophy is inconsistent with the teaching of faith;
*but philosophy only knows what natural reason is capable of knowing
about the natural order, and here it is the supernatural order that is in
possession of the truth.* We are therefore a long way from a doctrine
which says that natural knowledge is in accordance with supernatural truth. It is not even a question of a doctrine which says
that supernatural truth virtually implies the natural falsity of
natural knowledge. In Siger's opinion philosophical reason
describes nature as it is, or as it would be but for the existence
of a God Whose supernatural power has replaced nature with a
real order which Revelation alone enables us to comprehend.
How can we maintain that the natural order is the true one, when
faith assures us that the real order is also the true one? And
yet, rationally speaking, what philosophy tells us about nature is
precisely what natural reason should think when discoursing
on nature, even if what it thinks contradicts Revelation. The fact
that revealed truth is contrary to what natural reason thinks does
not entitle natural reason to think differently, because, being
natural reason, it *cannot* think differently.

That is why, in his three-point description of Siger's attitude,
M. F. Van Steenberghen seems to me to be quite right as regards
the last two points, but not, perhaps, as regards the first one,
viz. that "no inconsistency is possible between revealed truth
and the truth that is discovered by reason. For the truth is what

[1] P. MANDONNET, *op. cit.*, Vol. II, p. 163.

is, and God cannot reconcile things that are contradictory, or cause what exists not to exist, or make the impossible possible".[1] Siger's attitude cannot be properly expressed in these terms— not, at all events, on the evidence of the *Quaestiones* published by Father Mandonnet. The thing which strikes him is rather the fact that what presents itself to philosophical reason as naturally impossible is nevertheless real, and therefore true, from the point of view of faith, guided by Revelation. That there is, in Siger's eyes, no contradiction between the truth that is discovered by reason and revealed truth is a literal fact, but it is a fact only because Siger always ceases to describe a rational conclusion as true directly it contradicts Revelation. Now true or not, his conclusion none the less remains in his eyes entirely rational. Although there is no inconsistency to be found in his writings between a rational truth which he rejects, and revealed truth, in which he puts his trust, there is still an utter inconsistency between philosophy and Revelation, between the order of natural possibility known to reason and that of supernatural reality which faith knows to enshrine the truth. Hence, the world in which Siger moves, if, that is, his words are a faithful expression of his opinions, may be described as a natural order, as to the nature of which, in the vast majority of cases, reason and faith find themselves in spontaneous agreement, although, in a few cases, they are no longer so. In such cases what can the philosopher do? To him nature remains nature and, since philosophy is merely the description of the natural order by natural reason, his philosophy is neither obliged nor even able to change. To his way of thinking what has happened is simply that God has wrought a miracle, that Revelation shows it to us, and that through faith we should take it as a certain fact that in this instance God has freely replaced the natural order which ought to exist, but does not, with a supernatural order which, in a natural sense, ought not to exist and yet does. To the Christian Averroist the problem presents itself in the form of a choice, not between the false and the true, but between the natural and the miraculous.

One can understand now the nature of the reproach levelled by the Averroist against his Christian opponents; it is that they seek natural explanations for things which the philosopher can

[1] F. Van Steenberghen, *op. cit.*, p. 179.

only consider real if they are regarded as miracles. What, then, can he himself think of his philosophy? That it embodies the truth? Certainly not, since he knows that the true reality is different from the reality with which his reason is acquainted. It is nevertheless understandable that he takes care not to term his philosophy false, for, philosophically and rationally speaking, it is irreproachable and incapable of being changed. It accurately describes the world as it would be if the divine power had not endowed it with a structure which natural reason cannot comprehend or in any way explain.

Nothing could be more significant in this connection than the attitude adopted by Siger on the question (such a dangerous one from his point of view): "How is the intellective soul the perfect expression of the body and its mould?" In principle, the answer is clear: Philosophically speaking, the intellective soul is a separate mould. Undoubtedly Albertus Magnus and Thomas Aquinas assert the contrary, but *isti viri deficiunt ab intentione Philosophi, nec intentum determinant* ("these men betray the Philosopher's intention, and do not clearly indicate his meaning").[1] What, then, is the reproach that Siger levels against them? Simply that they want to make Aristotle say not what philosophy says, but what Revelation says. That is quite another matter! *Quaerimus enim hic solum intentionen philosophorum et praecipue Aristotelis, esti forte Philosophus senserit aliter quam veritas se habeat, et per revelationem aliqua de anima tradita sint, quae per rationes naturales concludi non possunt.* Sed nihil ad nos nunc de miraculis, cum de naturalibus naturaliter disseramus. ("For here we are seeking only the intention of the Philosophers and especially that of Aristotle, although perhaps the Philosopher's feelings were at variance with the truth, and there have been handed down through Revelation certain beliefs concerning the soul which cannot be confirmed by natural reason. *But we are not at present concerned with miracles, since we are discussing natural things in natural terms*").[2]

To stress this last sentence is undoubtedly a better course than to comment on it. We should not translate into terms of truth and falsity the opposition established by Siger between the reason-philosophy-nature group on the one hand and the

---

[1] P. MANDONNET, *op. cit.*, Vol. II, p. 152.
[2] P. MANDONNET, *op. cit.*, Vol. II, pp. 153–154.

revelation-truth-miracle group on the other. Siger *believes* that the intellective soul is the mould that moulds the body; but to him this is a miracle, and wherever miracles take place it is in them that the truth resides. But, it will be asked, what happens to everything else, then? Nothing: everything else remains what it was, *viz.* nature. Now, whether it exists or not, nature is the only thing with which we may as philosophers concern ourselves, *cum de naturalibus naturaliter disseramus* ("since we are discussing natural things in natural terms").

St. Thomas Aquinas does not seem to have replied to the new arguments employed by Siger. Yet no one doubts that the doctrine of the *Quaestiones* seemed to him practically as false as the one that he had refuted before 1270. As for Siger's attitude touching the relationship of reason to faith, it differs greatly from St. Thomas's, since what seems to St. Thomas to pertain to nature and philosophy presents itself to Siger's mind as something supernatural and miraculous. After 1270, therefore, the problem raised by St. Thomas's glorification of Siger in Dante's *Paradiso* seems to retain its former paradoxical character; and this, if it commends it to us as an object of curiosity, does not facilitate its solution.

V

Concerning the Thomism of Siger of Brabant

UNTIL very recently the presence of Siger of Brabant in the Dantesque paradise confronted historians with an intricate but clearly defined problem: How did Dante come to beatify and glorify an Averroist? Since the problem has been handed down to me in this form, it is on the basis of such an assumption that I have myself discussed it. Certain of Dante's expositors are convinced that the poet was a Thomist; accordingly they try to explain the fact that a Thomist has located an Averroist in paradise. Others, taking the presence of a well-known Averroist in Dante's paradise as their starting-point, regard it, on the contrary, as an indication that Dante was not such a confirmed Thomist as has been claimed; accordingly they scour the poet's works for anything that may be interpreted as a sign that he held non-Thomistic opinions. Moreover, they are not unsuccessful, but this fact is of little moment, for the problem has taken on a new aspect since the recent assertion of the Abbé F. Van Steenberghen, in the very stimulating book which I have already mentioned,[1] that at the end of his life Siger of Brabant himself was converted to Thomism. In that case there is no longer any difficulty to overcome: a Thomist glorifies a Thomist—that is in order, and nothing could be more natural.

I keenly regret that I only became acquainted with this work after I had completed my own. It is true that I should in any case have been in a weak position when it came to discussing it. Since its conclusions destroy the thesis which I uphold, I have too great an interest in deeming them open to question to be able to discuss them without being suspected of prejudice. Furthermore, we are concerned here with a problem of literary history, which should be dealt with for its own sake by specialists in the subject, regardless of any other consideration. I should

[1] See above, Chap. IV, p. 259, note.

therefore like simply to summarize the position in the matter as I know it, and then to offer a few comments suggested by the facts at present known.

In 1924 Mgr. Martin Grabmann, the scholar whose contribution to the historiography of mediaeval thought has been so outstanding, announced the discovery of a whole series of unpublished works by Siger of Brabant,[1] contained in the Latin manuscript 9559 at Munich.[2] These writings include some *Quaestiones in libros Aristotelis De Anima,* which M. F. Van Steenberghen published in 1931 in his *Siger de Brabant d'après ses oeuvres inédites.* The publication of these *Quaestiones* raised a curious problem, for if we refer to Book III, qu. 7—*Utrum intellectus sit idem numero in omnibus hominibus* ("Whether the intellect is one and the same in all men")—we establish that here the author of the treatise definitely opposes Averroes on this point: *Quamvis via Commentatoris probabilitatem habet, non tamen est vera* ("Although the Commentator's thesis is plausible, it is not in accordance with truth").[3] It would seem to follow from this that, at some point in his life, and probably towards its end, Siger of Brabant deserted Averroes and adopted the attitude of St. Thomas Aquinas, at least in one essential particular.

We should note, moreover, that in this first volume, which is devoted to the publication or analysis of Siger's unpublished works, M. F. Van Steenberghen did not need to discuss the problems of doctrinal history which this question raises. He therefore did not do so, rightly postponing the examination of the question until later. None, however, will doubt that he was aware of its existence. It was therefore with full knowledge of the facts that he published these Questions under Siger's name, without at the time expressing any doubt as to their authenticity.

---

[1] M. GRABMANN, *Neuaufgefundene Werke des Siger von Brabant und Boetius von Dacien,* in *Sitzungsberichte der Bayerischen Akademie der Wissenschaften,* philosophisch-historische Abteilung, 1929, 7, Munich, 1929; and the same author's *Neuaufgefundene "Quaestiones" Siger von Brabant zu den Werken des Aristoteles,* in *Miscellanea Ehrle,* Vol. I, Rome, 1924, pp. 103–147.

[2] See the table of the works contained in this manuscript in F. VAN STEENBERGHEN's *Siger de Brabant d'après ses oeuvres inédites,* pp. 5–6. Regarding the questions previously discovered by Mgr. A. PELZER, see *ibid.,* p. 6. Other works have since been attributed to Siger by F. STEGMÜLLER, *Neugefundene Quaestionen des Siger von Brabant,* in *Recherches de Théologie ancienne et médiévale,* III (1931), pp. 158–182. This article contains a detailed summary of this problem of literary history (pp. 158–162).

[3] F. VAN STEENBERGHEN, *Siger de Brabant d'après ses oeuvres inédites,* p. 133.

Mgr. Martin Grabmann had regarded them as undoubtedly
authentic and, whatever he himself may have thought at
this period, M. F. Van Steenberghen does not seem to me to
have evinced the least uncertainty on this point when publishing
them.

I leave it to the reader to imagine how Dantologists were
affected when their serenity was unexpectedly shattered by this
thunderbolt. If the Abbé Van Steenberghen had hoped that he
was going to be allowed to continue his work in peace until
he had published Volume II, he must have been bitterly disillusioned. The idea of Siger of Brabant as a convert to Thomism
that emerged from his book was precisely what Father Busnelli
was waiting for to enable him to crush Signor Bruno Nardi.
"Was waiting for" is not quite the right term, for undoubtedly
he had never dared to hope for such an eventuality. However
that may be, this fervent believer in the Thomism of Dante at
once anticipated some conclusions which, there is no doubt,
M. Van Steenberghen had already conceived as at any rate
possible, and declared that these Questions expressed Siger's
final opinion. If the philosopher was ultimately converted to
Thomism, the tercets which Dante devotes to him are easily
explained; we may even say, adds Father Busnelli, that "they
take on a definitely and profoundly true meaning, because they
imply that Thomas Aquinas (who eulogizes him in heaven)
knew of Siger's renunciation of an exaggerated form of Averroism in favour of the true Aristotelian doctrine as he himself
interpreted it".[1] In short, it is implied that St. Thomas was
glorifying his own victory over Siger in beatifying him in this
way.

A rejoinder was to be expected from Signor Bruno Nardi, but
undoubtedly its form had not been anticipated, for he countered
by bluntly disputing the authenticity of these Questions. Among
the various arguments which he adduced in support of his thesis
there is one which should be isolated on account of its importance,
for no one to my knowledge has hitherto disputed it and its

[1] G. BUSNELLI, S. J., *La Civiltà cattolica*, 1932, Vol. III, p. 135. This passage is quoted
by BRUNO NARDI, *Il preteso tomismo di Sigieri di Brabante* (in *Giornale critico della filosofia
italiana*, Second Series, III (1936–XVII), p. 29). A similar conclusion was at that time
offered for consideration by LEA PERUGINI, *Il tomismo di Sigieri e l'elogio dantesco* (in
Giornale dantesco, Vol. XXXVI, Nuova Serie, VI, pp. 105–168). The passage is quoted
by B. NARDI, *op. cit.*, p. 30.

opponents seem to me to confine themselves, even to-day, to limiting its field of application. This argument is as follows: In the Munich MS. 9559, the only work bearing the name of Siger is the group of Questions on the *Metaphysics* of Aristotle; as for the others, which include the now famous *Quaestiones in libros Aristotelis De Anima,* they are anonymous. Thus, Mgr. M. Grabmann, with the Abbé Van Steenberghen following in his wake, has taken it for granted that the author of one of these treatises was also the author of the others, although this is by no means obvious.

It might be thought that if the subject-matter of these Questions had been Averroistic in character, Signor B. Nardi would probably not have dreamt of bringing up this difficulty; but it is only fair to acknowledge that to attribute to Siger of Brabant, without any decisive external evidence, a treatise that contradicts his doctrine was a light-hearted interpretation of a somewhat heavy responsibility.[1] We ought, I think, to admit that, since the fact to which Signor B. Nardi calls attention is not disputed, we cannot expect him to prove that these Questions are not the work of Siger; it is the duty of those who regard them as authentic to prove that they are so.

In point of fact, the argument has gone home. When the Abbé Van Steenberghen declares that "not one of Signor Nardi's arguments constitutes a serious obstacle to the attribution of these *Quaestiones* to Siger of Brabant",[2] his observation may apply to the five objections that he discusses, but not to the one that he does not discuss, for the very good reason that its strength has led him to represent as only morally certain[3] the authenticity of a work which Mgr. M. Grabmann accepts as indubitably authentic, and which M. Van Steenberghen himself has published under the name of Siger of Brabant. Whatever Signor Bruno

---

[1] B. NARDI, *op. cit.*, pp. 31–35.

[2] F. VAN STEENBERGHEN, *Les oeuvres et la doctrine de Siger de Brabant*, p. 40.

[3] See above, Chap. IV, p. 259, note. Similarly, Lea Perugini, who had at once seen in the assumption that the *Quaestiones* are authentic all its implications as regards the Dante–Siger problem, hastened to declare, in face of B. Nardi's counter-offensive, that to discuss this point was, "if not idle and strange, at all events premature" (in *Sophia*, V, 1–2, pp. 159–161). Signor B. Nardi, who has re-opened the question in this connection, concludes afresh: "The *Quaestiones* on the *De Anima* published by Steenberghen are anonymous in the two manuscripts of which we to-day have knowledge; there is nothing, either in the technique or in the style, much less in the subject-matter, which entitles us to attribute them to Siger" (*Giornale critico della filosofia italiana*, Seconda Serie, Vol. V, 1937–XVIII, pp. 160–164, end of the article).

Nardi's opponents may say, they have felt the weight of the argument, for no one to-day maintains that the authenticity of these Questions is beyond dispute.

I too cannot feel disturbed by M. Van Steenberghen's observation "that Signor Nardi disputes the authenticity of these *Quaestiones* for the sake of his polemic with Father Busnelli and other Italian Dantophiles".[1] It goes without saying that Signor B. Nardi does not wish to see proven a thesis which, if it were valid, would considerably weaken his interpretation of Dante. That, however, is not the question. Ever since the appearance of his first essays on the rôle of Siger of Brabant in the *Divine Comedy* (1912) Signor B. Nardi has shown himself to be not only an erudite historian, but one whose opinions are remarkably well-balanced. Never has he been known to represent Dante as an Averroist. Even in those days he maintained simply that, "taken as a whole, Dante's philosophy does not indicate that he adhered to any of the systems already established." As an antidote to the belief that Dante was a thorough-going Thomist his thesis remains valid. I think so at all events, but even if his thesis were false I think it would be going too far to say that he disputes the authenticity of the *Quaestiones* for the sake of his polemic. M. F. Van Steenberghen knows better than anyone the terms of the problem. If there were a manuscript which attributed these Questions to Siger, Signor B. Nardi would perhaps continue to entertain doubts (for it is fairly common knowledge that such attributions are sometimes erroneous), but the problem would be transformed. It would be his duty to prove that these Questions *are not* the work of Siger of Brabant. To say, as he does, that there is up to now no proof that they are his work is to state a fact. No polemic on any question is needed to explain that if an anonymous treatise, containing a doctrine at variance with that of the philosopher who is regarded as its author, is attributed to him objections must inevitably be raised.

I find it hard to admit, moreover, that at this time of day even one of the parties involved in the controversy is wholly disinterested. In publishing these Questions M. Van Steenberghen claims that they are authentic; if they are, Signor B. Nardi will have to revise his interpretation of a whole series of facts of which he is certain; his very knowledge of these facts encourages

[1] F. VAN STEENBERGHEN, *Les oeuvres et la doctrine de Siger de Brabant*, p. 25.

him to shield them from the fact which is opposed to them. If he has good reason for regarding it as a pseudo-fact, why should he not say so? It is the same in my case. Ever since, in 1932, I became acquainted with the Questions *De Anima* published by M. Van Steenberghen under the name of Siger, I have felt convinced that they are not authentic. Prejudice? Certainly. The conclusions to which I had already been led by my study of the *Monarchy* encouraged me to regard Siger as representing in the *Paradiso* a separatist doctrine embracing Church and State, theology and philosophy, and envisaging something far more radical than the distinctions whose validity is upheld by St. Thomas Aquinas. Yet one could, without giving way to any personal predilections, feel astonished that a philosopher should have reversed his opinions so completely in such an important matter, and that he should have done so without even deeming it advisable to mention the fact. I had not thought of Signor B. Nardi's principal argument—that the manuscripts make no reference to authorship. I frankly admit that I welcomed it gratefully: it provided an objective justification of my feeling of incredulity.

Nor is the Abbé Van Steenberghen without an intellectual interest in this controversy. He published these *Questions* concerning the *De Anima* under the name of Siger, as if the problem of their authenticity did not even need to be brought up. Perhaps he proposed to bring it up later. However that may be, we may ask ourselves whether he had, in 1931, foreseen the objection that was to be raised in 1932 by Signor B. Nardi. If he did foresee it, he treated it as an exaggerated misgiving which could in practice be dismissed without discussion. His position is no longer the same to-day. Faced with Signor B. Nardi's objections, he pleads his own cause, bringing to his advocacy no less self-interest than his fellows bring to theirs, and able though his *Pro domo sua* is, it is none the less an apology.

It does not, however, follow from this that the Abbé Van Steenberghen's ripostes carry no weight. On the contrary, I for my part consider that pages 146–160 of his book on Siger's *Human Psychology* show an intelligence and an ingenuity that are truly admirable. It would be impossible to turn the hesitant strain in Siger's ideas as we know them to better account as evidence of the complete *volte-face* with which it is desired to credit him. Moreover, we are concerned here with an actual fact. If this philosopher had been an Averroist with no theoretical scruples throughout the preceding part of his life, his alleged renunciation of Averroism would be quite inconceivable; but Siger as he is described to us, on the evidence of his authentic works, is certainly indecisive and restless, and the possibility that he finally altered his opinions cannot be denied. In short, M. F. Van Steenberghen has shown very clearly that Siger's ultimate conversion to Thomism cannot be ruled out *a priori* as improbable, in view of what we know of him from other sources. And this is a fact of importance.

Nevertheless, the problem as to whether this conversion may possibly have taken place still awaits solution. We therefore find ourselves faced once more with the question of the authenticity of the *Quaestiones* which have been published under his name. Their presence in a manuscript which contains other works, of which one at least is attributed to Siger, while the rest are Averroistic in origin, certainly tempts one to attribute them to Siger. This, incidentally, is the reason why Mgr. Grabmann and the Abbé Van Steenberghen have done so. It is even possible that the copyist believed he wrote them, but this in itself by no means proves that he did so, and the theory still awaits confirmation.

The objections of a stylistic order raised by Signor B. Nardi leave me quite unmoved. If the *Quaestiones de Anima* are spurious, what may be inferred from the peculiarities of their wording? Seemingly nothing. M. Van Steenberghen's reply on this point seems to me unassailable, and in any case irrefutable.[1] In the same way, with regard to the psychological possibility that Siger finally altered his opinions, M. Van Steenberghen wins a point. That makes two—and they are not unimportant ones—in reply to the objections of Signor B. Nardi.[2] On the other hand, the positive argument which Signor B. Nardi has derived from the testimony of John Baconthorp, Gilles de Rome and Jean de Jandun seems to me to preserve its full force.[3] In fact, not only do these writings say nothing about Siger's adherence to Thomism, or even to a quasi-Thomism, but Baconthorp represents him as

[1] *Op. cit.*, p. 32.
[2] *Op. cit.*, pp. 35-36.
[3] The references are given in B. NARDI, *Il preteso tomismo* . . . , pp. 33-34. For the other side of the question see F. VAN STEENBERGHEN, pp. 37-38.

having been affected by the judgment of 1270, Gilles de Rome says that he knew him as an upholder of an Averroistic thesis and Jean de Jandun defends him against the enemies of Aristotle and of the Commentator.[1] If our philosopher later recanted, there is nothing to indicate that these three witnesses were ever aware of it. The objection that their testimony "in no way rules out a subsequent evolution of Siger's thought" is no more than the truth, but the fact that a hypothesis is not ruled out by what is known to be true leaves it wholly in the realm of possibility; it does not constitute a shred of proof. Moreover, the evidence adduced by Signor B. Nardi, if it does not render the hypothesis in question impossible, makes it far less likely. John Baconthorp died in 1348, Gilles de Rome in 1316 and Jean de Jandun about 1328; these three witnesses seem to know nothing of any recantation on the part of Siger of Brabant, who died before 1285, and their silence is rather a strong indication that such an event never really took place. To reply to this that "the fact that no marked traces remain in Paris of the Brabantine teacher's last writings and in particular of his last lectures is easily accounted for by the events of 1277 and by his premature disappearance"[2] is to take what is a very odd explanation as a matter of course. Thus, can it be that, because Averroism was condemned in 1277, the recantation of one of the principal Averroists, embodied in a treatise that is supposed to have come down to us, has passed unnoticed? How are we to believe that his opponents, overjoyed at their triumph, did not on the contrary proclaim it from the house-tops? It is rather as if one were to say that M. Alfred Loisy had recanted his biblical exegesis, but that, *because modernism had been condemned*, no one has ever mentioned the fact. This third round is all in favour of Signor B. Nardi.

It is the same with the fourth. M. F. Van Steenberghen considers "that there is no reason to locate the composition of the *Quaestiones de Anima* after 1277".[3] I regret this for the sake of his thesis. In any case, it is entirely to his credit that he upholds

---

[1] My copy of Jean de Jandun's edition of the *De Anima* (Venetiis, apud Juntas, 1544) gives the name "Remigius de Brabantia" (fo. 51, vo. a, foot of the page), but the *Incipit* of the treatise, as quoted by him, is certainly that of the *Quaestiones de Anima intellectiva* published by Father Mandonnet under the name of Siger (*Siger de Brabant*, Vol. II, p. 145). There is accordingly no doubt on this point.

[2] F. VAN STEENBERGHEN, *Les oeuvres et la doctrine de Siger de Brabant*, p. 38.

[3] *Op. cit.*, p. 38.

such an opinion. If, like him, I believed that these Questions were the work of Siger, I should certainly put them after 1277, for the simple reason that I do not see how they could be put earlier. The judgment of 1277 was, according to the manuscripts, directed *Contra Segerum et Boetium hereticos* ("Against the heretics Siger and Boethius"), or *Contra Magistrum Sogerum* ("Against Siger the teacher"), or *Contra errores Boetii et Sigeri* ("Against the false beliefs of Boethius and Siger"). The fact that a list of the condemned propositions describes Boethius of Dacia as *principalis assertor istorum articulorum* ("the chief advocate of these articles") does not mean that where Siger's name occurs it is suppressed.[1] Apropos of which I have already asked how Siger's arraignment, his condemnation, the summons served on him to appear before the Court of Inquiry and finally his flight are to be accounted for if he had already apostatized from Averroism on a crucial point involving virtually all the rest of that doctrine.[2] The reply given to this is that St. Thomas too was affected by the judgment. The two cases are, however, rather different. We are told of "the upshot of the trial", but we do not know exactly what it was so far as Siger was concerned and, in the case of Thomas Aquinas, a trial did not even take place. M. F. Van Steenberghen is entirely right in saying that, besides Averroism, the judgment affected Aristotelism, even in its non-Averroistic aspects, but not in the same degree or in the same way. Between a Thomas Aquinas who, though he has never repudiated any of the theses which he is accused of upholding, is not summoned before the Court of the Inquisitor of France or any other country, and a Siger of Brabant who, though he repudiated his false beliefs, is supposed none the less to have been summoned before that Court, it is not easy to make a comparison.[3]

---

[1] B. Hauréau, quoted by P. MANDONNET, *Siger de Brabant*, 2nd ed., Vol. I, p. 220. Cf. F. VAN STEENBERGHEN, *op. cit.*, p. 39, note 1.

[2] See above, Chap. IV, p. 266, note.

[3] M. F. Van Steenberghen suggests (*op. cit.*, p. 39) that Siger was still vulnerable in 1277, for he had not at that period "renounced any substantial part of heterodox Aristotelism". This is possible, but, if so, it is no longer clear in what sense Siger could have become that "disciple of Thomas Aquinas and an obedient son of the Church" (p. 183) the eulogy of whom, coming from St. Thomas in the *Paradiso*, "is no longer in any way disconcerting" (p. 182). In such a case, moreover, his condemnation would not have been due to "his past false beliefs" (p. 39), but to his present ones. If, therefore, his condemnation is accounted for, his presence in the *Paradiso* still raises a problem; it will only cease to do so if his condemnation remains unaccounted for.

Again, the writer adds, Dante's attitude towards Siger is easily accounted for "if the Brabantine teacher revealed a tendency to modify his false beliefs and especially his belief in the unity of the intellect, which was a flat contradiction of the Christian interpretation".[1] To be sure, Dante and St. Thomas are at one in their opposition to this thesis; if it is proved that Siger recanted it, we can understand more easily how Dante caused Siger to be glorified by St. Thomas Aquinas. But the removal of this difficulty inevitably gives rise to another. St. Thomas does not praise Siger for having repudiated false beliefs, but for having suffered in the cause of certain truths. I therefore ask: What are these truths? For my part, I can only conceive of one: the separatism advocated by certain Aristotelians. Whereupon it will be said that St. Thomas did not interpret it in the same sense. And this also is true, but, in any event, it is impossible to reconcile the political philosophies of Dante and St. Thomas Aquinas. Accordingly there is a difficulty either way. We may choose between several hypotheses: Dante glorifies Siger because he is not acquainted with his doctrine, but that is very improbable; Dante makes St. Thomas praise him for having suffered in the cause of the very truths which St. Thomas himself proclaimed—but it was for upholding other doctrines than these that Siger was summoned before the Court of Inquiry; Dante makes St. Thomas praise a philosopher who was converted to Thomism, but he himself did not everywhere give Thomism his support, and he extolled Siger in a context (Gratian, Solomon) which suggests that his interest might have been aroused by his separatism; finally, Dante might be extolling Siger as a representative of that separatism, but he does not accept his philosophy, and he causes his praises to be sung by one of his opponents, St. Thomas Aquinas.

There is consequently no solution to the problem that covers all the facts without leaving any unaccounted for. Whichever one we choose, we are bound to make an adjustment in order to show how, no matter what appearances may suggest, it will explain such and such a fact which stands in its way. I can therefore only repeat, in conclusion, what I first said in the introduction

---

[1] F. VAN STEENBERGHEN, op. cit., p. 39. I am disregarding the "Fifth difficulty" (op. cit., pp. 39–40), which seems to be of no great importance, for it involves a theory of personal psychology which the individual will always interpret in the sense suggested by his own thesis.

to this book: Our task is not to find one solution which fits better than the rest one or two of the facts of the problem—that is not difficult—but to find the one that best fits all those facts, at any rate as we know them. That Siger of Brabant became late in life a disciple of St. Thomas is not yet established as one of the facts of the problem; accordingly the time has not yet come to try to solve it on the assumption that such is the case; and even if it were, this new fact would certainly encourage us to seek the solution to the problem in a new quarter, but we should in that very process come up against new difficulties. Consequently, the hope that it may facilitate the solution of our problem cannot be held to constitute any presumptive evidence in its favour, for there is no guarantee that such a hope is well founded.

Index of Proper Names

N.B.—Dante's name is not included in this Index.
Figures in italics refer to names appearing in the notes.

Index of the Principal Questions Discussed